# LOSING TIME

## A TWENTIETH CENTURY FUND BOOK

The Twentieth Century Fund is a research foundation undertaking timely analyses of economic, political, and social issues. Not-for-profit and nonpartisan, the Fund was founded in 1919 and endowed by Edward A. Filene.

# LOSING TIME
## The Industrial Policy Debate

OTIS L. GRAHAM, JR.

A TWENTIETH CENTURY FUND BOOK

Harvard University Press

Cambridge, Massachusetts, and London, England

1992

*Library of Congress Cataloging-in-Publication Data*

Graham, Otis L.
   Losing time : the industrial policy debate / Otis L. Graham, Jr.
     p.  cm.
   "A Twentieth Century Fund book."
   Includes bibliographical references and index.
   ISBN 0-674-53919-2 (alk. paper)
   1. Industrial promotion—United States.  2. Industry and state—
United States.  I. Title.
HC110.I53G73  1992
338.973—dc20

91-18461
CIP

*For Lakin, Wade, Jim,*
*and Lady Dee*

# Contents

PART III   **The Past Speaking to the Future**   *241*

# Foreword

Few topics fascinate Americans as much as tales foretelling their own decline. We are a self-critical people, and a self-absorbed people, with all the strengths and weaknesses that preoccupation implies. Today, we are looking inward, focusing on the uncertainties of our economic place in the world. Americans now half believe that the postwar economic success of their nation is a normal component of this or, for that matter, any other country's heritage. And since we are slipping, even if only in a relative sense, we are rather furiously seeking answers, remedies, and, of course, villains. There is a certain national nervous disorder on this subject, one that might be calmed by a little more understanding of the realities of our own history as well as the facts of our current condition.

Near the center of discussions of these matters lies a controversy and perhaps a misunderstanding about the once and future role of industrial policy in shaping our economic destiny. Industrial policy, after all, is an American paradox. We have a tradition of rhetorical worship of laissez-faire economic policy, seldom more ascendant than over the past ten years. Yet we have always relied on interventions designed to spur development, innovation, and defense. And, more recently, we have introduced a variety of public policies designed to "help" the marketplace achieve outcomes that more accurately reflect true economic costs and benefits and certain noneconomic values of the society.

The future of American industrial policy remains uncertain. Should the U.S. government try to spur economic innovation by funding specific industries? Is an industrial policy necessary to the economic well-being of a nation? These questions will confront American policymakers at every turn as we enter a new era in which economic might overshadows military power.

The Twentieth Century Fund, therefore, is pleased to have sponsored the work of Otis Graham on the industrial policy debate in the United States. Graham, professor of history at the University of California, Santa

Barbara, has carefully and thoughtfully analyzed the evolution of this issue over the past decade. He brings a historical perspective to his analysis, which adds substantially to our understanding of this important public policy issue. We are grateful to him for his contribution.

*Richard C. Leone, Director*
*The Twentieth Century Fund*
*July 1991*

# Acknowledgments

Although this book has its roots in several long-standing interests, it originated in a definitive sense when James Smith, then with the Twentieth Century Fund, asked me one sunny autumn morning in Chapel Hill what sort of book I would write if history's policy applications were the issue. In arriving at an answer I have accumulated many debts.

The late Murray Rossant, then Director of the Fund, sustained the project at a time when I was still finding my way. Marcia Bystryn's commitment to the project was decisive, and I owe her a special debt. Ron Chernow, my editor at the Fund, brought superb insights; Susan Hess adroitly handled production; and Beverly Goldberg managed the end game with rare skill.

I benefited from two fellowships providing time, support, and congenial surroundings. The Woodrow Wilson International Center for Scholars in Washington, D.C., was a splendid place to conduct research and begin shaping the results. I am indebted to Director James Billington and to the unfailing professionalism of the entire staff there, including especially Michael J. Lacey and my good friend and history mentor since Marine Corps days, Samuel F. Wells. The academic year 1985–86 at the Center for Advanced Study in the Behavioral Sciences at Stanford, California, produced the first draft of the book, nurtured by many discussions with the fellows there, especially with Peter Eisinger, Nelson Polsby, and Stanley Engerman. The Center's staff provided invaluable support, and I am especially grateful for the climate of intellectual stimulation and comradeship established by then Director Gardner Lindzey, and by my good friend and Associate Director Robert Scott. Walks in the Stanford hills often clarified matters that resisted analysis within the walls of a library or study.

I am also grateful to the National Endowment for the Humanities for a Travel to Collections grant that allowed me to conduct research in the Jimmy Carter Library, in Atlanta, Georgia. This depository of primary materials was an oasis in a project that required an account constructed chiefly from secondary sources. George Eads, William Galston, John J. LaFalce, and Walter Mondale generously gave me interviews.

Two universities provided a nurturing environment across the life of this project, and I am fortunate to have called them both my academic home. At the University of North Carolina, Chapel Hill, I benefited from the ingenuity and patience of the staff assembled under Administrative Assistant Jane Lindley, especially Pamela Fesmire, who never met an eleventh-hour request that she could not handle with skill and aplomb. Chairman Colin Palmer was generous in support of the project. Research assistants Ken Siman, Christine Citrini, Ed Flowers, Yolandra Poole, and Wyatt Wells provided indispensable assistance. Eric Van Horne was a great help in this as in other endeavors.

And it was in Chapel Hill that I enjoyed what amounted to a nine-year seminar on the uses and misuses of history: from 1980 to 1989 the "history for decisionmakers" course at the UNC School of Business served as a testing ground for my ideas. My colleagues in that course over the years were historians Peter Coclanis, James Leutze, Joseph Tulchin, and Samuel Williamson and, from the Business School faculty, Les Garner, who helped convince his associates that history had a place in their curriculum, and William Fischer, who brought to the course his matchless wit and knowledge of things both worldly and Chinese. Deans Jack Evans and Paul Rizzo of the Business School, who understood at once the usefulness as well as the perils of using history, were staunch supporters.

My colleagues at the University of California, Santa Barbara, had sufficient faith in the project to invite me back to the site of my first university teaching position, and there the book was completed. I am especially indebted for the interest shown by Chancellor Barbara Uehling, History Department Chairs W. Elliot Brownlee and Hal Drake, and the advice of that pioneer in matters of "applied history," Robert Kelley. James Elliott, Lauren Jared, Christine Devine, and Betty Koed offered superb research and computer support.

The book was much improved by the skillful editing of Kathleen Lynch, who brought to the task a valuable command of international economics. Thanks to Aida Donald at Harvard University Press for wise executive decisions.

Along the way, I benefited from the good advice of Martin Neil Baily, Ross Baker, William Baumol, William Becker, Jack Behrman, William

Diebold, Stuart Eizenstat, Bernard Elbaum, Ernest Erber, Amitai Etzioni, Herb Fingarette, Edward Graham, Robert Hamrin, Bennett Harrison, Jerry Jasinowski, William Lazonick, Ernest May, Robert Reich, Bruce Scott, Robert Solo, Charls Walker, and Frank Weil. Sherrill Wells helped me to understand French Industrial Policy, and much else. James Sundquist has been a mentor and friend for more than two decades, and his influence is both evident and positive.

My brothers, though busy writing their own books, once again gave me invaluable help—Fred, especially by supplying timely questions and well-targeted skepticism; and Hugh, whose command of policy history and editorial skills greatly improved the product.

*January 1991*
*Santa Barbara, California*

# Introduction

The history of the United States may be seen as two or three subhistories, linked by eras of transition—the Civil War, the Great Depression, perhaps the 1890s. These turbulent zones of transformation were recognized as such by those passing through them, though few could discern the outlines of what lay ahead. This book is about what appears to be another such era of fundamental transition, and what to do about it.

The shift out of an era began in the 1970s, or so it seemed to an imposing number of social commentators who intensely discussed the nation's new circumstances and direction throughout the 1980s. At issue was the evidence of decline in the strength and well-being of the United States, by relative and possibly also absolute measures. With special relish Britons announced that history had finally caught up with the Americans living between Canada and Mexico, and began to teach them what the island former empire sadly acknowledged, the humbling law of cycles.

Thus in the 1980s national economic decline-revival became one of the foremost domestic issues, a new and uncomfortable prospect for Americans. By the latter half of the decade, vigorous public discussion had melded an impressively broad consensus that the erosion of U.S. economic strength was a reality, that it had not been and would not be stemmed by the Reaganite reforms, and that both relative and in some cases absolute decline had continued through even the remarkable years of expansion in 1983–1990. "You can feel America's eroding status in your bones," wrote the editors of *Business Week* magazine; and the noted economist Paul Krugman titled his 1990 survey of recent economic trends *The Age of Diminishing Expectations.*[1]

Yet through the 1980s the national public policy process for economic decision making foundered in irresolution and error. In just three years the world's leading creditor became the chief debtor, fiscal symbol of deep economic weaknesses compounded by policy mistakes. Whatever may be said about national policy fumbling on acid rain, energy, hazardous and solid waste disposal, global warming, and other areas of procrastination, the national economic policy through a decade of declining competitiveness stood out above all the other issues.

Societies just entering decline should especially interest us, Hegel reasoned, for we begin to understand an era only as the curtain drops ("the owl of Minerva spreads its wings only with the falling of dusk").[2] The following pages are an effort to describe and probe the behavior of the American national policy system in that moving zone between the advancing present and the more settled past.

Why was the public policy system so incapacitated as harmful trends gathered momentum? This is a topic attracting much scrutiny. The culprit was not ignorance or avoidance of the problem. There was vigorous debate, by new voices bringing fresh viewpoints and expertise, about economic matters in general and the erosion of industrial strength in particular. To a substantial degree the policy community began to abandon parochial outlooks and to move toward an internationalist range of vision, no mean achievement.

It is too soon to establish a convincing version of exactly what should have been done as, in the 1970s and irregularly through the 1980s, productivity slumped, savings rates decreased, investment was further skewed to defense spending, and industries became globally uncompetitive. Yet clearly, the wrong policy direction was taken—to evade hard choices, and to conceal their necessity by a binge of public and private borrowing.

Early, easy answers were offered to account for these policy choices and nonchoices. There was President Ronald Reagan's peculiar genius for combining inattention to bad news with euphoric talk of mornings in America. There was the calming, choice-avoiding influence of a remarkable eight-year expansion of jobs and output. There was a structural gridlock in the U.S. political and policymaking systems, an excess of Madisonian balance which prevented decisive initiatives of any kind in the absence of overwhelming crisis.

Acknowledging the complexity of the matter, this book concentrates on the unhelpful contribution of an important but neglected element in our public policy discourse—the role of history, as drafted into public service. The focus is the Industrial Policy debate, which commenced in 1980 and continued after 1984 under and somewhat obscured by the rubric "international competitiveness."

One of the many imports from Europe and Japan during those years, the Industrial Policy idea arrived on American shores with fuzzy edges and elastic boundaries. Governments attempt to influence their nation's economies in two ways: either with economywide policies, such as tightening credit or taxing capital gains; or with sector-specific policies, such as deregulating the airlines or protecting textiles from Asian imports. The latter are industrial policies; together aimed strategically toward certain national goals, they make up comprehensive Industrial Policy (IP). Industrial Policy denotes a nation's declared, official, total effort to influence sectoral development and, thus, national industrial portfolio. Industrial policies are the component parts of IP. In European practice, generally adopted in American discussion, "industrial" means the manufacturing but not the agriculture components of the goods-producing sectors.

Ronald Reagan and his allies came to Washington in 1981 to launch a bold, radical fiscal policy experiment, using economywide measures, specifically tax reduction and huge deficits. But another large idea, Industrial Policy, arrived in Washington a few months earlier, trailing a reputation as the central explanation for the economic success of our overseas economic rivals. The following chapters provide a case study of this second, microeconomic or sectoral approach. Industrial Policy is about important matters—among other things, which industries will remain on American soil and which will close their doors or set up in other societies, and what is the role of governments in such decisions. A broad-ranging debate began, centered on the question: Should the United States "adopt" an IP? Soon it was discovered that we already had one, in effect, an unacknowledged mélange of all federal, state, and local governmental policies affecting goods-producing sectors. The existing or de facto IP, once discovered, had no defenders. A nation should have either no IP, or an effective one; it should not have a de facto IP that no one would defend. The stage was set for change. The Industrial Policy debate, continued as the theme of competitiveness, built an impressive agenda of urgent reforms from whatever angle one viewed it. Microeconomic policy upon inspection emerged as an institutionally scattered, undermanaged, and error-prone set of governmental actions with substantial and, overall, negative influence upon regional and national economic development. Formerly ignored, industrial policies emerged as part of the problem. A more positive influence through more centrally coordinated management—Industrial Policy, not random policies—emerged as a concept, a hope, to many a possibility. To others, it offered an opportunity to minimize harm.

Yet the status quo, defended by no one, prevailed. Years of vigorous discussion led only to policy paralysis.

Many explanations for this outcome arise in the recounting. But a major agent of mischief was misuse of history, in many forms. Distorted versions of history inflated the important potential of industrial policies; onslaughts of counter-history lessons equally distorted what Industrial Policy was about. Together, these played a large role in preventing the degree of policy rationalization that was intellectually within reach.

Our policy system might perhaps have done worse, and people who think so might wish to leave well enough alone. I write from a more hopeful persuasion that if history was allowed its limited but invaluable uses, and if misuses of it were curbed, our policy system could improve upon this outcome. Hence this effort to build on and extend the growing body of research and thought that would discourage the policy misuses while charting the way to judicious policy uses of the past.

The debate over these matters did not end in 1990. This book is written in that hazard-filled zone between the beginning and the end of things. I was encouraged in this risk by an observation by two commentators on Britain in the early stages of Thatcherism, that "books generally come to an end before the problems they describe."[3] Historians usually reverse that dictum to read: "problems had best come to an end before books are written to describe them," but this book is directed less to historians than to the policy community—from voting periphery to the presidential center—who must make history-based judgments with or without expert advice. The past misunderstood guarantees future intellectual trouble. Policymakers are fated soon to reengage the Industrial Policy issue. This time error and delay may well exact a much higher price than the first time around, in the 1980–1990 indian summer of America's economic leadership.

# PART I

# Arguing Industrial Policy, 1980–1984

# CHAPTER 1

# The New Economic Order

We are passing over a divide . . . We are moving swiftly out of
the order in which those of our generation were brought up,
into no one knows what.

Alvin Hansen
"Presidential Address," *American Economic Review*

When, in 1941, Henry Luce, the publisher of *Life,* called upon his readers
to embrace enthusiastically "the American Century" of world economic
and political leadership, he mistook his place in time.[1] There was to be a
century of U.S. economic preeminence among nations, but Luce at the
time stood closer to the seventieth than to the first year of that century.
American Number Oneness seemed by many measures to come to an end
in the 1970s and 1980s, with economic dominance flagging along with
an erratic political leadership. The public perception that a historical
threshold had been crossed produced an outpouring of critical appraisals
of our economics, our politics, and the system of political economy in
which they were joined. From this intense self-examination emerged a
debate over Industrial Policy, the shadow-reform in the wings as long as
Ronald Reagan was on the stage.

## The Final Three Decades of the American Century

Luce was right about the 1940s, 1950s, and 1960s, and that is a long time
to be right. Through those decades the world's dominant economy surged
ahead, oblivious of the fast-approaching historical crest. The American
economy had been virtually isolated from external economic challenge;
the nation's only perceived competitor, the U.S.S.R., with its economy
hidden behind closed borders and dubious statistics, was incapable of
testing American markets. The president's annual economic report for
1964 found the nation advancing "toward our economic goals . . . full
employment . . . rapid growth . . . price stability," and victory in Lyndon
Johnson's new War on Poverty.[2] (The word *trade* did not appear in the
report's table of contents.) From 1920 to 1970 U.S. output per worker

7

rose at 2.3 percent annually, the highest rate in the world, for a projected doubling of wealth every thirty years. When the weight of the Great Depression was lifted, American capitalism generated product and production innovations at a stunning clip through years of only minor business-cycle fluctuations. Throughout the twentieth century Americans had enjoyed the highest per capita income in the world; by midcentury their economy produced 60 percent of the world's manufactures, sending out to domestic and world markets a stream of dominating products.

## The Ebbing of Economic Strength

In the 1970s the wind abated in the sails of American capitalism. Economic troubles changed in character, becoming more difficult to manage by either private or public authorities. The doldrum had many measures. After the oil embargo of 1972–73, American workers' aftertax income reached a historic crest. Real median family income, after expanding 38 percent through the 1950s and 34 percent through the 1960s, slowed to a 7 percent rise across the 1970s, and in 1980, a recession year, actually declined 5.5 percent.[3]

The economic craft ran onto the shoals of recession more frequently. Three recessions in the 1970s ratcheted the unemployment rate upward each time. Successive recoveries, less vigorous than in the past, left higher "normal" rates of joblessness. In the last half of the 1970s the low points for inflation (5.5 percent) and unemployment (9 percent) were the highest in 25 years, and the high points of inflation (8 percent) and unemployment (13 percent) had no precedent since World War II. The U.S. economy had seen higher rates of joblessness and inflation in the twentieth century, but formerly when one measure went up, something pushed the other one down. In the 1970s they ascended together, confounding both theory and experience. Many reasons were advanced and debated. External culprits included the Organization of Petroleum Exporting Countries. Internal maladies ranged from poor management to poorer government policies. Among many dour descriptions of the U.S. economy at the end of the 1970s, one summed up the nation's economic ailments in the form of an imaginary cable from the Soviet embassy in Washington to the Kremlin:

> The U.S. economy may be nearing the point contemplated by Marx when capitalism might strangle itself; the prime rate of interest is 20 per-

cent; the inflation rate is near 18 percent; the unemployment rate is headed to 8 percent; the prices of gold and silver are gyrating wildly; the dollar has been weak for several years; the trade deficit for the one month of February 1980 was nearly $5 billion; the federal budget deficit could be as high as $100 billion if the coming business recession becomes acute; the rate of capital investment in industry as a percentage of GNP [gross national product] is now the lowest of all the major industrial nations; the growth rate of productivity in 1979 was negative; expenditures for R&D [research and development] have fallen as a share of GNP.[4]

## The Realigning of Global Industrial Capacity

Such a report might have gladdened the heart of the Soviet embassy staff in Washington. But in Moscow the prospects for capitalism would have looked different to the authorities when placed alongside other reports from Tokyo, Bonn, Paris, Seoul, Singapore, Taipei. Whatever the perturbations within the American economy, the vital signs of world capitalism had for decades recorded health and vigorous expansion. Europe and Japan recovered quickly from World War II, and the industrial arts took root and flourished in new places—most especially on the Pacific rim. As the 1980s arrived the global economy was in its fourth postwar decade of growth. In the 1970s alone, world trade had expanded sevenfold, much faster than world GNP. The capitalist nations, taken together, were inventing, improving, producing, transporting, marketing, and consuming on a scale and with a vitality ever harder to reconcile with any of Marx's predictions.

Yet within the expanding perimeter of capitalist growth, basic structural changes took place. While trade expanded, more of the cargo in the sea-lanes was manufactures rather than raw materials—46 percent on the eve of World War II, but 61 percent by 1973. Yet the world's great manufacturing society, the United States, claimed a declining share of that trade, as the relative American position within world capitalism underwent a quiet transformation.

This transformation was willed by the U.S. government, to a point. The revitalization of war-devastated industrial economies was seen as crucial to the West's resistance to Soviet ambitions, as they were perceived in Washington at the beginning of the Cold War. The principal instrument in achieving this end would be the painstaking reduction of prewar tariff barriers, beginning with our own, which were pushed down from 60 percent in 1931 to 5.5 percent in 1985. Tariffs abroad moved in the same direction. Other instruments were the Marshall Plan and other foreign aid, and the dollar-based world monetary system constructed at Bretton Woods. Indeed, U.S. policy was part of a success so complete that by the 1980s it began to look more like a colossal mistake when viewed by import-besieged American industries.[5]

The U.S. economy grew, but virtually every other industrial or industrializing society in the noncommunist world grew faster, narrowing the huge postwar gaps in output, efficiency, technological prowess, income. U.S. exports were rising in volume, but still the American share of world production slipped in those 30 years to 35 percent. The U.S. share of total world manufactured exports shrank 23 percent in the 1970s alone. Other vigorous players were in the game, most dramatically, Asians. A primary overseas trading partner, Japan, absorbed a fivefold increase in U.S.-made imports while increasing its own exports to the United States eighteen-fold; and the world share of exports by the newly industrializing countries (in this case Korea, Taiwan, Singapore, Brazil, and Mexico) moved upward from 6 percent in 1970 to 11.4 percent in 1983.[6]

To American policymakers, these figures told good news, a tale of recovered economies, robust development, rising living standards everywhere. Trade was a vital part of this expanding well-being. Theory predicts and practice generally confirms that more things are available more cheaply in nations with high levels of exports and imports. The United States was drawn into the pattern, evolving from its relatively trade-isolated past to a trade-linked economic interdependence closer to the European and Japanese models. U.S. imports and exports combined were only 13 percent of GNP in 1960, but 24 percent in 1980.

That traded quarter of what was made and consumed in the United States had enormous leverage because of its changed composition as well as its growing size. American manufactures in 1950 had been stronger in world markets than goods made anywhere else, and were virtually unchallenged at home. By 1980 buyers at home selected from a range of products that now included foreignmade products competitive with our own in price and quality. American firms lost shares of expanding markets in London, Madrid, Mexico City, Buenos Aires, and Tokyo—but also in Los Angeles and Peoria—outdone by industrial rivals, the textile and toy manufacturers of the 1940s and 1950s.

Rising imports of manufactures attracted little official notice as long as they were perceived simply as reflecting consumers' growing appreciation of the price, quality, and availability of small Japanese cars and tape re-corders, shoes from Taiwan, electronic toys from South Korea. But the other face of import availability was import displacement of domestic goods, and thus a structural transformation, as American buyers exercised their choices. Import competition came first in low-wage indus-tries—textiles and apparel, toys, footwear. Soon the isolated Volkswagens of the 1950s became more numerous, with the Datsuns, the Sony record-ers, Olivetti typewriters. By the end of the 1970s, 70 percent of the U.S. market for manufactures faced foreign-made goods. American consumers who in the 1950s had "bought American" in all but French wines, Swiss watches, and other exotics now chose Japanese cars, European optical equipment, and Brazilian steel. Imports claimed 62 percent of television domestic sales in 1972, 94 percent by 1979. In 1980, 50 percent of all consumer electronic products, 90 percent of the cutlery, and one of every four autos bought in the United States was foreign made. In this year Japan for the first time sold more cars, worldwide, than the United States. Steel, symbolic heart of American industrial strength, traced a red line of decline as U.S. industry's share of world sales dropped from 26 percent in 1960 to 12 percent in the early 1970s.[7]

Foreign companies, also and unexpectedly becoming competitive in high-technology goods, cut away at the sales of domestic firms in indus-tries ranging from textiles, autos, and steel to electrical components, farm machinery, consumer electronics, machine tools, organic chemicals, and computers. The U.S. share of world high-technology trade declined in 1960–1983, from 25 percent to 20 percent; yet within that modest trend some competitors made greater leaps forward. Japan by 1981 held 44 percent of the world market in semiconductor 16K chips (chips holding 16,000 bits of information), 70 percent in 64K chips, and was so con-fident of domination of the emerging 264K chip market that several Japa-nese companies ran an advertisement in *Scientific American* late in 1981 in which they "quite simply declared victory."[8] Foreign firms were begin-ning to challenge the United States even in services such as insurance, financing, shipping, and engineering, denting its world share.

Contemporaries could scarcely grasp the meaning of this blur of eco-nomic change, conveying so many contradictory signs. American mer-chandise exports expanded tenfold from 1960 to 1985, from a dollar value of $19.7 million to $214 billion, telling a story of immense eco-nomic power. But merchandise imports expanded twenty-five times over those years, from $14 million to $338 billion, a feast for consumers but different news for producers. A few marks on the calendar told the story of structural shifts as comparative advantage in industry after industry flowed outside American borders. Imports of consumer textiles first overtook exports in 1955; household appliances crossed the line in 1962, industrial textiles in 1963, and auto products in 1968.[9] These successive sectoral thresholds suggest an inexorable passage from one economic era to another. "For the first time in American history, we can neither dominate the world nor escape from it" was Henry Kissinger's assessment.[10]

## Parallel Growth: Trade and Trade Politics

Domination had slipped away, but what had replaced it? Intense import competition had created a number of vocal, well-organized losers among American producers and workers in those industries. Their complaints and calls for help revived trade politics.

Once one of the most contentious of American political issues, beginning with the Reciprocal Trade Agreements Act of 1934 "the tariff" had been steadily shifted out of congressional debates and presidential politics, into executive branch bureaucracies. The new system matured after World War II, which members of both parties viewed as having arisen in large measure from economic nationalism (in which the United States shared, having enacted the highest tariff levels in its history with the Smoot-Hawley Act of 1930). World peace, it seemed, required an open world economy with capitalist economies strengthened through free trade. This bipartisan postwar policy of successive U.S. administrations pushed U.S. tariff barriers steadily downward in exchange for concessions negotiated with trading partners within the framework of the General Agreement on Tariffs and Trade (GATT). Lowered tariffs spurred the postwar trade expansion, which fueled an unprecedented (though uneven) human prosperity.

A key to this postwar liberalized world trade order was the ability of the executive branch, with congressional restraint, to contain domestic protectionist pressures. The unique circumstances after World War II—vivid memories of war and its link with autarchy, and an American economy's virtual isolation from international competition—made this possible. But by the 1970s trade volume and composition raised the number of American losers. Trade politics is the classic example of Mancur Olson's "logic of collective action," in which political pressures do not reflect real interests. Consumers (and importers) benefit from imports, but their sense of gain is diffuse and they are not organized for political action. Producers, losing sales to imports, are acutely aware of job and profit losses and aggressively seek political relief.

The changes sweeping through the world economy brought both benefits and costs to Americans, but those bearing the costs knew better who they were. The new international competition imperiously altered job patterns in the United States. Workers in manufacturing (including construction and mining), who had been 38 percent of the total work force in 1960, accounted for only 28 percent by 1981. Nineteen million new jobs were created in the 1970s, but only 5 percent were in manufacturing, with most of the growth in services. These lifeless figures translated into stunning job losses in particular industries and regions. Manufacturing jobs, which had grown in the Midwest and Middle Atlantic regions through the 1950s and 1960s, declined in the 1970s by 6 percent and 15 percent, respectively.

In the core smokestack industries the shutdowns moved some of America's best-paid blue-collar labor into unemployment. One-quarter of the 1970 work force in autos was laid off by 1980, when the four major auto corporations lost $4 billion, $12 million a day, idling 300,000 workers. The Chrysler Corporation was bailed out of bankruptcy by the government, and imported cars captured a record 27 percent of the market. In March 1980, 40 percent of Chrysler's peak work force (by one calculation) was laid off, 24 percent of Ford's. The labor force in the steel industry continued the decline of the 1950s; from 1974 to 1982, jobs in steel fell by nearly half, from 512,000 to 289,000. Many of the steel towns of Pennsylvania and Ohio had clean air again but also dark factories, and unemployed workers tied to mortgages and communities.[11]

Industries with stagnant or declining sales, losing market share to imports, generate protectionist pressures against the always-fragile system constructed to permit successive U.S. administrations to take the lead in lowering tariff barriers. Economists and others with no direct stake in the "mature" or "smokestack" industries could and did fashion an argument that this stagnation was natural, even desirable, and no cause for alarm. But imports were also cutting away the sales base of high-technology American firms. The Semiconductor Industry Association came to Capitol Hill with its worries about Japanese rivalries in 1979, along with executives from companies making fiber-optic products and consumer electronics. The number of trade-restrictive bills increased in each successive session of Congress after 1978, and references to trade in the House and Senate increased 70 percent from 1975 to 1980.[12]

## Taking Comfort from Economic Theory

There was an orthodox way to understand the new politics of trade disputes. Economic change made enemies at every stride along the road to progress. The ranks of those who had misguidedly attempted to obstruct the course of economic development included the British government as it contemplated the evolution of the American colonies, an endless file of American agrarians resisting industrialization, Luddites of various kinds who resisted labor-saving machinery, and every congressman who ever voted for a higher tariff. The path to progress brings entire industries to maturity, and in a healthy economy they are replaced by others. Makers of buggy whips, corsets, saddles, or player pianos go out of business or shrink to quaintness. Labor and capital then move on to make and sell radios, tennis rackets, video games, jet fighters, and sewage treatment plants. The central dynamic is technological innovation; a second theme, evolving tastes. In the process, "gales of creative destruction," in economist Joseph Schumpeter's phrase, periodically sweep across capitalism, releasing capital and labor to form new enterprises.[13] There is attendant pain, but the process is familiar, fundamental, and benign. Rising levels of affluence lie ahead if that process is unimpeded.

This view of economic change was buttressed by conventional trade theory. If an industry went into decline not because its products were no longer wanted by domestic consumers but because foreign producers undersold it, this was the way things were supposed to work. Two societies were richer as a result of trade-related shrinkage in an industry with a great past behind it. The result was mutually beneficial because nations possessed comparative advantage at making certain things, chiefly as a result of natural endowments of climate, resources, or location. They should specialize in their products of comparative advantage, and trade freely with others. Of course, comparative advantage might change. There was a "product cycle," so called by Harvard's Raymond Vernon, by which a product pioneered in advanced industrial societies became standardized in its production and could be produced less expensively in less-developed low-wage countries.[14] The originating economy should and would then move up the scale to yet newer, capital-and-knowledge-intensive production—

or perhaps not to goods production at all, but to Daniel Bell's "post-industrial" economy, based on services.[15]

This description of economic change seemed in some respects to fit the United States in the 1970s. The economy continued to expand across periodic recessions, to create jobs and new industries. New high-technology clusters grew in the Sunbelt or around Boston's collection of universities. America, in the orthodox view, was shedding obsolete ways of making a living, losing only those occupations best bade farewell as they slipped away overseas. Seen in this way, the bumpy road of change still led America toward a wealthier future. If corrective action was required, it was up to God to end the cartel of oil-producing countries so that petroleum might return to prices of fond memory, or for the electorate to send forward a new administration that knew how to macromanage the economy as Nixon, Ford, and Carter apparently did not.

This line of optimistic fatalism could be found in many texts, from Adam Smith's *The Wealth of Nations* (1776) on, but America's favorite text for optimists was our own national history. Our past abounded with examples of economic change on just such a progress model: economic growth replaced by decay meant that vital energies had shifted elsewhere. The South, once the home of proud agriculture-based societies centered in Virginia and South Carolina, saw economic leadership flow northward to New England, then to a larger industrial belt stretching from Boston to Minneapolis. National (if not sectional) welfare was increasing. Alarm, condemnation, and calls for political resistance had always sprouted where Schumpeter's gales of creative destruction blew—from the old South, then to New England's textile mills, and in the 1980s to Dayton, Buffalo, Gary, the Mahoning Valley in Pennsylvania's steel region, and the textile towns of the Piedmont.

If the past was a reliable tutor, then the changes of the 1970s must promise a future that would eventually be just as bright. This, at least, was the initial, privileged view in the community of economy-analyzers. Yet precedents could not exclude the possibility of the unprecedented. Never before had goods and services been traded around the world in such volume, industrial capacity been so globally dispersed, national economies been so commercially linked to others on such a scale. In itself, no threat to Americans' well-being was conveyed by the news that international disparities of income and industrial capacity were reported to be narrowing as poor nations caught up with the leaders. Reports that in 1978 U.S. per capita income had slipped behind that of the Arab sheikdoms and stood fifth, behind that of Switzerland, Denmark, West Germany, and Sweden, did not necessarily mean that Americans were or should feel worse off than before.[16] Optimists also suspected there was something wrong with the measures. In any event, trends that brought other societies to parity with the United States produced only relative decline. The American living standard would not thereby be diminished, only more widely matched.

This optimistic interpretation of global economic events rested upon a vision of the future structure of the American economy that combined clean, "high-technology" branches of manufacturing with "services," a broad category of endeavors that could be pictured as relatively well-paying mental work rather than physical labor at the low end of status and compensation. This vision was soon in difficulty. Evidence mounted that most of the new occupations evolving as a result of economic transformation offered low pay and little upward mobility. At the end of the 1970s the list of occupations growing most rapidly in new job production was headed by secretaries, nurses' aides, and janitors, with fast-food workers ranked eighth. Some fast-growing industries suggested a future of clean, high-wage work—robotics, laser technology, genetic engineering, computer operators and analysts. Other employment trends threatened to force unionized machinists, steel workers, and auto workers out of the middle class and into fast-food service, child care, office and warehouse security, vending machine supply.

## Is There a "Basic" Measure of Economic Strength: Productivity?

In the 1950s and 1960s, the public and its political leaders had judged economic progress almost exclusively in terms of growth of GNP, job production, and price stability. In the 1970s these simple aggregates, though still important, were displaced from the center of things.

By what indicators might we judge whether the course of the American economy was still optimal? A sailing craft may move forward but have fallen off the wind, while its rivals beat a harder, truer course. Trade figures convey important information about a nation's relative economic strength, and here the evidence pointed to a broad deterioration in the quality and price of American manufactures. A negative balance in merchandise trade was reported in 1971 for the first time in the twentieth century; this modest deficit of $2.3 billion doubled by 1977 and reached $25.5 billion by 1980.

Trade flows did not tell a full story. They might reflect either short-term or fundamental currency imbalances, and the difference was not readily discerned. In the 1970s negative merchandise trade balances also reflected the sudden rise of oil prices and America's slow adaptation. Interpretation of the nation's perplexing new economic circumstances required other measures besides trade flows. The esoteric terminology of business and applied economics suggested one measure—productivity.

Productivity, defined as output per unit of productive effort, is arguably the crucial determinant of wealth. Government statisticians measure it as the ratio of goods and services produced in relation to inputs of production, both expressed as dollars. To derive the measure on either end, output or input, is a formidable task, not well done in the United States before 1948, and after that carried on by an increasingly numerous and professional staff in the Department of Commerce. Normally the labor input alone is used (without capital or raw materials), since labor input indirectly reflects the machinery and resources used by workers. The productivity measure is reassuringly numerical, but its foundations are shaky. The value of output is measured in price, which does not necessarily reflect quality—and other intangible values like clean air and safe workplaces.

Yet productivity growth rates remain a useful measure of economic performance, however problematical. They report upon national and sectoral ability to increase wealth with the same hour of paid work. It is vastly revealing of modern American experience that the word virtually disappeared from general usage in the postwar era, even from the talk of many economists. In America, except to managers of workplaces or business consultants, productivity simply increased, and did not have to be thought about. In the 1960s Harvard sociologist Talcott Parsons reported on a trip to the Soviet Union with a group of American social scientists: "You know, we went over there, and we wanted to talk about theories of social organization. All that our counterparts wanted to talk about was productivity—how do you get it out of people. Well, you know, for us, productivity is like sunshine—we just have it, that's all. It's just there."[17]

American economic history makes that remarkable remark understandable. Labor productivity in the private sector grew steadily for 26 years, from 1948 to 1965, an average of 3.2 percent a year. Sunshine indeed! A thing growing at a steady rate of 3 percent per year will double every 21 years. Such fantastic rates had become "normal."

Abruptly, American productivity slowed, to 1.6 percent in 1965–1973, after the oil shock to 0.8 percent through 1978, to −2.0 percent in 1979, a year economist Lester Thurow called "unique in American economic history . . . the first year with rising output and falling productivity."[18]

The picture abroad put this news into sharper focus. A productivity growth rate slowdown had occurred at about the same time in the ten industrial nations monitored by the Bureau of Labor Statistics, even affecting the "miracle" economies of Japan and West Germany. In 1979, the Americans, at a productivity index of 100, could look back at Canada (92), France (85), Japan (62); the United States still led the world in productivity.[19]

The index was, however, a static measure of situation, not of rates of change. Other industrial societies had been closing the gap, even amid the general slowdown. Also narrowing was the price and quality gap between American and foreign-made products.

If productivity is the driving force behind wealth, slowdown means less wealth in the future. By one estimate, declining productivity since 1965 had made 1980 GNP, a sum three times larger than the year's defense budget, 20 percent smaller than it might have been.[20] Stagnant productivity rates at the end of the 1970s and a population growing nearly 1 percent a year yielded a formula for shrinking shares. A "productivity panic" rippled through business journals and the media as the decade ended, in anticipation of the coming struggle to distribute a nongrowing pie among a growing number of eaters.[21]

A public newly interested in "the productivity slump" might discover a large and complex literature on the sources of economic growth and decline. Suspect factors in the productivity slowdown ranged from the temporary or short-term—the shock of quadrupled oil prices, the slack economy of the recession-prone 1970s, poor macroeconomic management from Washington—to the excessive burdens placed by the welfare-regulatory state upon the capitalist ox, especially in the previous two decades. One could hear that American workers had become lazy, ill-motivated, some inclined to pilferage; or that corporate executives had lost touch with and interest in the actual production process, and spent time and energy upon financial and tax maneuvers to boost short-term profits while neglecting long-term investments. Students of the subject also suggested longer-term causes: the end of the century-long shrinkage of the agricultural work force, which had for so long boosted productivity figures by moving labor into more capital-intensive lines of work; or the entry of the baby-boom generation into the work force, diluting the reserves of experience and training; or a decline in savings rates, making capital scarce; or some inexplicable exhaustion of the American drive to innovate.[22] Political rhetoric made use of any and all such theories.

Prevailing wisdom on the causes of slowdown pronounced it "disturbing but also puzzling," essentially "a mystery."[23] To economist Lester Thurow this "ultimate determinant of our real standard of living" had gone flat at the end of the 1970s because many things had happened—or stopped happening—at once, bringing to his mind the metaphor of "death by a thousand cuts."[24]

Whatever the causes, nothing like it had occurred in the United States since the government officially started measuring productivity at the end of World War II. Combined with other economic trends, the news about productivity, this surrogate for social efficiency, deepened and widened the conviction that America had crossed some historic divide. The stage was set for a season of intense national self-examination, an outpouring of critical appraisals of our economics, our politics, and the system of political economy in which they were uneasily meshed.

## Visions of an Alternative American System

The American political economy in the 1980s encountered in Ronald Reagan its most radical presidential reformer since Franklin Delano Roosevelt. While Reagan presided over what he liked to call his "revolution," the Democrats developed an alternative doctrine, Industrial Policy.

Yet well before the emergence of Reaganism or Industrial Policy, the Keynesian, demand-side paradigm in economic management—so long accepted by both Democrats and Republicans as they alternated in the White House during the postwar era—had begun to seem increasingly inadequate. The 1970s brought energy-led resource shortages, intensifying inflationary pressures now combined with slowing growth. Keynesian measures in these circumstances would, at best, make something worse. In this setting, both parties began to develop a radically different approach to political economy. This was the Planning Idea.[25]

Every sixteen years or so, calculated Herbert Stein, Richard Nixon's chairman of the Council of Economic Advisers, the notion of national economic-social Planning captured the liberal mind and was pushed to the front of public discussion.[26] In the 1930s under FDR, Planning gained several beachheads against determined conservative resistance.[27] A brief enthusiasm for Planning was contained again at the end of World War II, and cycled through once more in the early 1960s when John F. Kennedy and some of his advisers cast a curious eye upon the French system of Indicative (soft, not command-and-control) Planning within a capitalist framework. Nothing came of Kennedy's brief curiosity, but the cycle came around hard again in the mid-1970s, just a few years before the "Reagan Revolution." This latest acute attack of the Planning virus remained fresh in the minds of all who followed public affairs and would strongly color the discussion of Industrial Policy.

### The Planning Movement of the 1970s

"Planning is a symptom of disorder," said AT&T Chairman Charles L. Brown in 1982: "When the future seems reasonably predictable . . . planning goes by another name: 'management.' When times are changing, there are planners everywhere." [28] Times were most clearly changing and disorders increasing at the hinge of the 1960s and 1970s, and forward again came the idea of national economic Planning. Liberal Democrats on Capitol Hill took the lead in the late 1960s, headed aggressively by Senator (and then Vice-President) Hubert H. Humphrey, who with unionists and academics helped form the Initiative Committee for National Planning and legislative proposals for a system of Indicative Planning. The political range of support for the Planning idea extended also to business leaders, academics, an occasional Republican politician like Senator Jacob K. Javits of New York or Governor John Connally of Texas—and Richard Nixon.

From the first months of his presidency Nixon had embraced the Planning concept and boldly added the term to presidential rhetoric. In 1970 he called for a National Growth Policy, a national land-use policy, a national population policy, a staff to plan for the attainment of national goals. He then unaccountably lost interest in these and other reforms aimed at bringing longer time horizons and greater coherence to national policy.

The moment of opportunity, if that is what it was, slipped away. Jimmy Carter, a self-confessed "planner," was elected president in 1976, but the sustained commitment to the necessary institutional changes for any form of indicative Planning was not to be found within his administration, and was only strong enough in Congress to force passage of an emasculated Humphrey-Hawkins Full Employment Act in 1978. The Humphrey-Javits indicative Planning legislation was shunted aside, and the broad interest in a "National Growth policy" limped toward its only embodiment, Carter's short-lived Urban Policy of 1978. [29]

The Planning movement had crested and would recede, frustrated at every point. It had been generated by a set of perceived economic troubles—unemployment with inflation, regional and urban decline, the inability of governmental machinery to anticipate resource shortages or much of anything else. The Planning idea did not ebb because these problems eased. They remained, along with a growing perception of governmental ineptitude in military as well as economic matters, sapping confidence in state intervention, the core of any dream of Planning. Somewhere near mid-decade the momentum behind Planning had been lost. Jimmy Carter had claimed to be a planner, but had not carried through. Judging him and the liberal-Keynesian approach to economic policy with which he operated to be failures, the electorate, without fully realizing what it was allowing, in 1980 opened the door of presidential power to the most radical doctrine of political economy since Franklin Roosevelt's system-changing reforms of the 1930s.

Reagan and the Republicans, and the Democrats who had resisted the Planning idea within their own party, had not forgotten that planners had, once again, been just outside the gates in the 1970s. When the Industrial Policy discussion began, they remembered that recurring ideological peril and quickly concluded that the periods of rest between battles was becoming shorter. Opponents of planning expected to meet again the familiar enemy under this opaque new label: Industrial Policy.

### New U.S. Import: Industrial Policy

Industrial Policy was at first seen as either a European import or a migrant, depending upon whether it was viewed as having been ordered by someone here, or as an invader. The phrase actually goes rather far back in the American past in isolated appearances—as the title of a book on trade issues published in Philadelphia in 1876 and another by economist Frank Taussig in 1898, and in a Twentieth Century Fund conference memorandum of 1931. One scholar believes that the term first occurs in Japanese writing before World War II. The term first gained official acceptance in Western Europe after the war but had a varied usage there and clarified itself only slowly. Andrew Shonfield had not used the term *industrial policy* in his seminal *Modern Capitalism* (1967).[30]

When the term arrived in the United States, in the late 1970s, it came with blurred edges that it would never lose. Industrial policies, by convention, were governmental policies affecting goods-producing sectors, though agriculture and extractive industries (mining, forestry) tended to fall outside the discussion—making industrial policies essentially the government's contact with manufacturing. Little of the Industrial Policy debate touched upon services, though one day that will surely change. Industrial policies were "micro-policies" as contrasted with macroeconomic policies, those fiscal, monetary, and other measures broadly affecting the entire economy.[31]

All advanced societies, it is at once obvious, have industrial or sector-specific policies—trade regulations, tax burdens and expenditures, promotional subsidies, workplace and environmental regulations, and much else. Some affect more than one industry; some are tailored for only one—textiles, shipbuilding, aircarriers. Postwar European economic discussion placed a high value upon national policy for sectors, to cushion the decline of older industries and promote new entrants in high technology.

France (like Japan) had deployed sectoral policies since the late 1940s in the hope of moving the structure of its economy in directions the state, in consultation with industrialists, thought desirable. In 1951 France and Germany launched one of history's most novel sectoral experiments. Joined also by Belgium, Italy, Luxembourg, and the Netherlands, the European Coal and Steel Community began to develop common policies for reorganizing two basic industries in a way that would "eliminate the age-old opposition of France and Germany."[32] This venture was extended in 1957 to other areas of the European economy.

The United States in the postwar era lacked official governmental discussion of sectoral policy. Sectoral policies were of course as old as the republic, and were vitally important to congressmen and various lobbyists for affected industries. But from the 1930s, when the federal government first consciously and explicitly took upon itself the management of the modern economy, top policymakers and economists hired to assist them were absorbed in macroeconomic analytic and policy efforts. Only in the rather isolated field of developmental economics, a subfield of the discipline concerned with promoting the economic well-being of the developing worlds, was there receptivity to the idea that explicit sectoral interventions by governments made good economic sense. Developmental economists were a different breed, convinced that governments could promote import substitution by nourishing certain sectors and thus lift Peru or Ethiopia out of poverty and dependency.[33]

The rest of the economists, however, concentrated upon this, the "first," the industrialized capitalist world with America at its center, and

the best and most ambitious of them tended to think only about macroeconomic management. Not for them, or for the front-rank politicians
and government officials who might hire or consult them, were the pid-
dling discussions of whether the machine-tool industry enjoyed correct
policy, or the textile industry was headed in the right direction, or footwear required a new policy regime. These were local issues (the tariff was
"a local issue," presidential candidate General Winfield Scott had responded to a question as long ago as the campaign of 1880), regional at
best, not attractive to minds attuned to larger, national or international
matters. Economic policy worth talking about in postwar America was
Keynesian macroeconomic management. Lord Keynes had said: "I see no
reason to suppose that the existing system seriously misemploys the factors of production which are in use . . . It is in determining the volume, not the direction of actual employment that the existing system has
broken down."[34] This statement well enough represents the stress upon
aggregate demand that was central to Keynesian thought. Economic policy meant manipulating spending and taxation, money and credit. The
government's function was to influence the *volume,* not the *direction,* of
investment. Consumers and industrialists would decide which industries
flourished or died.

Expanding world trade broke into this preoccupation with macroeconomic policy, allowing the terminology of Industrial Policy to migrate
across the seas from both West and East. The first signs of change came as
important goods-producing industries became serious problems rather
than periodic subjects of a subcommittee writing a tax bill. Textiles and
steel were the main import-injured major industries in the 1960s, autos in
the 1970s. Policies affecting those industries and others in special difficulty were increasingly said to need close national attention. Sectoral
troubles, even when their sources were not fully comprehended, pulled
existing sectoral policies from obscurity. At least one American businessman had seen this coming as early as 1972: "If the government has to
concern itself with adjustment on a greater scale than in the past, the government will have to formulate views about the desirable structure of
American industry. In Europe, Canada and Japan, "industrial policy" is
coming to be a central feature of national economic policy . . . May not
the same be happening, though a good bit more slowly, in the U.S.?"[35]

Presidents, aspiring presidents, top economists, and economic writers
had enjoyed the luxury of ignoring sectoral issues through decades of
expansion and little foreign competition. As late as 1975, the president's

Council of Economic Advisers, high priests of national economic policy, did not even gather data on sectors.[36] Yet events were impinging on this aggregate-engrossed, sectorally ignorant bliss. Large and leading industries were in trouble, and the term *industrial policies* would be needed in order to talk about them, to elevate their importance from the level of congressional subcommittees and trade association journals.

A second discovery siphoned the new terminology into U.S. discussion. Foreign governments, in concert with their corporations, were practicing Industrial Policy in the hope, and perhaps with the result, of underselling American corporations and eroding our industrial base in advance of the timetable decreed by the benign laws of economics. Especially important here was the U.S. encounter with a resurgent Japan.

Almost as if physical barriers against the terminology had been lifted at the end of the 1970s, the words *industrial policy* and *Industrial Policy*—usually undefined—began to appear in discussions of U.S. economic matters, from academic disputes to reports in the mass media. To this day the product is not standardized. People talking of industrial policy were often not talking about the same thing. A Canadian writer compiled a long list of definitions, indicating that Industrial Policy, for instance, can:

> [Concern] the structure of an economy . . . [refers to] discrete governmental measures as well as to the sustained pursuit of certain ends or the persistent use of certain methods or devices . . . [and covers] all economic activities. (Diebold)

> [Embrace] all acts and policies of the state in relation to industry . . . all aspects of State [*sic*] attitudes toward industry in its economic, social and environmental setting. (Baylis)

> [Mean] policies which are concerned in some way with economic innovation—with research and development, with new technologies and their diffusion. (Carter)

> Innovate rather than imitate, implying a broad industrial shift that modifies almost every single facet of industrial activity, from finance to research and marketing. (Shepherd)

> [Be] designed to encourage the growth of manufacturing and reverse the deficit in end product trade. (Lazar)[37]

Similarly, industrial policies range from "defensive" ("mainly concerned with keeping in being some structural arrangement, such as domestic production of certain goods that will not service international competition") . . . to the "adaptive" ("[concerned with facilitating] structural change by helping to shift resources to new uses that do not require protection or subsidy or by increasing efficiency in existing lines of activity"), to the "initiative" ("[in that policy] initiates change rather than simply responding to it").[38]

Such definitional confusion would never be entirely dispelled. Of Industrial Policy, economist Mancur Olson once irreverently asserted: "It is the grin without the cat," a phrase that could not be given form.[39] It was much more than that, concluded Aaron Wildavsky, who said: "Industrial Policy, if it is anything, is political economy."[40] It was the other reform idea; it arrived in the White House before Ronald Reagan brought his own, and was fated to be seen during those years as the Democrats' alternative.

# CHAPTER 2

# Emergence of the Industrial Policy Idea

The appeal of industrial policy to its supporters—and the source of apprehension felt by opponents—lies in the promise of coherence.

James Galbraith,
Joint Economic Committee

Jimmy Carter was a one-term president in part because he spent his first term preparing his government to be effective in his second, where he thought the payoffs lay. His managerial reform instincts were especially drawn to that distinctive, unruly feature of the federal government's organization—a fragmentation of assignments among many agencies carrying out inconsistent policies, while "cross-cutting issues" spilled across agency boundaries. In pursuit of coherence, of Energy Policy and Urban Policy and Ocean Policy, Carter and his aides invested thousands of hours of time and, more valuable, much fresh and innovative thinking.

Then Carter was abruptly discharged, with his appointees, the electoral majority deciding to forgo the accumulated intellectual capital of this experienced set of executive branch managers. The rejected administrators would have to reap the benefits of their training privately, in law firms or as the writers of memoirs. What Carter and his 1,000 top non–civil service helpers carried in their heads, the policy areas studied and the plans laid, was simply flushed away.

Industrial Policy was part of Carter's vanished legacy. Adopted and announced in August 1980, his Industrial Policy was all but ignored in the hectic last months of election and Iranian hostage crisis, and effectively obliterated by Reagan's succession. Even in the early memoirs of Carter and his top aides his Industrial Policy is more completely forgotten than the other fading policy landmarks of the Georgian's brief time in office.

### Jimmy Carter—Starting Out as a Keynesian

That Carter's involvement with the IP idea went virtually unnoticed is easy to understand. The administration never projected a sharply defined approach to economic matters. It was staffed by eclectic, moderate Keynesian economic advisers and on the whole charted a wobbly centrist and invincibly macroeconomic line of policy. Carter's four presidential reports on the economy abound with talk about the macroeconomic indicators as both definitions and solutions to problems: data on inflation, unemployment, interest rates, deficits—the usual aggregates that were thought sufficient to tell the nation how things were going. Aggregates, such as employment and inflation targets, were also the heart of the Humphrey-Hawkins Full Employment Act, which absorbed so much of the administration's time and negotiating energies in 1977 and 1978. The annual *Economic Report of the President* was absorbed with these economywide indexes even toward the end of the decade, when the new "supply-side" emphasis led the government to pay more attention to productivity and savings rate data, both economywide measures of economic condition.

Sectoral problems were not significant components of the government's economic agenda, to judge from presidential reports, news conferences, and the terms of discussion. Presidents and their aides preferred not to deal with sectoral issues. Economic policy in the postwar era was a matter of observing, and attempting to manipulate, the aggregates. John F. Kennedy had told his new appointee John Kenneth Galbraith: "Ken, you are my adviser on agriculture. I don't want to hear about agriculture from anyone but you. And I don't want to hear about it from you, either."[1] All postwar presidents operated in this tradition, but in this (as in much else) Carter was transitional, driven by events onto new ground.

### Jimmy Carter and "Troubled Sectors"

In 1977 steel was experiencing its own version of an increasingly familiar U.S. industrial story, the end of world dominance. The open-hearth, ingot-casting facilities of the United States, the world's most efficient as late as the 1950s, could not compete with new works, oxygen furnaces fitted for continuous casting, in Europe, Japan, Argentina, Brazil, Mexico, South Korea, and Taiwan. The U.S. share of world steel markets had dropped from 47 percent in 1950 to 17 percent by 1976. Americans used less steel and more plastics and other substitutes, and bought from abroad more of the steel they did use. Imports carved into the home market, from 2.3 percent of domestic sales in the 1950s, to 9.3 percent in the 1960s, 13 percent in 1973–1976, to 20 percent in 1977. Employment in the industry fell from 500,000 in 1970, to 450,000 by the mid-1970s, to 250,000 by the mid-1980s, as steel makers cut back capacity. In August and September 1977 alone, 14 mills closed, idling 20,000 well-paid workers whose incomes supported many communities.

The existing coalition of steel-interested politicians and business labor leaders from the most heavily affected communities in Pennsylvania, Ohio, and New York sprang into action. A Steel Caucus claiming 160 House and 30 Senate members demanded protection (again) from foreign competition, and this time a Democrat sat in the White House, a president most of them had helped vote into office.[2]

In 1977 the steel problem could no longer be contained by the elaborate machinery at lower levels designed to blunt and channel protectionist passions. Carter was forced to mobilize an unprecedented steel industry interagency task force, with Undersecretary of the Treasury Anthony M. Solomon in the chair. The resultant "Solomon Plan" established a "trigger price mechanism" (TPM), a price floor for foreign-made steel calculated on the Japanese domestic price. This complicated system bought the government temporary relief from protectionist pressures and in theory gave the steel industry time to invest and modernize, restructure, relocate, or shrink gracefully as surplus labor looked for other lines of work.[3]

The Solomon Plan was intended to be a broad policy framework for the steel industry, not a gift of protection for steel. A Tripartite Advisory Committee with five working groups was to ponder and recommend changes in the areas of capital formation, international trade, the environment, technology, and labor. The committee would have something to say about future federal loans for modernization and would influence policy changes in R&D, infrastructure, and aid to shutdown-affected communities.

On paper, one commentator observed, "this reads remarkably like a national industrial policy for steel and an enlightened one at that."[4] But the administration did not force the industry to animate the Solomon machinery. Without oversight of the new policy framework, this consultative system "failed both to relate the issues of concern to one another and to define an integrated plan of action to deal with them."[5]

Profits for a time returned to the books of the steel corporations—the industry's rate of return on equity vaulting from 4 to 9 percent from 1977 to 1979.[6] The TPM for a time held imported steel prices at levels that allowed U.S. companies to increase profits from $23 million in 1977 to $1.4 billion in 1978. Most of the profits went into capital diversification, not modernized steel plants. U.S. Steel closed production facilities and bought shopping centers, chemical firms, and Marathon Oil. Republic Steel diversified into insurance. The Carter administration, forced to invent industrial policy under pressure, had created for steel an interesting but barren structure for negotiation which amounted to protectionism for steel companies and their unions. The cost to the public was high—by one estimate $1 billion a year in higher steel prices—and imports would continue to leak around the government's flimsy barriers in the 1980s.[7]

Steel was Jimmy Carter's introduction to the new hazards in the political terrain of the 1970s—troubled industrial sectors, corporations, and regions, clamoring for aid from the federal government. The steel policy of 1977 succeeded in easing the administration past the political pressures generated from plant shutdowns, giving steel management and unions a temporary buffer from foreign steel imports but failing to add restructuring pressures to the protectionist subsidy it had granted.

The steel intervention of 1977 was a "bailout"—a government rescue going beyond routine trade policy relief—but it would not be called that. Helping steel entailed no direct federal expenditures or loan guarantees, as had the Lockheed (1971) and New York cases (1975–1978). Carter, understandably, regarded the steel negotiations of 1977 as an interruption, a messy business best put behind. No notice of it appeared in Carter's presidential papers for that year, and in his memoirs the steel episode is given not one line.[8] But Carter was not finished with the politics and economics of failing industries, for economic change was driving the administration along a troubled learning curve in the domestic implications of the new realities of world trade.

Unlike Abraham Lincoln, few presidents of the United States have been acutely aware of the nature of the major problems that would confront them upon taking office. Woodrow Wilson, the man who led America into belligerency in World War I and into a new world role, took office in 1913 talking entirely of domestic issues and remarked what an irony it would be if, bent upon internal reforms, he had to make major foreign policy decisions. Jimmy Carter was surprised by many of the issues that crowded his presidential agenda, but none caught him more unprepared than the incessant demands that the administration "do something" about industrial distress in particular sectors and regions. Macroeconomic matters such as inflation and employment were fully anticipated, but neither in the campaign nor in any of the bulky briefing books that Carter carried about before his inauguration was there attention to trade, international economic policy, or their sectoral victims.[9]

Other matters eclipsed trade issues, and there was after all a system for managing sick-sector problems, most of its tiers below and quite out of earshot of the Oval Office. The system's roots were in a history lesson, the memory of the depression that had followed and had surely been caused by the Smoot-Hawley Tariff of 1930. Raising tariffs in 1930 was seen in retrospect as an act of irresponsible economic isolationism. To prevent its recurrence, a system must be created to deflect trade decisions away from Congress. Thus in a series of steps beginning in 1934, Congress "legislated itself out of the business of making product-specific trade law" by shifting fact finding and policy recommendations to a series of executive branch institutions—notably the Special Trade Representative (USTR) and the U.S. International Trade commission (USITC)—in which protectionist sentiment could be generally contained.[10]

On a day-to-day basis, in I. M. Destler's words, this system was "cumbersome, inefficient, and frustrating" and made a lot of work for lawyers.[11] But few students of U.S. trade deny the postwar policy system a large part of the credit for the stupendous postwar expansion of world trade which seems clearly to have been the basis for decades of rising living standards and a cohesive Western alliance. Protectionist pressures within the United States and the European Economic Community remained strong and enjoyed some successes, but the general trend was clear. Multilateral negotiations sponsored by the United States had reduced the average U.S. tariff level on imports from 60 percent in 1931 to 5.5 percent in 1985.

The system was politically more fragile than suspected. It was also organizationally messy. A Senate committee looking at the structure of trade policy in the executive branch in 1979 observed:

> Trade is not given a very high priority in terms of commitment of resources and the attention to top governmental policy officials on a regular basis, other than the STR. Additionally, major trade functions are spread through the Executive branch, making formulation of trade pol-

icy and implementation of trade policy haphazard and in some cases contradictory. No single agency exists which clearly predominates in the formulation of trade policy to the extent that people with a trade issue know where in the Executive branch they can turn . . .[12]

The president at the time these words were written concurred: "No agency has across-the-board leadership in trade," said Jimmy Carter.[13]

### Trade and Jimmy Carter

The administrative untidiness of the system for containing trade politics would not in itself have distracted Jimmy Carter from his announced pre-occupation with human rights, abolishing nuclear arms, reforming taxes and the welfare system. Soaring imports lengthened the ranks of injured industries, however, and memories of the destructive Smoot-Hawley tariff of 1934 and of the Great Depression faded. The percentage of the U.S. GNP going into overseas trade, exports and imports, had been 9.3 percent when Jimmy Carter was born, 6 percent when he graduated from the Naval Academy in a depression year, but reached 22.6 percent in his final year as president.[14] Exports caused no domestic political problems, but the changed volume and composition of manufactured imports posed an eco-nomic and political problem of growing severity. In Carter's White House years, American buyers were selecting sophisticated consumer electronic products from Taiwan, small appliances and color TVs from Korea, auto components and steel from Brazil, and toys and footwear from Malaysia, the Philippines, and Sri Lanka.[15]

As international competition intensified, a growing list of U.S. indus-tries lost sales and cut employment, and a tide of protectionism washed into the Oval Office. A considerable increase in petitions for trade relief traced the rise of import penetration. Adjustment assistance petitions, which had averaged 25 a year in 1963–1974, rose to 967 in 1975–1978 and to over 2,000 in 1979–1981, while countervailing duty petitions went up from an average of 1 a year in 1963–1974 to 101 a year in 1979–1982. Trade disputes taken to the ITC rose threefold, and news items under the title "trade" increased 450 percent in the *New York Times* index in one decade. The president all the while was a Democrat with that party's special sensitivity to organized labor and the industrial Northeast. He thus found himself belabored for "lacking an effective trade policy," a charge not made against other postwar presidents, who could assume that trade issues were contained within the bureaucracy. For Carter they suddenly became ominous and demanded presidential attention.[16]

Carter eventually made some effort to reform the overall trade policy system, with unimportant results.[17] Yet he and his top aides underwent an important educational process as they tried to cope with the casualties of economic change. Trade problems were a part of something larger, and effective remedies lay outside the areas of import relief and export promotion—that is, outside the traditional areas of trade policy. Driven by trade disputes, the administration was headed, stage by stage, toward something that it could not label—Industrial Policy.

## National Growth and Urban Policies

The severe economic troubles of the Northeast and North Central regions and cities in the 1970s had produced a coalition of mayors, business executives, labor leaders, and an assortment of others behind the idea of a National Growth Policy. This movement brought together people concerned with national land-use patterns, urban form, encroachment of humanity's habitat upon ecologically sensitive areas, and much else. It became also a vehicle for those who had an economic stake in the Frostbelt cities, and who saw federal policy as both part of their problems and an element in their solution. Political pressure built behind this assorted coalition and converged upon a White House Conference on Balanced Economic Growth, in February 1978.

Top Carter administration officials devoted months to understanding this unfamiliar new issue cluster, rooted in economically distressed cities and regions. Could there be created a single National Growth Policy, coordinating the hundreds of policies affecting where people lived? Carter's answer was a sort of half-yes, when the first national Urban Policy was announced in 1978, amid much talk of "public-private partnerships" and the spurring of economic development through targeting "distressed" geographic areas with various federal interventions. The Urban Policy's merits and defects are now difficult to see, for it would have almost no track record. Congress rebuffed most of what Carter had asked for, and the 1980 election erased America's first Urban Policy from the scene.

The 1978–1980 Urban Policy died aborning, but the exertions that produced it influenced the administration's thinking for its remaining months in office. An attempt had been made to handle separately the problems of declining older industrial cities and of the steel industry, in both cases by inventing new institutions to manage them when the existing machinery did not fit the issue. The Carter government could have continued in this ad hoc fashion forever, but to some of his aides the steel and urban problems began to look like different parts of the same elephant.[18]

## Chrysler Corporation in Bankruptcy and in Washington

The shape of the animal became clearer when the chairman of the Chrysler Corporation, Lee Iacocca, came to Washington in 1979 with the news that a piece of America's major manufacturing industry was about to shut down, with what he estimated as the potential loss of 500,000 jobs. Iacocca reasoned that the same government that had rescued Lockheed in 1971 and New York City in 1975–1978 would surely devise some rescue for a corporation of Chrysler's size and importance.

Iacocca had first broached the matter of federal assistance to the auto company in June 1979, when he talked of regulatory relief and grants of money disguised as tax credits. He found Treasury Secretary William Miller firmly opposed and learned how little government knew about the auto industry and Chrysler. Nevertheless, nearly a deacade of bailouts, beginning with Penn Central in 1970, had deposited a certain expertise and set of assumptions in the civil service. This was especially so at Treasury, which usually took the lead, since Washington had nothing resembling a "federal bailout window" after the demise of the Reconstruction Finance Corporation (RFC) in 1953. Chrysler executives, backed by the United Auto Workers (UAW), wanted financial and regulatory aid with no strings, in the bailout pattern set by the many state governments that assisted distressed industries in the 1970s. But the federal officials who were listening in Washington in 1979 had some experience with supplicant corporations, and they displayed a sterner outlook than found in Michigan or Ohio. They demanded access to company information, insisted upon restructuring guided by long-term plans, and wanted institutional machinery to monitor compliance.

In September Iacocca, linking the company's economic difficulties to government pollution control and safety regulations as well as generally adverse trends in the U.S. auto industry, asked for up to $1.2 million in loan guarantees. When the bargaining was over, a package of aid combined with Chrysler-UAW concessions was enacted in January 1980, with $1.5 billion in federal assistance at the heart of a $3.5 billion infusion of capital.[19]

This was the largest government bailout of a single corporation in U.S. history, which suggested a certain uniqueness, but Iacocca cited precedent: "This nation has long since established the precedent of loan guarantees," the total coming to $409 billion in 1980 alone. "Our request breaks no new ground."[20] History provided also the scenario for the consequences of failure to act: "I look at this issue and I think of the bleak days of October, 1929, when I was a kid and the Crash came," House Speaker Tip O'Neill contributed.[21]

To judge from the congressional votes in the 1970s, bailouts were becoming a major and recurring component of national policy. Acceptance grew, over time, and resistance dwindled; on each new occasion the sums were larger. The 1971 Lockheed bailout went forward on a Senate margin of one vote, the first rescue of New York City in 1975 aroused only a ten-vote margin in the House but easily passed the Senate, while the Chrysler bailout vote passed comfortably in both houses. The federal loan guarantees in the three cases were $250 million, $1.65 billion, and $1.5 billion tied to twice that amount from other sources.[22]

Arranging the Chrysler package had been an exhausting business. It had occupied more than a third of the time of the secretary of the Treasury, had preoccupied Carter and White House Domestic Chief of Staff Stuart Eizenstat, and had claimed untold thousands of staff hours. Through 1980 the new Loan Guarantee Board, with its eight-person staff under Brian Freeman (who had learned about corporate finance and negotiation from his work on the creation of Conrail), doled out funds to Iacocca in return for concessions. The government was helping to run an auto company, pressing an irritated Iacocca and the Chrysler board to reduce the corporation's size, giving advice on car design, insisting upon changed investment plans and a wage freeze, pushing bankers and suppliers for concessions, and even making Iacocca sell the executive air fleet. Loan guarantees might not be new, but the government's role as co-manager through four years of the life of the Chrysler corporation was without exact precedent.

The Reagan administration, arriving in 1981, did not believe in such activities. Thus the Loan Guarantee Board rarely met thereafter, and Iacocca was given more managerial discretion. Yet this did not amount to a diminution of government's role, just a change in its composition.

Chrysler was given more assistance by Reagan than by Carter, in the form of favorable Internal Revenue Service rulings and a negotiated "voluntary" export limit on Japanese cars which was in fact an indirect tax on certain American car buyers with the funds sent to Chrysler (and the other auto companies).

This was activist industrial policy, "targeting," "loser fixing," and "bailing out," pursued under two very different administrations, leaving behind results and precedents that would be hotly argued. For some of the Carter top staff, it began to seem that there must be better ways to deal with sectoral problems.

## Carter on the Supply Side

Carter and his top aides had not been mentally prepared for such extensive White House involvement in sectoral matters. The domestic agenda of Democratic administrations was supposed to be jobs for the labor force, a demand-side assignment; civil rights for minorities; social services; environmental protection. Business was either regulated (generous subsidies might be and often were tucked under that term) or was on its own.

Carter's departure from this demand-side tradition was apparent in his handling of inflation, the foremost economic problem of the late 1970s, and one that Democrats did not find congenial. There were demand-side remedies for inflation, but they came drenched with Republican odors— tight money, efforts to balance budgets to dampen demand, admonitions about discipline and frugality. The Democratic alternative to these, over the years, had been controls, or jawboning about controls.

Carter did not want to slip down that old slope. A happier policy line was expansion of supply, and the administration set foot upon this road long before Ronald Reagan was taken seriously as a national political force. It was during Carter's term that Democrats began asking first-order questions they had not asked in living memory: How is wealth created? How are technological and business innovations generated? How are people motivated to invent, take risks, work, sell? How may American capitalists and the workers they hire put better products on the market than those offered by foreign capitalists and their employees, so that jobs and profits remain at home?

When the history of Carter's presidency is written, the chapter on supply-side efforts will be a substantial one. These might be divided into those Carter was pushed into by circumstances, which he did not much like to talk about, and those announced with fanfare by the White House and paraded in speeches. Sector-specific interventions on the supply side fall into the first group: the rescue and attempted restructuring of steel and Chrysler and then the auto industry generally. Time-consuming, of doubtful legitimacy in Democratic party doctrine, slow to take effect, these measures did not lend themselves to political bragging. The deregulation of airlines, banks, and trucking was better bragging ground, because the public at once saw their effects. Though continually involved with sectoral involvements, the Carter administration did not see them at first as a promising part of its general economic strategy.

In the other group are supply-side measures that affect all or nearly all of American industry, initiatives that Carter displayed proudly on ceremonial and political occasions. The length and variety of this list are noteworthy:

the 1978 establishment of a National Productivity Council
announcement of a national export policy; reorganization of the
   Commerce Department to expand trade promotion functions and
   create a new Bureau of Industrial Economics
a presidential message on innovation in 1979 and on science and
   technology every year
a report on economic competitiveness in 1980 along with a White
   House Conference on Small Business [23]

The significance of this record of activity did not lie in its immediate impact on the economy. Carter was a man of serious purpose, embarked upon a two-term presidency that would make a long-term difference. His supply-side program aimed at economywide processes, conceded to be fundamental to long-term national prosperity by every serious student of the economy.

He was also, to some extent, marching in step with advanced opinion. The general business press was full of reports about declining productivity rates and sluggish innovation, and the fact that patents granted per U.S. resident had declined every year since 1971 but to foreigners had risen every year since 1963 might be encountered in mainstream journals. A younger generation of liberal Democratic politicians, foremost among them California's Governor Jerry Brown, had begun to exploit the public uneasiness with underlying economic trends and to shape a response that stressed entrepreneurialism, thrift, and government support for high-technology enterprise. An interest in invigorating the almost forgotten dynamics of capitalism could be found here and there throughout the network of liberal discussion. At Robert Maynard Hutchins' liberal think tank, the Center for the Study of Democratic Institutions, in the summer of 1979, fellows who normally discussed civil rights, nuclear war, or press freedoms attended a meeting on "Innovation and American Industry: What Went Wrong?" in which businessmen, academics, and fellows worried about R&D expenditures, the availability of capital, tax rates, and the structure of corporate boards of directors.[24]

Meetings on innovation seemed consecutive in 1979—at MIT, at the Franklin Institute, at the National Academy of Engineering, on Capitol Hill as the Stevenson-Wydler Technological Innovation Act of 1980 worked its way through to passage. At a conference on innovation held in 1976 economist Robert Gilpin offered a historical interpretation of what was occurring beneath the figures on productivity: "The U.S. has now entered into the same cycle of decline that marked Britain's slippage as a world power in this century."[25] At Hutchins' Center in 1979, an attorney long active in liberal causes projected a scenario that others would echo in the 1980s: "The U.S. is headed back to where it was a hundred years ago: primarily an exporter of agricultural commodities and raw materials rather than manufactured goods."[26]

Given such currents of opinion, Carter may well have been on a promising track economically, but his supply-side initiatives were complex, slow, and thus "boring." Some way must be found to present such efforts as a grand strategy, and a winning one.

## The Economic Policy Journey of Jimmy Carter

The Carter White House had been struggling from problem to problem, staffing its internal task forces to handle crises in steel and autos and regional decline, to study innovation and competitiveness in general. Slowly, top Carter officialdom and Carter himself discovered that government was poorly organized to see the large industrial picture. One powerful lever prompting a basic revision of economic policy was political. The Carter administration was in serious political trouble by 1979, for many reasons; one was its inability to restore economic growth without inflation. An electoral test was coming in 1980, and Senator Edward Kennedy's challenge inside the party was anticipated well before he declared it on November 7, 1979. The study of technological innovation was launched in the fall of 1978 as an effort to regain the political and intellectual ground occupied by outgoing Governor Jerry Brown, who was plainly looking eastward. The study had occupied mountains of staff time, and the nine recommendations for policy reforms had the merit of having no enemies: "We have found no one against it," wrote an aide; "technological innovation may well be the one win-win game in town." [27] But no one was ardently for it, either. The study had produced no large ideas, slogans, or framework for addressing the economic tangles surrounding Carter. Something more arresting to the public eye, and with an earlier payoff, had to be offered as the administration's plan for its second-term economic management.

Congress gave a nudge in the Trade Agreements Act of 1979, requiring the executive branch to furnish a report on industrial problems. The administration launched another intense policy review, this one nearly eighteen months long, in an increasingly urgent search for a new economic strategy that would restore public confidence in Jimmy Carter's election-eve ability to guide the economy through the first half of the 1980s. Here the Industrial Policy idea surfaced, in a closed-door rehearsal for the public debate ahead.

## The Industrial Policy Study

An Economic Policy Group (EPG) of cabinet-level officials was instructed to conduct the review of "industrial policy" (uncapitalized in internal memos). Soon the group split on this issue nobody had satisfactorily defined. "As you know," Department of Transportation Secretary Neil Goldschmidt wrote to Treasury Secretary and EPG head G. William Miller in July 1980, "I am an avid"—then the last word was crossed out, and he went on—"a strong supporter of EPG's initiative on revitalizing American industry." [28] But not all Carter's top aides felt the same way. Secretary Miller, along with Council of Economic Advisers Chairman Charles Schultze, remained strongly skeptical, ensuring that the review would develop adversarial positions.

Since EPG was a cabinet-level group, its members busy with other duties, the review was in practice consigned to a group of deputies who worked hard through the spring and summer of 1980, and also became deeply split. There were enthusiasts, led by Arnold Packer from the Labor Department (who flew to Japan during the review to see IP for himself), Joshua Gotbaum from the Treasury, and Orin Kramer from State. They concluded, Kramer wrote, that "nothing is working," that the United

States already had "a 'de facto' industrial policy . . . one which . . . applies haphazardly."[29] In Commerce Department aide Jerry Jasinowski's words, since the days of Alexander Hamilton there has been in the United States "the widespread existence of what can only be called inadvertent industrial policy," but lacking an institutional mechanism to give it coherence, leverage, and defensible goals.[30] Packer, early in the process, had urged "creating winners," "restructuring less efficient industries," and "facilitating positive adjustment," a full menu of IP which he found to be working in Japan and in some of the other major industrial countries.[31] Frank Press, the president's science adviser, urged Carter to encourage "hi-tech" industries, and named a list of 19 products that Japan's Ministry of International Trade and Industry (MITI) was openly promoting for the next decades.[32] The administration had no shortage of activist ideas. The President's Commission for a National Agenda for the Eighties held hearings on the IP idea in Los Angeles and reported that a business-oriented audience displayed "a high degree of unanimity" on "the need to move in the direction of a more explicit and integrated industrial policy, though [there was] no consensus on the elements of such a policy."[33] Administration aides weighing such ideas must have known that in Congress, most notably in Senator Lloyd Bentsen's Commerce Committee, there was interest in a revived Reconstruction Finance Corporation.

There were also doubters. Peter Solomon spoke for Treasury Department skeptics, repudiating the idea of "a plan to pick or fund winners" or "a program for supporting losers," letting some air out of the development bank idea. Yet he still saw the need to move beyond such ad hoc task forces as had handled the steel and Chrysler problems, and he commended the idea of "a standing deliberative body (such as General Council)" of tripartite form and an "Office of Industrial Development" with the operating capability achieved by Japan's MITI.[34]

Other participants were more skeptical. "The potential for a successful massive program is low, for a large embarrassment, high," judged the staff economists from the Council of Economic Advisers (CEA).[35] The skeptics suspected that there were ample American precedents, perhaps sobering ones, for much of the apparatus being proposed for an Industrial Policy—national development banks, central planning councils, tripartite industrial forums. Some history must be hurriedly studied.

An institution from the American past, the RFC, kept intruding into discussion. Launched under Herbert Hoover, the Reconstruction Finance Corporation was transformed into a New Deal workhorse for funding various enterprises thought to be socially useful but overlooked by flawed markets, and was finally killed by a Republican Congress in 1953. The deputies group found so little written on the history of the RFC that it commissioned a history from the Treasury Department staff, along with a historical review of all federal credit programs. The State Department commissioned ambitious studies of the historical experience of Japan, West Germany, Sweden, and France with IP, all rushed to completion in less than a year.

These staff papers made the choices no easier, since their authors recorded historical facts and declined to interpret them. MIT economist Paul Krugman was hired as a consultant to derive the implications of State Department studies of overseas IP. If one assumes, Krugman wrote, that by "industrial policy" one meant "selective promotion of particular industries" as against general policies affecting manufacturing generally, then IP was practiced very differently in all countries studied and was "not nearly so important a factor as has been suggested" in any of them, not even in Japan. Krugman concluded: "Enthusiasm for a policy of selective promotion of growth industries does not seem to be warranted by the experience of France, Germany, Japan, and Sweden" and "should be treated with skepticism."[36]

This was not far from the thinking of the deputy most knowledgeable about the issues under study, economist George Eads, formerly of the Rand Corporation. In 1979 he was a member of the CEA and, with Jerry Jasinowski of Commerce, cochaired the review group. Eads knew that the IP idea had migrated from Europe, where he had encountered it as U.S. delegate to the Organization for Economic Cooperation and Development (OECD) Working Party 2 on "positive adjustment." This term, much in use in European economic circles, referred to "good" IP, which aimed to facilitate the movement of capital and labor into industries capable of growing tomorrow. ("Negative adjustment," not mentioned but implicit, must be industrial policies that blindly resisted the market, and thus, the future.) By the summer of 1980 Eads was thinking more clearly than most participants about this new set of issues, and an Eads-Jasinowski memo to the EPG principals, dated June 12, 1980, was a model of lucidity in the charged political atmosphere of that summer. Much of the talk of the next four years was foreshadowed in it.[37]

Noting the large political risks of discussing IP even internally in that preelection summer ("Our review of industrial policy, should we press on, may simply lead to decisions to reject anything akin to explicit industrial policy," and thus "may saddle us with unneeded controversy" or, if adopted, "may arouse false expectations"), the two men acknowledged that, "rightly or wrongly, the perception is growing that the United States is slipping into the status of a second-rate industrial power. Demands are mounting that the federal government 'do something.'" [38] The work of the Deputies Group to that point had been research; it was time to frame recommendations, but it was also politically the eleventh hour. The cochairs proposed to produce a study of the U.S. industrial situation, current policies here and abroad, with recommendations on this "industrial policy" idea and the options available. Four months might see it done thoroughly, six weeks in an emergency.

They must have known that the timetable of presidential campaigning dictated the emergency schedule. Indeed, in June they already knew the choices, for Eads and Jasinowski had summarized three broad policy approaches to improved industrial performance. [39]

1. *Process and management improvements* might include steps to enhance government information and expertise on industrial conditions, perhaps an annual report for the industrial sector and a coordinating unit for all government programs affecting industrial sectors, and a "high-level tripartite commission" for conflict resolution. None of these steps would require new powers. The last two "process improvements" seemed to imply substantial and continuing sectoral intervention and its management. Yet these measures to improve coordination could fairly be presented as nothing generically new nor troubling. The same could be said for the second approach.

2. *Cross-industry measures* "would be relatively neutral among factors of production and industries," such as strong tax incentives toward savings and investment, promotion of technological innovation, improvement of programs to retrain workers displaced by economic change, promotion of export trade, small business, and competition generally.

Neither option was seen as unpromising or reckless. Both promised to be sectorally "neutral," a concept held in much esteem by those with university educations in economics. The third option, however, was approached warily.

3. *"A set of approaches . . .* [would] lead towards what many regard as fullblown industrial policy . . . All [such approaches] leave behind neutrality. They need not entail greater cost to government, though those who oppose them argue strongly that once industries are favored or once instruments are used in non-neutral ways, the process encourages

the growth of interests and pressures which will surely lead to higher governmental costs." This would be "targeting sectors for special policy treatment."

The tone suggested that this third option was full of new hazards. Yet the authors conceded that sectorally biased measures were "not . . . an approach totally unknown to the U.S. What we have done in the agriculture and maritime sectors, and what we are now trying to do in the energy sector, represent specific examples of extensive sectoral intervention." They knew that the president had told a *New York Times* reporter in an interview in May that the administration had targeted the auto, steel, and shipbuilding industries for special study leading to continuous modernization "partnerships" between these industries and government.[40] The industrial policy horses were out of the barn, and presidentially acknowledged. Yet the deputies remained wary of taking the next half-step, from industrial policies to Industrial Policy. They reported "increasing skepticism" in Europe about continental national experiences in "picking winners," because of "Government's poor record." As for the United States, it all seemed to lead toward "planning . . . the end point on the spectrum of industrial policy," which "save for isolated instances in wartime . . . stands totally outside our economic tradition." These two brief historical judgments on European and U.S. experience dangled at the end of the equivocal draft report of the EPG Deputies Group on June 12. But Carter wanted recommendations within a month. He received them in late July; a covering memo by Eizenstat survives in the Carter Papers, but the final recommendations of the EPG have not been found.[41]

The documentary record does not disclose the options Eizenstat presented to Carter or reveal the president's thinking. It is clear that there was an internal tussle over labeling which anticipated the public debate to follow. Columbia University sociologist Amitai Etzioni, articulate and intense, broke into print with the "reindustrialization of America" idea he had pushed as a consultant to the EPG study. America, for Etzioni, had become "an underdeveloping nation" because of "two decades or more of overconsumption and underinvestment in both the public and private sectors."[42] Here, White House aides thought, might be that alternative large idea to do battle with Reagan's theory that too much government was responsible for all economic problems. The "reindustrialization" mission called for active government, and some people thought that Etzioni had found a way to urge Industrial Policy under a more fetching label. Stuart Eizenstat wrote to Carter in an undated memo, apparently in

May: "I believe an initiative on an industrial policy—under the rubric of the re-industrialization of America—would excite these [blue-collar] workers and offer the nation hope that our basic industries will remain competitive."[43]

Etzioni objected that there was confusion; industrial policy was "only a remote relative."[44] IP would move resources to politically chosen sectors, whereas reindustrialization in his conception would shift resources from consumption to untargeted capital expenditures through the tax system, and to governmental infrastructure investments.

Whatever Carter chose to call the new strategy it was not to be "reindustrialization," after Senator Edward Kennedy made a speech on May 21 calling for a "Reindustrialization Corporation" as the policy centerpiece of a government showing a new "boldness . . . Lincolnesque or Rooseveltian in dimension." Etzioni's terminology was dead inside the Carter White House, because Kennedy had stolen it.[45]

Only the label, however, would be abandoned. Carter's August 28 announcement of a new economic program made Industrial Policy the official economic strategy of an administration that turned out to be in its final months.

Carter's "revitalization" program bore a name less forbidding and confusing than Industrial Policy. A senior White House aide explained that the term *revitalization* was picked "to avoid any implication of aid essentially for declining industries that have no hope [and] because it embraced identification of growth industries as well."[46]

As it turned out, it was too late to convince the public that Jimmy Carter had finally hit upon the right formula or direction. The "Economic Revitalization Program" was briefly reported in the press, then vanished from discussion.

The occasion deserved more attention, for it was the first official espousal of a form of Industrial Policy, although Carter himself did not use that term in remarks announcing the program, and it appeared only in a minor place in a fact sheet handed out to the press. Carter's "Economic Revitalization Program" was introduced in meandering and soporific remarks about the lessons of history, the folly of expecting "simple and easy solutions," the need to increase productivity, Mark Twain's definition of an American, and the need to upgrade port facilities. Reporters hardly knew what to make of the program. Most news stories focused on the absence of proposals for large shifts in taxes or spending, and ignored the machinery for sectoral intervention proposed toward the end of

Carter's rambling talk. Yet the president had proposed: (1) a new institution, the Economic Revitalization Board, to institutionalize "cooperation" throughout the economy and to advise the president on the creation of (2) an "industrial development authority" (read "bank"). Along the way, he had proudly listed and stressed the great importance of sectoral interventions under way—building a new synfuels industry, doubling the size of coal output—and plans to "retool the automobile industry to . . . meet any competition from overseas," to modernize steel, and "to create a whole new industry to produce solar and other renewable energy systems."[47] These were by any definition targeted industrial policies, and new policy-shaping institutions would guide them: an Economic Revitalization Board, a national development bank, and tripartite committees such as those set up in the steel and auto industries.

This presidential speech capped eighteen months of intramural study, but for Carter it marked the end of IP instead of the beginning. The Economic Revitalization Board, under the chairmanship of Lane Kirkland of the AFL-CIO and Irving Shapiro, chairman of E. I. du Pont de Nemours and Co., never met. The industrial development bank was left in the cold print of the president's message. Carter plunged deeply into the reelection campaign, lost, and packed up for his return to Plains, Georgia.

The new economic program owed its rapid disappearance also to its weak roots within the administration itself. Top officials in the economic policy area had never supported its main elements. When the House Budget Committee held hearings on the Economic Revitalization Program in September, CEA Chairman Schultze and Treasury Secretary Miller talked without notable enthusiasm about the plan's attached tax changes, labor retraining, and the energy program. They virtually ignored the Economic Revitalization Board and entirely ignored the bank. Congressmen asked questions about the Comprehensive Employment and Training Act (CETA), the refundable tax credit, or the Kemp-Roth tax plan. Federal Reserve Chairman Paul Volcker talked about the money supply. Carter's Industrial Policy was stillborn.[48]

It had not been a "fullblown" IP, but rather a cautious, Carterite version, its outlines and significance submerged in distracting detail. Yet not everyone missed its significance. *The Economist* reported that Carter had taken "a leaf out of Europe's industrial book," noting that "suddenly, the Carter administration has decided to have an industrial policy."[49] Few commentators noticed the novelty of the problems addressed and the remedies suggested or the departure from Democratic party tradition. No immediate new jobs were promised, the tools were not Keynesian, the payoff was only in the long term.

Carter had twice referred to the past in his speech, in both cases to suggest that it was time to break free of it. This "journey toward a more productive and more competitive . . . American economy will be possible only if we regard the past not as a refuge within which we can hide, but [as] a treasury of lessons from which we can learn." But the only lesson he specified was the importance of going beyond symptoms to address causes. And Mark Twain was recalled, for he had "defined an American as a person who does things because they haven't been done before." [50] Jimmy Carter evidently saw himself as leaving the past behind.

# CHAPTER 3

# Ousted from Washington

The United States is in the middle of an economic disaster that is unfortunately not an economic crisis.

Lester Thurow
"The Productivity Problem," *Technological Review*

The voters in November 1980 consigned Jimmy Carter's presidency to history, along with his "Economic Revitalization Plan"—Industrial Policy—and his other attempts to turn the clock forward. But the IP idea had just begun its term of influence. Writing in 1980, economist John Pinder found that the term "industrial policy . . . not many months earlier, had seldom been in general circulation. More than one group of people said to themselves, 'it seems we have been talking about industrial policy all along and didn't know it.'"[1] In 1980 the idea emerged on a broad front. Assistant Secretary of Commerce Frank Weil, a deputy on Carter's economic policy review, used the term in an article in *Fortune* in March 1980, and *Business Week* devoted eighty pages of its June 30, 1980, issue to this new topic.[2]

## Business and the New Idea

*Business Week* stood squarely behind IP, though recognizing that some of its readers would find a "reindustrialization plan . . . dangerous because it requires an industrial policy which chooses which industries, sectors and product lines should be encouraged because they have a good chance in international competition." Without hesitation, the magazine endorsed government "targeting," picking of winners, the only choice left when other nations did not follow the rules. "The lesson of other nations [Japan, Germany] is that it will [work]." The United States needed "total reprogramming . . . a fundamental change [that] will require indicative planning," another term that held no terror for *Business Week*.[3]

*Business Week* spoke from a maverick position that no other business group immediately endorsed. The government, in the magazine's view, was plainly incapable of dealing with current economic problems; thus:

> The leaders of the various economic and social groups that compose U.S. society should agree on a program for reindustrialization and present that program to Washington. Neither Congress nor the Administration is capable of providing the leadership necessary to form a national consensus. Business, labor and academic leaders should establish a forum to hammer out a new social contract for the U.S. Special groups must recognize that their own unique goals cannot be satisfied if the U.S. cannot compete in world markets. The drawing of a social contract must take precedence over the aspirations of the poor, the minorities, and the environmentalists. Without such a consensus, all are doomed to lower levels of living, fewer rights, and increasingly dirty air and water.[4]

Other business leaders were beginning to move toward this new idea, although few spoke so explicitly about whose interests would come first or last in the new social contract. Alex Trowbridge, president of the National Association of Manufacturers, and Bethlehem Steel chairman Lewis Foy both advocated "a competitive industrial strategy."[5] The heads of 250 major corporations were surveyed about whether they favored an (ill-defined) "federal reindustrialization effort," the pollsters reporting that "the great majority of the top executives welcome government help."[6]

Still, the broader business view in 1980 was unsettled and wary. In August the *New York Times* ran a five-part series on "Reviving Industry," and in the Frostbelt found widespread anxiety among corporation and union heads, along with interest in any new forms of government help. "The industrial heartland is littered with closed plants," the paper reported on August 18. In the more buoyant high-technology regions, California and Massachusetts, it discovered what it subsequently found within the Carter administration—many doubters that "reindustrialization" or "industrial policy" was an intelligible or feasible response to industrial problems, which were in any event exaggerated. "The British tried that," was the history lesson offered by General Electric chairman Reginald Jones, "and it didn't work."[7]

At congressional hearings in September, experts were available to testify, a sign that the IP idea was maturing. Pat Choate, coauthor with Gail Schwartz of one of the first books on IP, urged "sectoral policies . . . jointly developed by government, labor and management" through a "consultative system . . . for each industry," supplemented by an Office of

Sectoral and Industrial Policy. Fletcher Byrom of Koppers Corporation heard in Choate's remarks a policy of "picking winners and losers." If this was IP, it was doomed out of history: "There are examples of failures in other countries which have attempted to follow this strategy (i.e., picking winners). Consider, for example, Britain's attempt to pick winners, under the National Industrial Development Board . . . I am sure there are some success stories . . . but experience both here and abroad tells us that as a policy for adjusting to long-term change it is most unlikely that any benefits from this approach will exceed the costs."[8]

Here appeared, at the outset, a fissure in the business community outlook on desired policy changes. *Business Week* demanded a procapitalist realignment of federal policies to rectify the errors of the 1960s and 1970s, but also envisioned some new institutional arrangements to allow federal aid to be targeted, as in Japan. There might need to be a public investment bank, some apex institution to coordinate policy and arrange sectoral consensus. Executives from mature, import-challenged industries tended to concur. Philip Caldwell, chairman of Ford Motor Company, asserted in 1980: "We need a new, sensible national industrial policy to provide an effective framework for action," since "in the auto industry, individual U.S. companies are competing against Japan as a country."[9]

Corporate spokesmen who wanted the procapitalist tilt but distrusted new institutions began to use the term *industrial strategy* as a substitute for Industrial Policy. An outline of a strategy was offered by the National Association of Manufacturers and in advertisements in major newspapers paid for by corporations—lists of easements of antitrust and regulatory laws, tax reductions, loosening of environmental and worker protections, in all a higher value to be placed upon "efficiency" and less on the overstressed "equity" issues.

## Learning Lessons from Japan

Caldwell had spoken the name on all minds—Japan. Nippon, formerly military adversary, then ward, then ally, forced the IP idea to the front. As a result of "the Japanese miracle," a surge of industrial prowess which carried Nippon's auto, steel, and consumer electronics industries past U.S. products in competitiveness, the business community became as preoccupied by Japan as the national security community and fundamentalist ministers were with the Soviet Union. The business media bristled with

stories of Japan's assets—national discipline and homogeneity, managerial innovations such as "quality circles" and lifetime employment, an educational system training engineers and technicians rather than lawyers—and a thing called Industrial Policy, orchestrated by the Ministry of International Trade and Industry. Ezra Vogel provided the authoritative statement in *Japan as Number One,* a 1979 best-seller. Vogel told of a formidable economic rival entering the 1980s with many advantages, chief among them a national strategy and MITI its chief planner.

Vogel reached a broad public. Other writers addressed congressional policymakers, as when Harvard law professor Julian Gresser told the Congress that the Japanese were ready for the competition of the 1980s, not only in heavy industry but also in semiconductors, computers, and telecommunications, the core technologies:

> History suggests that, in the past . . . control over the development of a core technology has permitted these entities [a firm or cartel] to influence critically the design, price, quantity, and time of introduction of other products; and ultimately, what new industries . . . would emerge . . . Our present piecemeal, uncoordinated approach will not meet the challenge presented by foreign competition in high technology, particularly semiconductors, computers and telecommunications.

Gresser left one further observation with the lawmakers: "We already have an industrial policy—it is just an ineffective one." [10] He offered more encouraging examples from the past—the War Industries Board of 1918, the National Recovery Administration (NRA) of 1933–1935, and the longest-running of them all, "agricultural policy."

The record does not show how important these examples were thought to be, but to those knowledgeable about American history it was an odd list. The War Industries Board had coordinated wartime production controls for a part of the war effort in 1917 and 1918, under circumstances that no one would want to repeat. The NRA had been a massive program of sectoral intervention affecting over 500 industries paralyzed by the Great Depression, an unprecedented effort in the planned limitation of production. In both general and expert opinion the NRA was thought to have been one of Franklin Roosevelt's not-so-good ideas, a policy misadventure killed (mercifully) by the Supreme Court. Naming it certainly did not strengthen Gresser's general argument. And what did he—and others—mean by citing all of agricultural policy? Apparently, Gresser was not seriously interested in past U.S. industrial policies, except to assert

that there had been many of them with some good results. He was, however, closely interested in the history of postwar Japan, as were Vogel and
a growing crowd of others.

Once seen from America as a nation of Western imitators, Japan was
now recognized as a country of innovators because of a record of recent
achievement—if not leading innovators in products, then certainly in the
systems that produce and market products. "The lesson of other nations,
particularly Japan," wrote *Business Week*, "is that it [Industrial Policy] will
work—if the U.S. can create a new consensus on goals." [11] It was time to
study, interpret, and learn from history. To judge from the discussion in
late 1980, that meant a superficial review of our own and a serious scrutiny of Japan's recent past. The library of books in English on the Japanese
political economy was a small one as the IP debate opened, but it was a
growth industry. [12]

### Autumn 1980: The Short, Unhappy
### Life of Industrial Policy?

The IP idea had made its sudden debut in the summer and fall of 1980, in
several places under several labels. Reindustrialization to some, industrial
policy or industrial strategy to others, the shifting nomenclature invited
a certain skepticism. Some commentators suspected that it might be
"merely a buzzword—an abstraction in search of a policy." [13] Others observed: "That term [Industrial Policy] and 'reindustrialization' have become shorthand to express a need to deal with an almost panoramic set of
problems, a rubric in search of a definition." [14]

The presidential campaign of 1980 generated debate on not much of
anything and shed no light at all on the IP idea. An inchoate concept at
this stage, IP could have become a framework for national discussion only
if a presidential candidate pushed it forward. Carter announced his "revitalization plan" but lacked a gift for communicating simple summaries
of complex ideas. His economic plan, like his energy plans, was in-
felicitously labeled, and, like everything else about Jimmy Carter in 1980,
boring to most of the public. The other presidential candidate, Ronald
Reagan, had at least one economic adviser, Charls Walker, who had publicly advocated some type of federal development bank as a better way to
handle bailouts than the ad hoc crisis management of the 1970s. Walker
continued on Reagan's Economic Policy Advisory Board after the election, but, as he recalled later, "I never discussed industrial policy with

him."[15] Reagan had other ideas, and they had nothing to do with a positive, nondefense role for government.

Thus, as the autumn of 1980 faded, the fledgling IP conception seemed adrift on a tide running out. A Senate Democratic Caucus task force was spurred by Senator Adlai E. Stevenson (D., Ill.), who held hearings on science and technology issues in 1979–80. Its report, published in early August, drew the headline: "Senate Demands Congress Produce Industrial Policy"; the lawmakers deplored bailouts but favored an industrial development bank for investment in infrastructure and "new processes," along with enhanced worker retraining programs and new tax advantages for capital investment. Carter was criticized for his lack of progress on the issue of industrial strength.[16]

But this small group soon disbanded, and in any event it did not seem to speak for most Democrats. The Democratic party platform ignored both IP and its supply-side thrust. "The one overriding principle must be fairness," the economic policy segment of the platform began, then discussed the rights of labor, followed by small business, minority business, women in business, and finally the well-being of consumers.[17] There was not a hint of the issue of international competitiveness, nor of policy approaches to especially troubled or promising industrial sectors. Democratic party platform writers remained oblivious to the issues so closely studied by Carter's policy review and surfacing in the media as reindustrialization or IP.

Apparently the Industrial Policy issue had peaked. The President's Commission for a National Agenda for the Eighties reported in December 1980 that "the slowdown of the past decade is not the result of systemic illness" and proposed a familiar set of macroeconomic policies as paths to noninflationary growth. On "industry-specific" problems, the panel found it an idea proven defective in "the experience of countries that have tried it." That sweeping and undocumented generalization stretched over several national histories was used to close the issue. But the panel could not have been unified, for the door was left ajar in the case of "basic industries . . . [which] meet national security needs," or "to prevent or reduce over-reliance on insecure sources of critical imports, especially energy."[18]

With this wary language about winner and loser picking, the commission's economic panel was apparently rebuffing the new IP idea, as it understood it. A final repudiation came from within the Carter administration, once nursery of the IP idea. Carter's last *Economic Report* appeared in January 1981, a small book sure to be ignored as new people and a new party moved into White House offices. To the few readers it may have had, the document appeared to settle the Democrats' internal dispute. It came down firmly in favor of the old macroeconomic verities, and against sectoral policies upgraded in importance and institutionally focused. The president's portion of the report, signed if not written by Carter, did not mention industrial policies, "reindustrialization," or the institutions for sectoral management invented in August. Yet in the analysis of economic trends by the Council of Economic Advisers, the issue was squarely joined. Economic troubles have "led some to propose an explicit 'industrial policy' to guide the broad collection of Federal activities affecting individual industries and sectors." This meant picking winners or supporting older industries, and was a bad idea:

> Attempts to pick winners or reinvigorate declining industries introduce considerations into strategic industrial decisions that, while not now absent, are certainly less directly felt. Greater government involvement in the detailed working of the economy has already increased the political aspect of economic decision making and led to constant pressures for the Federal government to aid firms, regions, and industries. Establishment of an explicit industrial policy . . . would intensify these trends.

This was surely the voice of Charles Schultze, CEA chairman and an opponent of the IP idea from its first appearance. He spoke last for the Carter government, in an apparent epitaph for whatever IP was, or had hoped to be. The report's final words on IP, however, were puzzling:

> In sum, recognition that the numerous policies of the Federal Government exert a substantial influence on individual sectors of the economy leads logically to a search for coherence in policy. The pursuit of such coherence is both justified and desirable when it involves the thoughtful coordination of policies in areas where government intervention is necessary. The danger lies in the unwise manipulation of policy variables designed for one set of purposes to attain goals which can be better achieved by the private sector.[19]

It is difficult to make sense of the passage, which appears to endorse "a search for coherence in [industrial] policy" while warning that there is a danger here which must not be risked. All in all, the Carter administration's final economic report concluded that this IP thing was a mistake to be avoided and a heresy to be firmly condemned. The same Jimmy Carter who had proposed a revitalization board and an industrial development bank in the late summer of 1980 sent to Congress in January 1981 a report that concluded in a section titled "The Dilemma of Industrial Policy" that "picking winners," "supporting older industries," and "supplant-[ing] the private sector in allocating capital" were "industrial policy" and "would go beyond the legitimate needs for balance, consistency, and flexibility in Federal actions affecting individual industrial sectors." [20] Carter has not again shown any interest in the topic. In his memoirs the term *industrial policy* does not appear.[21]

## Independent Advocates

Placing a bet upon the continuation of an IP debate as 1980 closed would not have been advised. The term still lacked clarity, and not all of its advocates were talking about the same thing. Although it was apparently a Democratic brew, some Democrats had refused it. More important, the new president, Ronald Reagan, couched his new ideas in the old language of macroeconomics—tax and spending changes, monetary policy.

Industrial Policy may have ebbed from political discourse after January 1981, but elsewhere spokesmen with impressive credentials in the worlds of economics and business were taking it up. In 1978 Walt Rostow, former aide to Kennedy and Johnson, now professor of economics and history at the University of Texas, published a book on the maturity stage of industrial economies. After discussing "the bankruptcy of neo-Keynesian economics" in the face of new realities in energy, raw materials, and international competition, Rostow insisted that the United States need not and must not go the way of Britain. "Economic decline is not a graceful process . . . It is painful, socially contentious, and potentially quite ugly." And unnecessary. "There are a good many examples of nations which successfully recaptured momentum after falling behind under the weight of mature industries with substantial obsolescent plant." France after 1945, New England after 1945, Germany after 1945 were Rostow's historical showcases. Many sources had contributed to the reinvigoration of these economies, but Industrial Policy had been omnipresent: "new forms of public-private collaboration," in "particular sectors, regions, cities and rural areas," doing a job for which fiscal policy was a blunt instrument. Rostow endorsed a development bank "like the old RFC," and a small planning office, such as Jean Monnet had created in postwar France.[22]

This was a voice from the liberal past, an economist concluding that the tools of his Keynesian generation were no match for the new circumstances. Another vocal advocate of this new stress on policy for regions and sectors was Felix Rohatyn. Born in Vienna in 1928, he arrived in the United States in 1942 as a man who "never took a course in economics."[23] By 1975 a partner in Lazard Frères and Co. in a New York City nearing bankruptcy, Rohatyn was made chairman of the state-established bailout agency, the Municipal Assistance Corporation (MAC). He published his first essay on U.S. industrial problems in late 1979, and by the end of 1980 he was a vigorous spokesman for a distinctive formulation of the IP idea. Rohatyn displayed no deference to economic orthodoxy, and he drew authority from his own financial success in the private sector, capped by his role in the artful bailout of New York City. His themes were unvarying: the nation is in serious economic difficulty, not unlike New York; existing political institutions lack the ability and public officials lack the will to discipline themselves or devise remedies for declining communities or sectors; the answer for the nation, as in New York, is to reach above legislatures to independent, qualified people exercising governmental authority to extend aid in return for restructuring.

Rohatyn's outlook blended economic gloom and policy optimism: "The thought that this Nation can function while writing off its basic industries to foreign competition is nonsense . . . What we have to do is turn the losers into winners, restructure our basic industries to make them competitive . . . This is a national security necessity . . . a social necessity."[24]

The answer was not isolated bailouts, such as the Chrysler "bandaid." What was needed was an independent organization, "free of political pressures," which at first he envisioned as a National Economic Planning Commission.[25] Soon his key institution looked more familiar, a new RFC, taking equity positions along with loans in exchange for "restructuring." Restructuring, a term central to Rohatyn's thinking, seemed to mean concessions from labor, perhaps also lower executive salaries. It would be arranged and imposed by the dedicated technocrats within RFC, an institution "publicly accountable but . . . run outside of politics, like MAC in New York state."[26]

Rohatyn had given IP a distinctive configuration. In his hands it was committed to the renovation of older industries and regions, had a technocratic cast, was institutionally centered in an RFC-type development bank guided by incorruptible brokers pursuing the public interest. "An RFC is not state capitalism," he wrote; "[it] is a temporary mechanism to restructure, on a sensible basis, those older, basic industries that otherwise will either disappear or be bailed out by indiscriminate government funding." The alternatives, he thought, were policy inaction, a continuation of industrial weakening, then class war, uprisings from the ghettos, where blacks faced 60 percent unemployment as urban economies stagnated. He, too, was a user of history. The experience of the United States was a replay of the experience of New York City ("New York is, in certain respects, a mirror of the U.S."), the RFC had worked and would again, the "examples of Germany and Japan should convince us that a genuine partnership of business and labor in government is required." To "cries of elitism or the fear of creating a new 'establishment,' I say that where we are going otherwise is infinitely worse." [27]

### The Varieties of Industrial Policy

Where was this IP idea to be located on the political spectrum? Versions of it were put forward by spokesmen for the older industrial sectors but also by those who foresaw a new governmental role in assisting "sunrise" industries. In 1980 MIT economist Lester Thurow spoke from the latter perspective: "Trying to help the losers doesn't work," but "the economic winners of the next 20 years" could be identified by a business-government collaboration on the Japanese model. [28]

Ideologically, the range was equally wide. Some people charged that IP was a "corporatist" plan hatched in the business community as a way to tilt federal economic policy away from the labor, consumer, and environmentalist gains of the preceding decades. It was Herbert Hoover's trickle-down theory, thought Sidney Lens, and "it looks a lot like Mussolini's Corporate State." [29]

One could move quite some distance to the left, however, along the stepping-stones of IP. Ronald Muller's *Revitalizing America*, published in November 1980, seemed to one reviewer to have established "the left-wing perimeter of reindustrialization." [30] Sketching his own version of the world economic crisis, Muller spoke of "equity" and "participation," and the need to "decentralize econopolitical decision-making" by expanding the boards of directors "of the 1,000 or so major corporations" to "include the new stakeholders" such as environmental and consumer groups. As for the mechanisms required to move to "an explicit industrial development policy framework," Muller borrowed an idea proposed by the chief economist of the New York business group the Conference Board. What was required was "an autonomous and quasi-public body," an advisory commission to "determine an agenda . . . suggest which sectors of the economy needed restructuring . . . make recommendations on equity versus efficiency trade-offs in industrial development . . . [monitor] global economic changes . . . provide an early warning to policy makers" and help select targets for a national development bank.[31]

Muller, almost alone among early writers addressing IP, had used the word *planning*. Were industrial policies planning? Was Industrial Policy Planning? The signs were mixed. People of the left are expected to like Planning, but many of them did not like Industrial Policy. Gar Alperovitz and Jeff Faux, analysts from the social-democratic edge of American politics, expressed considerable wariness about the talk about reindustrialization, since so much of it came from corporate sources—*Business Week,* Charls Walker, Felix Rohatyn.[32] But businessman (Ford dealer) Joseph Coberly, Jr., of Los Angeles did not like the sound of it either: "I cannot stress too strongly enough the danger of a national industrial policy. If the American Way means freedom of enterprise and voluntary exchange, nothing is more un-American."[33] Senator William Proxmire, also an amateur historian, expressed similar convictions: "I just wonder on the basis of past performance. Money will go where the political power is; it will go where unions are mobilized, where mayors and governors, representatives and senators have the power to push it. Anybody who thinks that the government resources will be allocated on the basis of merit hasn't been in Washington very long."[34] Similar skepticism was voiced by a top economic aide to two Democratic presidents, Charles Schultze, who offered journalist James Fallows a list of the 20 products or industries that grew fastest in the 1970s, and doubted that any government would have picked utility vehicles (ranked second), vacuum cleaners (ninth), cheese (eighteenth), or tufted carpets (nineteenth).[35]

Industrial Policy thus drew friends—and enemies—from across the political spectrum, from Wall Street to the Academy. At the end of 1980, the brief debate had peopled the stage with possibilities, the curtain half down and half up.

## Thoughts at the End of the Beginning

To this point, all discussants seemed either decidedly for or against Industrial Policy, whatever it was. This polarization reflected the combative and partisan atmosphere of an election year. In short supply was an informed understanding that the little that was known of the history of industrial policies, abroad as well as in the United States, bespoke multiple possibilities. An exception was William Diebold, senior staff member at the Council on Foreign Relations, whose *Industrial Policy as an International Issue* had been incubated through a series of conferences at Bellagio, Ditchley House, Florence, Paris, and Tokyo, with the help of the Japan Society and the Trilateral Commission, a shadowy institution coming to symbolize the eastern seaboard–internationalist conspiracy. Diebold addressed the domestic policy reactions within industrial economies as their global trade relations rapidly expanded. In response to trade opportunities as well as dislocation, "all countries" were taking a "variety of measures to shape the structure of . . . domestic economies [and to] determine long-run use of resources."[36] These industrial policies were designed to resist change, to promote adaptive action, or to encourage innovation. Thus the question about industrial policies could not be "Are they a good idea?" but "What kinds of industrial policies are we discussing?" Every nation employed them, Diebold noted, although the United States did not recognize its own. When asked by the Organization for Economic Cooperation and Development (OECD) in 1975 to report on its Industrial Policy along with other member states, the administration in Washington replied: "In line with American economic philosophy, the federal administrative structure is not designed to carry out an active, coordinated policy of promoting industrial growth," implying that Industrial Policy did not exist in the United States.[37]

Diebold hoped that Americans would learn not to make this error. But "if the world has lived this long with such a blooming, buzzing confusion of industrial policies, why should they now pose a major international problem?" The answer was: because of the expansion of world trade, resultant pressures upon older industries, and the threat of a surge of protectionism sufficient to shrink the world's enriching streams of commerce. The only alternative to this change-resistant form of industrial policy-making was different, superior forms: "One can make a strong case for an IP that mostly confines itself to helping instead of hindering adjustment, while at the same time easing the position of people who are hurt in the process," Diebold concluded from the European experience. Where industrial policies took that positive form, Diebold found several preconditions: reasonably good business-government relationships, continuity in policy, a banking community that understood and had historic ties to industry, labor leadership that was willing to play a constructive role in adjustment when not required to bear the entire burden of it. "The U.S.," he conceded, "has fewer aptitudes for conducting IP and more built-in obstacles than most countries." Still, Diebold cautiously argued for "a certain kind of action in the U.S.," and wished for an international forum in which member-state IPs could be nudged toward more economically rational (that is, less protectionist) forms.[38]

This was a prescient forecast of the rising importance of industrial policies in the American future, and of the pressing need to sort out their multiple possibilities. Jerry Jasinowski, leaving the government with the rest of Carter's appointees, had reached the same conclusion: "It seems increasingly clear that the government has always pursued industrial policies, and that the degree of government involvement has if anything accelerated over the past decade . . . [the debate] has shown that there are in fact pervasive industrial policies in the United States . . . Beyond recognizing this fact—which is in itself a major step—a central challenge is to improve the management of these ad hoc policies."[39]

Those were two major steps, and two early analysts who by the end of 1980 were ready to take them. The debate to follow would march for years in other directions.

## Prospects at the End of 1980

The 1980 election concluded one phase in the history of the Industrial Policy idea. IP and the Reagan version of supply-side economic policy were the two broad economic reform ideas to emerge from a decade of intensifying trade and regional problems that eluded traditional Keynesian manipulation. Together these two reforms went forward into the 1980s, one in the White House, the other in the wings. Diebold would recall: "I used to start talks by saying, 'You can have had an excellent education in the United States and never have heard the term "industrial policy"' . . . Then I had to amend it, 'but now you can't open the newspaper without reading it.' I don't know which is worse, probably the latter. It is at least more confusing."[40]

The IP idea evolved in parallel with Reaganism, given vitality not only by continued economic troubles and the discovery of rival industrial strategies abroad but also by the Democratic party's need for a supply-side strategy of its own. IP, a concept of beguiling versatility in 1980, might be shaped to the needs of Frostbelt or Sunbelt, and attracted both business and labor support. It seemed to promise a more direct response to the Japanese and European challenges. The IP debate became both more partisan and ideological in the political arena, while in other places and hands more technically informed and penetrating, as the Reagan presidency went forward, guided by other doctrines.

# CHAPTER 4

# Pundits at Floodtide

The new realism emphasizes . . . the suspicion that one of the reasons for the lack of success of the more-general economic policies is that there is some accumulation of structural difficulties.

William Diebold, Jr.
*National Industrial Strategies and the
World Economy,* ed. John Pinder

The word *hemorrhaging* was often used to describe the U.S. economy, the federal budget, or both as Ronald Reagan's team prepared to assume power in the last weeks of 1980. The U.S. economy had finished another poor year in the general recession gripping world economies. Noncommunist developed economies had grown an average of 1–2 percent in 1980, far below their 3–4 percent average gains in the two preceding years. Although "almost every country seemed to do worse [in 1980] than in 1979," only the United Kingdom did worse than the United States.[1] The American economy in 1980 "grew" at the negative rate of 0.9 percent; that is, it shrank. Unemployment stood at over 8 million people, or 7.6 percent of the work force. Inflation for the year had reached 12.4 percent, and the small merchandise trade deficit of 1971 had in 1980 reached a total of $25.4 billion.[2]

*Revolution* was the term the press used to describe the Reagan program, and at its enactment optimists made optimistic predictions. As 1981 ended, the economic indicators were mixed. A 2 percent rate of GNP growth reflected a strong first half, but the "Reagan recession" was soon shrinking the economy, with fourth-quarter growth −4.5 percent. Unemployment had risen to 8.9 percent, 9 million people, the merchandise trade deficit had reached $27.9 billion. Although the nominal inflation rate had dipped to 10 percent, the real rate stayed about where it had been a year earlier.[3]

President Reagan's economic report at the end of 1981 blamed these unsatisfactory results upon the long years of Democratic mistakes, and counseled patience and confidence. A year later, as 1982 closed, his

Council of Economic Advisers was forced to call that year, also, "a year of painful transition."[4] The now three-year recession was the deepest in postwar history; the U.S. GNP shrank by 2 percent until it was the size it had been in 1979, although the population sharing that output had grown by 7–9 million (depending upon the estimated number of illegal aliens one included). Total employment in all sectors was down by 1.7 million jobs; 10.7 million people were reported as unemployed as 1982 closed. Industrial production had fallen four times as fast as overall output, and exports moved in the same direction. Yet imports, which usually fall during recessions, surged to higher levels through 1981–82.[5]

This recession was unprecedented in postwar experience, both in its severity and in its ramifications. U.S. manufacturing was caught in a special ordeal of its own. The shrinkage of older industries was incessantly reported in the business and general press, with most of the bad news from autos and steel. As Ford Motor Company closed four plants and the seventy-year-old "Dodge Main" plant at Hamtramck, Michigan, shut down, the *New York Times* reported that "the people who design, make and sell American automobiles are living a nightmare whose outcome is anybody's guess." U.S. Steel closed fifteen facilities, several of them in Pennsylvania's Mahoning Valley, whose "steel towns have lost their reason for being."[6]

The larger picture emerging from the news about the shrinking basic industries of yesterday depicted displaced blue-collar workers whose prospects were not as good as their pasts. Was pervasive structural change inexorably carrying the American work force from high-paying jobs tied to the manufacturing core into either permanent unemployment or the bottom of the service economy? The Bureau of Labor Statistics predicted that by 1990 the major economic roles to be lost to technological change would be farm operators, teachers, compositors and typesetters, and clergy. People displaced from these occupations, or their children, would become waiters, office clerks, fast-food workers, or truck drivers. Such projections led to talk of declassing, of an industrial work force attempting, with the wages of cooks and sweepers, to buy from new manufacturers abroad.[7]

### New Crisis, New Remedies:
### "Minding America's Business"

These mounting economic difficulties gave the country at least one expanding industry—Industrial Policy talk. In 1980 the public had no book that both described industrial decline and prescribed the new IP remedy, but the authors eager to serve that market were even then at work. The harvest began in 1982.

"The best book yet about what industrial policy might be in the U.S.," Ira Magaziner and Robert B. Reich's *Minding America's Business* was declared in early 1982.[8] It was in many ways the prototypical Industrial Policy book, offering the basic structure of ideas upon which many variations would be spun. It began with a descriptive assertion of the realities of the new internationalized world economy; argued that comparative advantage in this new trade-saturated world was no longer a matter of natural resources or geographic position or the other traditional factor endowments, but could be created by societies employing neomercantilist systems of state-guided development; and contrasted successful systems of this sort, in Japan and Western Europe, with the unfocused U.S. system inherited from decades of unchallenged hegemony and preoccupation with welfare-state issues.

It was not a reassuring comparison, as Magaziner and Reich saw it. They described the investment decision-making process in U.S. firms and catalogued a series of misjudgments and failings institutionalized across the economy. These were rooted in American executives' short-term calculation of return on investment while foreign firms aimed at longer-term objectives and accepted lower profit margins; too much "asset-rearranging" by merger and acquisition (a point that Reich pursued in a subsequent book); poor quality control; inattention to production technology; unimaginative labor relations; lack of aggressiveness in pursuing international opportunities.

This argument bore some resemblance to the central message of popular books on how to be successful executive. Thomas Peters and Robert Waterman had just published *In Search of Excellence,* one of many books reaching the desks of an executive class more than usually anxious for guidance in an economy veering away from the old patterns.[9] Several other authors argued in the early 1980s that managerial errors and incapacities were the core and cure of the nation's slipping competitiveness— a thesis spread in the *Harvard Business Review* by Robert H. Hayes and William J. Abernathy in 1980 and in the *New Republic* by Ezra Vogel in 1981. In this view, the problems dotting the industrial landscape would respond to a differently educated and motivated top management.[10]

Magaziner and Reich concurred on these managerial shortcomings, but believed that the crucial changes required to improve economic performance must be initiated outside the company. Industries in other nations outperformed our own because governments abroad pursued a set of supply-side industrial policies to "address the pattern of investment, the mechanisms for industrial transitions, and the development of human resources, and not just entrepreneurial incentives and aggregate levels of savings and investment."[11] Nations with such government-orchestrated strategies put in the field companies that invariably outperformed American firms, whose government haplessly pursued an uncoordinated set of subsidizing, regulating, and harassing policies toward business. Thus the United States entered the 1980s as a slow-adapting, complacent society with an indelible memory of postwar dominance. It encountered foreign firms supported by market-invigorating, adaptation-facilitating national strategies found not in textbooks but in Tokyo, Paris, and Bonn.

Norton Long would observe that the advocates of IP assembled in two camps: the Preservationists, who wanted national assistance to shore up declining industries; and the Modernizers, who wanted government to work with market forces to encourage innovation and retrain the labor force.[12] *Minding America's Business* led off for the Modernizers, although only 37 of its 380 pages were devoted to the substance and design of an improved IP. Extending adjustment assistance to displaced labor, and state incentives to private investment in high-risk or long-term payback ventures were among the suggested improvements. The authors promised declining industries and regions no bailouts, only transitional wage subsidies, relocation allowances, and advance notification of shutdowns to ease adjustment. The thrust was toward accepting market decisions on the nation's industrial structure, cushioning but not preventing them. "In the long term," wrote Magaziner and Reich, "it is self-defeating to remain in businesses that are becoming dominated by developing countries."[13]

This was not a call for planning, for Industrial Policy was "haunted by the specter of centralized bureaucrats in capital cities who engage in picking winners and losers from among various industries, or oligarchies of industrial barons who systematically exchange campaign contributions for selective government largesse . . . The U.S. is not a nation of planners . . . But . . . economic success now depends to a high degree on coordination, collaboration, and careful strategic choice."[14]

In any case, industrial policies did not have to be invented. The United States already had an Industrial Policy in its existing collection of import restrictions and of aid targeted to various industries through the tax codes, loan guarantees, and subsidized insurance. MIT economist Lester Thurow, reviewing *Minding America's Business*, commented:

Whatever the rhetoric, no government does "nothing" . . . America now has an industrial policy. It just happens to be an industrial policy to shoot ourselves in the economic foot . . . [by] supporting sunset indus- tries . . . The strongest argument for industrial policies is not that they are needed, although they are, not that they can be made to work, al- though they can, and not that other countries used them to beat us, al- though they do; but that the U.S. is now developing a horribly inefficient set of industrial policies based on congressional investment banking. [It is time] to recognize what we are doing and start doing it right.[15]

### The Political Economy of Robert Reich

Magaziner continued to contribute to the IP debate by designing an in- dustrial policy for the state of Rhode Island—the "Greenhouse Compact" idea, of which more later.

Reich went back to his desk to produce a cascade of articles and books that established him as perhaps the leading advocate of Industrial Policy in the United States. In the spring of 1983 he published *The Next American Frontier,* a book crafted for the larger public.[16]

He framed the argument with two interpretations of history. According to the first, America's "singular history" among industrial nations re- vealed an uneasy combination of two competing ideals. America was the home of both a "business culture," concerned with efficiency and wealth making; and a "civic culture" concerned with justice, equality, and secu- rity. These deeply rooted cultures had long been adversaries, trading ad- vantage as political fortunes shifted: a reformist Woodrow Wilson followed by a probusiness Harding, a cycle of reform under Franklin Roosevelt fol- lowed by conservatism under Eisenhower. Americans had come to accept the idea of an inescapable trade-off between these two contesting ideals. A gain for the business culture was a loss for the civic culture; when one was dominant, the other must be eclipsed.[17]

In Reich's view, the unfortunate oscillation between these fundamental loyalties had prevented the emergence in the United States of collab- orative arrangements between the state and private interests such as were found in Western Europe and Japan. Ending this dualism, finding a way to combine the civic and business cultures—a break from history, a new cultural synthesis—was to Reich the key to economic revitalization.

Bridging or reconciling the two cultures was not, as he implied, a new idea. As the twentieth century has advanced, business and political leaders have often urged new accords and institutions through which the state and private entities would cooperatively steer society. The goals would be, first, efficiency, but also a modicum of nonbusiness goals that contribute to social order—equity, community stability, a perception of shared sacrifice. As secretary of commerce in the 1920s Herbert Hoover had developed an influential vision of his "American System," a new and cooperative relationship between government, business, labor, and scholars. Franklin Roosevelt experimented during the New Deal with several more-liberal versions of similarly dedicated business-government partnerships, making frequent use of the ideal of planned social development. He pursued such partnerships even as the Depression-driven antagonisms between "business" and "civic" cultures ran at their most intense. This business-government collaborative impulse has deep American roots and considerable persistence, though undeniably it has contended with and been often frustrated by that other, more adversarial dualism that Reich described.

Reich made much of this adversarial historical tradition, highlighting the legacy of state-capital division, to emphasize its painful dysfunctionality in the 1970s and 1980s. A second historical rail carried his argument, that the era from 1920 to 1970 was the successful age of long runs of standardized industrial production, a production mode which has been called Fordism and which once was the envy of the world. This, too, had become an encumbrance.

These two historical legacies—uniquely American ways of managing to live with the disruptive demands of dynamic capitalism, and of organizing industrial production for maximum efficiency—were once compatible. Grown obsolete, they were a part of the problem. America, successful through the modern era with its peculiar antagonism between the civic and business realms and with its Fordist industrial structure, had unwittingly entered a new era in 1970. Vigorous, sustained international competition for both domestic and overseas markets quickly exposed the weaknesses of inherited habits and structures.

The United States, in these vastly altered circumstances, had two choices, Reich thought. These did not include resisting the import invasions of the industrial heartland and the shrinkage of the mass-production industries. "We can continue to endure a painful and slow economic transition," futilely attempt protectionism, delude ourselves that a shift to service industries will sustain our standard of living, "and a nation of extractors, assemblers, and retailers—relatively poor by the standards of the rest of the industrial world . . . The alternative is a dynamic economy" shifting its production toward "relatively smaller batches of more specialized, higher-valued products . . . precision-engineered . . . custom-tailored," and toward the "high-value segments of more traditional industries (specialty steel and chemicals, computer-controlled machine tools, advanced automobile components) as well as in new high-technology industries (semiconductors, fiber optics, lasers, biotechnology, and robotics)."[18]

### The Institutional Binds

Reich's favored scenario was not unlike the one sketched so frequently in the business media, a song of excitement about new high-technology industries springing up around the American landscape, or of a technology-driven renovation of older industries, or both. But he did not believe, as did the managers of the Reagan experiment, that the American economy, its back lightened of governmental interference after 1981, would surge into that brighter future. The United States had not slipped into economic trouble because of high taxes or other governmental errors; the sources lay primarily elsewhere, in the economic structure. "The same factor that previously brought prosperity—the way the nation organizes itself for production—now threatens decline."[19]

"The way the nation organizes itself"—this was the language of the school of institutionalist economics, an intellectual tradition traced through the careers of Thorstein Veblen, John R. Commons, Simon Patten, Charles Van Hise, Wesley Mitchell, Rexford Tugwell, John Kenneth Galbraith. Institutionalists shared a conviction that in the modern industrial economy markets were so impaired by the growth of large organizations—corporations, unions, multilayered government—that the rules of classical theory no longer applied. Constrained markets yielded unpredictable and often suboptimal results, and the state must always be ready to make necessary adjustments. After World War II, the economic profession turned away from the institutionalist conviction. Keynesianism claimed the minds of many, and proposed the distant interventions of macroeconomic levers. Neoclassical dislike of the state attracted most others. Institutionalism held a small postwar foothold in the field of developmental economics, which harbored a stubborn faith that governments could promote development by targeting import-substituting industries and infrastructure.[20]

With Industrial Policy, institutionalism was coming home. Reich identified the problem as "the way the nation organizes itself for production" in the house of capitalism itself. "America's professional managers are ill-equipped to undertake the necessary shift" because "few of America's business leaders have been trained and selected for the role of guiding product and process innovation." In any event they are increasingly engaged in offensive or defensive "paper entrepreneurialism," devoting their innovative energies toward "accounting, tax avoidance, financial management, mergers, acquisitions, and litigation."[21]

Paper entrepreneurialism was not presented as a matter of moral failing. The structure of American credit markets and the increasing threat of hostile takeovers forced managers to concentrate upon short-run profit. There was no such ready supply of "patient capital" as Japanese firms enjoyed. If American managers made serious errors within this system, other segments of society floundered also: "There are no villains to this piece."[22] When managers turned to government for protection or subsidy, they found bureaucrats with no strong aversion to state-assisted "historic preservation" of existing industries, no vision of a different economic pathway, and inadequate sectoral information had such a vision emerged. Thus evolved the haphazard pattern of industrial policies—the state responding to industrial crisis with tariffs, quotas, "voluntary" market agreements, subsidies, occasional direct bailouts as with Lockheed or Chrysler, tax concessions, and an escalating defense budget that drained away engineering and scientific resources.

A set of institutional arrangements thus blocked "the superstructures of management" from seeing the need for or making the rapid and radical changes in organization of production which were required by international competition. The government for its part kept alive the false hope that these would not be necessary.

Reich acknowledged that American labor was caught in its own institutional gridlock—its skills rapidly becoming obsolete and "the signals of supply and demand inadequate to shift workers smoothly into the best jobs . . . Workers feel too insecure to leave family, friends, and familiar territory; they are unable to finance their own retraining." Even if they knew which jobs to retrain for and where to move to find them, "there would not be enough of these higher-valued jobs to go around." To the objection that the U.S. economy created 21 million new jobs in the 1970s, Reich asserted that "a large percentage of these jobs were dead ends"—cooks and waitresses, hospital orderlies, typists, security guards, clerks, janitors. All the existing mechanisms for raising the skills of the work force—public and private retraining programs, the nation's education systems—were either too small or too far behind the new technologies and failed to teach "collaborative and innovative problem-solving skills." American workers know they will pay most of the costs of economic change and its attendant insecurities, resist industrial change, and lend their political support to futile efforts at protectionism.[23]

American capitalism was thus depicted as too feeble a system of incentives and disincentives to break the cake of custom and find its way to the needed pattern and range of adjustments. If economics is the study of how people make choices, and sociology the study of how they have no choices to make, Reich wrote sociology through two-thirds of his book. Often he saw doom at the end of present trends, and expressed it with an aphoristic power that he did not always restrain: "meanwhile, with each passing month, U.S. business loses more ground . . . The U.S. economy is grinding to a slow, painful halt." More than once, in these 1981–1983 writings, he found the American economy, or society, to be "unraveling." At these points the reader might recall the comment of Goethe, "I thank God that I am not young in so thoroughly finished a world."[24]

Yet Reich's culminating vision was not doom, but rather the promise of rejuvenation. He sketched a buoyant and optimistic set of possibilities if certain choices were made: "If U.S. management and labor could break this economic gridlock—if management had access to patient capital, labor had adequate retraining opportunities and sufficient job security, and both sides willingly restructured the organization of production—what would the resulting new American economy look like?"[25]

The resultant changes would not reach many blue-collar and clerical workers, for there would always be jobs for unskilled labor. They would span the whole range of our economic activities, including the basic industries (steel, autos, chemicals), which would not be abandoned. Reich foresaw a wave of technological and organizational change, pushing American output toward "high-value niches" or "skill-intensive products and processes" in the world economy. Textile firms would shift from cotton to high-strength carbon fibers, chemical firms toward insecticides and herbicides custom-tailored to specific ecologies, pharmaceutical manufacturers toward new biotechnologies.[26]

Reich provided a shower of information on emerging high-technology innovations in product and process. If the intended readership of the book included liberal Democrats, they had never been asked to absorb appreciatively so much detail on how industrialists make and market their wares. Although Reich often spoke the language of the manufacturer, the labor force was at the center of his view of economic progress. In the new American economy "flexible-system production" would replace standardized production. As the quality of work became more important than quantity, it would be widely accepted that "workers' skill, judgment and initiative have become the determinants of . . . competitive success." Sharp distinctions between management and labor diminish in such production systems, hierarchies flatten, labor-management cooperation replaces antagonism. "The era of human capital" would arrive, in which America's assets would be cooperation, collective effort, and strategic approaches to decision making.[27] Equity would be the pathway to efficiency, not what must be traded off to achieve it.

Reich appeared to believe that the private sector was moving already in this general direction, but not as fast as the economies of our commercial rivals, and therefore not fast enough. Here emerged the role for public policy. Reich urged governmental issuance of employment vouchers to compensate employers for half the costs of retraining the low-skilled and unemployed; changes in the tax code to discourage paper entrepreneurialism and factory relocation while encouraging worker retraining and human capital investment generally; regional public development banks to replace the random patchwork of local-state-federal economic development schemes; and at the national level the creation of "the institutional capacity to view all its programs in light of the nation's long-term economic health," a public board to monitor all programs allocating capital in the economy and to advise the president and Congress on "changes in programs retarding national economic development." This would be that "national bargaining arena" in which government-business-labor would continually discuss restructuring plans that would regain the economic lead for many industries.[28]

Most expositions end after laying out such a broad and often novel agenda, but Reich asserted that his policy recommendations would provide only "a modest start." In order for flexible-system production—"collaborative, participatory, and egalitarian"—to develop throughout the economy, it must be "supported and sustained by a broader public framework . . . Economic policy will be linked to social policy . . . We will have one system" in which social welfare policies will promote economic ends while economic programs carry a large investment in human capital. Government must be the agent of such changes. "National governments will thus become bargaining agents for the least mobile factor of international production—human capital." They will be motivated not out of the earlier, New Deal desire for humanitarian relief of poverty, but by the realization that a labor force that participates in decisions and is not required to bear the entire brunt of change is the key to innovation, productivity improvements, and national economic power.[29]

Reich did not expect changes of this sort and on this scale to flow merely from the rearrangement of governmental units and assignments he proposed as "an explicit industrial policy," but, more important, from a release of energies that the reformed organizations would help to channel. Reversing a nation's decline, throughout history, has depended on politics more than on policy, a quickening of the spirit of citizenship, and a broadening of participation. "History is filled with examples of societies whose economic decline paralleled the decay of their civic cultures." Reich cited the Italian city-states of the twelfth and thirteenth centuries, the Dutch of the seventeenth century, Britain in the nineteenth century— all, in his view, succumbing to enervation and an inability to adapt. These were avoidable fates. Reich envisioned a civic culture invigorated by participation in economic renewal, a new sense of social collaboration, bringing about a synthesis of the equity concerns of liberals and the efficiency concerns of business. Liberals must become interested in the problems of production and marketing, and the business community "must accept that claims for participation and fairness are not obstacles to their mission, but ultimately its very substance." [30]

### Doing It for the Democrats

"This'll do it for the Democrats," Walter Mondale is said to have exclaimed to his wife upon reading galley proofs of *The Next American Frontier.* Mondale called Reich in Cambridge and "offered to plug Reich's forthcoming opus as doing for this generation what Keynes did for the previous one." The comparison with Keynes was, at least, premature. And the book did not "do it for the Democrats"—certainly not in the year Walter Mondale had in mind.[31]

Reich had undeniably given vigorous expression to one version of the emerging supply-side liberal economics. He combined solicitude for the capitalists' core task, producing and marketing competitive products, with a critique of corporate decision making that proposed a larger role for labor and the state: "If liberalism is to regain ideological predominance in the 1980s it must re-establish a rational connection between prosperity and social justice . . . This is the only supply-side theory that makes lasting sense."[32] He proposed that the two goals of efficiency and equity were not in perpetual trade-off, but could be maximized together.

Reich's assertive writing at once attracted critics. His diagnosis of ills, it was said, was far stronger than his design of IP remedies, and his call for a broad political renewal was unconnected to his economic analysis. Impressively knowledgeable about industry, Reich, the former Federal Trade Commission bureaucrat, "virtually ignored the state" and, in the opinion of economic historian Robert Solo, showed far less grasp of the government's internal evolution and current capacities than he did when observing America's corporations.[33]

Reich's vigorous advocacy had nevertheless given the IP idea a formulation especially attractive to the large community of liberal Democrats losing confidence that Keynesian tools could deal with problems of contemporary capitalism.

## The Deindustrialization of America

The Industrial Policy idea was extended to the left of Reich by economists Barry Bluestone of Boston College and Bennett Harrison of MIT, in *The Deindustrialization of America*. "On June 30, 1980, *Business Week* finally sounded the alarm" began a book that displayed a special northeastern-urban ear for pain in the old industrial heartland. The subtitle bore their central message: *Plant Closings, Community Abandonment, and the Dismantling of Basic Industry*. Not only had the U.S. economy "for all practical purposes ceased to grow," they wrote at the bottom of the recession that ended the next year, but during the 1970s the American standard of living had slipped behind that of ten other industrial nations by several measures. This reflected "deindustrialization . . . a widespread, systematic disinvestment in the nation's basic productive capacity."[34] The book was intended to explain deindustrialization, convince the reader of its enormous social costs, argue that corporation executives making plant-closing or relocation decisions were not responding to iron economic necessity, and offer alternative ways of reaching decisions about plant location and profitability.

A blind Samson asked to be led to the pillars that supported the temple, but Bluestone and Harrison knew exactly where capitalism's pillars stood. They were labeled "Management Always Knows Best," a proposition rarely questioned in good times but requiring some reinforcement when plants close and industries shrink. Conventional economic wisdom was ready with a defense of plant closings: capital was moving in order to deploy labor to more profitable, and therefore more socially beneficial, enterprises of the future. National efficiency increased as a result of such mobility; the costs of community disruption and employee relocation were a necessary price and not one to dwell upon. Bluestone and Harrison concentrated on those costs, with a few brief and skeptical looks at the gain side (those new communities and Greenfield plants), where they also found costs.

Were plant closings so large an economic phenomenon in 1980s America as to justify this sudden concern about what conventional thinking took to be that small amount of timely dying that a healthy and growing organism requires? Bluestone and Harrison calculated that, from 1969 to 1976, plant, shop, and store closings ended 100 million jobs, while openings created 110 million. Thus about 3.2 million jobs were lost per year, on the average, while 3.6 million were annually created. This amounts to 32–38 million lost jobs across a period of net job expansion.[35]

To the Schumpeterian eye, this was probably good news—like the jobs "lost" on farms in the late nineteenth century as workers moved to better opportunities in the cities. In that view, look to the growing new urban economies, not to the abandoned farms, and be reassured that the process of change is also progress. Bluestone and Harrison suspected that the new occupations and economic sites selected by capital in its wisdom were inferior to the old, and doubted that the service economy into which capital was shoving America's work force was as desirable in basic respects as the industrial economy that was emigrating to overseas bases. This point became a dispute over "the declining middle," which they vigorously joined in subsequent essays.

The stress in their 1982 book fell elsewhere. The main argument of *The Deindustrialization of America* did not rest on calculations of individual workers' exact losses (or gains) in the industrial transformation. Hoping to encourage a clearer sense of society's own balance sheet (or the balance sheet it should be keeping, but did not) in such matters, Bluestone and Harrison moved beyond individual workers' personal anxieties about occupational structures and wage levels, where they were sure the costs were heavy, and asked: What happened to entire communities left behind by the decisions of profit-seeking executives?

The costs were lowered life income for many, especially the older workers; reduced or lost pension rights; savings depletion in the search for new employment; the physical and mental disorders that come with unem-

ployment; the community strains of overbuilt infrastructure, falling reve-
nues, and the many psychological costs of sudden decline. Where the
new jobs appeared, usually in the Sunbelt, they paid lower wages, provided less job security. There were boom-town costs also, primarily du-
plication of infrastructure, environmental damage, and crime, matters on
which they did not expand.

On corporate balance sheets, "deindustrialization" made sense. Managers relocating or rearranging capital were seeking higher profit, and
also another private good that was to them virtually the same thing, a
nonunion work force. The costs that interested Bluestone and Harrison
did not appear on corporate balance sheets, but were placed upon the
shoulders of workers, communities, and a nation whose "production system is moving toward a state of atrophy." "When historians look back on
the decade of the 1980s," ventured the two economists into historical
comparison, "they may very well classify it in the annals of economic history alongside the 1930s." [36]

*The Deindustrialization of America* urged different measures of economic
success from those used by corporate decision makers. "Growth per se is
not enough . . . Any acceptable plan for revitalizing the American economy must embrace a commitment to greater security, along with a commitment to equity and the democratic process." Suspicious of calls for an
IP built around national investment banks or boards, judging the history
of the RFC to have been that of a "millionaire's dole" because capitalist
interests had captured public policy, Bluestone and Harrison offered an
alternative set of governmental policies, "a radical Industrial Policy." It
would reject "private profit as the sole criterion" for making economic
decisions, and seek more "economic democracy." Goals would be "a
rising standard of living for working people . . . the adequate supply of
useful goods and services, whether or not they can always be made at a
profit . . . more hospitable, more interesting, less authoritarian, and safer
work environments." Admitting that they did not know exactly how to
reach that goal, they urged a broad debate over both the values that
should guide decisions and over the individuals and groups that should
make them. They suggested an expansion of "the social wage" (welfare
benefits, broadly speaking), enactment of income maintenance and job
replacement provisions as tested in Europe, and adoption of plant-closing
legislation that would protect labor through advance notification. [37]

Bluestone and Harrison had hoped to stimulate debate over their central idea, that economic decisions ought to be made on the basis of broad

social accounting rather than corporate profits, and that an economy so organized would reap productivity increases from a more "secure" and participating work force. These ideas were launched in the context of the 1979–1982 recession, and their reception must have disappointed the authors, despite wide notice.

To judge from reviews and published rebuttals, *The Deindustrialization of America* stimulated debate, not upon the strategic issue of whether corporate cost accounting and decision making would achieve desirable social ends, but upon one of the authors' tactical suggestions. This was plant-closing prenotification, a limitation on the traditional freedom of capital. Prenotification proposals before the Ohio and New Jersey legislatures and in Congress provoked such sharp dispute as to upstage their larger argument about who should make investment decisions, and on what basis.

On one central issue Bluestone and Harrison were squarely confronted by critics. Several economists challenged the idea that the United States was "deindustrializing" at all. The U.S. manufacturing sector employed roughly the same number of workers in 1980 as in 1970 while its output had increased, noted Brookings' Robert Z. Lawrence. This pattern presented quite a contrast to such truly deindustrializing economies as Great Britain's. The American economy, in Lawrence's perspective, retained its industrial base despite changing its composition, and was no cause for alarm. The lack of job generation from manufacturing was more than compensated for as the economy shifted to services. Bluestone and Harrison had wished to ignite an argument about the need for greater social control of industrial investment decisions, given the heavy personal and social costs hidden within the stagnant or declining total of manufacturing jobs. The response of Lawrence and other critics, however, made the national portfolio of jobs the issue, not the more difficult-to-measure transitional costs, and the suggestion that the enormity of those costs argued for a revised decision-making system. Those who would stake out the left edge of the IP debate would find that critics had an unexpected ability to move the stakes.[38]

### Industrial Policy: Left or Right or Center?

What, now, was Industrial Policy? Jimmy Carter's administration had divided over it, the journal *Business Week* had called for it, Robert Reich gave it a formulation that Walter Mondale liked, and Bluestone and Harrison offered a radical version that few liberals and no capitalists could accept.

The recession of Reagan's first two years had been a hothouse for the IP idea, producing incompatible versions. Many people who endorsed their own vision of IP were distinctly uncomfortable with what they heard of other versions.

Bluestone and Harrison were critical of "bailouts" or "lemon socialism," and wary of IP versions that offered "a new corporatism," which they took to imply a committee of businessmen, government bureaucrats, and a token labor delegation that would run an investment bank to assist complaining industries. They voiced the time-honored uneasiness of the left with planning proposals that originated from "big business" or "technocratic" sources. Samuel Bowles, David M. Gordon, and Thomas E. Weisskopf argued in *Beyond the Waste Land* for a worker-directed and planned economy not much different from Bluestone and Harrison's, but explicitly rejected whatever they took Industrial Policy to be.[39] Writing in the liberal *New Republic*, Michael Kinsley responded to Felix Rohatyn's stream of essays on the need for a new RFC: "It [the RFC] would give unprecedented power to an unelected group of dignitaries chosen from established elites . . . Am I off-base to wonder what royalist language like this is doing in a supposedly left-wing journal like *New York Review*?"[40]

Thus IP could be and was imagined as a leftish venture with workers running their own factories forever fixed to their communities, or as part of a liberal program for the formation of a more highly skilled and consulted work force, or as a businessman's tool for repealing two decades of consumer and environmental regulation in the name of "competitiveness." As more versions were formulated in 1982 and 1983, it appeared that IP could be any, but in practice surely not all, of these.

# CHAPTER 5

# Industrial Visions and History Lessons

I'm concerned about . . . we don't go back and look at the things that we have already done. Instead . . . we forget what we have already done.

Congressman Daniel Lundgren, June 30, 1983

More than once, President Franklin D. Roosevelt threatened to lock a group of squabbling advisers in a room and not let them out until differences were resolved. The Industrial Policy idea was a candidate for that treatment, for its multiplying friends did not agree. Felix Rohatyn, the AFL-CIO, and a Senate Democratic Task Force promoted the idea of a national development bank, while Robert Reich was dubious about the bank, and Lester Thurow objected that a new Reconstruction Finance Corporation sounded destined for futile bailout missions. And there were other knots of confusion.

It occurred to someone to repeat FDR's device and to put these diverging friends of Industrial Policy on a committee together, to resolve their differences. A newly formed think tank with close ties to the Democratic party—the Center for National Policy—enlisted a study group on Industrial Policy whose members included Rohatyn, Lane Kirkland, Irving Shapiro, former Carter cabinet members W. Michael Blumental and G. William Miller, and Stuart Eizenstat, with Walter W. Heller and Robert S. McNamara from the Kennedy era. Their report made the now familiar basic points: the economic recovery of 1983 had not reversed the decline in industrial competitiveness; fiscal and monetary policy must be put right as a prerequisite to economic health; all governments had industrial policies, and those of the United States required "a new approach."

This new approach must not be misunderstood as "central planning" and "picking winners . . . the myths of the industrial policy debate." Nor should it be "a single all-inclusive 'industrial policy' [for which] we have neither the capability nor the need"; nor should it be coercive or based upon adversarial relationships. The core idea was to organize what was already being done in a scattered way. Since "in virtually every sector of the economy, government officials regularly determine tax, antitrust, trade, education and training, regulatory and procurement policies that combine to shape the competitiveness of the affected industry's products," it seemed to the group that "what is often lacking . . . are efforts to coordinate or even to recognize the effects of all these different policies on a particular industry." The institutional innovations proposed were an Industrial Development Board, on which the group agreed, and an Industrial Finance Administration (or bank), on which, despite spending so much time in the same room, they did not.[1]

While Felix Rohatyn may be assumed to have favored the bank, Carter's former secretary of the treasury, G. William Miller, would not sign a report that endorsed it. Stuart Eizenstat admitted to reservations about it and thought the bank idea "needs more review." Morton Meyerson of Electronic Data Systems Corporation worried that it would become "a feed trough" for ailing corporations. This division within the Industrial Policy community would never disappear.[2]

### Lester Thurow: The Uses of Government and the Uses of History

One collaborator in this study was Lester Thurow, who published a series of essays in the early 1980s which marked him as one of the articulate proponents of the IP idea. "Industrial policies," Thurow wrote, "start from the observation that American industry is being beaten up in international competition and that America's productivity growth has died. If it were not for the stench of economic failure, no one would be talking about industrial policies."[3] To Thurow, the economy was more vulnerable to aggressive foreign competitors after enactment of the 1981–1982 Reagan program than before—huge deficits and an inflow of foreign capital led to an overvalued dollar against other currencies, making imports more and exports less attractive. Worse, an administration that denounced the idea of industrial policies refused to recognize that "we already have industrial policies." In Thurow's view, Reagan had repeatedly joined Congress in making industrial policies worse, as when in early 1983 the administration ordered an increase in the tariff on motorcycles to "save" a market-selected loser, Harley Davidson. This helped to give an even more protectionist cast to the array of industrial policies whose core Thurow saw as $244 billion "in existing loans or loan guarantees."[4]

The case for an IP began, then, with the preference for an explicit rather than a back-door process of setting policy for economic sectors. An effective Industrial Policy to Thurow was "not a form of central government planning . . . [was] not designed to slow down the workings of the market but to speed up the workings of the market and remove some of the economic pain and suffering that would occur if the market alone were relied upon." Further, "industrial policies are not substitutes for a good education system, adequate savings and investment, low interest rates, a competitively priced dollar, or better macroeconomic policies." They constitute something additional, a "basic strategy" for "maximizing economic growth and meeting foreign competition . . . an expression of and a vehicle for bringing about a strategic consensus among government, industry, and labor as to the basic directions in which the economy ought to move." It required any one or all three of these operating arms: an industrial research and development arm, an investment banking arm, and a restructuring arm that would engage in what he was willing to call "industrial triage."[5]

There was nothing new about such proposals, Thurow emphasized: "American history is full of examples where we have in the past made industrial policies work." He cited the Erie Canal, the western railroads, the Tennessee Valley Authority and Bonneville Power Administration, and agriculture. As late as the 1930s, "agriculture was an industrial loser—a sunset industry" transformed by "an elaborate industrial strategy" into "the industry where we now enjoy our greatest competitive advantage in world trade." In Japanese history he also found the positive contribution of industrial policies to economic leadership.[6]

### History Lessons

This spray of history lessons blew past so quickly as to seem frivolous, not seriously meant. But Thurow only packed more analogies into a shorter space than others did. Felix Rohatyn, in congressional testimony, was asked if history did not contradict him about the successes of the RFC: "Didn't the RFC fail because of political pressure?" asked Congressman Wortley. "If the track record shows in the past it did not work, what makes you think . . . ?" Rohatyn broke in with an unambiguous counterinterpretation: "It worked extremely well, if I recall, from 1932 to 1944. It worked extremely well . . . during the period when it was needed the RFC did some very good things." But Rohatyn had lived in Europe during the time he was recalling. "It did not work," countered the congressman, offering even less authority than "as I recall."[7]

Though no one remarked it, virtually every advocate of IP had cited history lessons, and if the record of the RFC or other designated episodes in economic development policy were to be taken seriously, that would be a serious matter, for the debaters seemed both confused and not very well informed. The patterns of history use begin to demand attention.

Confusion first appears in the selection of those parts of the past claimed to be comparable to current choices. Was the Erie Canal an industrial policy? Industrial policies were typically explained as policies affecting individual firms or sectors. The Erie Canal admittedly had something to do with economic development, but was an example of regional infrastructure. What drew Thurow and many others to the Erie example was not any particular industry that it stimulated, but rather the fact that it was a bold decision by a government (in this case, of New York State) to attempt something technically formidable, physically stupendous, and of potentially great benefit to a society of capitalists who would not have built it as a private venture. Economic historians commend the vision of the New York politicians. The social rate of return was quite high; the Erie linked the Great Lakes and eastern seaboard and greatly quickened development. And the project, "possibly the most successful American developmental enterprise of the 19th century," earned a profit on tolls after one year (1819), and the entire Erie debt ($7 million) was retired by 1837.[8]

But citing such an example only muddied the IP discussion. Was Industrial Policy really investment in transportation infrastructure? The Erie example carried a lesson that ill-fitted the larger IP discussion debate. Further, if seriously studied it would have led to a set of parallel cautions. Envious residents of other states watched New York with great interest, a canal fever spread, and Pennsylvania as early as 1825 thought it knew the lesson: Pennsylvania must build a canal from Philadelphia to Pittsburgh before New York outstripped the Keystone State. Several other states joined in a burst of canal projects, just at the moment when technology, in the form of the railroad, was making canals uneconomical. Most state canal projects were financial failures, and by the 1850s the Erie's own golden run was essentially over.

Though the sponsoring states lost money, the social rate of return upon the investment in a canal network still made it a bargain for society, but a costly one to taxpayers west of New York. The lesson New Yorkers learned

was this particular canal was a good investment on everybody's books—
for about 20 years. But the situation was fast changing, and the lesson in
important respects lost portability. Neither Thurow nor anyone else
dipped into the Erie Canal story deeply enough to wring out all its
insights.[9]

But Thurow and others were in search of emboldening stories; they
cited also the TVA and Bonneville dams and power systems as historical
cases encouraging some sort of public activism, though no one suggested
that America should build more dams in order to cope with the Japanese.
The cited pasts often did not seem to connect well with present circumstances, yet no one seemed to raise objections. The TVA was a unique venture in federal regional development, a public corporation with many
missions. Bonneville was a huge power-generating facility on the Columbia River. What did these cases prove? From the several admiring references to the TVA experience one would not guess that historians of the
agency raise serious doubts that it should still be regarded as an overall
success in its mission of economic development, and its environmental
side effects as a power generator have been decidedly negative. But even if
earlier positive assessments of TVA were valid, what is the lesson here for
sectoral activism in the 1980s? But Thurow's volley of analogies did not
lead the mind so far from pertinent knowledge as other arguers would do.
Former congressman Richard Bolling and collaborator John Knowles
cited the Marshall Plan, the Employment Act of 1946, the Hoover Commission, and the federal highway program.[10]

The confusion at this early point was deep and wide. Were industrial
policies sector-specific, or did the term extend to include just any economically beneficial measure governments might take? William Diebold,
Jr., could have enlightened all participants in the discussion. He pointed
out that governmental measures with significant impact on the nation's
industrial structure add up to its Industrial Policy. Over the years, the core
of these have been the explicitly targeted, sector-specific ones—tariffs,
subsidies, bailouts. In addition there is the multitude of "economywide"
measures that in practice are not sectorally neutral and probably cannot
be made so—taxes, antitrust decisions, R&D, procurement, labor law.
"Think structurally," he suggested, and the boundary of Industrial Policy
will sketch itself.[11]

A simple matrix clarifies the issue (see Figure 1). Elements affecting
economic performance are grouped along a horizontal axis dividing the
private from the public sector, and are divided into quadrants by the
vertical axis separating macroeconomic or economywide from micro-

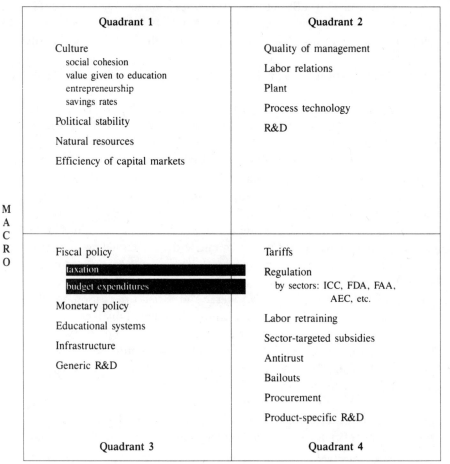

PRIVATE SECTOR

|  | Quadrant 1 | Quadrant 2 |
|---|---|---|
| M A C R O | Culture<br>  social cohesion<br>  value given to education<br>  entrepreneurship<br>  savings rates<br>Political stability<br>Natural resources<br>Efficiency of capital markets | Quality of management<br>Labor relations<br>Plant<br>Process technology<br>R&D |
| | Fiscal policy<br>  taxation<br>  budget expenditures<br>Monetary policy<br>Educational systems<br>Infrastructure<br>Generic R&D | Tariffs<br>Regulation<br>  by sectors: ICC, FDA, FAA,<br>       AEC, etc.<br>Labor retraining<br>Sector-targeted subsidies<br>Antitrust<br>Bailouts<br>Procurement<br>Product-specific R&D |
| | Quadrant 3 | Quadrant 4 |

PUBLIC SECTOR

Figure 1. Components of national manufacturing competitiveness. *Note:* These examples illustrate the untidiness of the effects of public policy. Some government policies and programs thought to be economywide or "macro" have some sector-specific impacts, and vice versa.

economic or sector-specific elements. Everything in quadrant 4 is clear-cut industrial policy—public sector, micro. Some policies in public-sector quadrant 3 are effectively sectoral policies to some degree, even though designed to touch the entire economy.[12] Think structurally, Diebold counseled, and you will find them.

Reference to the quadrants clarifies matters only retrospectively. The IP discussion proceeded without any such clarity. Hurried citations of historical analogies referred to governmental ventures that were not sectoral policies at all, but regional development policies, and whatever the Marshall Plan can be called.

Here we enter a larger puzzle. The debate bristled with borrowings from history. But while references to policy pasts were frequent, they were also carelessly chosen, perfunctorily made, simplistically interpreted, and rarely followed by any kind of challenge. Were arguers serious about these history lessons? Was anyone listening? "That's history," George Bush told a news correspondent, "that doesn't mean anything anymore," expressing one view of how Americans sometimes see the past.[13] But Ronald Reagan's political success bore witness to history's contemporary power, at least as offering rhetorical rallying points but also apparently for expressing and fortifying one's own deepest convictions. In the intellectual and political climate of Reagan's first term, proponents of some positive economic activity by government felt it essential to remind listeners that there was another American tradition, one of state-led economic development with many positive results. For Reagan, the master of the warfare of history lessons, had for many voters destroyed that past and replaced it with its opposite. IP advocates acted as if they knew the past to be part of the battleground, and followed Reagan's example in another way. They appeared to assume, as did Ronald Reagan with his pockets of note-card anecdotes and erratic memory, that the factual requirements were not strict.

In Lester Thurow's hands, however, the uses of history became more sophisticated. Having argued that American (and Japanese) history contained many encouraging examples of governmental activities that boosted the rate of economic growth, Thurow concluded that, looked at another way, history no longer applied. The United States in the 1980s had jumped the older historical track that had moved the nation from strength to strength. There had been "a sharp divergence in experience between the 1970s and the 1980s." Economic weakness was no longer associated with a few older industrial sectors whose phaseout should be welcomed, as in our industrial past. Weakness was more general; the United States was being "whipped on the tail end of the economy, but . . . also whipped on the front end of the economy" in high-technology areas such as semiconductor chips, robotics, consumer electronics.[14] Economists were accustomed to explaining the decline of industrial sectors as the "product cycle," that now familiar and beneficial process by which

low-wage industries were handed down from industrial leader to fol-
lowers. Thurow insisted, however, that something new was taking place.
The Center for National Policy's working group, on which Thurow sat,
concluded: "The normal product cycle of the past, where high-tech/high-
wage products are introduced in America but gradually become low-tech
low-wage products that can be produced more cheaply abroad, may be
replaced by the far more threatening process in which the U.S. is beaten at
the beginning of a product cycle as well."[15] "What used to work won't
work," Thurow told Congress that year, "for the world has fundamentally
changed."[16] Americans had no experience with the new path toward permanent industrial decline.

## The Lengthening List of Worries and Worriers

The IP idea was squarely before the public by the spring of 1983. In early
1980, when the Carter administration decided to study the issue, indexes
to books and periodical literature did not contain the term, and in any
event would have led Carter to precious few American "experts"—perhaps only one, William Diebold, Jr. By 1983 the term was heard everywhere, think tanks and business groups convened conferences around it,
and the stable of authorized, published experts was full and restless for
the gate. If a conference organizer could not get Reich or Magaziner,
Rohatyn or Thurow, Bluestone or Harrison, there were Harvard's Bruce
Scott and George Lodge, the University of Pennsylvania's Michael
Wachter, Berkeley's John Zysman and Stephen Cohen, policy analysts
Gail Schwarz and Pat Choate, former Carter officials Stu Eizenstat and
Frank Weil, and many others endorsing some version of IP.

When CBS journalist Fred Graham asked, "What the hell is Industrial
Policy?" his puzzlement reflected the divergence of policy remedies
among its proponents.[17] Yet all IP advocates agreed that the American
economy and polity were ailing; general decline was expected inexorably
to follow industrial decline, despite hopes that a "service economy"
might offer an affluent replacement. There was also agreement on what
Yale economic historian William Parker has called "the international
horse race" perspective on social change, which assumed that an acceptable economic future for Americans required the United States to remain
the world's lead horse.[18] Perhaps the lead had already been lost. Ezra
Vogel implied as much with his *Japan as Number One: Lessons for America*.[19] Barry Bluestone and Bennett Harrison reported that "the average
Swiss or Danish family enjoys a higher standard of living than that of the

average American," a development naturally "disturbing to a generation raised on the unchallenged perception of America as Number One."[20] Two economists in 1982 calculated an "economic performance index" for nine Western industrialized nations (plus Japan) over the period 1974–1980, and found the U.S. fifth in rank order, behind Ireland and only a shade above Italy.[21] These were, indeed, uncharted waters.

Some might say that the future was not so different from the past so long as there was economic progress, that it did not matter if the nation placed second, or fifth, or seventh in the international horse race so long as the entire field moved forward. Even this scenario seemed unlikely to many—to Lester Thurow, for example, whose *Zero-Sum Society* (1980) assessed the consequences of static wealth per capita or even decline, with the likely intensification of social conflict.

Whatever the direction of per capita wealth for American society at large, a structural worry, a "declining middle," preoccupied Robert Kuttner, among others. Kuttner saw the middle-class occupation base eroding as manufacturing gave way to a service economy requiring vastly more hamburger servers than high-skilled professionals.[22] A labor economist foresaw "a two-tier work force . . . At the top will be a few executives, scientists and engineers, professionals and managers performing high-level, creative, high-paid full-time jobs . . . At the bottom will be low-paid workers performing relatively simple, low-skilled, dull routine, high-turnover jobs."[23]

These themes predominated in the discussion of America's economic direction, together with the fear that intense global competition amid slack demand and industrial overcapacity would stimulate mercantilist protectionism and stall international trade. Public and policy leadership must realize that a choice had to be made between what William Diebold had called "Preservationist" industrial policies such as were everywhere evident, and industrial policies that promoted adjustment out of industries doomed by foreign competition and did what could be done to modernize the rest. "Domestic political support for a liberal economic order," wrote two Berkeley economists, "requires that the U.S. government arm itself with a variety of instruments to promote economic adjustment at the sectoral level rather than to impede it with protectionist measures."[24]

### The Industrial Policy Gap

On all these matters the diverse Industrial Policy designers and promoters were in agreement as well as on their interpretation of what history had recently done to the international economic rules of the game. A nation's place in the international horse race was no longer determined solely by starting positions, possession of the economic factors conferring comparative advantage. Handicaps—governmental systems, political economies—also conferred or reduced advantage. An "industrial policy gap" had opened between nations and companies doing well and those doing less well. Firms that beat American corporations in the marketplace were something more than well-run organizations employing disciplined, saving, institutionally loyal workers in societies mindful of the importance of the values of craftsmanship, social cohesion, education, those assets found in quadrants 1 and 2. These winners were also firms married to helpful governments, collaborating with the state to push American-made products aside. These sectoral collaborations were industrial policies; their strategic sum was a nation's Industrial Policy. The new rivalries between capitalist states reminded more than one writer of the Atlantic community mercantilism of the seventeenth and eighteenth centuries. "We do not live in the world of Adam Smith," wrote Jimmy Carter's former domestic policy chief Stuart Eizenstat, who endorsed the IP idea in public after his departure from the White House in 1981. We live "in a world in which other foreign governments engage in heavily mercantile policies, with products subsidized at every level."[25] A labor-industry coalition found that the "industrial policy gap . . . between the trade and industrial policies of other countries and those of the U.S. . . . has put American industry at a systematic disadvantage."[26]

Even to experts, industrial policy overseas presented a complex and confusing picture.[27] The kit of policy tools used in industrial countries included direct or indirect subsidies for equipment or research, aid for overseas marketing, state-arranged mergers, tariff protection, and labor force retraining. The institutional tools took different forms in every country, basic elements being a ministry taking the lead in setting strategic direction for sectors, a national development bank, and forums for continuing tripartite consultation. Information piled up about the activities of a range of industrial rivals, but most attention went to the two island nations: Japan, imitator turned tutor; and Great Britain, the society that could not seem to get Industrial Policy right.[28]

### Japan, Inc.

American interest in Asia had traditionally been focused on China.[29] Americans cared less, and so knew much less, about Japan—as measured by the coverage given it in magazines and professional journals, books, and university and school curricula. World War II initiated no major national curiosity or reappraisal, where Japan was concerned. The postwar stereotypes survived the war in full strength—of the Japanese as a people of innate cruelty, duplicity, and imitativeness (the Japanese, for their part, held equally stubborn and invidious stereotypes of Americans). As for the economic abilities of the Japanese, in 1954 Secretary of State John Foster Dulles stated bluntly: "The Japanese don't make the things we want."[30]

Change was even then hurrying past Dulles' assessment of Japan's potential. In 1965 Americans for the first time bought from Japan as much as they were exporting there, and the mix was changing. At the time of John Kennedy's election, 30 percent of Japanese exports to the United States were cheap textiles and apparel. By 1979 textiles had fallen below 10 percent, while machinery had risen to 61 percent. These were the decades of "the Japanese miracle," when that island's growth rates averaged 9–10 percent annually.[31] By the early 1970s Japan had replaced Great Britain as the world's number-two producer of industrial goods.

In the process, the stereotypes changed, and condescension turned to grudging admiration—on which was founded at least one American growth industry, writing and selling books about Japan. Such accounts, along with rising journalistic attention, invariably noted the importance, in the Japanese formula, of something larger than the sum of the parts. The Japanese had forged out of both indigenous cultural advantages and borrowed elements a new "system of government-business interaction [which] is so close and constant that the system is often dubbed Japan, Inc."[32]

### Japan according to Vogel

How that system worked remained an Asian mystery to most Westerners, until Ezra Vogel's *Japan as Number One,* a book so enthusiastic about the Japanese formula for economic success, and so explicit about the relative decline of the United States, that it became a best-seller in Japan. Vogel's account of Japanese IP was at once the most substantial yet to appear and the most approving.

What was the Japanese formula? Poor in natural resources, Japan became the world's second industrial power by drawing upon its social resources. These were acknowledged to be: a remarkable social cohesion and national consensus upon the basic goal of international competitiveness; a well-educated, industrious labor force, loyal to company and nation; aggressive management with a strong entrepreneurial bent; non-adversarial labor-management relations, encouraged by and reflected in "lifetime employment" and flatter organizational wage structures than in other industrial nations; high domestic savings and investment rates; close involvement of investment banks with industry, providing debt structures that allowed Japanese industry to avoid the heavy equity capitalization that made American firms vulnerable to stock market pressures for quarterly dividends; and a competitive home market, fostered by the partial dismantling of the industrial cartels (*zaibatsu*) during the U.S. occupation. Last but not least there were Japanese managerial techniques, translated for American executives in popular books.[33]

These were the Japanese secrets, carried back to the West. But was there one large Secret? The entire Japanese economy had moved with extraordinary rapidity up the scale to capital-intensive, high-technology production, taking commanding positions everywhere in the world and deep in the American market—in consumer electronics, autos, computers and their internal memory chips. Such a successful transformation of a national industrial portfolio was not accomplished by the interplay of market forces alone. There was something especially purposeful about Japan's postwar vault upward. Vogel emphasized more strongly than earlier writers the guiding hand of a national economic strategy, an Industrial Policy orchestrated primarily by the Ministry of International Trade and Industry (MITI). Yet that strategy did not repose in any document or single agency, but inhered in "a web of relationships" forming Japan's public-private partnerships. It had evolved out of Japan's unique past, with an American assist. During the MacArthur occupation Japan had been pressed into economic planning, and for this task postwar Japanese governments inherited important advantages. They also displayed a remarkable institutional inventiveness as they experimented with the means to influence the national portfolio of economic assets. The starting point was a well-paid, skilled, and respected senior civil service, an elite corps of bureaucrats possessed of "group esprit . . . self-confident and dynamic leadership," a description that the word *bureaucrat* does not evoke in the American mind.[34]

These civil servants are professionals in the Bank of Japan or one of the economic ministries. A small planning agency produces an occasional volume expressing economic, environmental, and other social hopes. The chief agencies are the Ministry of Finance, which sets both monetary and fiscal policies; and MITI, which exerts a less formal but larger informal role in shaping the Japanese economy. MITI's role has changed over time.

It is a complex mixture of influences in which the agency's ability to offer or arrange tax and direct subsidies, permits, and tariff or other trade protection is less important than its pervasive "administrative guidance." MITI convinces, cajoles, and persuades other parts of the government—and Japanese industry, organized in four major associations—to move in directions that make Japan's products always more competitive. Vogel likened MITI to the National Basketball Association or the National Football League in the United States, as an organization seeking to place in competition the strongest possible companies. Like the NBA and the NFL, MITI operates with limited powers and is forever dealing with refractory owners and labor who do not see the whole picture. Producing every year (since 1975) a *Long-Range Vision* of the Japanese economy in the world setting, MITI attempts (never with full success) to assist unusually promising industries, to convince banks and managers to enter new production areas, and to nourish these winners of tomorrow with protected home markets and other subsidies. The agency is also active at restructuring industries experiencing difficulty, arranging mergers or acquisitions, suggesting new technologies, and shrinking unwanted capacity by apportioning quotas among companies.

MITI's guiding strategy has been to move the economy rapidly toward a knowledge-intensive structure and high value-added production. This reflects an astute postwar judgment of Japan's real comparative advantage in a world economy in which rivals will ceaselessly attack established positions. Often MITI is fought by business interests or by other parts of the government, but then consensus comes after the prolonged Japanese methods of talking their way to accord, the Diet, no match for the expertise of the executive branch, usually agrees to whatever policy change has been worked out. Japanese IP is a collaborative product, but on the government's side the architects are the executive branch civil service, Japan's "permanent government." It is not made, as in the United States, by the political operators who arrive with each new president (or, in Japan, with their prime minister), people who will leave when he departs; it is not made in Japan by their deferential and understaffed legislature. Vogel conceded that these technocrats are not always right. The Bank of Japan refused to extend the first loan to a nonexistent and (to the bank) unpromising steel industry in 1951. MITI tried to discourage Sony from going into transistors, and was following conventional wisdom in the 1960s when it feared American power and attempted to shrink the Japanese auto sector and avoid international competition in a product line so dominated by the United States. On balance, however, the marketplace has confirmed the judgments reached through Japan's public-private decision-making process.

This process is remarkably accessible, to those who learn Japanese. An American businessman wishing to know what his British rivals (in the nonnationalized sectors) intend to do in the next five years can turn only to industrial espionage or intense socializing in London. The business challenge coming from Japan can be read—in Japanese—in MITI's annual *Long-Range Vision*. There in the late 1970s one could have seen the Japanese semiconductor industry being maneuvered into a battle with American firms, a contest that ten years later the Japanese were clearly winning. The Japanese strategy did not seem complicated: "The semiconductor is American in origins. With an eye on its great future, we imported it from America. However, the IC (integrated circuit) industry required enormous resources for investment in production facilities and R&D. For this reason, government and business became one body [*kanmin ittai*] to promote R&D for this industry. In this way Japan made rapid progress."[35]

Vogel's *Japan as Number One* bore the subtitle *Lessons for America*. Here Vogel was cautious. America should borrow the idea of an active Industrial Policy and some of Japan's "communitarian vision," but it should not emulate certain social habits that seemed to come attached—the smothering of individual rights and creativity, excessive nationalism, social conformity.

Another forceful statement of the importance of the Japanese state to the success of that nation's corporations was Chalmers Johnson's *MITI and the Japanese Miracle* (1982).[36] Reflecting upon the formidable cultural and institutional resources the Japanese had mobilized, Johnson saw "the U.S. . . . in danger of ending the 20th Century as the leading producer of ICBMs and soybeans while the Japanese monopolize the production of everything in between." The United States should not attempt to copy, but should move promptly to "match" Japan's public-private collaboration and strategic capacity. "Foreign enterprises must of course expect to compete with their Japanese counterparts," Johnson said in 1982, "but they haven't a chance unless foreign nations also compete with Japan on the level of the government-business relationship," where that nation had made "a genuine and emulable contribution to capitalist economics."[37] Drawing from the American past, he suggested the Manhattan Project and the Federal Reserve Board as models of institutions possessing the required independence from meddling hands in Congress.

### The Other Island History Lesson

If serious attention was to be directed to the historical experience of Japanese economy and government, on the claim that a key to Nippon's success could be found in that history and imported to America, then eyes must also go to that other island economy and former economically preeminent nation, where the Industrial Policy aspiration seemed in most trouble.

In 1886 Britain led the industrial world in the output of iron, steel, and coal, in manufacturing productivity, dominated world markets for manufactured goods, and was the financial center of the Atlantic world. That was the year of the *Final Report* by the Royal Commission on the Depression of Trade and Industry, prompted by worries that rival powers were overtaking Britain. A best-selling book of 1884 had been *Made in Germany*, touching nerves of a capitalist community anxious about falling rates of profit and loss of market shares to German and American manufactures. The commission deplored poor management, insufficient investment, poor labor relations, and the inability of British salesmen to speak foreign languages. There was no call for Industrial Policy, but with some alterations in names and places, the commission report might have sold well in Washington in the early 1980s.[38]

Great Britain's long decline left a wake of books and white papers. After World War II Britain briefly kept pace with her two major war-damaged rivals, France and Germany, but by the 1960s these and other societies had clearly bested the British in the arts of making and selling goods. From 1967 to 1978 the British economy grew at 60 percent of the average OECD rate, in the words of one British scholar "a staggering relative decline" that pulled the British people below the standard of living of even the northern Italians.[39]

Successive British governments throughout this period busied themselves launching remedies, which they were much slower than the French to call industrial policies. Still slower were they to perceive them in their entirety as a national IP, but such it was, a cobbled-together affair generally acknowledged to be a model of ineffectiveness. "If at First You Don't Succeed, Don't Try Again" was the title of an essay on IP in the United Kingdom. The authors went on: "British experience . . . suggests, perhaps, what other nations ought not to do."[40]

Governments in the U.K. did not lack imagination as they took up the task of administering tonic to British industry. In the first decade after the war there were tax concessions for certain favored forms of industrial investment, educational reforms to increase the supply of trained engineers, the establishment of business schools on the amusing notion that their proliferation in the United States had conferred upon the former colony some sort of advantage. In the 1960s Britain's economic performance worsened, with large balance-of-payments deficits, inflation, rising unemployment, and import penetration. A Tory government in 1962, inspired by the French example, launched an experiment in avowed indicative planning, setting up the National Economic Development Council. "Neddy" was to have been that forum, so often found at the center of modern IPs, for tripartite discussion between government, management, and unions. Sectoral working parties were attached to Neddy, and put to work devising production targets.

This apparatus launched Britain's first formal economic plan, in 1965. The tangled history of that planning effort disappointed friends and advocates. Neddy working parties could often locate what appeared to be the structural problems of an industry, but there was resistance to suggested changes. Economic rejuvenation eluded the government. Perhaps the institutional form of Industrial Policy was not right. A white paper from the Department of Industry in 1974 called for an "Industrial Strategy," and led to the National Enterprise Board (NEB) of 1975. The idea was to pick "winners" and create packages of government aid—loans for development of new products, or to modernize equipment, or to finance takeovers to gain larger scale. This was Industrial Policy, unmistakable and out in the open.

After five years, none of the NEB-backed new companies in electronics, underwater engineering equipment, or genetic engineering had made a profit. Most of the government's attention went not to picking winners but, under heavy political pressures to save jobs, into bailing out losers—British Leyland, then Chrysler. Subsidies went to many firms in difficulty, such as steel and shipbuilding. According to Lawrence Franko, these activities had the usual purpose and effect of "reinforcing the existing structural characteristics of U.K. industry instead of helping industry reform along the lines of national comparative advantage."[41] Again in 1979 came another lurch in British politics, this time to the Thatcher form of free-market faith, and the NEB was reined in.

British Industrial Policy was always under revision, careening from one mix of institutions and hopes to another with every election. Little institutional or policy substance survived each change of government. In the 1980s, Conservatives and Laborites continued to share almost no common ground on what industrial policies or Policy should be. The left took a curious turn toward a faith in protective tariffs; the right continued to hope for economic revival from some combination of monetarism, North Sea oil, and the disciplining of the labor force to be expected from high unemployment and a scaled-back welfare state. British economic difficulties persisted through all these policy eras, and the nation experienced absolute deindustrialization—a shrinkage of both industrial jobs and output. The United Kingdom slipped on down the list of nations, as ranked by technological prowess and standard of living.

This was a story unlikely to attract the advocates of an American IP as they built their arguments in the early 1980s. The United Kingdom, with the weakest postwar economic record of the large industrial nations, was giving industrial policies a bad name. "The story of industrial policy is a depressing tale" in Britain, ruefully admitted Sir Arthur Knight, who had been active in much of it.[42] The story would seem to convey a negative verdict on this Industrial Policy idea to residents of a former British colony who feared that they might repeat the pattern of industrial decline and who entertained the hope that governmental industrial policies might reverse economic trends.

As it turned out, this was not the role assigned to British history in the American IP discussion. Some of those hoping for an IP in the United States not only did not shun the British experience, but attempted to use it, interpreting it in ways compatible with their own aspirations for reversing American economic decline. At the very least, this piece of British history provided a lesson in the dangers of complacency: "History does not treat kindly those societies that diagnose their structural weaknesses only after those weaknesses have become irreversible . . . For the historical analogy . . . with Britain . . . to hold, all that is necessary on our part is a comparable lack of timely attention to the danger signals."[43] Or, as Harvard dean and historian Henry Rosovsky told an early conference on industrial problems in Cambridge in 1980, in a passage worth extensive quotation:

> People from different walks of life are assembled here to ask a question that some will consider astonishing, and others frightening: Can the United States remain competitive? That this question even has to be asked certainly is regrettable; that it is being asked is a hopeful sign. Becoming less competitive may be the symptom of a serious national disease. If [it is] recognized, analyzed, and understood, one can perhaps suggest some remedies.
>
> Just for a moment, look back at the world one century ago—really

not such a very long time in historical terms. In the 1880s, Great Britain was, by a considerable margin, the leading industrial power in the world. The Industrial Revolution was born in Britain during the second half of the eighteenth century, and one hundred years later the British Empire was at its zenith.

In the 1880s, very few people realized that Britain's economic decline had already begun—that for a great variety of reasons, Britain would not remain competitive. The principal challengers were the United States and a recently united Germany. Russia also was becoming a factor in the world economy, although that development was effectively halted by the Communist Revolution. Japan had just opened herself to international contact after nearly 200 years of virtually total isolation. No one—except perhaps some Japanese—believed that Japan would ever be a major economic power, least of all the leading industrial power of the world: for that is what Japan is today.

Why this bit of history? Because I wish to stress a number of points.

1. Between the start of the Industrial Revolution in the eighteenth century and today, approximately twenty countries have experienced modern economic growth. New countries are joining the parade all the time, and the early industrializers—primarily Britain, France, and the United States—are continually facing new challengers. At present, the most rapidly growing area of the world is in northeast Asia, and it may be elsewhere in the future. The point is simple: remaining on top or in contention is not a static process.

2. It takes a long time to become aware of decline. Although most economic historians agree that Britain's climacteric occurred about one hundred years ago, this fact did not really become a matter of public concern until after World War I, and forty years of relative decline may have been an insurmountable obstacle.

3. Although a great many reasons have been given for Britain's economic decline, in my opinion the principal factors were internal and human, and therefore avoidable: British entrepreneurship had become flabby; growth and industries and new technology were not pursued with sufficient vigor; technical education and science were lagging; the government-business relationship was not one of mutual support.

When we look at our own country today in the perspective of history, the danger signals seem obvious. Productivity growth is slow; quality frequently low; capital formation is inadequate; all too often the latest technology is not used; in many parts of the world our export markets are deteriorating; and the communications gap between business, government, and the public is vast. These are the issues that have brought us together . . . The hope is to build a nonpartisan coalition . . . that will suggest policies for improved productivity and steady growth and press for their adoption.[44]

Rosovsky drew from British history the lesson that decline is best recognized early, and concluded that Britain's decline had been "avoidable." This was a particularly American view, that things broken can be fixed, even entire economies.

In the United Kingdom, where this issue had been seriously studied for some time, opinion was deeply divided over both the root causes and the slim possibility, at that advanced moment, for revitalization. Might there yet be "a spring offensive," a government-led (or divinely inspired?) renewal of all the social values and institutions required for economic strength? British writers were themselves weary and divided. "So much that caused Britain's dismal economic performance since the war seems to derive from the dead weight of the past, beyond the power of anyone alive now to alter," wrote Sidney Pollard: "Nothing stands in the way . . . of rejoining the advanced countries of Europe," but "optimism . . . is difficult" and one is drawn to a "terrifying hopelessness."[45] In another view, "The burden of history weighs heavily against successful industrial policy."[46] "While new interest in IP has recently emerged in the U.S. and some other countries," wrote Michael Davenport in 1982, "the characteristic British reaction to this is cynicism."[47] When an American and a Briton thought the matter over together, the most positive reflection was a question: "Whatever Britain lacks, it is clearly not brains in the public sector. Is it possible that brains are not enough? Or perhaps it is the public sector that is not enough?"[48]

These were good questions, and the very different answers found in Britain and Japan sent Americans deeper into both histories. For the IP idea was gaining momentum in the United States. As 1983 arrived, Industrial Policy stretched along the wide range of formulations given it by a growing chorus of professors, New York bankers, heads of corporations, unionists, and publicists in government and out. It appealed chiefly to Democrats, in whose hands it was simplified—for speeches by presidential candidates—and codified—for legislative hoppers. Intended to bring about change, the idea continued itself to change as a presidential election approached. Increasingly it was being taken up by people who, unlike Harvard or Berkeley professors, might actually give it tangible form.

What form would it take?

# CHAPTER 6

# Alternative Designs

We have two ways to go, the way of the British or the way of
the Japanese.

Arnold Packer,
Assistant Secretary of Labor

From the widening range of ideas on what IP should be, policymakers in
1983 could have constructed many designs. One analyst has devised a
simple taxonomy consisting of Modernizers and Preservationists.[1] Modernizers, such as Reich and Thurow, stressed that policy must work with
market forces rather than resist them, to accelerate change and shift labor
and capital into new roles, new industries. Policy should look ahead, financing risks with payoffs unanticipated by the market and easing the
transitional pains of dislocation. Preservationist conceptions of IP began
with doubt that market forces, supplemented by foreign industrial policies, should be allowed to erase entire industries. No individual or group
walked under that banner, but perhaps the label was intended for the
AFL-CIO, Felix Rohatyn, and Bluestone and Harrison.

William Diebold, Jr., suggested a more accommodating set of categories, pointing out that IPs could be distinguished by their goals, and might
thus be categorized as defensive, adaptive, or innovative. Defensive policies were usually the first deployed, most often in the form of import protection. Regrettably, this history had caused most people to see Industrial
Policy as "a denial of market forces," preservationism, when "this should
not be so."[2]

There were two other alternatives. Adaptive IP assists labor to move to
new sites and tasks, thus reducing the political pressures for defensive industrial policies. The other, innovative policy, nurtures innovation in general and subsidizes the growth of sunrise technologies and sectors. The
two were often characterized in Europe as "positive adjustment," the
state helping to move capital and labor out of weak positions into strong
ones. This was vastly preferable to preservationism, which was costly in

the short term and in the long term futile—though exceptions might have to be made for "national security" industries, whatever these might be. Definitions of this category were few and vague.

### Industrial Policy as Targeting: Making Winners, Remaking Losers

These terms clarified some choices, but confusion counterattacked through the widespread use of another term—*targeting*. The "hallmark of industrial policy," economist Robert Solow wrote, is selectiveness. Not all industries or companies are to be treated alike or to have access to the same array of assistance." [3] For the central purpose of IP was to engineer outcomes different from those being produced by markets plus foreign Industrial Policies. The hopes of different outcomes extended in two directions: spurring the growth of national champions or "winning" industries that promise to be dominant, and extending aid to industries in difficulty. The media, in their incessant search for simplicity, associated Industrial Policy with "picking winners" and "fixing losers," a partial truth that became a lightning rod for dispute.

Indeed, the Industrial Policy community was quite divided on the matter of how and when to target sectors, products, or production processes. In the increasingly frequent instances in which a large company slipped toward bankruptcy or a shrinking industry trailed a cloud of layoffs and enervated communities, how was the state to respond? Many advocates of Industrial Policy, especially those from Sunbelt regions or whose hearts were with entrepreneurial ventures, did not see IP as addressing declining industries at all. It would not work, led to costly bailouts and "lemon socialism," the nationalization of sick industries. Government should target, but only toward the sunrise.

Others saw a role for the state in the case of established but troubled industries. It was said that U.S. agriculture was an industry that exhibited many signs of becoming a "loser" in the second half of the nineteenth century, but instead evolved into a world-envied industry. Assisted by national policies—R&D, an elaborate system of price and commodity controls, export subsidies—agriculture grew smaller (in employment) but remained large (by output) and became successful (by productivity, export sales, world market share). Troubled industries such as agriculture were seen by some as an opportunity for government, one to be seized with confident remedial purpose. Felix Rohatyn often cited the Chrysler episode as another positive example, along with New York City's rescue, of what could be done by a government willing to extract from labor, management, and creditors the reorganizing concessions that these players could not agree to among themselves. Lee Iacocca, after Chrysler paid off its warrants, publicly and often made the same case.

Robert Reich, with other friends of IP, was less sure that the Chrysler history should give bailouts a good name. Congress in that episode had lacked reliable data, and the bailout was shaped "in the back rooms of the Treasury Department." This was ad hoc crisis management, when there ought to be a permanent and open process for handling industrial emergencies. What should have been openly discussed were such issues as the relationship of Chrysler to its suppliers, the future of the auto industry itself. "There was no opportunity to develop these themes," Reich commented, "no place, no forum, no data. No real participants."[4] The meaning of Chrysler bailout history was unclear. Yet public interpretation of that episode might shape future policy. Reich began to write a history of the Chrysler rescue.

The Chrysler case was too recent, and its results too ambiguous, for decisive use as an arguing point. Policy histories could be more easily appropriated for today's debates if they reached back beyond most memories. The nation's longest-running bailout machine, the Reconstruction Finance Corporation, had been born fifty years earlier and its end came in 1953. Surely, many lessons could be found decorating its grave.

Yet advocates of a rescue policy for failing industries soon disagreed about the RFC precedent. In 1980 Amitai Etzioni viewed targeted aid to specific industries as a mistake. By 1981 he was advocating a revived RFC.[5] Senator Adlai Stevenson (D., Ill.) had the same difficulty with his compass needle that year, as the IP idea emerged bristling with all its contradictions. When asked about "a renewed Reconstruction Finance Corporation," the senator replied sharply: "Not the reconstruction finance idea! That's the bailout machine . . . It's the Chrysler route—bailing out firms, the endless subsidization of the geriatrics. It's a hospice program for coporations." Stevenson proposed instead an industrial development bank that would, in return for aid, insist that a suppliant industry make "some progress toward restructuring that got rid of excess capacity, or offered modernization." It would be "an independent credit instruction, one that is politically insulated," to "offer needed capital in large amounts in exchange for concessions to undertake restructuring. Maybe it can start on a regional basis . . . I really haven't begun to think through the details."[6]

The senator had much company in his inability to separate his IP from that monster so easily punctured by critics, a "bailout machine" run by an arrogant bureaucratic elite that thought itself better at selecting tomorrow's successful industries than capitalists with their own money at stake. Felix Rohatyn was against one kind of bailout and aggressively for another: "It is . . . counterproductive for government to bail out large, inefficient or noncompetitive organizations," he wrote in 1981. Restructuring was another matter. The state could "exact concessions . . . impose fundamental reforms," as it intervened in troubled sectors.[7]

As for targeting in the other direction, toward the industries of the future, investment banker Rohatyn, for example, was not much interested. "Attempts by government to 'pick the winners' are for the most part futile. No government agency is capable of doing so." Lester Thurow agreed: "The problem is not to pick the sunrise industries of the year 2,000. No one can do that."[8]

Many others urged a more active governmental role in exactly this search for tomorrow's winners, citing what were said to be encouraging precedents—governmental aid to the airframe and telecommunications industries, and in the development of the computer.

Criticisms of targeting in any direction were widespread, but some debaters thought the issue should not be posed as "whether to target." The phrase was "an intellectual dry hole," thought the Democratic majority on the Joint Economic Committee, since "every country, including the U.S., has, at the least, an implicit industrial development policy"—that is, is already targeting in both directions. The issue was how to choose.[9] Since "the hallmark of industrial policy is selectiveness," in one economist's words, "how that selection is to be made is what differentiates one version of industrial policy from another."[10]

### How to Decide: Criteria, Institutions

Policy targeting, in the existing system, was done chiefly by congressmen in a process of denying or granting sectoral interventions without any central, guiding perspective. If a first objective of IP was to shape such decisions by means other than raw political power, countervailing influences must be introduced. "Let us have clarification as to aims, results and criteria by which to judge" industrial policies, wrote the authors of the Trilateral Commission Task Force on Industrial Policy. They suggested economic efficiency, maximization of economic freedom, "social" considerations such as community stability, national security, and the health of the world economy, in that order.[11]

This brief list implied a radical change in the national policy agenda. Placing economic efficiency first seemed to dethrone job creation, the central economic policy focus of postwar liberalism and of many congressmen who called themselves conservatives. But there was much evidence that advocacy of such a shift was not confined to the Trilateral Commission. In 1983 a study group of liberal lineage offered its own list of criteria to guide Industrial Policy. "Strengthening U.S. competitiveness" came first; "promoting full employment" came fourth.[12]

"It's hard for me to use a long run performance criterion for industrial policy other than international competitiveness," William Diebold stated in late 1980. "Of course societies want more than efficiency . . . stability, even at the cost of efficiency . . . less disturbance, lower unemployment . . . national security. Society doesn't live by efficiency alone." But to him the art of successful IP was first to respect the market and move toward competitiveness, and only very sparingly to pursue those other goals of community security or equity which required that change be slowed and buffered. Threatened industries always prefer a defensive IP, but the state's protective powers must be used to buy time, not to preserve the status quo in a government-built sanctuary but to make adjustments. "You must use the time . . . and avoid getting caught in your own arrangements."[13]

This advice went only a short way toward criteria for targeting. Might Japanese targeting offer guidance? MITI, Harvard's Bruce Scott observed, had "decided to establish Japan in industries which require intensive employment of capital and technology" and which have strong export prospects and promise rapid productivity increases.[14] These convincing criteria should not be too difficult to adapt to American uses.

While discussion of guiding criteria continued, some sought strategic direction in changes in policy process. Current policies were essentially protectionist, reasoned Berkeley's John Zysman and Stephen Cohen, "in part because we have no apparatus for developing . . . policies that actively promote American international competitiveness."[15] Senator Edward Kennedy argued in 1983 that the right sort of IP could derive only from "a capacity to ensure coordination . . . a capacity to build and sustain cooperative relations among all of the participants . . . a capacity to target investment on those strategic . . . industries that are fundamental to our future."[16] From this formulation of "process needs"—a capacity for coordination, for sustaining cooperative relations, for targeting resources—came the institutional concepts that would anchor the IP debate:

  a coordinating and analytical instrumentality at the apex of the
  executive branch (hereafter, the Council, although it would often be called other things)
  a consultative, information-sharing, public-private, tripartite body (hereafter, the Forum, though it would often be called other things)
  a national development bank (hereafter, the Bank, by general agreement)

## Institutional Infrastructure of a New Industrial Policy

Council, Forum, and Bank—these were the institutional building blocks so frequently mentioned and variously designed. Although in 1982 and 1983 these were presented as institutional innovations on the governmental scene, there was nothing entirely new about them. The need to coordinate scattered military, intelligence, and foreign relations activities had engendered the National Security Council in 1947. Tripartite bodies—business, labor, government—within various industries had long been a part of the American polity, and Jimmy Carter had announced (and then not established) an apex national industrial Forum in late 1980. As for the Bank, the RFC had operated for more than twenty years, and there were in the early 1980s government banks for farmers, exporters, small business, and much else. The only novelty would be to have them freshly remade, with a national mandate for a more strategic approach to industrial development.

Despite extensive precedents, Congress must decide on the details of any institutional innovations, and this work was concentrated within a House subcommittee in 1983–84. Many volunteer architects offered models of the required institutions, clarifying choices. Former Carter official Frank Weil, along with others attracted to the independent positioning of the Federal Reserve Board, folded Council and Bank together in a "semi-autonomous Federal Industrial Coordination Board."[17] Both White House and Congress would face a giant new rival source of power under plans of this design, and the idea did not fare well in either place.

More politically acceptable proposals were soon available. Robert Reich endorsed "the creation of a single bargaining arena" to "provide government with the institutional capability of achieving a broad-based consensus about adjustment policies" for industries in decline (a Forum) and a coordinating Council ("Board") to arrange some coherence in sectoral interventions. He conspicuously left out the Bank.[18] The Center for National Policy proposed a Council ("Industrial Development Board") that would "generally respond" to sectors rather than initiate action, selecting those "crucial to the national interest" and then participating in the negotiation of a development strategy. This entity had power only to recommend, not to act. In recognition of the need for some muscle in sectoral negotiations, it was to be the policymaking body for a Bank (some members of the CNP task force dissented here) whose resources would often tip the balance in negotiations over "restructuring."[19]

After the Council, Forum, and Bank, other ideas for institutional innovations were churned up by the debate over industrial troubles. The Reagan administration allowed Commerce Secretary Malcolm Baldrige to testify on the Hill in favor of reorganizing all trade functions within the Commerce Department, which would become something like an American MITI. A White House adviser on competitiveness seemed a good idea to many. A periodic report to Congress on Industrial Policy seemed to some a useful mechanism to enhance policy "transparency," a word that Europeans used to denote visibility, forthrightness, and clarity. Stephen Cohen offered what sounded like a whimsical idea for a "Factory Extension Service" modeled on the Agricultural Extension Service, but by 1985 fifteen states had established programs for technology diffusion within industry.[20]

"God is in the details," Frank Weil quoted an architects' maxim.[21] It would fall to Congress to craft the institutional design from the ideas swirling about in 1983, and there was much from which to choose.[22]

### Policy Reform without Institutional Change: Industrial "Strategy"

Or perhaps the struggle to sort out the institutional details could be avoided altogether. "Do we need some kind of super industrial coordinating what-have-you?" one skeptical machine-tool executive asked a congressional committee, while claiming to favor an Industrial Policy. "I don't think so."[23]

This question, arising from some who supported the IP idea, should have been no surprise. To propose new institutions was to suggest the formation of yet another government agency, unthinkable in the Reagan climate. Even if acceptable in principle, new institutions reorganized power, and very specific and powerful people would object. Those now making industrial policy decisions, in Congress and the executive branch, as assisted by organzied private groups, would lose power as the new Council, Forum, and Bank gained it. Politically this was unpromising, even if one favored something like it in principle.

Congressman John J. LaFalce (D., N.Y.) (who in 1984 would sponsor legislation launching a veritable baby boom of new institutions) held hearings on IP in 1983. Most witnesses favored the general idea of an American IP, but only a few had new institutions clearly in mind. What they wanted could be secured, most seemed to think, if enough national leaders made inspiring speeches about "innovation," "entrepreneurship," and "competitiveness"; stressed that saving was more important than consumption, graduating engineers more important than graduating lawyers; and in similar ways led American culture back to basics. Beyond this, a new Industrial Policy seemed to consist of changes in some or all of a familiar list of existing federal policies or programs: trade policy—especially export promotion—merger and antitrust policy, R&D funding, tax policy, business regulation, small business promotion, government purchasing, science and technology policy, patent policy.

Inevitably, the witnesses did not agree on the substance of the changes that would give the United States the right sort of IP. Each industry's lobbyists could quickly list the tax and regulatory changes, R&D and export assistance augmentations, that would make it a national champion. Many thought the road to this new idea, Industrial Policy, led through a series of discrete reforms of existing policy and did not require new institutions.

An important alternative path to IP had surfaced here. If strong new institutions for sectoral management were politically hazardous or of troubling potential, perhaps the real objective—an assemblage of governmental policies that promoted global competitiveness of U.S. corporations, to replace the current policy muddle heavily weighted toward social, political, and environmental missions—could be achieved merely by pressing incrementally for a whole range of desirable statutory and administrative changes.

This might be called Industrial Strategy, urged, for example, by the Committee for Economic Development.[24] Congress should revise all economic policies affecting industry, aligning them with the true principles of capitalism, and there would be no need for "new government programs and planning boards." Government, together with business, should "develop a *strategy,*" said *Business Week,* "without risking the strictures of a government-legislated *policy.*"[25] In the climate of the Reagan presidency, lobbying existing institutions seemed to promise more than creating and empowering new ones. The use of the alternative word, *Strategy,* was a tactic to get probusiness policy changes in quadrants 3 and 4 without the risk of reconfigured mechanisms of decision. A larger conception of Industrial Strategy was that of Harvard's Bruce Scott, who saw Strategy as an all-quadrant effort: "[Strategy is] the whole tilt of a nation, its goals or priorities, its policies toward education, labor, credit . . . We need a reordering of priorities almost as fundamental as that which began in the New Deal . . . a set of priorities which strikes a balance between the consumption oriented 'entitlements' of the welfare state and the increased levels of work, savings and investment which are required to meet the new competitive challenge."[26]

## Planning in Disguise? No, and Yes, and No

A debate so rich in alternative terminology kept the confusion level high. And this was not the end of the distracting labels. Was IP really Planning? IP advocates gave a vigorous "no" in two forms—refusal to use the word *planning,* and emphatic denial of the association. The word appeared neither in the index to Ira Magaziner and Robert Reich's *Minding America's Business* nor in Reich's *The Next American Frontier.* To meet the issue squarely, Reich, Thurow, and others frequently denied that planning was what they meant by Industrial Policy. "Central planning and 'picking winners' are myths of the industrial policy debate," said the Center for National Policy: "We reject them."[27] "I am opposed to government planning and to government-owned industries," said Felix Rohatyn.[28] "We do not talk about central planning," were the reassuring words of Congressman John LaFalce.[29]

These were the dominant reactions to the accusation, frequently heard in the debate, that somebody wanted to plan something. Only a handful of those endorsing IP did not object to the association with the forbidden word despite the intellectual climate of the 1980s. "We feel that there is the need for . . . an institution—call it planning; I'd like to call it planning," said Arnold Cantor of the AFL-CIO in 1983. Congressman Charles

Roemer then tried another maneuver through this minefield: "Planned economies are not what I want . . . and an economy with a plan is something I think we need." [30] This was about as much clarity on the planning question as the IP debate would achieve.

### Choose Your Tilt: Industrial Policy, Right and Left

The IP idea was now stretched across widely divergent values and social priorities. Sternly conservative cultural values could be heard in the call for a reformed and more strategically aggressive political economy. The nation could no longer afford the luxuries to which it had unfortunately become accustomed in the era of the great aberration between the New Deal and the 1960s: there were too many welfare-state entitlements; wages were artificially high as a result of union power; business was harassed with unnecessary environmental and safety regulations and high taxes. Sentiments of this sort pervaded much of the IP discussion and led some to conclude that this new thing was the old familiar corporatism, an attempt to capture the state for the purposes of large corporations—to form legal cartels, gain governmental subsidies, enforce social discipline.

But other values and priorities lived under the IP tent. Cutting taxes, wages, and social benefits was one path to economic development. Another derived from the conviction that "we must invest in our people"— their education, training, health. [31] An extension of this emphasis on investment in human capital was a conviction that rising productivity began with the work force, not just in providing people with better machines but also and more importantly with a sense of participation and reasonable job security. Here the stress was on a far wider and deeper participation of labor in managerial decisions, combined with sharing of the fruits of enterprise. These themes were inherited from the left, along with the frequent criticism of business leadership for "paper entrepreneurialism" and fixation upon "short-term profits," the charge that markets provided a flawed vision; that more communal, national and long-term, considerations must be included in corporate decisions.

### Choices: Maximalism or Minimalism?

Such diverse norms could produce many and divergent Industrial Policies. If numerous people by 1983 were talking of IP, they were not talking of one thing, but of a range of choices ahead. One last distinction was difficult to see, and no helpful labels were invented to mark it out. Some people advocated an explicit American IP, were eager to begin, and were confident that they knew how to construct and implement a policy framework that would suffuse the nation's manufacturing sectors with strength. Correct policy would awaken new industries and renovate old ones, and to begin the work the full range of institutions should be at once established—the Bank, the tripartite national Forum, the apex coordinating Council. This maximalist approach was adopted early on by, for example, the AFL-CIO, which proposed a tripartite public member-dominated Council that would do more than study and analyze. Such a Council would "intervene" in rulemaking and other procedures of federal agencies where it would have "standing," and would help a Bank target industrial aid to regions of high unemployment and "excess infrastructure." The Bank would assist both "mature or linkage" as well as "emerging" industries. Workers would be retrained. The AFL-CIO expressed no doubts that all these tasks were well within the abilities of Americans and their institutions.[32]

In contrast, a minimalist conception was preferred by people who expressed trepidation about constructing, through American political institutions, and in a rapidly changing world, specific sectoral policy responses to the shifting and varying circumstances of industries ranging from acoustical materials to zippers. Many advocates of IP reminded themselves and their hearers that the United States was not a society that would find successful industrial policymaking easy to devise in a competitive world.

> The difficulties that stand in the way . . . should not be underestimated. Unlike Japan and many West European countries, the U.S. lacks a tradition of an expert and independent civil service that could provide the business community and the general public with a high level of advice and analysis. It will be difficult for the U.S. to achieve the sort of consensus upon which industrial policy must rest . . . Consensus-forming institutions in U.S. society have deteriorated over the last two decades . . . coalitions are fleeting, attention spans are short . . . there is so much "noise" in the system. In short, the U.S. is not a nation of planners.[33]

The same realism marked the Industrial Policy advocacy of, for example, William Diebold, Jr.: "The U.S. has less aptitude for industrial policy and more obstacles to overcome than most other democratic countries."[34] To Bruce Scott, the way that the Reagan administration had pushed its preposterous and inept economic program was proof enough that America might easily botch an Industrial Policy: "Industrial policy . . . risks being turned into a painless quick fix, the Laffer-Kemp-Roth bill of the next administration . . . By asking our government to do something which it is exceedingly ill-equipped to do [portfolio management] risks . . . not only adding to the business problem but diverting attention away from painful but badly needed reforms." [35]

Was this counsel tantamount to a recommendation against attempting this thing for which America was so poorly equipped? No, since "efforts will be made," Diebold went on; indeed, efforts had already been made, to wit the de facto Industrial Policy we operated under and yet denied. A Reagan administration official in the office of the U.S. Trade Representative moved along similar lines to his minimalist position: "There is a dilemma. It would appear that the U.S. cannot function as an industrial democracy with industrial policy nor compete in world markets without an industrial policy." For those of this mind, there was, he thought, "a middle course." [36] Others also envisioned a minimal IP, consisting of the few short steps this unplanning society could be expected to take without sliding into bad Industrial Policy.

What steps? Perhaps only the institutionalization of a continuing review of existing industrial policies, to ensure that they did not indefensibly impair U.S. industries' trade and domestic performance. Such a review would expose the de facto IP to sustained scrutiny, develop knowledge of its impacts, and lead to recommendations for changes. An annual report from such a review would give the oversight process visibility, would gather together what had been scattered intellectually and bureaucratically. Coordination of existing industrial policies might be added to this review assignment. Such ideas led toward the conception of the Council—a very small Council with advisory powers only; others proposed merely a White House–based adviser to the president.

Another small step was attractive to some. If industrial policies were to be accepted as a reality and reviewed, perhaps coordinated within the executive branch, why not base them upon the strengths of informational exchange and consultation already available in existing forums for management-labor-government interchange? Such sectoral forums, overarched by a national body, would mobilize years of experience with tripartite bargaining and create an institution with the advantage of partial or total independence of Congress and the executive branch. Such a body could gather and exchange information, analyze industrial problems and current policy, enlarge horizons, strike bargains, and recommend policy directions. In the maximalist conception such a Forum would be granted operational authority, perhaps direct the activities of the Bank. In minimalist schemes, there was no Bank, and the Forum would be confined to an advisory role.

Yet its potential contribution might be considerable. One of its functions, and the boundary of its authority in the minimalist approach, was suggested by C. Fred Bergsten, director of the Institute for International Economics. To create in the United States a "mechanism" for producing "visions of the future" for "particular industries," projections of where key industries were going, Bergsten would emulate the Japanese. "If you didn't like where it [an industry] was going" and there was " 'consensus' about this." Here minimalists hesitated at the edge of something bolder. Bergsten would first build "visions," while also analyzing industrial policies abroad, something not now being done. This would be an improvement over the status quo, quite short of Planning. Congressman LaFalce interjected: "Industrial plans are no good but visions are good?" "Well, semantics are difficult," the economist conceded, but he saw a difference "between visions and plans" and preferred the more limited beginning.[37] "Visions" were an effective industrial policy tool, Harvard's Bruce Scott argued. Although business might upgrade industries in desired ways, government studies of where sectors are heading "can reduce the courage needed . . . [while] adding an official blessing to the new activity."[38]

Here was the boundary zone between two conceptions of IP. Minimalism preferred to take the limited steps sketched above, leaving the rest ahead on the learning curve. IP in this mode would be disciplined by the rule that "when we confront . . . a sector problem . . . there should be a clear order for policy preferences: aggregate policies first; policies to improve the workings of markets second; and finally—and only as a last resort—industry-specific policies."[39] Council and Forum would formulate such policies, on a modest scale (and without a Bank), unencumbered by exaggerated hopes and hubris.

### The Economy, 1981–1983

As the Industrial Policy symphony warmed up, these harmonies and disharmonies reverberated. A conductor was required onstage to establish order and direction—a president, in the American system. As the IP idea fluorished in the early 1980s, however, a president was already trying other remedies. Ironically, Reagan's first term was a hothouse for the IP idea. The recession that settled in by the end of 1981 turned out to be unusually long and deep. The year 1982 was not a good one for the OECD industrialized nations as a whole, with average growth at a sluggish 1.3 percent, but the U.S. posted a 2 percent shrinkage of GNP. Industrial production dropped 8 percent over the year, the last two quarters both recording a downward trend. By the end of 1982 the GNP had sunk to the 1979 level, though the population sharing it had grown by 7–9 million (excluding illegal aliens). Unemployment ended the year at 10.4 percent, or over 11 million people, a pool of idleness not matched since World War II. The merchandise trade deficit was also larger than it had been the year before—at $33.1 billion for 1982. That the inflation rate for 1982 declined to 5 percent seemed small compensation.

Certain structural features of this recession were unprecedented. Imports in all previous recent recessions had declined with domestic buying power; but not in 1981 and 1982. Exports did fall, since the recession was worldwide; but imports surged into the hands of U.S. consumers and producers, intensifying the dislocations within American industry. Nontraded goods were somewhat buffered from the pressures of recession, but an estimated 70 percent of American-made products were by the 1980s exposed to some degree of foreign competition, which translated into intense pressure upon industries such as machine tools, consumer electronics, textiles, footwear, steel, and even beer and wine, for years essentially unchallenged in the home market.

Like the hospital emergency room on national holidays, the Washington offices of the U.S. International Trade Commission (USITC) was a central point where industrial strain could be readily measured. Housed in a dilapidated building constructed in the 1860s on Seventh Street, the USITC found its work load propelled upward by the economic changes of the early 1980s. Some 94 investigations of trade violations associated with manufacturing imports had occupied the USITC staff of 347 with its $7.4 million budget in 1974; 400 member-of-Congress requests had to be handled. By 1980, 142 investigations and 1,300 irritated requests from members of Congress busied a staff of 401, with a $15.5 million budget, still mostly ignored by the public and the White House in their forlorn quarters.

The avalanche came in 1982–83: 188 investigations were dominated by complaints from the steel, chemical, agricultural, and textile industries. More than 18,000 angry member-of-Congress inquiries came in

1983. Twenty percent of the ITC's growing staff of 430 had to be transferred to the Bicentennial Building a block away. The agency's annual reports for 1982 and 1983 were filled with the distress cries of American producers injured by imports—Harley-Davidson motorcycles, stainless steel, mushrooms, bicycle tires from Taiwan, cement from Australia, sheet glass from Switzerland, color TVs from Korea, hot-rolled carbon steel from the United Kingdom, toys, sneakers, fungicides.[40]

The economic experience of 1981 and 1982 rendered a dismal early verdict upon Reaganomics and stimulated the search for alternative policies, principal among them IP. Then economic expansion began in the first quarter of 1983. By year's end the GNP had grown at a rate of 3.5 percent, unemployment had dropped to 8.8 percent. Productivity had also resumed positive growth, and inflation had fallen further, to 3.8 percent.

These encouraging signs did not end the interest in alternative policies, for the recovery appeared to have weak foundations. Some analysts said it was driven by consumer spending not only generated by a willingness to assume larger private debts but also stimulated by federal tax cuts, which enlarged the government's debt with growing annual budget deficits, a record shortfall of $206.7 billion coming in 1983. Supply-side economics had promised that savings rates would go up after tax reform, but they declined. It had also promised that investment would flow to productivity-increasing channels rather than to vacation homes or tax-sheltered investments; but it did not. The trade deficit for 1983 jumped to $56.8 billion, the last two quarters of 1983 recording the largest deficits. And to symbolize the weakening grip of the American nation upon her former technological preeminence, the Perth Yacht Club took the America's Cup to Australia in 1983.[41]

Thus the 1983 recovery neither confirmed Reaganomics nor ended the debate over political economy, but supplied ammunition for every school of thought as the election year arrived.

### Rendezvous with the Democrats

The approach of a presidential election heightened an irony of the career of the IP idea in the United States. Inherently antipolitical in aspiring to shift economic decision making away from legislatures toward the technocracy and the endless meetings of tripartite forums, the idea found itself deeply ensnared in a partisan conflict. IP in the 1980s was a vehicle upon which needs climbed—capitalists wanting a more supportive government and a rationale for lower wages and less burdensome regulation; unionists hoping somehow to stop, slow, or influence the wringing out of industrial jobs; and Democrats, their New Deal–Keynesian inheritance worn unconvincingly thin, desperately needed a supply-side alternative to Reaganism. Industrial Policy, as the newest large economic idea that had not yet been tried, would be pressed into political service. By 1983 Industrial Policy was called the central economic program of "neoliberalism," the term Morton Kondrake of the *New Republic* coined for a generation of younger, supply-side Democrats. "Neoliberalism aims to repair the private economy rather than expand the public sector," Kondrake wrote: "Neoliberals tend to hold that the country's most urgent national business is the revival of American industry, which requires investment . . . The neoliberal solution is some form of government intervention to direct investment."[42]

In other words, Industrial Policy was "the Democrats' answer to supply-side economics—a pithy phrase with a thousand definitions."[43] The need for such an answer was acute: "Without industrial policy, there's no coherence to the alternative to Reagan," Congressman Timothy Wirth conceded. It was "the leading issue for 1984," Congressman John J. LaFalce announced as he began subcommittee hearings on IP: "Don't get me wrong—I'm not talking about government planning," but "whatever we do or whatever we don't do is our national strategy."[44] "An industrial strategy" was the phrase Senator Gary Hart (D., Colo.) used in his 1982 book, *A New Democracy,* and he was quoted in 1983 as saying: "Industrial policy is a moral issue . . . Policy isn't sawdust. It's about people"; and if Senator Robert Kennedy were alive, Hart was sure that he would "make people understand."[45]

Hart's views were more than senatorially important. He, along with five other senators and one governor, made up the Democratic party's shortlist of candidates for the presidential nomination. Six of the seven had endorsed "the industrial policy concept" by the fall of 1983. The doubter, Governor Ruben Askew of Florida, was said to favor "many specific steps advocated by those who want a formal policy."[46]

In the preelection skirmishing, the candidates endorsed a nebulous concept. Eventually, someone would be required to put it into words, eventually into legislation. A group of House Democrats reconnoitered at a weekend issues conference soon after the dismaying defeat of November 1980, and shortly they were formed by Caucus Committee Chairman Gillis W. Long into the Committee on Party Effectiveness. Meeting through 1981, led by younger and nationally ambitious members such as Richard Gephardt and Timothy Wirth, the committee produced *Rebuilding the Road to Opportunity* in September 1982. The "Yellow Brick Road," so called because of its yellow cover, was a new road for the Democratic party, declared one journalist, for it "had assembled behind a report that meekly but unmistakably replaced the politics of redistribution with the politics of investment." The report talked of productivity decline, the need for public-private partnerships, the rise of international competition, the need for a coordinated trade policy—and, specifically, for a tripartite Forum ("Economic Cooperation Council").[47]

In the Senate one year later, a Democratic Task Force led by Senator Edward Kennedy made "the need to maintain competitiveness . . . our unifying theme" and recommended creation of a Council of twenty members serving six-year terms and fulfilling an advisory role as a "forum within which the Nation's industrial strategy will be debated and formulated." A development Bank was mentioned as a possibility but was not endorsed, for that way lay the unraveling of party consensus.[48]

Committee documents could evade or elide the hard choices that drafting legislation would expose. But 1983 was the year when the draftsmen began to give the IP idea form, or forms. By a Library of Congress count of November 1983, at least 17 bills proposed an armada of national development boards, commissions on competitiveness, and the like, 9 of which would reestablish the RFC in one form or another.[49] An alarmed researcher at the Heritage Foundation found the 98th Congress facing more than 30 bills "that collectively would forge a national industrial policy"; 5 of them would reestablish the RFC.[50] Most attention went to Richard Gephardt and Timothy Wirth's bill to take a minimalist course by establishing an advisory Economic Cooperation Council. "It would be premature to start with a Bank when nobody is sure of what is needed and where we are going," Wirth was quoted.[51] The sponsors were from west of the Mississippi River. More activist instincts produced the maximalist effort by Stanley Lundine and David Bonior (from New York and Michigan) to establish the Bank.

Hearings were held in several committees in both houses, on the topics of trade, high-growth industries, and export promotion. When some likely legislative vehicle moved within reach, Democrats attached an Industrial Policy element to it. A reorganization of the Department of Commerce into a Trade Department was brought forward in 1983 by the administration and Senator William Roth, and Democrats added a proviso that an "industry sector competitiveness council" be convened for trade-threatened sectors of national significance. But the Senate, in Republican hands by the narrowest margin, was an unlikely place for a new policy of any kind. Neither a Department of Trade nor an attached industrial pol-icymaking Council reached the Senate floor.

### Congressman LaFalce Incubates Industrial Policy

The House, where the Democrats predominated, produced the Industrial Policy bill, the work of John LaFalce's Subcommittee on Economic Sta-bilization of the House Banking Committee. In 35 days of hearings over five months, beginning in June 1983, the members heard how the Japa-nese make IP work but also that they don't, that the RFC had been a huge success and also that it had been a failure. They heard Timothy Wirth de-scribe his Council, and Robert Reich express doubts about the desirability of a Bank. The de facto Industrial Policy was described and its principal institutional nexus located in the Defense Advanced Research Program Agency (DARPA) just across the Potomac River. The hearings were a feast of information and opinion on this sprawling new topic, and everyone who could listen and count knew that this subcommittee intended to send forward an Industrial Policy bill. The principal elements of what be-came H.R. 4360 could be discerned at the end of 1983. LaFalce's bill called for a Council and, despite the congressman's doubts that it was po-litically wise, a Bank. Industrial Policy was in the Democrats' pipeline and moving, wavering between maximalist and minimalist forms.[52]

### White House Defense: Encapsulate the Idea in a Commission

The political surge of the IP idea forced the Reagan administration to posi-tion itself for conflict. Prominent economic policy spokesmen who had ignored the idea now had to denounce it. Treasury Secretary Donald Re-gan called Industrial Policy a proposal for "having economic allocation decisions made by . . . 20 or 30 Government planners."[53] A limited offen-sive could also be mounted as part of the defense, so that it would not appear that all of the apparently serious study of industrial sectoral troubles was being monopolized by the Democrats. On June 28, 1983, the president appointed a Commission on Industrial Competitiveness to identify sectoral problems and recommend changes in governmental policies to improve the private sector's competitive ability in international markets; its report was timed for release after the 1984 election. The administration wished the issue to be officially but unobtrusively under study, sanitized away from the current electoral struggles.

To all but the White House navigators, this must have seemed a transparent and futile maneuver. No presidential commission reporting after election could sterilize this new idea, which sprouted everywhere. Whatever Republicans did, the idea had been nurtured and was sure to be harvested by the Democrats, and seemed on its way to a central place in the presidential contest of 1984. This was, however, an appointment that the presidential candidates did not keep.

### The Past in Service to the Future

Of the more than 200 witnesses who testified during the 35 days of the LaFalce subcommittee hearings, there was only 1 historian, Professor David Noble of MIT—and one might add economist Richard R. Nelson of Yale, an authority on economic history. History was present, a thousand times and in as many forms, but 2 experts at most were called to escort it. Every congressman seemed a historian on active duty, as did the many testifiers from business, labor, the academy. Amateur historians were busy everywhere, for the past was often at issue. The advocates of IP deliberately tried to establish the proposed reforms as progeny of the American experience. The Founders had been the first industrial policymakers, most especially that activist in guided economic development, first Secretary of the Treasury Alexander Hamilton. His *Report on Manufactures* (1791) set out an early rationale for public intervention which was frequently quoted:

> Capital is wayward and timid in lending itself to new undertakings, and the State ought to excite the confidence of capitalists, who are ever cautious and sagacious, by aiding them to overcome the obstacles that lie in the way of all experiments.
>
> It is well known . . . that certain nations . . . enable their own workmen to undersell and supplant all competitors in the countries to which those commodities are sent. Hence the undertakers of a new manufacture have to contend, not only with the natural disadvantages of a new undertaking, but with the gratuities and remunerations which other governments bestow. To be able to contend with success, it is evident that the interference and aid of their own governments are indispensable.[54]

State and federal governments throughout our history have repeatedly acted upon that advice, Industrial Policy advocates pointed out. Lane Kirkland's list of successful case histories stands as a summary of those most frequently mentioned—the Morrill Act, the land-grant colleges and farm credit institutions that propelled American agriculture to unmatched productivity, the Federal Reserve system, the RFC, "atomic energy."[55] Others confirmed or extended the staple list of past industrial policies: Felix Rohatyn:

> We became the world's dominant agricultural producers as a result of deliberate policies which included credit related policies. The REA [Rural Electrification Administration] and a whole series of inter-related policies. The RFC, before and during World War II, helped create a number of industries including much of the aluminum industry and the synthetic rubber industry . . . We have seen here in the last decade examples of what can be accomplished with the correct combination of policies and actions. Lockheed, New York City, and Chrysler were all doomed to bankruptcy by the financial markets. They are all thriving today.[56]

Gail Schwartz and Pat Choate:

> Government and industry . . . must sit down together . . . Models for such cooperative mechanisms exist. In World War II, American production took off like a rocket under the guidance of industrial committees.[57]

Lester Thurow:

> American agriculture was an industrial loser—a sunset industry . . . The shift from failure to success depended . . . upon an elaborate industrial strategy that heavily depended upon government funds and cooperative arrangements . . . [Agriculture today] is an American success story. And it is not alone. Similar stories could be told about the Erie Canal . . . the western railroads . . . and the TVA or Bonneville Power Administration. American history is full of examples where we have in the past made industrial policies work.[58]

*Business Week* looked abroad while looking back:

> The lesson of other nations, particularly Japan and Germany, is that it will [work]—if the U.S. can create a new consensus on goals.[59]

These and other oft-cited case histories defined the landscape of precedent said to invite a new venture in state-led development.

The first remarkable similarity in these history lessons is that they are a logical shambles. Many of the cited success stories were not sector-specific interventions at all, but rather investment in infrastructure (the Erie Canal) or regional development (TVA). And the bona fide sectoral policies cited contained curious omissions. Where was the mention of tariffs, that archetypal sectoral policy? Apparently trade policies were too complex, or insufficiently triumphant, to be paraded as triumphs or disasters. Among bailouts, besides Chrysler and Lockheed, where were Conrail and Continental Illinois Bank? The most noticeable omission from the past was any explicit attempt at Industrial Policy itself—nationally coordinated sectoral interventions. At least four such attempts had been made in the twentieth century, as one congressional consultant pointed out: wartime mobilization in 1917–18, 1941–1945, and the Korean War; and the National Recovery Administration (1933–1935) of Roosevelt's early New Deal.[60] Where were mention and study of these? Perhaps wartime experience was unique. But the NRA, America's first and only adventure with a peacetime IP? It had slipped from memory.

And if the Erie Canal was so clearly remembered, why was there complete amnesia about the busy economic interventionism practiced by every colonial and state government from the beginnings of European settlement of the New World? Colonial governments were, of course, mercantilist in outlook and practice, notwithstanding the colonists' growing resentment of the long-distance mercantilism from London. Thus the entire colonial era was festooned with industrial policies. While Adam Smith published that fountainhead of laissez-faire principles, *The Wealth of Nations,* in the same year as the Declaration of Independence, state governments during the early decades of the republic did not act as if legislators had read or agreed with Adam Smith's ideas. Instead, they followed Hamilton's injunction, and states acted as agents of economic development, promoting and protecting commerce, manufacturing, agriculture. Laissez-faire may have been an ideal held by some, but it is a myth that Smith's minimal government was the American model at the level where most government took place, the states. Throughout the nineteenth century the reality was aggressive state regulation and promotion of enterprise, its extent limited not by objections from the ideologists of "free markets," who were virtually nonexistent, but by state governments' puny administrative and fiscal capacities.

When Lord Bryce came to the United States on the tour that inspired his *American Commonwealth* (1888) he found that "though the Americans have no theory of the State and take a narrow view of its functions . . . [and] though they conceive themselves to be devoted to 'laissez-faire' in principle and to be in practice the most self-reliant of peoples, they have grown no less accustomed than the English to carry the action of government into ever-widening fields."[61] As the nineteenth century closed, a national system of tariffs and subsidies violated all laissez-faire principles, and at the state level a buzzing profusion of laws (both punitive and promotional) regulated and subsidized banking, agriculture, mining, lumbering, the professions. State governments extended and broadened those activities through the twentieth century, compiling a massive record of economic development policies, most of them with sector-specific incidence.[62]

Did none of them "work"? Did they all "work"? Those debating Industrial Policy in the 1980s did not ask, and their conspicuous silences on the long record of state economic intervention bring to mind "the curious incident of the dog in nighttime," perceived as curious by Sherlock Holmes:

"Is there any point to which you wish to draw my attention?"
"To the curious incident of the dog in the nighttime."
"The dog did nothing in the nighttime."
"That was the curious incident," remarked Sherlock Holmes.[63]

State and local governmental industrial policies were among the dogs not barking in the days, let alone the nights, of the Industrial Policy debate in 1980–1983.

Thus much relevant American experience was not mentioned, while selected policy case histories from the Erie Canal through RFC to Chrysler were cited as instances in which governmental intervention had "worked," an argument undergirded with the flimsiest supporting evidence of research and analysis. Further, and most important, it was asserted that these histories were analogies with tranferrable lessons, that they applied, "proved" something about the response to be expected tomorrow if such actions were repeated.

There were abundant but unremarked difficulties in all of this. The cases were different, the positive weight to be given governmental policy varying; but within policy histories there were also stretches of time when policy appeared to "work" and times when it did not. These anomalies suggest questions that might have led to useful knowledge, but they were almost never asked. On rare occasions, someone would show an interest in actually exploring some historic industrial policy. Former secretary of agriculture Ray Marshall remarked that "the analogy that people frequently give of agriculture is inappropriate for the kind of changes taking place now." The massive shift of labor out of agriculture had not been the painless experience sometimes implied, he reminded his urban audience; and in any event rural labor had been absorbed into an economy robust in productivity growth and not facing substantial foreign competition. The analogy with agricultural policy should not be made if it implied accepting massive displacement of millions out of traditional sectoral employment, as in the past, without provision for the costs of that displacement. In any event, think of the differences, he stressed, to a committee eager to move on: "Because of the differences . . . we ought to be very careful." [64]

This was astute and historically informed advice, rarely heard in the quest for analogies to serve as success stories promising to repeat themselves. As the arguments unfolded, few objected as the procession of simplistic analogies marched on, escorting the argument for (and, we shall see, against) industrial policies.

### The Past's Other Side

"A lot of trees died this year for the cause of industrial policy," a journalist remarked at the end of 1983, and "at times the *Washington Post* seems to write about nothing else." [65] The core argument was by then familiar: the era of U.S. industrial dominance was over, ended by capitalist economies guided by neomercantilist strategies. Ahead lay relative and possibly absolute economic decline unless, among other fundamental adaptations in private behavior, the United States realigned its industrial policies into an effective Industrial Policy. Many versions were offered, from the limited to the sweeping. Was Industrial Policy, whatever it was or might be, an idea whose time had come? We don't have a law yet, said Congressman LaFalce at the close of his hearings in late 1983, but if our goal was to stimulate debate, "let me now declare victory." [66] Certainly he sensed more success than a mere enlargement of the argument.

At a conference in Jackson Hole, Wyoming, economist Paul Krugman agreed, at pain to his preferences: "At some point in the next decade, the U.S. will probably adopt an explicit industrial policy" because "it is favored by nearly all Democrats and many Republicans, nearly all liberals and many conservatives, nearly all unions and many businesses." Only economists, he thought, stood against the tide. [67]

Krugman gave the idea a decade to win explicit acceptance, and he may yet be proved right. But the Industrial Policy idea, modestly framed and cautiously put forward by some as a limited part of the required national response, had taken on larger dimensions and bolder claims in other hands. Democrats needed a large economic idea badly, and by the end of 1983 they were drafting legislation. Grafted to partisan alignments, a magnet for ideological passion, Industrial Policy would attract more opponents than a few academic economists. At the same Jackson Hole symposium, one economist called it "chiropractic economics—at best ineffectual and more likely wrenching."[68] And Krugman himself, after predicting IP's adoption, condemned it out of economic theory, and then out of history. The debate was joined.

# CHAPTER 7

# The Critics

"Industrial policy . . . Is it just a shell with nothing in it?"

Congressman Sander Levin

The opening and closing words of all Industrial Policy appeals expressed the need for cooperation and consensus. Ironically, the idea produced division and multiplied antagonists. Born of a desire to remove industrial policymaking from incoherent dispersal in Congress and executive agencies and to formulate it within new institutions immune to partisan politics, the IP idea remained a canvas stretched on a partisan frame. It arrived in the critical early years of the Reagan "revolution," and no ongoing revolution welcomes another. Friends of Reaganism equated IP with Democrats wielding Big Government, a familiar enemy by any name. This trojan horse at the gate was built by the Democratic National Committee, an idea for targeting which was "targeted on one problem . . . that Walter Mondale, Gary Hart and others are not in the White House but would like to be." [1]

## The Unfolding Critique

The skeptics naturally began with first principles of political economy. Free markets, Reagan's secretary of the Treasury would say in his first speech against Industrial Policy, were "the most knowledgeable judge of economic winners and losers known to man" and "more sensitive than any computer." [2] In sharp contrast to this reliable guide for allocating society's resources was the idea of Planning, now called Industrial Policy. "I see little substantive difference between industrial policy and . . . planning," wrote a Cato Institute fellow. [3] Another critic thought that the one led to the other if there was any distance between them in the first place: "Industrial Policy . . . would put . . . the U.S. on the road to central economic planning." [4] Perhaps another book on the follies of Planning would bury this IP idea. Cato commissioned one.

Some small element of the public might find such an argument persuasive. But to influence the policy community the critics of the IP idea must engage its inner logic more closely. The beginning point of the IP argument was that market forces were producing in America an economic structure inferior to those created abroad by governments craftily supplementing markets. There was significant market failure—perhaps inadequate investment in risky R&D—which governments had the capacity to correct. Foreigners understood this; doctrinaire Americans held back.

Calling this line of argument socialism or Planning was an ineffective counterargument, especially for those who knew something about the Japanese system. A better line of attack was to deny that governments had such abilities at the sectoral level. No one made this case more effectively than Charles Schultze of the Brookings Institution. Industrial Policy, Schultze wrote in 1983, always translates into "systematic government policies designed to produce an industrial structure different from what the market would have produced." It builds on two theoretical assumptions: "The first . . . [is] that government has the analytical capability to determine with greater success than market forces what industrial structure is appropriate . . . The second is that the American political system would (or could) make such critical choices among firms, individuals and regions on the basis of economic criteria rather than political pressures." Things do not happen this way. Under capitalism, as economic change adds up to progress, businesses occasionally fail on a scale large enough to cause noticeable pain in whole industries or regions. Its victims often wield political influence, and when geographically concentrated they tend to turn to government to alter market outcomes. "But the one thing that most democratic political systems—and especially the American one—cannot do well at all is to make the critical choices among particular firms, municipalities, regions, determining cold-bloodedly which shall prosper and which shall not . . . [since] a cardinal principle of American government is 'never be seen to do direct harm.'"[5] Lacking defensible criteria for overriding political pressures when protecting losers, the government chooses poorly.

Schultze's views drew added strength from his credentials—Democrat, former White House official, Brookings economist. He had constructed a model for counterargument, a blend of economic theory and political realism. The stress fell upon the latter, the inability of American government to make hard choices, or wise ones. Along the way, in a brief passage, Schultze denied that the United States was "deindustrializing," apart from the unique difficulties of steel and autos. Others recognized that this question required more sustained analysis.

## "The Myth of Deindustrialization"

The *Economic Report of the President* for 1984, compiled in late 1983, squarely addressed the question. Since manufacturing's share of total output was the same in 1980 as in 1960 (24 percent), the Council of Economic Advisers answered that the United States was "definitely not" deindustrializing. There were of course structural shifts from labor-, capital-, and resource-intensive industries to technology-intensive ones, shifts painful to some communities and workers but "not a threat to our economy or international competitiveness." Compared with European economies, continued the CEA, the U.S. manufacturing sector "grew faster" than most others in 1960–1980, while some industrial sectors in Europe declined absolutely—that is, truly did deindustrialize. Reagan's economic advisers attributed the severe sectoral problems of the 1981–82 recession to the business cycle, reversible errors of management, or government deficits. These were all remediable, if business and government were not distracted by notions of sectoral manipulations. Confidence in U.S. industry would be revived if one raised one's sights from the hard months of 1981–82 and considered the 1950–1980 stretch, when 5 million jobs had been created in American factories. Constructing the right frame of time did wonders for one's frame of mind. Looking at the 30 years from 1950, Reagan's economists saw industrial growth, not deindustrialization.[6]

Equally optimistic was another institution with an interest in economic cheerfulness. The New York Stock Exchange (NYSE) was alarmed at the "central theme" of those who "march under the broad banner of industrial policy," that "government must play a more active role in the planning and guidance of the economy," meaning "major surgery" of a risky sort. So the managers of Wall Street sponsored a study of the assumption at the heart of such a belief, "that the [U.S.] economy suffers from a widespread lack of international competitiveness." The NYSE found that the U.S. trade performance of 40 industry groups over the decade 1972–1982, as measured by world market share, had been reasonably good, apart from a "relatively small number of industries which have hit upon hard times" (motor vehicles, iron and steel, textiles, shoes and leather, apparel). Services were expanding to take up the slack, a natural and beneficial stage in the economic evolution of advanced economies, not to be resisted or feared. The structural composition of the economy should be unimportant to policymakers: "It should not really matter whether the source of our economic growth comes from the goods-producing sector or services sector." As Herbert Stein put the same point, "If the most efficient way for the U.S. to get steel is to produce tapes of 'Dallas' and sell them to the Japanese, then producing tapes of 'Dallas' is our basic industry."[7] Both the NYSE and the former CEA chairman expressed a basically orthodox view, always scornful of worries about industrial structure.

The Stock Exchange study revealed with special clarity that what one sees in economic trends depends on where one decides to stand—in time. The study argued that people such as Robert Reich and Lee Iacocca had wrongly assumed "that the recent (1980–82) past is the most reliable guide to the future" when in fact "the mid-1980s is not a particular turning point in U.S. economic history . . . but merely another dot on the continuum." For the NYSE, the correct span of time for analysis was 1972–1982, not 1950–1982; the exceptional years (1950–1972) had to be stripped out, for then our economy did not face the caught-up industrial rivals or stagnationist environment that must now be considered normal. The study's authors understood this selection of time frame to be a critically important judgment; they set aside an entire page for that famous quotation from George Orwell: "Those who control the past control the future. Those who control the present control the past."[8]

Unfortunately for its lasting value, the Stock Exchange's brief study was based upon an economic model developed at the University of Maryland into which the NYSE's authors inserted dubious assumptions about the future. They arrived at a 3.5 percent annual growth rate for the U.S. economy (to 1995) based largely upon a projected 2.2 percent productivity increase, which was arrived at by extrapolating forward the 1969–1982 rate, after doubling it in anticipation of the invigorating effects of the Reagan reforms! These hopelessly indefensible assumptions led the study to predict that the mosaic of occupations would not be as Lee Iacocca gloomily foresaw, "a nation of video arcades, drive-in banks and MacDonald hamburger stands," but "will be much as it is today," with some continued relative shrinkage of manufacturing jobs and no significant diminution of earning power—in other words, a future resembling the past. Radical measures were not called for.[9]

### Deindustrialization Denied—Reassurance from Brookings

The CEA and NYSE studies were brief and suspect of institutional bias. Any thorough and dispassionate airing of the deindustrialization argument would require a book-length study by some person or institution neither friendly to Reagan's economic program nor committed to the maintenance of an optimistic investment psychology in and around Wall Street. As if on cue emerged Robert Z. Lawrence's analysis of structural change in U.S. manufacturing, and from the Brookings Institution, where Reaganites knew well that their aspiring successors were restlessly housed.

As we have seen, speculating about what the future holds is much influenced by what piece of the past one selects as a base for establishing dominant trends. Lawrence conceded that a focus on 1979–1982 invited the conclusion that the U.S. was shedding its industrial base, as employment in manufacturing had fallen every year, cutting the total by 10.4 percent in just three years. Even with reference to the longer time frame, 1950–1980, writers such as Robert Reich and Lester Thurow had easily derived a striking impression of a relative decline in productivity and world market share which, if extrapolated as if that past were to become a flipped-foward future, implied industrial inferiority with all its deplorable but inevitable by-products. But Lawrence preferred to set aside for comparative purposes the two catch-up decades when our competitors made such spectacular gains, and to look for enduring trends in the "new era" of stagnation that ensnared all industrial economies after 1973.

After a technically formidable discussion, Lawrence concluded unequivocally: "America is not deindustrializing." Although manufacturing's share of employment had slipped, from 35 percent to 21 percent in 1950–1982, Lawrence did not see this as "an erosion of the U.S. industrial base." For manufacturing's share of output remained almost the same—23 percent, down from 24.5 percent, a slight drop caused not by competitive weakness (imports) but by general economic stagnation, whose cure was correct macroeconomic policies.[10]

In this view, the United States was not on a new downslope of international economic competitiveness, but simply caught in a new era of slow growth that gripped all industrial economies, some less adaptable than America's. Industrial employment had dropped in most industrial countries (including in Japan), but not in the United States; only Japan has achieved larger output growth than the United States, amid the general sluggishness. As for that worrisome indicator productivity, Lawrence thought the emphasis should fall upon the fact that U.S. output per employed factory worker remained the highest in the world, rather than upon the unsurprising fact that societies catching up to our lead had for some time sustained higher growth rates of productivity than our own.

Such increases had not yet brought European economies to industrial strength rivaling America's. "It is . . . Europe," Lawrence wrote, "rather than in the U.S. that . . . is undergoing [absolute] deindustrialization"; "the structural problems facing European economies far exceeded those in the U.S."[11]

What of the rest of the 1980s? The heart of Lawrence's challenge to the idea of deindustrialization lay in his explanation for the admittedly poor performance of U.S. industry in 1979–1982. His econometric model returned the answer that the causes were an overvalued dollar and a sluggish U.S. economy—both reflecting budgetary (and to a lesser extent monetary) policy in the United States. For ills caused by flawed macroeconomic policies, the nearest and most obvious remedy was not microeconomic intervention. If corrected macropolicies removed these basic causes of uncompetitiveness, older industries would still contract, but Lawrence denied that such an inevitable transformation of economic structure would lead to lower incomes, to a "declining middle."

Lawrence concluded his economic treatise with his own views on government, without the authority of tables of data. Any criteria used by government to target resources differently than would the market were "inherently flawed and likely to be inefficient."[12] This sounded like a denunciation of an approaching calamity that might yet be averted by right thinking: "Before taking the irreversible step of conferring enormous benefits on big business and labor," we ought to consider the overwhelming evidence that the culprit was poor macroeconomic policy. Lawrence opposed this new deviation called "industrial policy," which he took to be the effort to "protect and subsidize our firms for fear that they cannot . . . compete."[13]

### Manning the Guns of History

By 1983 critics had done much to quash the idea of Industrial Policy by vigorously restating how free-market capitalism works and by citing the systemic inability of the U.S. government to make more rational economic allocation choices than Wall Street and Main Street. The ideological troops were in the field. Historically, however, the free-market faith had not held back the advancing tide of governmental activism that had steadily narrowed the scope of economic liberty since the 1880s. Lawrence, Schultze, and others were countering the IP idea's empirical claims about "deindustrialization." Yet the case for some kind of IP had rested on the lessons of history, where successful precedents had been found. Those lessons could not be allowed to stand unchallenged.

To a considerable extent the terrain on which the struggle would take place had been dictated. Proponents of IP had focused on certain historical episodes; those opposed to IP and its supporting history lessons felt compelled to provide a different view of the same histories, or to cite other histories that carried government-discouraging lessons. For the most part they offered personal opinion or recollection, with few serious attempts to conduct or review research.

Thus, if people claimed that federal interventions to spur economic development had been successful in opening up the interior, in pushing agriculture toward mechanization, in modernizing the Tennessee Valley, or that a national development bank had enjoyed a long and useful run and that auto companies could be restructured when the market seemed bent upon bankruptcy, then at least some of these interpretations of history must be turned to point another way.

There were many willing hands, for little study seemed required to play this game; generating history lessons appeared to be easy work. Congressman Frank Guarini (D., N.J.), submitting a bill to reestablish the RFC, said: "Remember the history of the RFC . . . [It] never cost the government any money," had "a long successful history of government helping industries to reindustrialize," and "helped boost American productivity and employment for nearly two decades." Although he cited not a single authority, no one dissented.[14]

Anyone could play in that sandbox. Two economists, one of them President Reagan's first CEA chairman, offered a historical interpretation of the RFC: "Its history shows that government subsidy of business encourages a misallocation of resources and provides opportunities for political favoritism . . . [and] also demonstrates that government programs develop a life of their own and persist long after the problems for which they were created have been solved."[15] Another economist offered a novel view of the RFC's origins and then easily extrapolated its successor's future: "The original RFC was inspired by Mussolini's Instituto per la Riconstruzione Industriale (IRI) . . . The lessons of the IRI should not be lost on the American people if an "Americanized" version of the IRI is presented as part of the Democratic economic program in 1984 . . . European experience shows that the real myth is the notion of an efficient industrial policy in the first place."[16]

James C. Miller, Reagan's appointee as chairman of the Federal Trade Commission, recalled "our own brief experience with industrial planning during the great depression. It included the Smoot-Hawley tariff and the NRA . . . [which] tried to pick 'winners' [but] did not work." [17] The tariff was industrial planning? How did he know that the National Recovery Administration "did not work"? But no one asked these questions. A broader brush was used by historian-congressman Daniel E. Lundgren (R., Calif.), who, in pondering the proposal for a national Council, "would go so far as to analogize it to the lessons we have learned from the entitlement program formula. Once the government giveth, it is more difficult to take back what it gave away." [18]

Such hit-and-run history minilessons abound in the official record. Critics of Industrial Policy busily assaulted its case-history foundations with the same casual and primitive tools used to construct them.

This was the predominant pattern, but there were exceptions. Efforts were made to offer more substantial alternative interpretations, especially for the most dubious cases. Four recent and much-publicized cases— Lockheed (1971), New York City (1971), Conrail (1974), and Chrysler (1979)—were instances of that most suspect of federal interventions, the bailout, and presented problems for both sides. The Lockheed Corporation had returned to financial health after many federal transfusions, and arguably was a special case of a permissible bailout, since the firm was a principal supplier of defense hardware. New York City rested in another special niche, as the nation's largest city and financial center, its post-bailout health much improved by painful retrenchments forced by the city's lenders, mobilized by New York state officials. Advocates of IP with the exception of Felix Rohatyn and Lee Iacocca had never made much of these two incidents, or of Conrail, another "unique" case of an industry with a peculiarly public character. But Iacocca and others talked enough about the social benefits of the Chrysler loan guarantee that some critical effort had to be directed to that case.

### Chrysler: Bailout History Revised

This was a case history difficult to turn to the advantage of anyone but Chrysler executives, workers not fired, and shareholders. By 1983 Chrysler was solidly in the black, and it paid off the last of the guaranteed loans in September. A thin scattering of critical appraisals appeared that autumn, presenting the downside of an episode that Iacocca was frequently praising on television commercials. A quickly produced Heritage Foundation pamphlet pointed out that most of the damage anticipated under the averted bankruptcy occurred anyway, that creditors had lost an estimated

70 cents on the dollar, and that one-third of Chrysler's workers had been fired in the belt-tightening of 1980–81. Taxpayers absorbed the interest-rate subsidy on $1.2 billion of guaranteed loans, and the company's 1983 profitability could be attributed less to marketplace-proven virtues than to "voluntary" Japanese import limitations and a tax carry-forward of earlier losses.[19]

Apparently, the Chrysler piece of policy history could not easily be made to yield unambiguous judgments or applications. A congressional committee heard one participant in the Chrysler affair testify that "federal restructuring of industries as a whole is misguided and would not work." He conceded that Chrysler might be called an isolated policy success, but the company must be at the brink of disaster, as Chrysler was, before concessions necessary for successful intervention could be extracted. The history lesson was that the policy was successful for Chrysler but should not be repeated outside those exact circumstances.[20]

The General Accounting Office studied all four bailouts and drew up four "guideline" lessons to allow such efforts to be repeated successfully. On whether it was a good idea to attempt replication, GAO came down on both sides: "Some of those lessons are undoubtedly transferrable to a more general, institutionalized approach such as a resurrected RFC," but on the other hand "what appears to have worked in crisis-oriented, unique situations may be less successful if it becomes routine."[21]

This had an intelligent sound, yet it could not have satisfied those who hoped that bailout histories would discredit the idea of the state as industrial savior. Single-company bailouts were not such a dangerous precedent as that ever-ready bailout machine, the RFC. The claim that the RFC had been a beneficial institution could not be allowed to stand unchallenged.

## Learning the Lessons of the RFC

The proposal to reestablish this celebrated New Deal–linked government development Bank was a stubbornly recurring idea. An RFC had been called for by prominent national figures as early as 1969, and the notion drew support through the 1970s from such pillars of capitalism as Treasury Secretary John Connally and Federal Reserve chairmen Arthur Burns and William McChesney Martin.[22] The Ford administration may have had the RFC in mind when in 1975 it called for an "energy independence authority" to finance innovations in energy supplies. In the 1980s a revived RFC was endorsed by Henry Ford II, Lee Iacocca, and the AFL-CIO, all of whom would have agreed with Felix Rohatyn that the RFC "saved thousands of banks, railroads and businesses, financed public works and ultimately defense plants in World War II." [23]

It is not clear what the evidence might have been for such laudatory appraisals. In his autobiography, *Fifty Billion Dollars* (1951), Jesse Jones, chairman of the RFC board from 1932 to 1945, claimed to have disbursed $35 billion by the time of his resignation in 1945, and to have returned to the public a $500 million profit after the loans were repaid. [24] This was hardly a disinterested or adequate assessment of this remarkable, enormously powerful, and long-lived federal bank, and the only historical account of the agency, published in 1983, covered only its first three years under Herbert Hoover. [25] For some critics of the concept of a federal development Bank, judgment could not wait for research and analysis. The Cato Institute found two authorities who were happy to offer decisive conclusions: "The old RFC was a dismal failure at rejuvenating American industry," wrote one; the other called it "a dismal failure that most assuredly made the Depression worse." [26]

For some interested in the RFC, the failure of historians and other policy scholars to provide the public with adequate retrospective analysis meant that they must quickly do it themselves. Finding historical scholarship on the agency very thin, the Carter IP task force requested, and received within months, a written history of the RFC from the Treasury. Much was learned.

Jesse Jones had been a bit off the mark; the agency disbursed $40.5 billion, whether at a profit or not being a question "somewhat difficult to answer." On the whole, the report concluded that "a useful role was served" during the Depression and war, but there was much reason for a negative appraisal thereafter. In any event, the RFC was hardly dead. Fragments remained in Jimmy Carter's day, such as the Export-Import Bank, the Small Business Administration, the Federal National Mortgage Association, and the Commodity Credit Corporation. "RFC-type federal financing activities," found the Treasury report, amounted in 1979 to 6.5 percent of the GNP, much higher than in either Depression or wartime. [27] This historical review contained neither policy judgments nor recommendations, and was an unremarked part of the staff work preceding Jimmy Carter's decision not to pile a new RFC atop this mound of credit in 1980.

This unpublished study was not available to guide others. Two researchers at Washington University published a short study in 1984 based on the records of a Senate investigation of the RFC conducted by Senator J. William Fulbright in 1950–51, in the wake of charges of politicization of loans, graft, and waste. The researchers argued that there had actually been three RFCs. The activities of the first had been "necessary and performed with reasonable efficiency" in the Depression decade, when the agency shored up an entire banking system along with the railroads. Few loans to industry were made in this phase. During wartime the second RFC purchased strategic materials and financed the early building of war production facilities, "useful and vital services" in a national emergency.

The third phase seemed to them a different story. With poorly defined objectives and little accountability, the bank entered its most aggressive lending period, channeling money to auto firms that subsequently failed; to the metalworking, sugar, concrete, lumber, steel, and housing industries; to Western Union; and to Miami hotels. It lost $57 million in a venture to market steel frame houses during what it thought was a permanent timber shortage.[28] Paul Craig Roberts, a Reagan appointee in the Treasury Department, had the pleasure of quoting the 1950 Fulbright investigation to a congressional committee, reminding them that the "third RFC" had invested in snake farms, movie houses, a rainbow trout factory, and a roulette room in a Nevada hotel.[29] This had been the RFC's unfinest hour. With Jesse Jones gone and the Truman government overburdened with foreign policy problems, the RFC drifted on as the fraud-bitten bureaucracy that conservatives see in every federal building except the five-sided one on the south bank of the Potomac. It was an agency that richly deserved its dismemberment at the hands of Congress in 1953.

After this closer look at the RFC, Arthur Denzau and Clifford Hardin concluded that "in the light of the experience of the original RFC" a new Bank "does not appear to be the answer."[30] Which experience—RFC 1, 2, or 3? Apparently, history would repeat itself, and to them this meant the especially painful phase 3; the successes of phases 1 and 2 did not entice them.

This was not the only conclusion that could be drawn. Yet the level of research and analysis was improving. The Business Roundtable also decided to put a spike in this IP idea, and its task force on industrial policy took the unusual step of hiring a historian, William Becker of George Washington University, to prepare a historical analysis of recent federal economic interventions. He produced an informed, though brief, assessment of the RFC's history and its meaning for contemporary policy. The

RFC had been useful, the historian wrote; but it failed to "get the U.S. out of the depression," and expanded beyond its original functions with an ease that should not be forgotten.[31]

When the quality of historical inquiries improved, the "lessons" became increasingly complicated and proliferated on both sides of the controversy. At times a national development Bank seems to have been a useful policy instrument. Under Jesse Jones's tough-minded leadership, the RFC shored up the banking system of Depression America with loans and stock purchases, and private investment was not "crowded out" because savings were abundant and idle.

The RFC did little winner-picking in the 1930s, although it financed public works projects such as the Oakland Bay Bridge, when the marketplace and local governments would not. The bank's usefulness during wartime has probably been understated. It created the Defense Plant Corporation, which went on to build and lease to operating corporations some 30 percent of the plant capacity on which American mobilization depended. To that RFC-launched subsidiary the United States owes the Big Inch pipeline eastward from Texas, aluminum capacity sufficient after the war to break Alcoa's monopoly, rapid expansion of the aircraft industry, and much else.[32]

Yet parts of the RFC record are decidedly chastening. Economist Robert Solo's painstaking research on one of the RFC's wartime sunrise industries, synthetic rubber, displays government-business collaboration at its worst. Standard Oil nudged the government into taking the financial risks of developing synthetic rubber technology, and because that industry eventually flourished and supplied the tires under American armies, the synthetic rubber case is often mentioned as an encouraging episode in winner-picking ahead of the market.

The reality was quite otherwise. Under oil industry pressure, untalented bureaucrats (bankers and oil executives on loan from the private sector) in the RFC and War Production Board stubbornly insisted on using petroleum as a feedstock when alcohol from grains was abundantly available. So serious were the delays in rubber production that only the Russian victory at Stalingrad bought the necessary time to avert a disastrous shortage. After the war the RFC-born Rubber Reserve Corporation poured $40 million into what Solo calls "a grant-eating industry" that would not prove to be the hoped-for sunrise industry. Synthetic rubber made from isoprene was eventually patented and marketed by B. F.

Goodrich and other domestic tire makers, drawing substantially upon technology from abroad. The new tire industry grew from roots almost unrelated to all the RFC-financed R&D.[33]

Thus even the wartime, second RFC compiled a record marked by mismanagement in winner-picking, as well as by success in increasing national industrial capacity in critical industries. The third RFC, however, offered critics the clearest target. That record is a rich vein of technological and economic incompetence by RFC bureaucrats and of waste, corruption, and false bookkeeping to hold a less-than-vigilant Congress at bay.[34]

## Applying RFC History

Even if all could agree upon this interpretation of RFC history, where would that leave future policy? "The analogy is wobbly," remarked Herbert Stein, reviewing the case for reviving the RFC in the 1980s on the grounds of its usefulness (which he conceded) 50 years earlier in the Depression.[35] Whatever the judgment on the RFC, first, second, or third, today's circumstances are different, and substantially so. Some versions of the development Bank proposed for the 1980s were different from the RFC. For example, Ronald Muller urged Congress in 1983 to establish a national development Bank to promote industrial strength, although he had concluded "that the RFC proposal suffers from two extremely important deficiencies." The RFC model did not operate through regional development banks, as Muller preferred, and its governance structure consigned decision making to a narrow elite.[36] Others urged versions of RFCs with other differences, such as its subordination to a National Economic Council, or the addition of an industry-restructuring mission that required the Bank to extract quids pro quo from client applicants.

Reflecting these refinements, Congressman LaFalce's House subcommittee drafted legislation for a different agency from the one Jesse Jones had managed for so long and in a different era. This does not make the history of the RFC irrelevant to LaFalce's labors, but too much of the discussion asked the wrong questions of that history. "Did it work?" should at the least be refined to "When it produced useful, or harmful and unintended, results, why? How?"

The RFC "worked," when it worked, when certain conditions were present. These began with reasonably clear goals: achieving banking system liquidity and railroad solvency in the Depression; financing the building of obviously needed national security–related production facilities in wartime, and of certain large public works during both periods. Equally important was high administrative competence—that repeated lesson of policy histories. Unlike most Depression-era agencies, the RFC actually inherited an experienced civil service, veterans of the old War Finance Corporation. It enjoyed strong leadership from Jones, a hard-nosed bargainer and good judge of people and banks. The agency's administrative competence was diluted during its wartime expansion to a maximum size of 36,000 staff, many of them bankers or executives on loan from industry. During part of the second and all of the third phase, the agency's managerial talent was overextended—its technological expertise woefully thin, its economic purposes unclear to itself and especially to field staff, its personnel recruited prevailingly from the private sector and lacking that clear sense of public purpose that might have contained the political and industrial pressures for cheap loans. This peacetime, non-Depression third RFC story conveys far more caution than emboldening results.

Such insights and questions are much to learn from an agency history. After early claims that the RFC history would provide a green traffic signal, or a red one, some were beginning to realize that deciding about a new apex credit institution was not going to be a simple matter. "If we don't do anything," said Congressman Ed Bethune of Arkansas, "if we don't form an RFC, we have a first class problem. If we form one, we still have a first class problem." [37] Quick histories and counterhistories were nurturing the beginnings of wisdom.

### Japan: An Alternative History

The underpinnings of the case for adopting an Industrial Policy included other historical analogies besides the RFC. There had been successful canals, regional river valley authorities, the Atomic Energy Commission, the Manhattan Project, and other moments in American policy history which were thought to glow even now with the success of economic invigoration through government. Critics paid little attention to most of these as they made their counterarguments, perhaps rightly because they were not examples of sectoral policies. Yet one large historical example was the reinforcing steel running throughout the IP foundation, and it could not be ignored. The postwar history of the Japanese system was displayed as the quintessential achievement of the mercantilist state guiding capitalist development.

This was a pivotal history lesson. If Ezra Vogel, Frank Gibney, Henry

Rosovsky, Chalmers Johnson, Robert Reich, and Lester Thurow were right about Japan, U.S. Industrial Policy seemed inescapable. As long as informed authorities could say "Japan has been practicing the most efficient type of industrial policy the world has even known" without informed rebuttal that his claim misinterpreted Japanese history, the IP idea would be a very attractive import.[38]

An alternative history of the Japanese postwar economy could hardly question the reality of economic success, but it could present a different version of the causes. Perhaps a deeper knowledge of the Japanese system would reveal that the sources of Japanese strength were broadly cultural and in the private sector, in private work and saving habits, managerial ingenuity, and other extragovernmental resources. The role of the state, if positive, had been so only because of unique "catch-up" circumstances. Industrial Policy is inherently easier for nations with a leader to pursue and imitate.

Only in 1983 did scholarly accounts of the Japanese experience convey such conclusions in writings accessible to the lay audience. Philip Trezise assessed the policy instruments wielded by the Japanese government in its effort to accelerate the rate and alter the path of industrial development. These policy tools he found to be primarily fiscal, along with the MITI-generated "vision" of the future, derived from an elaborate consultative procedure played out among MITI technocrats and industrial councils. The "vision" had unmeasurable but not primary influence upon business decisions, because it was derived from soundings into what businessmen intended to do anyway. Most national spending and tax incentives in Japan appeared to be aimed at broad social purposes unrelated to "picking industrial winners," and trade policy was no longer more protectionist than those of other industrial states, even if protectionism was assumed to be a beneficial policy tool. He concluded: "To attribute to industrial policy a crucial role is an expression of faith, not an argument supported by discernible facts."[39]

Trezise offered an explanation that he found better than the MITI myth for Japanese commercial vigor. The heart of the revisionist case was the view that the principal sources of Nippon's advance had always been in private society—in a vigorous market that nurtured aggressive corporations, in high savings rates and low capital costs, in social solidarity, in fewer lawyers and less paper-shuffling than in the United States. There were also the Japanese management techniques praised and retailed in the United States through books such as William Ouchi's *Theory Z,*

Richard Pascale and Anthony Athos' *The Art of Japanese Management,* Robert Hayes and Steven Wheelwright's *Restoring Our Competitive Edge.*[40] In none of these accounts, each of them a strong seller, was IP found to be an important ingredient in the Japanese story. What needed to be imported from Japan were behavioral changes targeted toward corporate headquarters and business schools, not toward Washington.

Several paths led to this MITI-minimizing conclusion. One of them began with the concession that the state in Japan had once been a vital and active part of industrial decision making, but only in the immediate postwar era, the 1940s and 1950s. From the mid-1960s to the early 1970s there was "a distinct shift" toward a greater reliance on competition and less-intrusive controls.[41] The economy had never been so rigidly controlled as the label "Japan, Inc." implied, and MITI in the latter 1970s was an agency of receding influence, in one account its "role as cartelist and rationaliser . . . eroded . . . its role as research co-ordinator . . . curtailed . . . its role as protector . . . diminished by international pressures."[42]

Time had thus carried Japan into new circumstances that produced a less influential and effective IP than the earlier one that American scholars had recently and admiringly discovered. The catch-up period coming to an end, the Japanese economy in the 1970s encountered the difficulties of all advanced industrial societies. Environmental costs intruded, domestic politics became more contentious, the earlier clear sense of national direction showed signs of splintering. MITI's gradual retreat to a more passive role had been missed by most but not all observers: "To adopt instruments that the Japanese are discarding seems . . . illogical," thought an American analyst in 1982, and one Japanese economist concurred: "Having learned some hard lessons in the last decade, the government will probably leave most aspects of economic development to the private sector."[43]

By 1983 the English-language literature on the Japanese system spanned a substantial range of interpretation, whereas four years earlier there had been essentially one view, and before that almost no knowledge at all except among a handful of academics and Pacific-traveling businessmen. By 1983 informed accounts accorded the role of the state in Japan a relatively small and probably diminishing place in the postwar "miracle" as frequently as they saw that role as central and continuing. Most specialists on Japan came down somewhere in the middle. The British historian G. C. Allen, for example, presented such a complicated and multifactored picture of the role of the state as to preclude any clear conclusions about the relative importance of cultural as against politicoeconomic elements. The role of government could be esteemed quite highly and some emulation by the United States endorsed, and the formidable strengths of the Japanese national character and social institutions recognized at the same time. For Frank Gibney, a successful businessman in Japan for many years, the government had been an "absolutely critical factor in Japan's postwar economic resurgence."[44] Yet in 1982 he allocated only one chapter to IP in his *Miracle by Design;* the rest of the book stressed Japan's work ethic, management styles, and social solidarity.

Finding that Japanese postwar history was complex and the mechanisms of the nation's economic success elusive was a sure sign of a maturing body of historically focused analysis. There were at least three discernible positions taken on whether Japanese history held lessons for the United States. First came the view, associated with Vogel, Johnson, and Gibney, that the Japanese state-led, neomercantilist system greatly accelerated national economic progress. The state's strategic role was and remains crucial and, with some modifications appropriate to our own culture, should be tried in the United States.

In the second view, even granting the effectiveness of Japanese IP in defiance of economic doctrines holding that governments could not improve the workings of capitalism by sectoral intervention, their system could not be imported by Americans or any other non-Asian society. "Japan is a radically different case," George Gilder wrote, and its Industrial Policy in any event less important than low taxes.[45] "A nation's industrial policy is inseparable from its history," wrote Robert Ozaki, arguing that the United States, because of its own history of economic "hegemony," incurably lacked the historic positioning and motivation, along with the habits of social consensus, which Japan had inherited.[46]

This "Japan is no model" thesis was offered as good news. The social price paid by Japan for its economic efficiency and societal discipline was high social conformity, little space for the deviant individual, high environmental costs, business opinion's overwhelming power in governmental counsels.[47] Japanese IP was corporatism with an especially procapitalist tilt, and many warned against importing it, even if some economic gains came in the bargain. "If the Japanese system resembles anything the West has ever seen," wrote a reviewer of six books on contemporary Japan, "it is fascism in its early days in Italy, or Germany's war economy of 1917–1918."[48] This extreme statement marked the far edge of a growing understanding that the Japanese maximization of economic efficiency exacted costs elsewhere in society. Americans should "borrow with caution" from Japanese values and institutions, Jared Taylor advised, for these "may not travel well."[49]

Finally came the view that Japan had moved into an era in which IP would not do for that nation what it once had done. Industrial Policy was for catching-up societies. The United States was not (yet) such a society—nor was Japan, any longer.

The meaning of the Japanese miracle had thus been made problematical. By 1983 the understanding of Japanese political economy—so thin among American elites as the 1980s opened—was becoming somewhat broader, and sometimes deeper. Nonexperts at congressional hearings in the fall of 1983 could discourse for several minutes on the inability of the technocrats at MITI and the Bank of Japan to "pick the winner"—Commerce Secretary William Brock, for example, cited Brookings' Trezise as authority for the importance of MITI.[50] History lessons about Japanese economic success with MITI at the center of the story were now matched with reputable scholarship interpreting Japanese IP as an insignificant and at any rate a declining factor. Checkmate.

### Interpreting Nations' Histories

The Industrial Policy proponents had also found instructive lessons in neomercantilist policy in Western Europe and elsewhere. Skeptics rapidly produced counterhistories, or at least counterinterpretations. An early effort was consultant Paul Krugman's paper, circulated within the Carter administration in the summer of 1980. Acknowledging that the study did not take into account national security or "equity" aspects of IP, he had concluded that "the available evidence does not support the view that selective industrial policy has played a crucial role in economic growth in any of these . . . countries," and "enthusiasm . . . does not seem warranted."[51] Carter aide George Eads shared this view. The British record, an unrelieved story of subsidy or nationalization, showed not one single industry nurtured to competitiveness. The French had had somewhat better results in computers and commercial aircraft, but only the Japanese had shown any significant success in fashioning IP that fostered adaptation rather than endless defense of losers. Even the Japanese, remembering MITI's effort to steer resources away from auto production in the 1950s, may be said to have a mixed record, which was also the best the world could show. "The main lesson" of this foreign experience, Eads said, "is to suggest skepticism . . . What lessons there are tend more in the direction of emphasizing the importance of . . . designing government interventions to minimize their intrusiveness."[52]

To other minds, history's lessons were less complicated than that. Melvyn Krauss, a senior fellow at the Hoover Institution, analyzed the industrial subsidies of five Western European nations through the 1970s and pronounced them all to be forms of "hidden protectionism" designed to protect jobs that the market wanted to end, the industrial equivalent of the welfare state.[53] "Anyone presenting Europe as a model of successful economic readjustment ought to have his head examined," wrote *New York Times* economic writer Robert Samuelson in critique of Robert Reich's *Next American Frontier.*[54] Unemployment rates were climbing faster in Europe than in the United States, and the European economies as a whole had produced almost no job growth in the 1970s while the United States had added nearly 20 million jobs. Europe, in fact, was truly declining in industrial capability. "Europessimism" was Europe's own verdict upon its economic performance. It was unconvincing to tout European systems of political economy at this unimpressive stage in European economic history.[55]

Here were unequivocal judgments for those in search of them. Industrial policies in Europe made economies feeble, in all times and places. Yet such dogmatism shared space with more balanced and more convincing assessments. In an essay tilted against IP, for example, Theodore Eismeier declined to force history into the role of an unfailing ally: "The broad diversity of foreign economic experience permits no easy generalization . . . the evidence is decidedly mixed"; and while the French record in picking national champions "is still a slender reed on which to lean the case for an American imitation," the "lessons are complex" and "ought not to be overstated."[56] To knowledgeable analysts not caught up in the heat of political combat, the varied historical experiences of many European societies under different political regimes and IP configurations, when reviewed, rarely if ever communicated a simple "it works" or "it doesn't work" verdict. Those who continued to hope that there yet be at least one decisive history, one clear case of Industrial Policy's pernicious influence, turned their minds toward Great Britain, our cultural ancestor and kinsman, formerly preeminent, now lagging and deindustrializing.

## Lessons from the United Kingdom

The government of the United Kingdom had operated one of the most extensive IPs of all industrial states since the 1960s. It seemed to critics a good case to work with, one in which an inept and probably harmful Industrial Policy had run parallel with continuing, remorseless decline. The record invited anti-IP observations, and opponents of a sectorally active state quickly obliged. "If at first you don't succeed," one essay admonished, "don't try again."[57] After the expenditure of billions of pounds and "virtually every institutional arrangement imaginable in an effort to pick-the-winners," concluded George Eads, the British attempt to stimulate new industries has been a "dismal failure" and the effort to revitalize failing sectors "a textbook example of how not to aid disinvestment—or to revitalize."[58] "The lessons American leaders can draw from Britain's experience with industrial policy are for the most part negative," in the view of two New York business consultants, a finding that "has particular relevance for American leaders because of the similarity of the constraints which policymakers face on both shores of the Atlantic." The "burden of history" in both societies was the same: "weak state" traditions, deriving from laissez-faire faiths of unusual strength, the relative absence of co-operative linkages between government and industry, the achievement of industrialization without active governmental direction, a civil service with little industrial expertise. In such circumstances, Industrial Policy could not possibly succeed.[59]

So ran the counterinterpretation of the British case history—a record of an IP that turned always toward self-defeating protectionism as it was captured by threatened elements of both the capital and labor sides of the private economy. The inescapable conclusion must be that the United States, with similar traditions and political institutions, would necessarily repeat that experience and reap the continued economic weakening that went with it.

British history was thus enlisted on both sides. Used one way, the interpreted record warned against relying merely upon market forces to lead a strong nation out of gathering difficulties, and supplied an object lesson in how not to construct the IP that the United States had to construct. Used another way, it predicted that any Anglo-Saxon society commencing experimentation with Industrial Policies would bring to the task a burden of history always defeating the effort.

### Debaters' History Lessons Reconsidered

Both interpretations could not be correct. Did British history imply a closed IP option for its English-speaking ex-colony, or an open one?

The first discovery in the historical scholarship on British industrial decline is that the subjects had attracted analytic attention long before two world wars had stripped away the empire and exposed national eclipse. The signs of decline were evident by the late nineteenth century as writers lamented the precocious development of German and American manufactures, and a worried royal commission paid visits to both countries to inspect their technology.[60] With national confidence further shaken by the military and organizational fumblings during the Boer War and by the vigor of German and American industrialism, Britain at the turn of the century surged with both social anxiety and reform energies. Books appeared on the superiority of German, Japanese, and U.S. social systems, and everywhere were heard cries for better nutrition among the working classes, government by skilled experts rather than liberally educated amateurs, an overhauled education system to favor engineering and public administration, in all "a universal outcry for efficiency," said *The Spectator* in 1902; "give us efficiency, or we die."[61]

This was an awakening of sorts, but without a seismic shock such as defeat in a war to focus national attention. The average Englishman who did not read alarmist books or essays on national decline could still see British life in a favorable light. On the eve of World War I the economy had continued to grow, and England was still the world's largest foreign investor and producer of 25 percent of the world's manufactured goods. There was no standard economic indicator that reflected decline, apart from cyclical perturbations. Basic indicators such as productivity, growth, and innovation showed improvement, though slowing historic rates of improvement.[62]

The Great War interrupted the clamor for a more competitive society, Britain completed its construction of an advanced welfare state, and the opening decades of the twentieth century brought their gauntlet of shocks. Beneath it all, the relative eclipse of British economic and technological power inexorably continued. Post–World War II Britain was forced to confront the mounting evidence of economic decline, and in the early 1960s a Tory government led the way into a new political economy deploying indicative planning, which did not last long, and Industrial Policy, which was to be permanent.

In serious writing on the British economy there was scant support for the simplistic lessons appearing in the debate. Two Brookings economists delved beneath inept government policy, shortsighted management, and obstinate labor, and found that "the productivity problem" originated "deep in the social system."[63] "The preoccupation with past and academic pursuits, the obsession with honors, the contempt for workaday trade," and the crippling nostalgia for lost imperial and military glories reminded Anthony Sampson of the twilight of the Spanish empire.[64] A longer list came from a noted writer associated with the London *Sunday Times,* Peter Jenkins: "The litany runs through the decades: generational decline in entrepreneurial spirit; social prejudice against manufacture and trade; education bias in favor of liberal over technical education; failure to apply science and technology to commerce; concentration on traditional and easy but slowergrowing markets; complacent management and obstructive trade unions; industrial relations poisoned by class discrimination, and resistance to change all around."[65]

Serious inquiry thus leads to government-business relationships, but also, beneath them, to the roles of education systems, class relations, and ultimately the social values that underlie them. Historian Martin Wiener traced a cultural bias against industrialism through the long history of British economic success.[66] Harvard's David Landes has illuminated the special British ambivalence toward the industrial regime through a comparison with Germany in the nineteenth century as these rivals moved at the head of industrial advance, Great Britain for a time in the lead. In the islands a disdain for technical education mingled with widespread elite feelings that education for the masses might not be such a good idea. A mystique of the superiority of "practical experience" over formal schooling for those destined for lives in business kept the British system of public and private technical schools a skeletal one, even as the Germans put in place a substantial network of such schools. In Great Britain the brightest of the young were sent off for liberal arts educations.

British savings rates were high enough to supply capital for rapid industrialization, but lenders were cautious, and borrowers who might have used venture capital "did not want it or know enough to seek it out." The British manufacturer typically made "the tacit assumption that tomorrow would the same as today," with "estimates on the conservative side." By contrast, in Germany "a different kind of arithmetic . . . maximized, not returns, but technical efficiency. For the German engineer, and the manager and the banker who stood behind him, the new was desirable, and not so much because it paid, but because it worked better." The British businessman adapted; the German counterpart took risks to move in new directions, displayed greater entrepreneurial intensity.[67]

Despite the cultural dissonance between industrial and preindustrial values, which some think authors such as Wiener exaggerate, the British brought together many assets as they achieved commercial, industrial, and military predominance. Whatever the drag of an anti-industrial strain in national values, British industrial power had a long run. Britain's eventual decline from preeminence was only in part an internal matter; it was also ordained by the superior resources of the two superpowers that emerged after World War II. Yet the internal features of British society impeding economic development loomed larger as the race with the Germans and Americans stretched on. Looking back at the United Kingdom's fall behind the progress and the material standard of life of West Germany, Japan, France, and then a lengthening list of European neighbors, scholars tend to conclude that the ever-present British cultural resistance to industrial capitalism's relentless mandates somehow gained the upper hand in the twentieth century. Nelson Polsby and Geoffrey Smith described a postwar faltering of national confidence, a pessimism about the future which, "far more than the economic malaise, is . . . a prime cause of economic failure." [68]

## Lessons?

Where in all of this are the lessons for policymakers? Historians were parsimonious. "How comforting it would be," Landes wrote, "to be able to draw unambiguous lessons from this rich tapestry of human experience and present them for the guidance of the industrializers of today." He found no unambiguous lessons. The evidence scattered and shrouded by time, the experience impossible to replicate for experimentation, historians of modern comparative economics concede that they cannot with certainty know why economic change occurred as it did, let alone whether it could have occurred otherwise. Opinions will differ, and "neither empirical evidence nor theoretical reasoning is likely to settle the dispute; sharp differences of opinion will always remain," Landes concluded. [69]

From this reality derives the necessary modesty of our hopes for guidance from the study of historically similar situations. There are no plainly applicable formulas. Still, reflection upon the pasts of other societies thought to be in analogous situations produces what all comparison grants the mind—things exposed to view for the first time, matters illuminated from another vantage, a realignment of levels of significance. He knows not England who only England knows, as Maccaulay reminded us. Recalling that the Japanese have consciously twice remade their political economy provides an antidote to American fatalism. On the other scale, the history of those other, Atlantic islands clearly reveals that the United Kingdom has not yet devised a set of strategies for interrupting a century of waning economic strength. Since this had been true both before and after Industrial Policy was added to the mix of remedies, this reflection serves as an antidote to the overestimation of IP's potential for either good or ill.

Reflection upon that experience also breaks free a perspective not provided by any other industrial nation's history, one that interested no one in the U.S. debate through the 1980s but may yet fall on fertile American ground. Some Britons say of their experience that the path they are on is not without attractions. Those postwar decades of "decline," after all, saw only relative loss. The British are today wealthier than ever, their wealth more equitably distributed than in the prewar era, the welfare state spreading more broadly and securely the benefits of education, housing, health care, security in old age. They may be seen as the first society to enter the postindustrial world, perhaps rationally choosing to emphasize leisure, community stability, and civil peace even at the costs of allowing competitive economic superiority to slip away to more materialist and restless societies.[70]

This perspective is irritating to many British observers scornful of such a "dream . . . of a Venetian twilight: a golden-grey steady state where staid arts and moderate politics join to preserve the tenor of things English."[71] Even a century after rivals began to perform more strongly and the wounds to national pride spurred cycles of introspection mixed with spurts of renovative energies, British attitudes remain a shifting combination of resignation and some residual saddling up for a fresh start. If there is a British consensus on their own experience which Americans might add to their examination of the U.S. situation, it seems distilled in the comment of one Briton at a Philadelphia conference on IP: "Humility and realistic aspirations" were the "major lesson of British experience."[72]

## The Emerging Case against IP

By 1983 each facet of the Industrial Policy concept had been met with a critical rebuttal. A substantial literature carried the skeptic's case—that the vision of a neomercantilist state playing a positive role in resolving American industrial difficulties misunderstood the empirical economic realities, rested upon mistaken economic theory, and misread the plain lessons of our own and others' national histories.

The argument from economic theory, in the form of repeated assertions of the supreme wisdom of markets, at best confirmed those already convinced. If vigorously affirmed True Economic Principles had been sufficient to repel government intervention, however, the American political economy would have looked in 1980 as it had a century before, when such theories were everywhere dominant. As it turned out, true principles of economy had not held back the advance of the welfare and regulatory state. The case against IP must be strengthened by a critical dissection of claims of deindustrialization and, after 1982, by pointing to the recovery under way. Yet the economic news was so mixed that neither side could crush the other through its interpretation. Because the IP appeal rested in substantial measure upon history lessons, anyone who would undermine it must become, at least for a day, a historian.

Thus the air in congressional hearing rooms and the print in editorial pages, policy center pamphlets, chapters of books, and entire books soon carried counterhistory lessons—usually of the handful of policy episodes that had become the lead cases—the boondoggling RFC, Chrysler's costly rescue, MITI's limited and diminishing role in Japan's surge, the United Kingdom's futile policies. After these, the critics liked to draw lessons from a handful of recent policy experiences thought to deserve universal scorn—Model Cities, the Small Business Administration, and especially the Economic Development Administration (EDA). These made easy prey for Herbert Stein, for example: "Experience with government economic development programs for depressed regions, with small-business assistance programs and with tariff protection, demonstrates what should be obvious a priori, the dominant influence of personal or regional political considerations."[73] John Albertine of the American Business Conference cited EDA as what one gets from governmental targeting, with 93 percent of U.S. counties qualifying for some sort of grant. This is the way our system works: programs are invariably "captured by those who don't want resources to move out of the declining sectors of the economy."[74]

From such materials could be compiled a memorably simple and eternal lesson of historical experience, as Secretary of Commerce Malcolm Baldrige summarized it: "Interventionist government policies have really not worked in the past, and there is no reason to believe that we can make them work now . . . No government agency is astute enough to target the right industries."[75] Or, in the words of the Heritage Foundation's Robert McKenzie: "The historical record reveals a strong coincidence between growth in government economic intervention and growing severity of inflation, unemployment, and lagging productivity improvements."[76]

### Dogs Not Barking

Such universal truths were grounded in a remarkably small and selective set of policy histories. One is struck by what Sherlock Holmes noted about the dog that did not bark in the nighttime. Many arrows of policy failure would have fit the critics' bow. Why not condemn federal aid to the maritime industry, a sunset sector adopted by the government long ago? A Brookings economist had published a stinging appraisal: "Two centuries of assistance in one form or another have . . . failed to create an efficient, competitive merchant marine or shipbuilding industry." This history of direct and indirect subsidies, combined with protective regulation, had formed U.S. industrial policy for shipping and shipbuilding. Gerald Jantscher found it "demoralizing" (to the industry) and sadly devoid of performance standards or goals on which aid should have been contingent.[77]

Or why not make much of U.S. industrial policy for steel, where a consensual assessment was that "public policies [from 1945 to 1960] had as much to do with subsequent industry decline as did other factors"?[78] If Jimmy Carter's Synfuels Corporation (1978–1985) was too new to serve as a glaring example of flawed winner-picking, why was there no effort to look further back in the federal dream of sponsoring a synfuels industry? The beginnings would be found at least as early as 1943, when the secretary of the interior, advised by an 85-member advisory committee of oil industry executives, took the first steps in a costly research program into coal gasification and other technologies which failed and was terminated in the 1950s.[79] And why not scrutinize the record of nuclear power, the government's special winner, by the end of the 1970s an industry building no new plants and defending its aging and costly generating capacity against encircled critics?[80] Above all, why so little reference to the history of the only peacetime governmental effort to pull the nation's industrial policies into one coherent Industrial Policy, Franklin Roosevelt's ill-fated National Recovery Administration, 1933–1935? Here, surely, was the most chastening episode of governmental incompetence and hubris, as the New Deal attempted to plan production in more than 500 industries, and in the end alienated all participants. Historians had done substantial work on the NRA; no excuse there. Policymakers of an anti-IP outlook should have been especially drawn by the title of one such study, Bernard Bellush's *The Failure of NRA*.[81]

None of these policy dogs was asked to bark for the opponents of IP. More remarkable was the absence of references to that bristling universe of industrial policy histories, the efforts of American state and local governments at economic development. Policymakers seemed unaware of the range of case histories available from subfederal policy history. In any case, most advocates and critics alike chose recent federal policy episodes that their intended audience might personally recall. Past policy efforts not barking were often those beyond the memory of the American policy community, broadly defined. As Walter Sellar and Robert Yeatman announced at the beginning of their classic, *1066 and All That,* "History is not what you thought. It is what you can remember. All other history defeats itself." [82]

### The Antis at Full Strength

The advocates of IP, the first out of the gate in 1980, had left the opposition surprised and far behind. A conference organizer in 1981–82 knew whom to invite to present one version or another of the IP idea, but who had the credentials to oppose? This question faced the conveners of a March 1981 symposium on Industrial Policy at the Wharton School at the University of Pennsylvania, and they found few committed opponents with some reasonable mastery of the subject matter. [83] By 1983, the number of critics with a claim to expertise had grown; the skeptics included not only many associated with Republican politics but also four economists from the Brookings Institution. [84] The idea-cluster that was Industrial Policy had been brought under serious ideological, empirical, and historical challenge. As 1984 arrived, some critics sensed that the tide had been turned. "Intellectual support for the notion of an industrial policy is unraveling," announced a Heritage Foundation release. [85] Jerry Jasinowski, then chief economist for the National Association of Manufacturers, thought that the argument for an industrial policy "has already peaked." [86] IP would soon be gone, a rejected abstraction.

### The Unremarked Convergence

Seen from one aspect, the discussion had polarized along increasingly partisan lines. From another, a zone of agreement or potential consensus seemed to take form as a placid eye at the center of this growing tropical storm of argument. The proponents had asserted that the United States already had an Industrial Policy made up of industrial policies put in place over the years. These could not be made to go away, even with eight years of Reaganite trimming, if indeed he was trimming sectoral interventions, which was far from certain. Existing policies ought therefore to be managed in some more explicit fashion.

On this point alone, among all the points of dispute, the opposition was virtually silent. On one occasion Reagan's Council of Economic Advisers acknowledged the "claim that the U.S. already has an industrial policy" but dubbed it a "pointless" argument. What should be discussed, the CEA thought, was not the IP now in existence, but the proposals for a formal policy, for these posed the critical question: "should the U.S. government have a larger role than it now has in deciding the composition of U.S. industry?"[87] This was an evasion of the issue, as well as a questionable characterization of the IP idea; but it was the administration's only response. Few other critics of IP responded at all to the "de facto IP" problem. Three Democrats, all former high-ranking aides to Jimmy Carter, and all dubious about the IP concept, were more forthcoming. On separate occasions Charles Schultze, George Eads, and Jerry Jasinowski frankly conceded that the United States already had a powerful, unacknowledged, and generally unsatisfactory IP. Each went on to deny that it was therefore a logical or desirable step to move the monster from the shadows toward legitimation in some visible institutional and statutory form.

Schultze, senior and best known of the three, argued that the best machinery for occasional bailouts and the annual allotment of industrial subsidies was exactly the political machinery already in place: "The ad hoc approach is the best approach," he thought. Industries and companies eager for governmental aid must laboriously run the gamut of congressional committees and executive agencies each time, a discouraging level of effort.[88]

As Jasinowski put it, "institutionalizing the process by which the special interests can make their claim on the Federal government" would be to allow that function to grow, legitimating what had formerly been a rare event. To Schultze "the surest way to multiply unwarranted subsidies and protectionist measures is to legitimate their existence under the rubric of industrial policy."[89]

Eads recalled the Chrysler episode, which he had witnessed from inside the bailing-out government, and noted that it had been "unpleasant" for the corporate executives who appeared before Congress and in the end were forced to accept the receivership and dictates of a committee headed by the secretary of the treasury. Because the process was extraordinary, it discouraged resort to that sort of misguided industrial policy so much in demand.[90]

Unlike the CEA evasion, this was a direct reply to the assertion that the de facto IP should be brought out of the shadows and organized. The advice was: whatever is to be done, do not bring the beast out into the open, or it will grow larger and more arrogant. But was the entire de facto Industrial Policy more dangerous if openly acknowledged, or kept in the shadows? Or did only the bailout function deserve to be hidden? Should the potentially more positive elements of sectoral policy, including coordination of sectoral initiatives and tripartite forums, be kept in the shadows that the Bank-bailout idea deserved?

Eventually, the logic of the issue drove Brookings' Robert Lawrence to recommend what should be done with the many sectoral policies that his opposition to a formal IP left in place. He conceded that there would indeed always be "industrial policymakers," and offered advice on how they might improve upon their performance: avoid so far as possible the effort to select viable industries; keep industry-specific programs to a minimum in any case; "focus on recognized cases of market failure and on improving performance in industries in which government intervention is already widespread"; improve policy coordination and transparency; and emphasize the promotion of adjustment.[91]

This was remarkable advice from someone who had soundly rebuked the IP idea. It could have been written by, or culled from, William Diebold or Robert Reich or Lester Thurow. Lawrence went on to regret the absence of a "comprehensive inventory of all government policies or a detailed analysis of their net effects," which resulted in industrial policies based on inadequate information and lacking transparency, difficult for either Americans or foreigners to analyze for their real costs and benefits. He thus recommended the establishment of an "independent analytical agency . . . charged with the responsibilities of maintaining records and issuing reports on governmental assistance to industries and firms in all sectors of the economy for the purpose of bringing greater coherence to the totality of policies."[92]

Welcome to Industrial Policy!

Assuredly, it was IP of the minimal variety, built around a small version of the Council, without a Bank, lacking even a toothless, moneyless, advisory Forum. But it was significant that one of the leading critics of the concept had worked his way to a margin of agreement with industrial planners who lined up "for" Industrial Policy.

Lawrence had some company. George Eads told the Joint Economic Committee that although he was "an opponent of some of the more grandiose proposals for industrial policy," those deriving from "infatuation" and arriving with too much "enthusiasm," the 1974 Commission on Supplies and Shortages of which he had been staff director had recommended establishment in the Executive Office of the President "a small group of sectoral specialists whose job would be to help coordinate microeconomic interventions" and an analytic capability in the Department of Commerce. Micropolicies are needed and should be coordinated. Call that IP if you like; it was one without "infatuation," "too much enthusiasm," "expecting too much from any industrial policy."[93]

Even Charles Schultze, when asked in late 1983 about the advisability of an independent agency to analyze sectoral policies and their impacts, responded that "it would not be too bad and it might be useful sometimes. If that is what industrial policy is, I cannot get terribly excited about it."[94]

## Getting Excited about Industrial Policy

Useful sometimes. Not exciting. Had the debate led at last to that elusive animal, Industrial Policy, and found it to be a smallish, useful, but not exciting necessity?

Here were the materials for a negotiated end to the conflict. But the smoke of battle obscured them. The tone and substance of what was being said and written had the ring of ideological war, not of compromise or negotiation toward common ground in some incremental reform. Industrial Policy, most of its critics insisted, was not a new, market-respecting, economically beneficial use of the state and could never in the real world become so. It was the old liberal planning dream and must be defeated so that it would go away. As one critic said, people such as Robert Reich might profess their trust in markets, but, like all IP-ers, "he has a thorough disdain for the market," "does not believe that markets provide sufficient signals" to management and labor to lead them to necessary changes.[95] Advocates of Industrial Policy may sound as if they offer only market-respecting improvements in the coordination and effectiveness of the inevitable sectoral interventions, but the IP idea itself is Pandora's box, and out of it will climb protectionism, planning, Lane Kirkland, and Felix Rohatyn. There are two distinct spheres: the marketplace, which makes wise decisions about where economic resources should go; and the government, which theory predicts and history confirms cannot make such decisions. Government should stay clear of the marketplace.

This tenor of argument smothered the prospects for compromise. Somewhere in its voyage from Europe and Japan to the United States, the Industrial Policy idea had gathered around itself something not found in the countries of its origin—the high emotions of ideological combat. The debate was thus bent away from the illumination of policy reality and revision and toward a political event—the autumn 1984 decision to vote it (and its advocates) up or down. There was the general sense that the judges of the debate would rule on election day, November 3. "The key economic issue of the 1984 elections," wrote an anxious conservative in the *Wall Street Journal*, "regardless of who the candidates are, will be the establishment of a national industrial policy for the United States."[96]

CHAPTER 8

# The End of the Beginning

Industrial policy is one of those rare ideas that have moved swiftly from obscurity to meaninglessness without any inter-vening period of coherence.

Robert B. Reich
July 1984

Had the economy tipped in 1984 toward either extreme of recovered strength or depression, the Industrial Policy dispute might have been de-cisively resolved. Yet the year made famous by Orwell's novel appeared at its wintry close to have carried trends that confirmed parts of conflicting predictions for the U.S. economy. The *Economic Report of the President* for 1984 found a growing economy shaking off the problems thought so critical two or three years earlier. "The strongest recovery in 30 years" had pushed GNP up 5.6 percent over the year, unemployment had come down to 7.1 million, inflation was a third the rate of four years earlier, and "the American economy is once again the envy of the world."[1] These words appeared above Ronald Reagan's signature, and the report offered data to demonstrate strength born of his "policies that broke the awful pattern." An average of 300,000 jobs a month had been created since the upturn of late 1982, "the envy of Europeans," who simply "cannot get over it."[2]

Here warning signs intruded, even in the administration's assessment. Farming labored under multiple difficulties, and bank failures were high. Not all industries or regions shared equally or at all in the overall expan-sion. The official view read these stresses as signs of an economy stirring again with entrepreneurial and adaptive vigor, shedding the old skin of uncompetitive industries and continuing to shift toward a mix in which services and high-technology manufacturing expanded their roles. But most of the job expansion had come in eating and drinking, grocery, and data-processing workplaces, while goods-producing jobs had shrunk by

850,000 over the year. The worry persisted that America might become, in Lee Iacocca's words, "a nation of video arcades, drive-in banks and McDonald's hamburger stands."[3]

Productivity trends could also be read in divergent ways. Official data showed that labor productivity had risen 3.2 percent in the larger business sector in 1984, and 3.5 percent in manufacturing; these figures led one productivity expert to announce that "the decade of slow productivity growth that began near 1973 is over."[4] Others reading the productivity figures found such optimism premature. Yale economist Peter Clark placed the 1981–1984 record against the longer historical span from 1890 and found the recent productivity recovery "rather weak by historical standards," only half as strong as the long-term average. Energy costs had moderated, and the baby-boom cohort was largely absorbed into the work force; yet the economy had reached only half its historic rate of productivity advance.[5]

The pulse of commerce at ports of entry showed an acceleration of imports into the United States in 1984 in an ever-broadening variety. The nation's import bill reached $340 billion that year, with capital goods the fastest-growing category of things American bought from foreign producers. American high-technology industries such as communication equipment, office machinery, and computer chips were beginning to feel the same kind of foreign competition that had so long battered metals, leather, and textiles. When the year was over, the merchandise trade deficit totaled $123 billion, the current account deficit was $101.6 billion, and the Commerce Department conceded that the nation's 71 years of surplus in investment overseas would end sometime in the spring of 1985, leaving the United States a debtor nation. "Imports are beginning to hurt," conceded the constitutionally optimistic editors of *Business Week* in the fall, after 90,000 industrial jobs fell away in September.[6] Protectionist pressures could be measured in any congressman's office, or in the media, or at the offices of the U.S. International Trade Commission, where an "ever increasing workload" of 13,000 filings for relief from imported steel, copper, tuna, cardiac pacemakers, optical fibers, green olives, and cotton yarn piled upon the swamped ITC staff in their 140-year-old building with its "cracked masonry, bad roof, no central heating, and faulty electrical power." The USITC took up twice as many investigations of unfair trade practices in 1984 as in 1980, three times as many antidumping complaints, four times as many countervailing duty cases; and its percentage of findings in favor of relief increased.[7]

Thus America's economic transformation hurried on, spreading speculation about where it would carry its people.

> Hog Butcher for the World
> Tool Maker, Stacker of Wheat,
> Player with Railroads and the Nation's
> Freight Handler[8]

That had been Carl Sandburg's Chicago as America wrested industrial
leadership from Europe. The description had fitted the entire nation for a
long time but was fast ceasing to do so. A food basket America remained,
but the tools were increasingly being made in other nations and shipped
here. Global economic change brought to American public life in the
1980s its central questions: what work would Americans do, if they did
not make tools, or steel, their own shirts or shoes? Would the service
economy, which now provided the living of three-quarters of the population, sustain the climb toward increasing wealth, as the industrial economy had done? Or would economic change divide the society between
the hamburger cooks, sweepers, clerks, and security guards who were
trapped below that middle-class wage zone where social strength had
once rested, and those lucky few who found their way to the remunera-
tive roles within the new knowledge-driven economy?

"The American people," wrote journalist Joseph Kraft near the end of a
lifetime that almost spanned the transition from Sandburg's Chicago to
Ronald Reagan, "have plunged into a new adventure in the national saga
. . . a wholesale restructuring of basic industry." Would there be "energy
left over" for "such large affairs as Europe and Asia," or would there be
"neoisolationism" as America struggled with internal economic transformation? The veteran journalist feared that economic matters had forced
their way to the front of his preferred foreign policy agenda in this election year.[9]

### Industrial Policy: Repetition, Progress, and Detour

Given an extended life by such mixed economic trends, the debate entered its fourth and most politicized year. Would the arguments be the
same, in content and in quality? Or would there be intellectual progress?
The answers would be yes.

The arguments that had crystallized for and against Industrial Policy in

1983 were repeated in 1984, often by the same people, some of them perceptibly tiring as they repeated themselves. Yet it was also the best year of the discussion, as more substantial and sophisticated analyses were published, and gaps in research and argument were filled in by a widening circle of participants. If in 1982–1983 it had been difficult to escape the perception that there were two opposing camps, those "for" or "against," the tides of discussion in 1984 washed up on the beach a third position—"Industrial Strategy." Paradoxically, a cautious version of Industrial Policy would gain wide acceptance in the very year the idea suffered a decisive political defeat. Even the manner of the autumn defeat would come as a substantial surprise.

The continuing discussion at times seemed to reflect minds frozen at the lower levels of thought, as when the Republican staff members of the Joint Economic Committee dismissed the IP idea in all of its formulations as nothing more than "a misguided effort" by Democrats hoping "to shed an antigrowth, antibusiness image" when the idea only meant "more government spending, higher taxes and more government regulation" along with "a further extension of the welfare state."[10]

In fact the IP idea led to quite the opposite result, said Harvard professor George Cabot Lodge. More bluntly than Felix Rohatyn, he argued that the first implication of a necessary Industrial Policy was sacrifice of the untenable pleasures of recent enjoyment, including artificially high wages and the welfare state.[11] These were not entirely unfamiliar perceptions, reminders that IP might be many things. Familiar also was the appearance in Cambridge and Washington of a tag-team debate between, on the one hand, Barry Bluestone and Bennett Harrison, who presented new data reinforcing their view that millions of workers were slipping out of the middle-class as corporations unnecessarily gave up on manufacturing; and on the other, Charles Schultze and Robert Lawrence, who held to the convictions of 1982–1983 that U.S. industry would hold its competitive position when macroeconomic policy returned to sanity.[12]

The year also brought Robert Lawrence's book-length statement of views he had expressed in 1983 as one of the Brookings Institution skeptics about "deindustrialization" and the rising enthusiasm for sectoral interventions. Lester Thurow, reviewing the book, pointed out that Lawrence rejected industrial policies in one chapter and "essentially embraces industrial policies without being willing to use the name" in another; Lawrence regretted the absence of a "comprehensive inventory of all government policies" offering industrial assistance, and suggested that the United States urge upon all nations the establishment of "an independent analytical agency . . . charged with the responsibilities of maintaining records and issuing reports on governmental assistance to industries and firms in all sectors of the economy and for the purpose of bringing greater coherence to the totality of policies." [13] The desirability of coherent sectoral policies was affirmed by a skeptic, a minimalist IP from Brookings!

There were shifting positions and new information elsewhere. A long-awaited Data Resource Industries study emerged as a sober and fact-filled analysis of 20 industries over a 30-year period, built around a computer run on the DRI econometric model in which the U.S. economic performance after 1955 was simulated using different policy variables. Policy changes alone worked dramatic effects in the model, strengthening the nation's industrial performance virtually across the board. Most of this movement the DRI study attributed to different macropolicies that would have reduced budget size and deficits, thus aligning the dollar more fairly against foreign currencies and lowering the cost of capital.

According to DRI, because of wrongheaded fiscal policy "a decline of the position of manufacturing" had occurred in the U.S. economy and was "a major historical development for this country" and a cause for concern. The nation had a competitiveness problem in manufacturing, even after Reagan's remedies. If economic policy continued to be made "without an industrial viewpoint," the DRI authors foresaw by 1996 a set of national difficulties that included a slowing of general economic advance, regional disparities more intense than in the 1980s, an enfeebled national defense, domestic discord. The history of Britain, they thought, "is a warning to us." [14]

The policy implications of this unsettling report remained unfocused at the end of it. Congress had mandated a White House Productivity Conference, which met in April 1984, bringing Industrial Policy talk as close to Ronald Reagan as it would come. The meeting was carefully balanced politically so that neither party's agenda would predominate, with the result that the IP idea was not voted up or down. The conference affirmed the existence of a serious American productivity problem, canvassed the range of suggested causes and remedies, and, when the IP idea was allowed to surface, found it "a general term having many connotations" whose discussion at the meeting "reflected the wide variety of opinion in this area." This was not quite stalemate. The conference transmitted, without specific endorsement, the suggestion that there be established, or at least studied, some mechanism for "better coordination of governmental intervention" in industrial sectors. [15]

## The Question of Criteria

One of Charles Schultze's unanswered assertions in 1983 had been that no concrete economic criteria had been proposed to guide industrial policy decisions, leaving only political pressures from interest groups, or the whims of technocrats down from Harvard eager to make things hum— with deplorable results likely either way. To economists this must have seemed the central issue. The criteria for private investments were clear in the texts, if less clear in the street—profit maximization, blended with targets for return on invested capital and market share maximization. Public policy on industrial sectors abandoned these criteria without specifying any others of comparable concreteness, which seemed to economists a formula for surrender to mere political power. The point went without a direct and substantial response until well into 1984, although it might have been pointed out that most public policy lacked rigorous guiding criteria.

A substantial and direct response came from Julian Gresser, a lawyer who had written about the Japanese legal system and electronics industry. Gresser offered "a specific method of how to select and launch 'critical' sectors, an explicit rationale to justify those choices." The method was derived from "the writings of historians," especially David Landes' work on the British cotton textile complex; Albert Fishlow on railroads in nineteenth-century America, Landes on the German chemical industry and the shift of watchmaking from England to Switzerland, and Nathan Rosenberg on machine tools. Gresser blended historians' insights with borrowings from economists Joseph Schumpeter, Kenneth Arrow, and others. The result was a "theory of strategic industries," which Gresser acknowledged to be virtually embodied in the Industrial Policy of postwar Japan. He presented a nine-step "trigger method" for selecting "strategic industries" and proposed a novel plan for consultation between Japan and the United States so that their resultant industrial policies would be to the highest degree complementary. Both ideas deserved a discussion they did not receive.[16]

## Learning the World's New Ways

Intellectual progress in some areas was undeniable—most especially in comparative international political economy. In 1984, unlike five years earlier, any adequate American university library offered readings, in

English, about the formulation of industrial policy for steel, robotics, or electronics in Japan, France, or Italy. The Brookings Institution devoted a conference in September 1984 entirely to French IP and had no difficulty assembling knowledgeable panels of experts and filling a large hall with listeners. One anthology brought together the comparative histories of fifteen national systems of industrial policymaking, finding a policy apparatus of varying coherence and differing techniques from Switzerland, Malaysia, and Mexico on the minimal-intervention end of a continuum, Japan and France on the other end. The industrial policies of the United States were allotted a chapter, since they exerted significant influence.[17]

The expanding expertise on overseas economies and industrial policies was impelled in part by the energies flowing to the trade issue. In conventional trade theory, no nation could for long enrich itself at the expense of trading partners by targeting subsidies to its exporting sectors (or protecting its domestic industries from imports). Targeted exports might flourish, but they should be seen as a subsidy to foreign consumers. Protectionism, like export promotion, could not be defended within the prevailing economic theory.

These convictions were unsettled by Asian export-oriented strategies and their apparent success, but the theoretical case for what the Japanese and others were doing was not well developed in the West. This situation visibly changed in 1984, as the professional literature on international economics stirred with ideas that the media came to call "new wave" or strategic trade theory. A conference in October brought together several of those who argued that certain imperfections in international markets combined with the learning dynamics of high-technology production made successful state interventions possible under specific conditions. An activist trade policy could, in principle, benefit a country relative to others; it was less clear, even in theory, whether this must necessarily beggar someone, or could conceivably be harnessed to a general advance. In any event, "the standard economic analysis of trade policy has begun to look a little wobbly" because "the world has changed," commented MIT's Paul Krugman, who would edit conference papers for an influential volume published in 1986.[18]

The most conspicuous example of a nation doing what theory had predicted it could not do was Japan. IP would have lost much of its impetus if Japan's success could have been attributed to something else or if the success itself were to end. Here, too, the trends of 1984 were not kind to the opposition. Despite annual predictions that the Japanese surge was ebbing, the European Management Forum produced a complex system of ratings of international competitiveness from 1978 on, and Japan ranked first in every year, including 1984.[19] The editor of *Industry Week* confessed that the mounting problems that he saw on a visit to Japan in 1973 had not brought an end to national vitality. "The picture of a Japan stumbling over its own successes," he wrote, "was wishful thinking . . . From a competitive standpoint, the Japanese are hardly missing a beat."[20] Chalmers Johnson foresaw that if the United States did not improve its industrial policies America would "become the world's leading producer of ICBMs and soybeans, while Japan produces everything in between."[21]

### The Inevitability of Industrial Policy

Johnson in this essay had taken his turn ringing the loudest bell in the carillon of 1984, the discovery of the long history, size, and irrationality of the de facto IP of the American nation. "There is no such thing as a government's not having an industrial policy," was his irrefutable conclusion.[22] Former White House domestic chief of staff Stuart Eizenstat added convincing recollections of his own engagement with "microeconomic decisions," which "are inevitable," "as old as the Republic," and are not confined to the lower levels of government. They were waiting when he and Carter entered the White House in 1977, most of them rising from trade-troubled industries. Eizenstat found himself passing up to the president decisions on citizens' band radios, shoes, color televisions, autos, steel—and not just trade relief but bailouts, unmentioned in the briefing books studied by President-elect Carter. But behind trade relief and bailouts were decisions on regulations, taxes, R&D spending, and rolling over parts of the $100 billion in loans and loan guarantees the federal government carried every year. It was "a crazy-quilt—a makeshift industrial policy of often contradictory individual decisions."[23]

On the other side of Eizenstat's desk at one time had been Lee Iacocca, an auto maker without much prior education in matters governmental who had at one time throught the government wasn't in and didn't belong in the auto industry business. He learned very quickly about government's role in industry after coming to Washington for help in 1979, and in 1984 thought he would "probably be one of the few guys who would immediately be granted a doctorate in industrial policy." Loan guarantees, he discovered, "were as American as applie pie," gratefully accepted by his corporate friends even as they condemned Chrysler for abandoning the principles of laissez-faire. "We have an industrial policy," it began far back in the colonial era, and today "it's a bad one." The American people want the country strong, "but they want it to happen without any planning. They want America to be great by accident! . . . In our heads, we're still trapped in 1947."[24]

Here the IP debate was almost grotesquely asymmetrical. No one responded to these announcements that America had an Industrial Policy, one with a long lineage and indefensible incoherence. After all, what could be said? The reality could hardly be denied. Yet to concede it would allow a fatal shift of ground beneath the argument, to the advantage of those favoring IP. For what must follow if this de facto Industrial Policy were acknowledged? Bruce Bartlett managed a plaintive "we ought to be dismantling our existing industrial policy, not enhancing it." However this might have sounded in 1981, by 1984 an end-of-term realism had arrived; the dream of a Reaganite stable-cleansing had faded. Many government intrusions were apparently eternal, sectoral interventions among them. The next step was logical—to call for greater coherence. Richard Newfarmer of the World Bank concluded: "The U.S. should understand and make transparent the extensive role of its own government in promoting industry . . . decide more forthrightly" what that role should be, which could only mean steps to "create a government vehicle . . . [to] perform analytical tasks," publish "a public agency to evaluate authoritatively private claims about an industry's situation."[25] The longer the debate went on, the stronger the tacit convergence toward the necessity to manage sectoral interventions, even if there was no agreement upon whether to expand or contract them.

### "Never Call Anything Industrial Policy"

Yet even a minimalist IP had two political drawbacks. It had that off-putting name that Lee Iacocca so emphatically rejected before a House committee: "Well, the first thing we do is we get a new name for it . . . Never call anything industrial policy."[26] In addition, the IP idea, first hailed in the pages of *Business Week* in 1980, appeared to have evolved away from its original business constituency and toward the labor unions and their Democratic allies.

A prominent journalist offered to remove both handicaps, reasoning that Industrial Policy should not simply be repudiated as a liberal scheme, as Reagan spokesmen and other conservatives were doing. Instead, it

should be given another name and recognized for its conservative promise. "The term 'industrial policy' has gotten a bad name," Kevin Phillips
declared, "because it was associated with notions of excessive government interference in the economy." In this new world of globalized manufacturing and state-guided export drives, something like IP was needed,
however, and American businessmen understood this. At least seventeen
corporation-led task force reports on the industrial situation had recently
appeared, and all agreed on the need for a newly activist economic policy
configuration, but no one knew what to call it. They assumed that positive government had to be part of the solution, and most of them used the
term *Industrial Strategy* for this realignment of policies and policy machinery. Phillips thought the emerging business program ideally suited to
the public mood in the 1980s. "Businessmen are now taking the lead in
invoking government power and assistance," he reported, quoting trade
associations, *Business Week,* and *Industry Week,* the chairman of the board
of Du Pont, the head of the American Business Conference, the Committee for International Trade Equity, the Business–Higher Education forum,
and a new group whose program Phillips found especially cogent, the
Labor-Industry Coalition for International Trade.[27]

In 1984 Phillips perceived "the possibility that business can co-opt
the industrial strategy issue." Industrial Policy had managed to sound
like more liberal government than Americans in the mid-1980s would accept (Phillips never argued that IP "would not work," indeed found it
"exceedingly effective . . . from Tokyo to Brasilia"). But a "lesser version" would offer a "middle way . . . between neomercantilism and su-
pineness." He condensed various business proposals into an agenda of
15 elements: a list of tax and regulatory easements, more aggressive trade
policies, more R&D support, antitrust law revision such as would be familiar to anyone who had in 1981 or 1982 heard an executive from industry tell a congressional panel what ought to be done about his company's
troubles. "Unlike the central planning ambitions of left-of-center industrial policy proponents," an Industrial Strategy would not require Forums, Banks, or Councils. Yet Industrial Strategy still involved "targeting"
of aid to "basic industries like steel or automobiles, or high-technology
industry."[28]

## Defining Industrial Strategy

What, by 1984, was the distinction between Strategy and Policy? IP, some
would have said, was what the antibusiness Democrats were proposing to

do regarding the nation's economic situation, which would of course be "too much government." Its intended beneficiaries would be labor, communities, and some firms in the old smokestack regions. IP's targeting was formulated by new institutions, the dreaded Council, Forum, and Bank.

And Strategy? Apparently, it was what probusiness Republicans would do, and thus would not be too much government but one with the right beneficiaries—a government that was, in one economist's words, "a service sector for firms."[29] Whereas Phillips embraced a Strategy of targeting specific sectors, another version of Industrial Strategy envisaged a government with all policies cleansed of sectoral favoritism and the only targeting being "targeting the process of innovation."[30] No dangerous new institutions were required. Apparently the advocates of Industrial Strategy had not read or did not concur with the noted historian of American business, Alfred D. Chandler, Jr., when he argued that large corporations in the twentieth century had been able to change direction only when a change in strategy was accompanied by structural reorganization.[31]

### The Political Calendar Takes Control

As anticipated, congressional Democrats, building upon the endorsing groups in and outside government, were ready to give legislative form to this new idea, which some Democratic presidential nominee would carry into the fall campaign. House Resolution 4360 cleared Congressman John LaFalce's subcommittee on February 8, and was endorsed by the Banking Committee on April 10 by a vote of 25 to 16. Every Republican had opposed it. The bill would establish:

- a 16-member tripartite Council on Industrial Competitiveness, assigned to conduct sectoral analysis, act as a public-private forum to discuss sectoral issues, convene subcouncils for industries, and provide policy advice to
- a Bank for Industrial Competitiveness, to bring a "coordinated and strategic approach" to governmental financial assistance in order to "upgrade" the nation's industrial structure.[32]

The Democrats had decided to ask for a Bank, although LaFalce prepared for compromise with statements such as "it [the Council] would still be an excellent process without a bank."[33] Focusing on the controversial Bank, observers ignored another unusual decision, to conflate the separate concepts of an executive branch coordinating and analytical mechanism, often (and in my usage always) called the Council, with the tripartite (business, labor, government) Forum with "consensus-building" and the making of industrial "visions" as its main assignment. The Council proposed in H.R. 4360 would do all of these, and was a monster of menacing influence.

LaFalce was said to hope for House floor action prior to the Democratic convention. All Democratic presidential hopefuls except Reuben Askew and John Glenn were reported on record "for" Industrial Policy. Gary Hart had called IP "a moral issue." Walter Mondale had said that Robert Reich's version of IP would "do it for the Democrats."[34]

What IP in fact did for the Democrats, when the time came to move from isolated proposals sponsored by individual legislators and give the idea a legislative form with party imprimatur, was to divide them. LaFalce's bill split the party's Sunbelters, enamored of "high technology" and "entrepreneurialism," against the party's Frostbelters, attached to mature industries and labor. Against LaFalce's better judgment, H.R. 4360 contained "the Bank," capitalized at $8.5 billion; this measure alienated western and southern centrists. The Bank represented "dollars in search of a problem," said Congressman Timothy Wirth from Colorado. "I never liked the bank idea," commented a southwestern Democrat, "because . . . it looked to us like another bailout type of operation . . . going to support firms on the way down rather than firms that are on the way up . . . It had a regional flavor . . . you know, save the smokestacks."[35]

The bill's sponsors defensively pointed out that the government was already a bank responsible for one-fifth of the credit activity in the United States and the holder of $1 trillion in loans or loan guarantees. LaFalce privately agreed with Lee Iacocca, who said that the Bank "will just confuse everybody," but the AFL-CIO was ardently for it.[36] Of the unions' insistence, LaFalce would say later that "they almost had to be taught a lesson."[37] Political scientist Ross Baker, after interviewing Democratic representatives and House staffers, concluded that the Bank was seen as "a reversion to the interventionism that Democrats had resorted to so readily in the past."[38] When H.R. 4360 emerged from the Banking Committee with the Bank attached, Walter Mondale began to balk, and in a meeting of his campaign staff in April he decided to distance himself from legislation. The House Rules Committee stalled, and at a "climactic meeting" in Room H-137 of the Capitol in June, it was decided to scuttle the legislation in order not to "split the party" for the fall campaign.[39]

"The controversy over a bank should not obscure the key issues in the discussion over industrial strategy," Senator Edward Kennedy wrote that summer, even as exactly that was taking place.[40] The idea of a visible new spending institution had become a symbol of the Democratic party's history as Ronald Reagan had successfully fashioned it—"tax and spend." Mondale backed away because he assumed, it seems, that Reagan and the Republicans had already won the history debate. LaFalce was at pains to design the Bank and to explain it as unlike the RFC and more like the International Monetary Fund, in that it would take equity positions along with private investors, insisting upon conditionality and concessions. No matter; the Bank proposal evoked a larger past. "The [older] Democrats basically had no credibility," commented a younger Democrat from the Southwest.[41] Industrial Policy had emerged unexpectedly burdened by a certain interpretation of one party's history.

### June Swoon—Grassroots Choice?

In retrospect, June was the political highwater mark of the IP idea of the early 1980s. In and after that month, "the whole approach seemed to pass from fashion," in Ross Baker's words.[42] This reality would first be glimpsed in Rhode Island, where the IP idea was further advanced than in Washington. The smallest state's "Greenhouse Compact" had been devised by a special commission appointed by the governor in 1982. That plan, modified by the legislature in early 1984, was transmitted to the voters in a referendum scheduled in June. The name "Greenhouse Compact," a recommendation for four research centers called "greenhouses," hardly captured the boldness of the package compiled by the 1982 commission. Rhode Island, the statistics seemed to report, was in the 1970s losing more of its young people to job opportunities elsewhere than any other state, and it seemed time for bold departures.[43]

The Rhode Island plan deviated sharply from those hatched in other states. One reason was the involvement of Ira Magaziner, a former Brown University undergraduate leader of uncommon influence, then a business consultant operating out of Providence, and coauthor with Robert Reich of *Minding America's Business.* In any setting, Magaziner was a man of remarkable energy who originated reform movements wherever he found himself. Inspired by Magaziner, the Rhode Island Strategic Development Commission did not submit its recommendations in the form of a list of good ideas to be disposed, insofar as each had merit, by the legislature. Their recommendations were to be taken as a unit, a plan—a potential "compact" with the citizens of the state. The commission asked that the state legislature transmit their proposals without change to the voters for adoption as a package, by referendum, leaving the implementation to a new state planning board endowed with $250 million in new money. The board would be guided by expansive goals: to reduce unemployment 25–30 percent below the national average, raise average wages to within 25–30 percent of the national average, and create 60,000 new jobs. All of this in seven years.

Who would benefit, who would pay? According to the commission, "the community as a whole" would move to a stronger economic base; there would be no losers. The payoffs, as with any investment, would come only in the long term. The Greenhouse plan was complex; its 900 pages offered smothering detail about subsidies to high-wage firms, to entrepreneurs who would develop new products, to companies in need of assistance with product development and testing. It even specifically targeted industries in which Rhode Island was thought to have comparative advantage—tourism, fishing, boatbuilding, jewelry.[44]

No reform so sweeping had ever emerged from state development planning. The Greenhouse idea broke radically with the older economic development efforts, in which any industrialist promising to create jobs was seduced to plant his payroll inside state lines. Now Rhode Island would target technological innovation, promote it in every industry, and attempt to move the state's industrial structure toward knowledge-intensive occupations judged by state officials to be promising engines of growth. This was a far cry from the old formulas of cutting business taxes, touting low labor costs, and weakening land-use and other environmental regulation. "We must invest in our people," said Magaziner as he stumped the state; "we must develop skills" for the long-term payoff. We must also move economic development decisions up a level, from the incompetent legislative pork-barrel arena to a knowledgeable commission, for "development must be above politics."[45]

For the first time, a state economic development plan received both broad public debate and then a statewide vote. Just as the IP idea brought out the professional economists at the national level, so too the economists took the lead in Rhode Island as critics of the Greenhouse idea. The Brown University economics department, according to report, was unanimously opposed. One of its members, Professor Allan Feldman, joined with disgruntled business leaders to organize "Common Sense," the only organized resistance. Greenhouse, they argued, was "an elitist scheme," since the plan entrusted an unaccountable commission with vast public sums.[46] Some of the critics' language could have been borrowed from the national debate: "We think the program is risky," said a Common Sense member who was the president of a boat company. "It's the public sector getting into the marketplace . . . picking winners and losers in the marketplace. We don't think it'll work."[47] This was a remarkable sentiment in a state whose governments for decades had been meddling in the "marketplace" to help "winners" come to Rhode Island and prevent "losers" from folding. But the Greenhouse went so far beyond the usual state development efforts that this time the ideological opposition came out fighting.

Greenhouse supporters traversed the state, appearing at citizens' meetings to build support. There was endorsement from labor and civic leaders, but advocates found the public confused about the plan's complex features. "It's very hard to explain this to everyone," Magaziner confessed.[48]

It was not a good time, if there ever was a good time in Rhode Island, to carry such a proposal to an electorate with no knowledge of state economic development issues. Turnout for such special elections averaged 8–12 percent of the eligible electorate, allowing small groups who were especially affected to decide the result. The Greenhouse idea was intended to benefit the entire citizenry, and a major effort to mobilize support was matched by efforts to mobilize opposition, and the turnout reached 30 percent. Like the rest of the American public, Rhode Islanders in 1984 were in a mood to distrust "politicians," and it was not difficult to focus their suspicions on a new commission whose members and intentions they did not know. It did not help the Greenhouse cause that the mayor of Providence had that year been convicted on charges that he assaulted his wife's lover, or that on the day before the election the state's public works officer was led away by police officers for questioning on corruption charges. "You can't trust politicians," one worker was quoted. "Who are these guys, anyway?" was a question repeatedly directed to those who wanted the Greenhouse plan to go forward.[49] And in 1984 the Rhode Island economy was showing the same signs of improvement buoying the national economy that spring. The vote on June 12 rejected the Greenhouse plan by four to one.

The vote was the best-covered news of state-level economic policy in the national media. There was much speculation about the meaning of the Rhode Island vote for the larger debate. Some observers declared the Rhode Island outcome a harbinger of a national verdict. "Those enthused about the idea of government 'industrial policy' . . . received a cold shower last month," summarized a *Washington Post* writer in July. "Today, Industrial Policy is dead as a political idea," exulted Allan Feldman. Four days before the election, the Republicans on the congressional Joint Economic Committee had predicted that "state and local governments are moving away from industrial policy."[50]

There was another view: The Rhode Island vote had been a unique event, and the outcome meant nothing in particular. State industrial policies would continue to expand. A writer for the *Wall Street Journal* observed that, in contrast to the national discussion, "in the fifty states . . . industrial policy has met with a much more enthusiastic reception." Even in Rhode Island, industrial policy seemed to gain muscle, as a newly elected Republican governor borrowed pieces of the Greenhouse Compact and promised to invigorate state economic development activities in 1985. Wrote two academic state-watchers: "while politicians debate it [industrial policy] and academics analyze it, state and local governments DO it."[51]

Certainly the Rhode Island outcome was no harbinger of trends in subfederal government. It did nothing to slow the movement of state and local governments toward more aggressive and expansive intervention to shape the industrial structures within their borders. But although the vote had been a poor predictor of state trends, it coincided with an ebb tide for similar ideas at the national level.

### Ending with a Whimper

"The great industrial policy debate predicted for election year has not ignited," noted *Science* magazine on June 29. Nor would it in the following months. Walter Mondale became the Democratic presidential candidate in July. Neither he nor President Reagan uttered the words *industrial policy* during their debates or in any formal speech. A writer for the *National Journal* noticed Mondale's September announcement of a plan to revitalize the steel industry through a tripartite council that would exchange a five-year period of restricted imports for a restructuring agreement. He saw in this "a sharp contrast with President Reagan's announcement on September 18 that he had instructed his aides to negotiate agreements to reduce steel import levels but had not imposed any requirements on the steel firms." In view of these events, the journalist declared that "a big idea is back."[52] Planning for sectors; Industrial Policy.

But the big idea of IP was not back. The brief flurry of activity on the steel industry's problems had produced sharply divergent approaches to sectoral problems between the two candidates, but nothing was made of it by them or anyone else. The episode did not establish a larger framework for economic policy debate. House Democrats did attach Mondale's plan to an omnibus trade bill, but no more was made of the contrast between his approach to sectoral problems and Reagan's. Histories of the 1984 presidential election confirm Robert Kuttner's comment: "The great industrial policy debate ended with a whimper"; indeed, judging by the presidential campaign, "that debate was never had." [53]

### The Strange Disappearance of "Industrial Policy"

Why did the Industrial Policy theme deflate in or around June, making no mark at all on the long campaign between the two nominees, contrary to the informed judgment of people like former Democratic National Committee chairman Robert Strauss that the voters would back the candidate who made "industrial policy" a centerpiece of his campaign? [54]

Such predictions rested on the assumption that the Democrats would press their new idea against Reagan, making it part of the electoral agenda. Since the president opposed the idea, it had at the outset only a 50 percent chance of making the 1984 electoral debut predicted by so many.

The decision thus rested in large part with the Democratic nominee. William Galston, Mondale's issues coordinator, reveals that the former vice-president had decided in April that he did not like the package in which the idea emerged from the House that spring. Mondale was a convert to the Industrial Policy idea, but he thought of it mostly as a way to handle bailouts, and preferred restructuring bargains as struck in the Chrysler case and as he proposed in September for steel—deals guided by the White House, toughly bargained with "a quid pro quo" extracted from the petitioners, and all this on a case-by-case basis. Mondale also thought macroeconomic policy errors under Reagan to have been far more important sources of mischief than sectoral blunders, in which he was of course correct. He wished to focus his argument here, on irresponsible taxing and spending patterns, which he would blame mostly on Reagan. [55]

Even this macroeconomic focus was difficult to establish, for there were diversions. Congressman LaFalce recalled: "For one whole month, you couldn't talk about anything but Ferraro's finances. Then Cuomo and the abortion issue. Then Mondale had to shy away because it had the bank in it and sounded like big government."[56] As Mondale recalled in 1985, "the more I thought about it [Industrial Policy] and listened to those guys— you know, Reich and the others—I came to see that they were simply advocating more government, essentially. So I backed away from it" and stressed Reagan's macroeconomic sins.[57]

"Advocating more government, essentially." This was Mondale's eventual judgment, and, since it was also Reagan's, Industrial Policy made no appearance in the campaign. With Reagan's reelection, it was questionable whether it would ever appear again.

This was an unexpected outcome after four years of debate. Mondale and other leading Democrats knew that unmanaged sectoral policies, the de facto IP, belonged on the agenda, and for a time they had imagined that it might *be* the agenda. At the eleventh political hour it was Mondale's judgment that the IP idea would not carry that weight in the fall election. Whatever his exact reasoning, it surely combined an awareness of several pitfalls ahead. There was Ronald Reagan's ability convincingly to preach the history lesson with which he had won in 1980, that "more government" had never worked and was the problem. There was also the inherent difficulty in translating the notion of different sectoral interventions, in all their complexity, into something with which to excite voters in a year of economic expansion. Voters unconvinced that this new thing was without risks or that it was a magic bullet, would of course be justified. At best, the immediate economic payoff was sure to be modest, and most of the benefit could not be immediate. A politician wishing to promise early improvements should be talking about macroeconomic corrections, as Mondale intended to do, and the microeconomic theme might even be seen as a diversion, given the public's short attention span.

So Mondale in April decided to cut his losses, detach himself from IP, and look elsewhere for political themes. "The term [IP] has never been an organizing principle for talking about reform or changes in the political economy," Robert Reich reflected in 1985. "There continues to be a great deal of confusion among economists and journalists about the term's meaning," and "a significant number seem to think the term implies centralized economic planning. Much of the blame, I think, can be placed upon the 1984 presidential election and the two years leading up to it."[58] Added Ira Magaziner: "We couldn't explain industrial policy very clearly. It's a complex economic idea . . . I guess a lot of people just saw it as more taxes and more government," that is, would remember it from the Democratic past as Reagan interpreted that past.[59] As the election neared, the political risks inherently associated with the IP idea had suddenly become more impressive than the policy promises. It would be dropped from politics by important former sponsors, its future jeopardized as a policy idea.

### Contrary Signals

Was IP in full retreat? It seemed so when Treasury Secretary Donald Regan released his plan for a sweeping revision of the tax code a week after the voting. The announced intentions were to simplify the tax code, reduce the cost of capital, and move the tax system as close to sectoral neutrality as possible. If the discussion of industrial policies had generated any influence, one would expect to see its marks on the new tax bill.

The existing tax code was, of course, a collection of industrial policies (among other things), and it contained wildly divergent tax obligations across the economy. Under Regan's plan, "Treasury I," costs of capital would rise for producers of durable equipment, transportation, communications; capital costs would decline for services and construction. A former Reagan official became so agitated as to predict that, should the Treasury's proposal be adopted "in its present form, the U.S. would be deindustrialized within a decade."[60] A part of the administration, with White House blessing, had been at work revising the nation's tax industrial policies toward less favorable treatment for manufacturing. It was painfully obvious that "the industrial viewpoint" spoken of in recent debates was no part of the administration's perspective. Lawyers and tax experts in the Treasury Department were in charge of taxes and had created reforms that appeared to amount to an anti-industrial industrial policy.[61]

Then, in late December, with the election safely behind, came the report to the president of his own Commission on Industrial Competitiveness (PCIC), conveying virtually an endorsement of the central arguments of the Industrial Policy community. The commission delivered its conclusion at the beginning: "The U.S. is losing its ability to compete in the world's markets . . . While it is still the world's strongest economy . . . a close look at the U.S.'s performance during the past two decades reveals a declining ability to compete [with foreign-made products]." The commission concluded, in language formerly associated with Reich, Thurow, and others, that productivity gains had been "dismal" since the 1960s, and the post-Reagan upturn noticed in 1983 had "only approximated the long-term averages of other nations" and had then flattened in 1984.

Real per capita income was growing very slowly; the merchandise trade balance, when analyzed "with great caution" as an indicator of competitiveness, brought disturbing news of a declining share of even high-technology world trade. Reporters, upon release of the two-volume study, especially liked a simple graphic displaying the U.S. as having "a major advantage" over competitors in only one of eight "key factors in improving U.S. competitiveness."[62]

Commissions are supposed to propose remedies, and the White House surely hoped that this one would announce that Ronald Reagan had already put forward all the economic reforms America needed and had gained acceptance of most. Stay the course was, after all, the annual message of the Council of Economic Advisers. But the Young commission was not on the president's payroll, exactly, and it had developed a wider view. That view viewed with alarm. It rejected the idea, central to the administration's optimism, that if the dollar were to be brought down, the resulting "level playing field" would end industrial problems. It conceded that Industrial Policies seemed to work, abroad—at least in Asia.

What to recommend? Certainly not Industrial Policy, the dragon the commission had been asked to help slay. "The Commission rejects active government participation in the development of specific industrial sectors," came the expected denunciation. What was needed was "strategy," and "we are submitting," said Chairman Young in a letter of transmittal, "an overall strategy for U.S. competitiveness . . . a long-term, action plan which can play a useful, positive role long after the Commission ceases to exist." Thirty-two recommendations could be found, almost hidden in an appendix to the second volume—tax incentives for private-sector R&D, increased support for university research, regulatory relief, assistance to exporters—the usual laundry list familiar to readers of Kevin Phillips' business-led task force reports.[63]

Industrial Policy? Not yet—until the commission turned its attention to managerial institutions. Here the nation could not go on as before. "The President is hindered in the consensus-building process by a lack of independent data on competitiveness," they found. The commission urged a cabinet-level Department of Science and Technology, endorsed the earlier administration call for a Department of Trade, added support for "a more effective coordinating mechanism under the direction of the President for integrating, balancing, and reconciling differences between domestic and international policies," and spoke favorably of "mechanisms . . . for building consensus among key sectors."[64] Coordination—that was the

Council idea; building consensus—that was the Forum idea. Minimalist Industrial Policy.

This insidious idea was proving hard to kill. Driven underground in the summer and fall of 1984, it had somehow landed in December upon the president's very desk, woven through the pages of the Young Commission report. Ronald Reagan made no comment on the document, and in the rest of his presidency he would do nothing at all with it, to the disgruntlement of many U.S. senators (the Senate passed a futile resolution demanding that the White House respond to the PCIC report), and eventually of Young himself. What of the commission's recommendations? a reporter asked a White House official. "This is not the time to propose a major reorganization," came the answer; the matter was "on the back burner." [65]

It was indeed on the backmost burner, after five years of boiling debate. It had been a dangerous idea, this IP notion, only at the eleventh hour pushed to the perimeter of politics and policy. The pusher most responsible was that interpreter of the American past, Ronald Reagan. He had asserted his own history lesson in the message in which he announced the Young Commission's appointment: "The history of progress in America proves that millions of individuals making decisions in their own legitimate self-interest cannot be outperformed by any bureaucratic planners." [66]

The first phase of the Industrial Policy debate was now history, its future importantly decided by selected interpretations of the past.

# PART II

# The Persistence of Industrial Policy, 1985–1990

CHAPTER 9

# America's Unconscious Industrial Plan

We've got an industrial policy, but it's about the sorriest
you've ever seen.

Senator Ernest F. Hollings
(D., S.C.), 1990

The Industrial Policy debate, a dispute over the evolution of national economic structure and its policy implications, had arrived at a familiar
result. A community of reformers had urged that scattered policies be
consciously shaped into coherent Policy. They were defeated. This left a
Policy in place nonetheless—revealed Policy, de facto Policy, the incoherent one exerting undetermined sectoral influences as before, without a
central monitor or manager.

The same result had obtained after discussion of energy policies, urban
policies, growth and population policies—all areas in which reformers in
the 1960s and 1970s had urged a more deliberate policy process in the
hope of greater coherence and rationality. All had failed. The winner, in
these disputes, was the unreformed status quo.

In the case of industrial policies, evaluating the results of the debate require us to analyze the winner, the status quo that survived the reformers.
Here the difficulties are formidable, for no agency was charged with the
analysis of IP; no government report or process encompasses the issue.
The concept of IP is homeless. Still, the debate had produced much illumination of this elusive thing, and even an emerging consensus on its
overall quality. An Aspen Institute study concluded, for example:

> In the controversy over whether or not the U.S. should have an indus-
> trial policy, it is often forgotten that our government is already interven-
> ing like a brain-damaged octopus.[1]

Or, in the view of a congressional committee:

> This country currently has an extensive and expensive array of industrial policies . . . neither coordinated, cohesive, nor consistent . . . a melange of stop-gap measures.[2]

Or, from an auto executive well known to the public:

> America already has an industrial policy, and it's a bad one.[3]

Or an electronics executive, not well known to the public:

> To steal a classic line from a play by George S. Kaufman and Moss Hart, "It stinks."[4]

These comments reflect the general tone of contemporary assessments of the Industrial Policy status quo, the winner in the IP debate.

How did they know that "it's a bad one"? The auto and electronics executives drew upon their experience within import-besieged industries. Elsewhere a body of more dispassionate analysis was building to respectable size, sketching the outlines of this entity in hiding, the revealed IP of the United States.

## Industrial Targeting by Cash and Credit

The first thought of such targeters, it would seem, was to send money. An early report by the Urban Institute, *The Federal Entrepreneur: The Nation's Implicit Industrial Policy* (1982), turned up 329 discrete "program aids to business" in the form of financial subsidies, of which 265 (81 percent) were sectorally targeted. The study found these federal incentives to industry poorly reviewed for their performance, costly (amounting to $303.7 billion, or 13.9 percent of GNP, in 1980), and frequently neither task-effective nor cost-effective.[5]

This huge patchwork of industrial assistance was dispensed through 29 different agencies, although 40 percent of the favors flowed through the Department of Commerce and the Small Business Administration. It went principally to the agriculture, transportation, energy, and maritime industries, and to small and minority-owned firms. These subsidies reflected "no comprehensive national objectives," only the result of lobbying by distressed industries, groups, and regions.

There was no evidence that such aids to capitalist enterprise might be done away with—indeed, the trend was the other way: they had grown by $44 billion in Reagan's first two years. This "complex system of federal supply-side interventions," in the view of the Urban Institute authors, resulted in "a massive expenditure of increasingly scarce federal fiscal resources"; its "massive costs" and "often conflicting objectives" begged for reordering and rationalization.[6]

Of these 265 "aids" aimed at various parts of the American economy, the fastest-growing instrument was provision of credit, either directly or through loan guarantees. The camels of federal credit had long been inside the private-sector tent. When Jimmy Carter's aides examined Industrial Policy in 1980, the Treasury Department commissioned a study of the Reconstruction Finance Corporation and found that its termination in 1954 had been only the beginning of separate lives for the Federal National Mortgage Association, the Export-Import Bank, the Commodity Credit Corporation, and the Small Business Administration. Congress continued to add pieces to these dispersed heirs to the RFC as the years went on—the Farm Credit Administration, the U.S. Railway Association, the Economic Development Administration, the National Consumer Cooperative Bank, the Federal Aviation Administration, the Farmer's Home Administration, credit programs in the Department of Energy and also Interior and the TVA. These agencies busily targeted public money to railroads, sugarbeet farmers, college students, Georgians wishing to establish a peanut cooperative, owners of Arizona acreage arable only under irrigation, experimenters with coal gasification, and other interesting and needy enterprises.

Reagan's Council of Economic Advisers complained in 1982 that such a large portion ($86.5 billion, 24 percent) of the total capital raised in U.S. credit markets in 1982 ($361 billion) was diverted to federal clients through loans or loan guarantees to citizens (and foreigners). Whether the government was in the hands of Democrats or Republicans, Reagan or LBJ, many winners had been picked, many losers shielded from their fate by federal financial subsidies since 1953. None of this had required the help of the long-dead RFC. Asked if a new RFC would be a good idea, the executive director of the National Governors' Association responded: "No, not unless you, in fact, get rid of one you are already doing which is totally unfocused."[7]

Commercial enterprises received some funding, but industry took a large share. The 424 identifiable programs of this genre were, however, not dispersing funds evenly across the industrial landscape. Despite the lack of central analysis of the patterns of lending, let alone the results, it was readily apparent that the leading recipients were the construction and agricultural sectors. (Whatever the patterns, moreover, such lending increased during the Reagan years.) The Export-Import Bank was especially partial to the aircraft and nuclear power industries, and after·those, to the makers of electrical and construction equipment. The Eximbank's criteria for this targeting were not closely scrutinized, but it seemed bent upon making winners of four companies that, in the 1970s, received from 53 to 84 percent of the sales deriving from Eximbank loans: Boeing, McDonnell-Douglas, Westinghouse, and General Electric.[8] The federal loan portfolio as a whole, a Congressional Research Study concluded in late 1980, represented "a revealed preference for certain types of industrial activity" over others, and was thus "the industrial policy implicit in Federal business assistance programs."[9] Carter was leaving the White House as this report was issued, but the de facto Industrial Policy would remain.

### Discovering the Revealed Industrial Policy: Taxes

The most dedicated searchers for the revealed IP were the members and staff of the LaFalce subcommittee. By 1984 they had concluded that the de facto Policy had three legs: direct spending and credit programs, trade policy, and taxes. There were in fact more than three, but the tax code was indeed a master targeter, treating industrial sectors differently, making judgments about winners and losers.

What parts of American industry were favored or burdened by the tax code, and why? There are no official answers, since no entity was charged with producing one. Unofficially, it seemed that before 1981 the tax code favored machinery over structures, and commercial structures over factory structures. After Reagan's 1981 reforms, somewhat altered by a contrite Congress in 1982, real estate and utilities were favored over other sectors, and little else was clear. Various groups estimated the tax burden of firms and sectors, and found irrational and indefensible inequities. Aerospace, in 1982, paid half the taxes paid by retailing; chemicals were taxed at three times the rate of paper and wood products.[10] Some $70–90 billion in tax expenditures to industry were distributed according to no understandable logic. By Lester Thurow's analysis the effective tax rate of the computer industry was 26 percent, railroads 8 percent, electronics 13 percent, chemicals −5 percent.[11] An analysis published by the Urban

Institute found sharp changes in the patterns of sectoral taxation in the 1981–82 Reagan era tax reforms, without any apparent rationale. Effective tax rates increased for office machinery and computers (from a rate of −27 percent in 1980 to 1.3 percent), whereas automobiles were favored (from 9.9 percent to −4.7 percent) and agricultural machinery found its rates unchanged.[12]

Experts contested the data, but not the reality that the tax code was doing industrial targeting. Even the Reagan administration conceded the point: "Our current system promotes some economic sectors over others . . . We have, I believe, an industrial policy through our tax code. I do not favor that," said Treasury Secretary Donald Regan as he introduced the reform called "Treasury I" late in 1984.[13] "We find that the current tax policy is a de facto industrial policy and not a very good one," concluded Hewlett-Packard's John Young.[14]

### Discovering the Revealed Industrial Policy: Trade

In trade policy, the existence of federal microeconomic policy was so unconcealed and traditional, and beyond hope of repeal, that it was openly discussed as a set of industrial policies. What industrial strategy did the mélange of trade policies add up to?

The official doctrine was the promotion of free trade; the practice was selective protectionism and export promotion. Did a strategic pattern give order to the details? One trade specialist expressed the informed consensus that the apparent objective of contemporary U.S. trade policy "has been to maximize consumer welfare" on the import side while increasingly granting protection to politically powerful declining industries, but protection of a "leaky" sort. On the export side, there was "relatively little special assistance" in comparison with other advanced economies, but a persistent strategic purpose could be discerned in frequent State Department curtailment of export licenses where the Soviets might be the beneficiaries.[15]

If this could be termed a national strategy, it was not planned, had many authors, and was subject to change. Indeed, U.S. trade policy in the 1970s and 1980s had experienced a progressive "domestication," as the growing import vulnerability of home industries forced Congress to advance toward ever-greater protectionism, and the foreign affairs bureaucracy in the executive branch to reactively retreat. The Reagan White House gave up considerable ground to pressures for import restriction, tightening sugar import quotas, protecting the Harley-Davidson motorcy-cle company from Japanese imports, arranging an extension of "volun-tary export restraints" (VERs) on Japanese autos and some types of foreign steel, broadening relief against textile imports, and mounting stiff resistance to Japanese semiconductors.[16] The administration's language suggested that it was on the offensive and was winning victories, Treasury Secretary Baker making the awkward boast in 1987 that in the previous two and a half years Reagan "had granted more import relief to U.S. in-dustry than any of his predecessors in more than half a century."[17] The discussion of what was or was not being achieved by the tilt toward pro-tectionism was confined to the familiar macroeconomic language of jobs saved as against costs to consumers.[18] The government claimed to have goals, usually justifying protection as providing "time" for complaining American corporations to take whatever steps they saw fit. The admin-istration exacted no commitments, had no independent conception of what firms or sectors should do as they came under pressure. Congress was sporadically more active, as when it required the steel industry to re-invest only in steel for five years after 1984.

The administration claimed to have at least one goal in all of this, pro-motion of a free-trade world economy, even as it moved tactically in the opposite direction. Like its predecessors, however, the Reagan admin-istration conspicuously lacked goals associated with economic structure; it merely responded to political pressures from declining industries and regions. Protection was granted without performance requirements, since the government did not see sectoral performance as its continuing re-sponsibility. Whereas the Japanese frequently required downsizing in re-turn for aid to declining industries, U.S. trade policy was rarely linked to such state strategies. An analysis of three major U.S. industries granted protection from the 1960s to the 1980s—textiles, steel, autos—found that only textiles had managed to combine downscaling with other effi-ciencies sufficient to raise productivity across the period of protection.[19] As one trade expert put it, "the government does not view its role as being responsible for strengthening the competitiveness of individual U.S. in-dustries, it does not act as a catalyst for seeking industry-wide solutions"; this was a "direct consequence of government's lack of both detailed knowledge about an industry and substantial analytical capability to choose an appropriate course of action." "At some point," continued Alan Wolff, an experienced specialist on both the private and public sides of U.S. trade negotiations, "the U.S. must abandon its ideological excuses for continuing to ignore the fate of its major industries," for if it continues to let random events and foreign industrial policies decide the outcomes, these industries "may become permanent wards of the state."[20]

## Others Sites of Revealed Industrial Policy

Sectoral targeting could be and was accomplished by other, less visible tools than direct financial subsidy, taxes, or trade regulation. Influential aid, or burdens, were routinely conveyed by antitrust law, government procurement, R&D spending, worker retraining and relocation programs or their absence, control of technology transfer, and government-sanctioned forums for purposes ranging from discussion and information exchange to covert cartelization.

Are any of these tools sectorally neutral? Where they are not neutral, we have found an industrial policy.

Consider R&D activities. The marketplace generates a certain level of research and brainstorming about tomorrow's opportunities, but from the beginning of the republic it was assumed that the market underinvests in some forms of knowledge, and that a role for government derived from this market failure (the Founders did not use such terminology, but the idea was the same). On this assumption, President Thomas Jefferson sent Lewis and Clark westward on a fact-finding expedition. Recognizing that farmers underinvested in basic and applied agricultural science, the federal government began agricultural research in the 1860s. Still, as late as 1930 the Washington government was funding only 14 percent of the nation's R&D. With World War II and the Cold War came a shift in the respective shares for public and private R&D: in 1947 the federal share was 54 percent, in 1967, 61 percent, peaking at 65 percent in 1964 and declining to 48 percent in 1980 before an upturn pushed the federal proportion back above half.[21]

No claim could be made that this industrial aid was sectorally neutral. Whether the targets chosen were product champions (rockets), problems (heart disease, cancer), or technologies (nuclear energy, lasers), the government's R&D managers were promoting industrial sectors. Federal R&D spending in the Cold War did not entirely abandon farmers in their (once) declining industry, but the favorites were now some winners selected chiefly for their contribution to staying ahead of the Soviet military—aerospace, computers, scientific instruments, telecommunications, nuclear energy. Picking such as these, all considered high-technology areas, the government was at the same time deciding that other industries deserved little or no research support—among them automobiles, steel, pharmaceuticals, and textiles.

The revealed strategy of national science and technology policy was to remain militarily ahead of the Soviet Union. This military focus distinguished U.S. governmental R&D from the pattern in other nations. The United States spent 54 percent of its R&D on defense-related projects in 1981, while France spent 39 percent, Sweden 15 percent, and Japan 2 percent. Ronald Reagan's budgets reversed a late-1970s decline in military-related R&D, pushing military projects ahead by 15 percent a year in his first term while holding civilian technology investments steady.[22]

Subordinated to this drive for military supremacy, a goal common to all postwar governments, minor themes in our national science and technology strategy were the pursuit of medical discoveries, agricultural productivity, new energy supplies. Winner sectors were being picked, and one loser, agriculture, had been transformed into a world leader.

In this brief reconnaissance of R&D-industrial policy we have found another part of the elephant of de facto IP, busily shaping national industrial structure inside an administration ritually denouncing even the idea of such activities. To examine R&D is, at least, to find industrial policy made by people trained for the work they are doing; in another arena where sectoral policy is manufactured, antitrust law and antimonopoly regulation, the power to decide industrial futures had been entirely conferred upon the occupational group most often named as least qualified to make them. Antitrust law is made by a lawyer-dominated Congress, then is turned into policy by the lawyers in the Antitrust Division of the Department of Justice, in the Federal Trade Commission, and on the bench. In the summer of 1981, when the fate of the world's largest telecommunications company was being decided, the president of the United States "was utterly uninvolved," according to a recent history.[23] The active deciders were lawyers in the FTC and the Justice Department, and the actual head decider was Judge Harold Green. Informed people do not agree at this early stage on whether the decision to break up AT&T was good economics from any standpoint, or good social policy on any other grounds. The head of the company found the process "chaotic, costly, disorderly, contentious;" and the author of a 1986 study of the episode added that "precious little in that history . . . was the product of a . . . genuine, reasoned consensus"; the decision was "driven by opportunism, short-term politics, ego, desperation, miscalculation, happenstance, greed."[24]

This spreading thicket of industrial policies was the version that had evolved by 1984, flourishing in Reagan's prime years. As anyone could see, even a Reagan-led government daily implemented industrial policies, by merely continuing to act in certain familiar areas such as taxation and antitrust. But surely some of the proposed elements of Industrial Policy could still be beaten back, had not yet found a foothold. The idea of a tripartite national Forum had been squelched by mid-1984, and with it, presumably, the whole concept of sectoral tripartism. And surely the Reagan government did not harbor programs designed to move labor from sector to sector?

But the de facto IP of the 1980s had both components. The president's own Commission on Industrial Competitiveness (PCIC) looked into the "micro-policy . . . dialogue mechanisms" placed around the industrial landscape by the national government, and found in 1983 that 884 sectoral advisory commissions engaged 17,980 members from business, trade associations, labor, the Academy, and government. These industrial policy mechanisms, most of them under the Commerce, Labor, and Treasury departments and the Office of the U.S. Trade Representative (USTR), brought together people with unique knowledge won by manufacturing and marketing goods—semiconductors, coal, plums, aerospace equipment, Atlantic tuna. Here might have been the foundation of a national mechanism for building industrial vision and consensus. Instead, this network was found to have "little effect on the agencies, the Congress, or anyone else"; met "infrequently, often hearing of important policy issues after decisions have been implemented"; and upon close inspection was composed disproportionately of political appointees.[25] Yet it was just such a network of sectoral discussion forums which IP advocates had urged— with an important difference, that it be capped by the national Forum, the only part of the institutionalization of tripartism which was not already in place.

Not only did the Reagan government, like its predecessors, unconsciously and ineffectively practice tripartism; it also, on a daily basis, acted against its professed principles of noninterference by becoming involved in bailouts of industries that the markets judged should be allowed to decline. There was the notorious Continental Illinois Bank bailout in 1982–83, and in its final hours the administration was preparing for the largest bailout of them all, involving the nation's savings and loan institutions. One might see these as intermittent and relatively rare breaches of the faith, but the Reagan administration nonetheless continued the government's involvement with declining industries begun a century before, facilitating their shrinkage through programs of aid in relocating and retraining displaced labor. The effort began in 1887, with a small program of assistance to railroad workers laid off as a result of mergers. Workers displaced by urban mass transit systems were given income supplements in the 1960s to facilitate their shift elsewhere, and when the administration of John F. Kennedy moved to liberalize trade in 1962 it tied its request to a new program to assist displaced labor—Trade Adjustment Assistance (TAA). The program expended no money for seven years because of poor design, was expanded in the Trade Act of 1974, and surprised the policy community by growing rapidly during Carter's presidency: from 1977 to 1981, federal income-support payments and retraining programs reached 1.2 million trade-displaced workers and firms. Loans, counseling, and technical help went to footwear, textile, and apparel companies; their workers received cash allowances and retraining. In 1981 the Reagan administration inherited a cost-overrunning TAA enterprise four times as large as it had been four years earlier. David Stockman's knife made severe cuts in TAA, slicing the number of enrolled workers to below 25,000, but in 1982 the administration agreed to a new Job Training Partnership Act, whose Title III dealt with trade-displaced workers through grants to state governments to do pretty much what TAA had already been doing, ineffectively.[26]

Thus Ronald Reagan would spend his entire term in office in charge of, or at least responsible for, what insiders call "microeconomic manpower policies." However distressing to the dream of governmental neutrality, these are sector-specific programs to assist labor adjustment. The president's own secretary of labor asked a task force to look into this activity in 1986, and these (mostly) Republicans agreed that manpower policies of this sort were a worthy policy purpose. If displaced workers were left to the marketplace—that is, their own efforts—they proved not to be a frictionless resource. They tended to be older workers, tied to community, and a source of protectionist sentiment. Trade-related labor adjustment programs should be embraced as "an antidote to protectionism," in the words of the task force chairman, but neither past nor current programs had lived up to their potential.[27] This expressed a bipartisan assessment by the few people interested in the history of a sound policy idea "perverted from a program of adjustment into one of compensation" with tardy benefits not effectively tied to useful retraining.[28] But the Reagan administration continued to act as if manpower policies for declining sectors did not exist and and could not possibly have a positive potential.

### Interpreting America's Orphaned Industrial Policy

However many policy tools are available and busy at work as parts of the de facto Industrial Policy, there is no need to frisk them all for their sectoral winners and losers. May we gain a larger view, based on the information available at mid-decade, and discover the larger impact of this unassembled assortment of many industrial policy parts?

Appraising the revealed IP in 1984, Robert Reich found its tax-industrial component biased against internationally traded manufacturing industries. This did not seem true of R&D spending. The subsidized loan-industrial policy area formed a different pattern, while procurement policies seemed to generate another set of winners and losers. The patterns of advantage and disadvantage did not suggest any simple theory of corporate domination of the state. The auto industry was dissatisfied with its mix of favors and burdens, while construction was invariably favored. At the bar of R&D judgment, the government apparently valued fisheries five times more highly than steel, and timber far above semiconductors at tax time.

As the state picked these curious mixes of winners and losers it appeared to Reich to act not as the purposeful executive committee of dominant capitalist interests, but as a confused agent of many propertied and some nonpropertied groups, a government on a random walk through industrial precincts. He thought the winners and losers "anointed inadvertently," could not discern any national purpose or controlling strategy animating the American state as it fashioned industrial policies—until he took a close look at very recent years. He concluded that "the U.S. already is moving at a rapid clip toward the institutionalization of a more centralized and strategic industrial policy," with at least high-technology policy "increasingly . . . being planned and executed by the Pentagon" during Reagan's buildup.[29]

"Increasingly" meant new magnitudes, not new patterns. The Defense Department had directed a large portion of the nation's scientific and engineering resources throughout the postwar era, frequently picking winning technologies and products by supplying the military's clients— chiefly the weapons, aerospace, telecommunications, and data processing industries—with R&D support and purchasing of output. The Pentagon had nurtured entire new industries into robust life and had prodded others into dramatic transformations.

For two decades after World War II, the hardware cost of information processing in the United States had dropped at an astonishing 28 percent a year, "without doubt one of the steepest sustained declines in an important price in the history of industrial society," in the summary of an analyst of the rise of the computer industry.[30] In this undeniable success story of winner-picking by government, its military arm dominated the industry's development from wartime through the 1960s, when merchant suppliers proliferated to serve a fast-growing commercial market. In the 1940s and 1950s, most computer R&D was launched by contracts from five federal agencies—the Atomic Energy Commission (and its successors, chiefly the Department of Energy [DOE]), the National Science Foundation (NSF), the National Aeronautics and Space Administration (NASA), and the National Institutes of Health (NIH); but by far the largest sums came from the Department of Defense (DOD), acting through the Defense Advanced Research Planning Agency (DARPA) and the Office of Naval Research.

At the other end of the R&D process stood that same nurturing government, ready to purchase the new computers for purposes ranging from guiding rockets to tabulating the census. U.S. world leadership in computers might have come through the workings of the private marketplace, but would there have been technological and entrepreneurial "efforts of approximately the same intensity," asked Brookings' Kenneth Flamm? The question "may be answered with a fairly clear, No," he concluded.[31] Computers offered a classic example of a technology that presented investors with high risk and with difficulty in protecting closely held secrets. Because of the widespread impact upon other industries, there were also extensive positive externalities (spillovers) that could not be entirely appropriated by the sponsoring firms. Computers were thus an emerging industry where the social rate of return was higher than the private, and justified the social investment on a scale that only the military could conduct in the postwar era. While nurturing the computer industry, the Pentagon was transforming an older industry, machine tools, as the Air Force's Manufacturing Technology (Man Tech) program encouraged the development of numerically controlled machine tools beginning in the 1950s, followed by programs to accelerate development of laser welding, isothermal forging techniques, and robotics.

The success stories of America's world leadership in aircraft, computers, and communications equipment had created a comfortable consensus that civilian-sector spillovers from such DOD winner-picking were substantial. Only a few critics, such as Columbia University's Seymour Melman, had insisted from the 1950s onward that the civilian economy was being injured by the Pentagon's manipulation of industrial structure. Government support for R&D declined slowly but steadily from the mid-1960s to 1979, as a part of the general reduction in the defense portion of the federal budget, and not as a result of any concerted intellectual attack upon the notion that government support for new technologies and products thought desirable by admirals and generals was an expenditure with not one but two positive results, military and civilian.

When the defense budget began to grow again in Carter's last year, both absolutely and as a percentage of GNP, so, too, did the military investment in—or claim upon—the nation's scientific and engineering resources, and thus its influence on industrial structure. Industrial policymaking might be blocked elsewhere but was unchecked by ideological resistance when generated from the Pentagon.

This meant that the revealed IP during Reagan's military buildup was changing both in form and direction. The Pentagon in the 1980s enlarged its portion of national R&D from a quarter to a third, and asserted more vigorous influence over decisions made by the chief civilian R&D sponsors (congressional committees, NSF, NIH, NASA, and DOE). The Pentagon's chief sunrise, high-technology industry picker continued to be DARPA, which in the 1980s launched programs to hasten development of very high speed integrated circuits (VHSIC), advanced lasers, fiber optics, computer software, and composite materials.

Winner-picking was only one side of the military establishment's attentive role in the evolution of the nation's manufacturing base. It was a nanny reluctant to let client companies face the ultimate penalty of mistakes or bad luck, and thus was active in bailouts. The Lockheed rescue of the early 1970s was widely noticed and was understood to have a national security rationale, but few suspected how widespread the practice had become. By 1973 the Pentagon had used Public Law 85-804 3,625 times since 1959, in order to assist ailing companies. The cost to taxpayers had been, at that point, $89 million.[32]

In the 1960s and 1970s few people asked if Pentagon winner-picking, done for the purpose of remaining the most advanced weapons and aircraft-making economy in the world, was the best road to civilian spillovers, or if Pentagon bailouts of faltering client firms was the best approach to the modernization or planned shrinkage of declining sectors. An occasional heretic such as that persistent skeptic Seymour Melman from time to time objected that military spending was economically harmful in multiple ways, and that no rich harvest of spillovers with commercial application came with military R&D spending. In the 1980s, at least parts of Melman's message began to look more plausible.

The American computer industry, an infant nurtured to maturity by the Pentagon, came under strong assault in the 1980s by European and Japanese firms, leading others to take up Melman's theme. Academic experts joined industry spokesmen to urge the government to move from military toward civilian-justified R&D investments on a broad technological front. "Support for industrial technology ought to be decoupled from a volatile military budget," wrote a Brookings scholar, since "military specifications and textbook procedures sometimes drive technology in the wrong direction," toward products and processes selected for military applicability with little or no concern for commercialization and its core interest, price.[33] The Young Commission went so far as to announce that the military in the 1980s was a "net user" of the pool of civilian research, and no longer a net adder to it. The commission concluded that the days of an automatic positive spillover to the domestic economy from military and space-aimed R&D were past; the nation's stock of scientific and technological talent was a resource from which the military was now subtracting.[34]

This observation seemed especially true after Reagan's 1983 conversion to the Strategic Defense Initiative (SDI), the "Star Wars" dream of a defense shield deployed in space. The diversion of money and scientific resources to SDI was so potentially massive that even conservative estimates were breathtaking. Harvard's Harvey Brooks confessed SDI to be "virtually unique," there being "no parallel from the rich and diverse menu of the past."[35] He foresaw a program that in its exploratory phases alone would probably be from 10 to 100 times as expensive as the Apollo program. Another estimate was $5 trillion.[36] Even in 1986, SDI claimed 28 percent of the government's R&D budget, and doubts were widespread about the extent of commercial spillover. "Almost any other type of R&D program would be likely to yield greater return on investment," concluded one analyst for a business audience.[37]

Concern about the wisdom of a military-dominated national strategy in the areas of science and technology policy and in procurement, two powerful sectoral levers, had sources deeper than the SDI fad. The Pentagon, with its singleminded interest in military performance, almost entirely lacked the commercial sector's interest in cost effectiveness. As a leading expert on military procurement put it, "maximizing performance regardless of cost is a philosophical virus that could infect the commercial side" of any business taking military contracts. Moreover, the Pentagon procurement specifications had by default become a substitute for national product standards. Pentagon-led Industrial Strategy thus had "its dark side," a discovery made during the IP Debate.[38] "While we and the Soviets [are] draining our resources in military competition in space," observed the head of a corporation that stood to gain some of the contracts, "our economic competitors will be eating our lunch."[39] Seymour Melman, doubtless cheered by all the new converts to his view, rephrased his old indictment to utilize the new terminology: "A choice is being made, not simply between guns and butter, but between guns and competitiveness in the means of production themselves."[40]

## The Dual Pattern of Revealed Policy

Two overriding impulses appeared to animate the evolving industrial strategy of the Reagan years. At one level, reflected in R&D spending and procurement decisions, the government's sectoral interventions continued the bipartisan focus on maintaining military supremacy over the Soviet Union. In another area the administration and Congress alike were shifting toward more activism—trade policy. Yet both the executive branch and Congress, despite the impression of purposefulness, continued to lack any sense of where the industrial part of the economy should be moving. Trade policy was thus all tactics and no strategy, "a whole series of benefits," in Bruce Scott's words, "for which there is no performance expected."[41]

Indeed, in both areas the government appeared as characteristically reactive—to what it thought the Soviets might do, to what remaining number one in military power required, to protectionist pressures. There resulted a trend toward a more expansive revealed Industrial Policy than had been in place a decade earlier, but it was neither guided by new institutional analytic capability nor directed toward the goal of economic competitiveness. The Pentagon guided one component, affecting mostly high-technology industries of certain types; the trade machinery directed another part, doling out protection to declining industries at the front of the trade complaint line.

Increasingly, inspection of the revealed IP brought to mind the convergence of the great postwar adversaries, the United States and the USSR. They remained very different societies and economies, the United States surpassingly robust, but many observers noted how their military rivalries had led both into economic development paths leading away from strength into relative weakness. By the mid-1980s this unnerving comparison was a frequent theme in public discussion, and suggested an ironic historical positioning that struck historians attempting to gain some perspective on the postwar era. Berkeley's Walter McDougall recalled that Edwin Land, the developer of the Polaroid camera, had warned President Dwight D. Eisenhower that the trend toward state direction of so much of the nation's scientific and engineering resources was bringing the United States to resemble its Soviet adversary. That comment helped motivate Eisenhower's celebrated warning against "the unwarranted influence of the military-industrial complex in our domestic councils," in his last State of the Union address (1961).[42]

Yale economic historian Paul Kennedy declared that the joint economic decline of the United States and the USSR—the first relative to other capitalist societies, the second threatening to be an absolute decline—was attributable in the main to the decades of preoccupation with military supremacy, and was irreversible. "Imperial Overstretch," he called these rivals' shared error, and paraphrased Shaw: "Rome fell. Babylon fell. Scarsdale's turn will come."[43] Kennedy found in historical experience little reason to believe that either empire could reverse its decline, and urged a graceful accommodation to a world in which Japan and other societies would have a larger and more nearly equal share of global power. If there were any economic hegemony, it would reside in Japan and other Asiatic societies with low defense budgets and different national priorities.

"More and more, the balance of power, at least as it is determined by technology, will tilt toward Japan," Robert Reich concurred, while "the military-encrusted bureaucracies of the Soviet Union and the U.S. tend toward the preservation of the economic status quo."[44] "Firm USA is spending a lot just to guard the plant," added Air Force defense contract inspector and fired "whistle-blower" Ernest Fitzgerald, "so naturally the Japanese get ahead of us." "I would contrast this [Japanese IP] with the major goal of American industrial policy," observed Japan expert Hugh Patrick, "which has been to maintain the industrial basis for military strength in terms of quality and quantity, but not of price."[45]

Thus emerged in the 1980s the outlines of the structure and influence of the unintended, unacknowledged American Industrial Policy, the one left behind after the defeat of the Industrial Policy idea.

## Activist Government in the American States

James Bryce's observations of America while touring the states in 1886 became the classic *The American Commonwealth* (1888). Like all other educated Europeans (and Americans), Bryce knew that the United States was, among all advanced societies, the citadel of laissez-faire, that doctrine of minimal government born in England in 1776 but more honored in the former colonies than anywhere else. Yet Bryce became convinced by his travels, and by the research reports on state government prepared for him by a young Johns Hopkins University Ph.D., Albert Shaw, that not all levels of American government steered by the doctrines of Adam Smith. Shaw had found American state governments, especially in the transappalachian West, busy with "undertakings, restrictions, and interferences" affecting private enterprise.[46] They regulated railroads and grain warehouses, lumbering and insurance; they licensed doctors, pharmacists and dentists so as to exclude the unqualified and assist the qualified toward respectability and higher incomes; they protected dairymen from the new product "Butterine"; they attacked monopolies, and much else.

Every session of state legislatures in the late nineteenth century expanded these governmental activities. Shaw found that "the one common and striking characteristic of this huge collection of new statutes is its utter disregard for the laissez faire principle." Yet Adam Smith's "theory is already accepted by these legislators." They regulated not in accord with an alternative theory of political economy but in the teeth of the one they held. "The average American has an unequalled capacity for the entertainment of legal fictions and kindred delusions" and easily "lives in one world of theory and in another world of practice," Shaw observed. As an academic he seemed somehow to disapprove, but he was also an American, and in the end he saw in this anomalous behavior "the true genius of social and political life in the American provinces."[47]

Bryce, alerted by Shaw's report, observed state government for himself and added some examples of state intervention of his own. It was "too soon" to determine if this state-level intervention was successful, he wrote in 1888 (and in subsequent editions). But to Bryce the Americans who believed in laissez-faire and nonetheless legislated so much governmental involvement in economic life were "these unconscious philosophers" making a new political economy by daily actions.[48]

Bryce published his observations on American society just a year after there was was enacted in Washington, accompanied by intense debate, the founding statute of the regulatory state—the law establishing the Interstate Commerce Commission. Subsequent steps toward the regulatory-welfare state were to be taken so slowly that it was not in place until the end of the 1930s. All the way, in agonized debate, the opposition insisted that each step was an unprecedented and disastrous breach of laissez-faire principles; it was not often noted that some of the states had preceded Washington in this alleged error. Bryce may be credited with the discovery of a law of American federalism—in the United States, whenever some new venture in national policy arises in debate, look to the states; some of them are already doing the thing being debated on the north bank of the Potomac River but without the theoretical soul-searching.

Bryce's Law was not announced at the time, and would not have had high predictive power over the coming decades, for the activist state governments observed by Bryce in the late nineteenth century atrophied somewhat over the next few decades. The national government became so active in social interventions that citizens (and historians) who had any inclination to follow public affairs had more and more justification for a bad habit they had even in Bryce's day, of ignoring happenings in states and communities on the assumption that social change was initiated and could best be observed from the three capitals, political (Washington), financial (New York), and intellectual (New York or Boston). True, in some policy areas, the states were, by the twentieth century, manifestly backward, either unengaged or unimaginative—in environmental protection, science, the arts, civil rights. They remained active in their traditional domains of education, infrastructure, and (less noticed) business and professional regulation. Bryce's Law was unformulated and unappreciated, especially in and after the 1930s, when Franklin Roosevelt's New Deal made the federal budget for the first time a more significant influence than all state budgets combined, and in other ways shifted national energies and attention toward Washington.

Bryce's insight took on new potential as state government in the 1960s and 1970s experienced an unprecedented renaissance of capacity and energy. When the 1980s arrived, most of the American state capitals had been transformed from seats of rural-dominated, incompetent, and not infrequently corrupt governments into centers of greater activity and competence, where governors with strong powers and larger ambitions attempted to lead legislators who were better paid and supported by staff resources, all operating under modernized constitutions. Given these changes, it should not have been surprising that Bryce's Law correctly predicted the course of industrial policies in the United States. While at the national level an intense and almost theological debate ended in the decision not to take this new step, the states had done it and were, as always, ignored in their heresy. "National industrial policy is already being implemented by the states . . . [which] have their own industrial policy," concluded the Office of Technology Assessment in 1983.[49] The *Wall Street Journal* glumly reported: "In Washington, the notion of 'industrial policy' seems to be falling into a kind of disrepute . . . In the fifty states, however, industrial policy has met with a much more enthusiastic reception."[50] "When the Reagan revolution crushed the industrial policy boomlet in Washington," observed a southern editor, "the notion migrated to the states."[51]

### State-Led Economic Development: The Evolution of Buffalo Hunting

The states had a long history of economic intervention even when Bryce arrived in America to discover contemporary practice. In the decades before the Civil War it took the form of the sort of regulatory prohibition that Bryce had seen but also of many positive efforts to spur economic development. But although, according to Bryce's Law, the states were, are, and may be expected to remain active economy-manipulators, he had never claimed that this was good public policy, producing the ends it sought. The states' long road to the 1980s led through much dubious territory, even as they continued to innovate. The state-level economic regulation of the late nineteenth century was accompanied by some (in retrospect) promising ventures in nurturing economic development— state investment in colleges of agriculture and schools of mining and textiles. In the meantime, a new and retrograde path to economic progress within state boundaries was discovered and explored in the 1920s and 1930s and in the nation's poorest region—the South.

These interwar years were an especially experimental time for state governments in the American South. As in other regions, the political futures of governors and state legislators were importantly tied to their efforts to provide jobs to some of the voters and a necessary core of campaign workers. Traditionally this job-creation function came through power over what was to politicians a limited ability to spend in the traditional areas of schools, penal institutions, road building, and government jobs. In the 1920s and 1930s, however, in the South especially but not exclusively, the idea dawned that state (and local) governments could produce or appear to produce jobs by luring them in from the outside— "buffalo hunting," as it came to be called. South Carolina's Balance Agriculture with Industry plan of 1935 was followed by the establishment of state agencies in every southern state by 1943, dispensing subsidies in the form of land and buildings financed by local bonds, capital subsidies through loans, loan guarantees, or tax-exempt bond financing, tax off-sets, reassurances that the local work force and community were anti-union. All of this invariably came with reams of favorable publicity about mild climate and docile workers.[52]

This activity expanded in the South and to other states in the postwar years. Even so, "state economic development (SED) policy" remained a low priority for governments. In all states having a development office or commission it was a small unobtrusive agency, busy compiling promotional brochures or wining and dining visiting or visited industrialist. As late as 1965 the popular textbook *Politics in the American States* by Herbert Jacob and Kenneth Vines did not mention economic development as it dealt with the core of state governmental efforts in education, taxation, welfare, and highways. A survey of the issues dominating governors' "state of the state," inaugural, and budget messages did not find economic development until 1976, and then it stood sixth in importance.[53]

This obscurity was justified—or, more accurately, merciful. The few scholarly studies of SED policy in the immediate postwar era came close to contemptuous dismissal. State (and local) efforts to lure industry were generally found to be ineffectual, since the locational decisions at the level of the firm apparently accorded little weight to the small subsidies offered by the states—lower local taxes, a bit of help with land acquisition and plant construction, a road or a sewer. The constant hunt for a relocatable industry was in reality a subsidy to business financed by the rest of the community—some locals paid more taxes because new businesses paid less, and every citizen, through federal taxes, subsidized the industrial development bonds (IDBs) beloved by local governments. On the rare occasions when SED policy managed to lure a new payroll within state borders, any benefit went to one American community at the expense of another, a zero-sum game leaving national well-being the same. Wealth-making capacity was not being created by SED policy but, at best, redistributed within national borders as states chased smokestacks in a minor way; it was not being "developed."[54]

Two things not noted in the small literature on SED policies after the war may be said in retrospect. Although it was far from their minds and beyond their analytic capabilities, state and local officials were engaged in picking winners, for they expected the incoming firms to flourish and stood to lose heavily if it turned out otherwise. They were also sometimes bailing out losers; many state subsidies went to resident industries in real or feigned economic difficulty which had announced an intention of re-locating unless governments came to their assistance.

Second, such economic development policies met no ideological or doctrinal opposition on the grounds that true principles of political economy were being violated. The American states were still the home of Unconscious Philosophers, policy pioneers without a justifying theory.

### From Buffalo Hunting to the Entrepreneurial State

In any case, change was on the way. In part it was driven by the same convergent forces that had produced the IP debate nationally—the economic sluggishness of the 1970s, rapid decline of certain older industries in the face of international competition, an intensification of regional economic rivalries as components of a more footloose industrial apparatus began to migrate toward the Sunbelt. These changes in economic environment and geography forced state governments toward policy re-evaluation and activism and coincided with enlarging horizons and capabilities in state government. One result was a shift in the composition and a marked increase in the visibility of SED policies.

"Economic development is our highest priority," announced Governor Richard Thornburgh of Pennsylvania in the early 1980s, reflecting the rise of SED policy to a high place among state policy concerns.[55] At first glance, the novelty appeared to be merely one of scale. States continued to fund agencies whose mission was to persuade companies inside their borders to stay and to entice outsiders into relocating. A principal policy tool was some sort of capital subsidy, a sum (for all states) totaling $18.9 billion by 1981. Most of this was not state money but a gift from Washington through the IDB, that suction hose into the federal treasury. In 1975 $1.3 billion in such tax-exempt bonds had been issued; state (and local) governments raised $8 billion from the market through this federal subsidy in 1980, $27.4 billion in 1984.[56]

A "program binge" was under way, launched in the 1970s and little noticed nationally until the 1980s.[57] The $18.9 billion estimate of state financial aids to business, an early effort to keep track of such things, came in 1983 in the Urban Institute's *User's Guide to State Industrial Incentives*, which "became an immediate best-seller." That estimate was quickly out of date; a successor volume in 1986 reported that the total value of corporate incentives offered by the 50 states had reached $300 billion by mid-decade. Buyers of these thick and formidable reference books may have included executives from Japan's Mazda Corporation, who soon applied successfully for a $120 million assistance package to establish a plant in Michigan.[58]

## Sources of the New Policy Entrepreneurialism

Given the economic environment of the late 1970s, and a generally activist trend among state governments assuming new roles in environmental and social regulation, it should have been no surprise to find the SED function expanding. But there would also be innovation; state and local governments went well beyond capital subsidies and tax breaks.

In the 1950s and before, most governmental officials in the development (or buffalo hunt) field were from southern, western, or nonindustrial midwestern states. They were hungry for industry and were inclined to defer to corporate executives and to share business sentiments about unions and the environment, defining their task as pleasing those industrialists restless for a geographic relocation, whatever their product or pay scale. By the 1960s the industrial states of the Northeast and Midwest had joined in the economic development efforts, although this trend produced no immediate change in the conduct and content of what was in any event minor activity. SED officials remained typically deferential to America's corporate leadership, unaccustomed to making prior judgments on the type of industry their part of the country should be seeking. Theirs was to lure or retain payrolls, to increase total jobs irrespective of wage levels. They offered such tax subsidies as they could add to local scenic or infrastructure advantages and, in South and West, the relative absence of unions and of prolonged cold weather.

This remains the dominant pattern in municipal and county economic development efforts. But many of the states have begun to go a new way, toward what has been called "the entrepreneurial state."[59] The first signs of a new approach appeared in the industrial Northeast. There, political elites had been intensely caught up in the "national growth policy" movement with its commitment to the ideas behind the phrases "targeting" and "business-government partnerships for development" and "balanced growth," all invitations to a new governmental activism. In states like Massachusetts, Connecticut, and Pennsylvania, the tiny cadre of economic development officials found that their domain was being invaded by citizens' coalitions, statewide commissions, and politicians up to and including the rank of governor. These newcomers to the development game brought with them the planning instinct that had always been strong in developmental economics—an inclination toward broad social diagnosis, projection of alternative futures, and the devising of specific program and institutional responses. Their core assumption was that there were gaps or bottlenecks in capital and labor markets which public policy could remedy. From such impulses grew the new entrepreneurial state.

The buffalo hunt would not in any state be entirely repudiated as a tactic in the search for prosperity, but it would move over to make room for very different approaches. Perhaps four decades of almost unrelieved scholarly criticism of SED policies in the beggar-thy-neighbor mode had convinced many state officials to shift their efforts in more positive directions. Perhaps a few policy and business leaders, and even an occasional politician, had read or absorbed critiques of what they had been doing, data-dense studies by people no governor had ever heard of: Glenn McLaughlin and Stefan Robock, John Moes, Leslie Papke, and Michael Wasylenko. Robert Goodman's *The Last Entrepreneur* (1979) was a popularized version of this critical view of SED subsidies as both ineffective and socially reactionary.[60]

A source of change more influential than books conveying critical evaluation was a new breed of economic development officials emerging in the Northeast. In David Osborne's account of the rise of the "new paradigm" in SED policy, an "intellectual revolution" took place in the late 1970s, led by a younger generation of planners and development officials with roots in Massachusetts and an early base in Jerry Brown's governorship in California. Among these active essayists, traveling advocates, and wordsmiths for governors—men such as Michael Barker, Belden Daniels, Michael Kieschnick; women such as Gail Garfield Schwartz— the most quoted was MIT economist David Birch.

Birch and a team of researchers analyzed data from 5.6 million American firms and found that the difference between stagnating and growing regions of the country was not job loss—which averaged about 8 percent a year across all regions—but job creation. Where new jobs were generated an incipient stagnation was turned into growth, and new jobs were overwhelmingly created by small (52 percent of jobs by firms with 20 or fewer employees) and young companies (80 percent of new jobs by firms less than four years old). Birch's first paper on "the job generation process" had not even been published when the news of his findings raced through the world of SED policy: jobs did not migrate into a region; they were born there, in small, start-up ventures! Buffaloes, the new evidence indicated, should not be lured from the outside, but grown from the inside.[61]

New strategies circulated within policy circles by energetic young converts were a catalyst for change. More important, probably, was the politicians' sense that the new ideas about development policy allowed them to attach their careers to the mystique of the new high technologies—computers, telecommunications, biotechnology, and the latest promiser of miracles, superconductivity. After all, where in the slow-growth era of the 1970s and after, where in America, was the economic excitement and vitality, especially after the boom in the oil-producing states deflated in the mid-1980s? The media reported that economic vitality resided in the much-publicized high-tech Golcondas: the booming Silicon Valley south of Stanford University (which also deflated somewhat in the mid-1980s), the belt of companies along Route 128 swinging past university-rich Boston, and the Research Triangle Park between three universities in North Carolina's piedmont. Why should the states lure polluting, smoke-stack industries, now said to be dying and certain to give rise to environmentalist protests? The future was plainly with high-technology industries making tiny computer chips or wonder drugs to cure AIDS or acne or cancer and operating out of sleek glass buildings where highly paid workers functioned in comfort. Why should a state governor confine his or her efforts to luring outsiders, now that the idea of self-help and local initiative was in the air?

Whatever the combination of sources behind policy realignment, fundamental reorientation was occurring as the effort expanded, visible first in the policy processes of economic development, and then in the output. The shift was seen first in areas hit hardest by the slowdown of the late 1970s and early 1980s—the Northeast, Midwest, and parts of the Southeast—but by the early 1980s, every state had institutionalized development policy in larger and more visible bureaucratic niches, whether a department, agency, or cabinet council; about half of these were thrust onto line after 1970. In at least 27 states the routine work of these permanent and enlarged line agencies was augmented by the reports of a special state economic development (often the word *planning* was added) commission. Here were 27 versions of the brainstorming, consensus-building forums for private- and public-sector representation that had been so frequently proposed in the national IP debate. They provided governors and legislators with programmatic advice, in 17 cases (by 1986) with formal state economic plans, always with marching orders and an implied public mandate for an activist economic policy. "In some states," Governor Bruce Babbitt of Arizona leaked the news to those who had not been paying attention, "the recommendations of these commissions amount to a state industrial policy."[62]

Exactly so. State governments moved to adopt some of the agenda set out for them by their commissions and task forces, selecting from the same range of possibilities found in the national IP debate. Some states shunned new planning institutions, advisory or permanent (Tennessee's economic development strategy was formulated in Governor Lamar Alexander's head, for example), and their strategy was simply to pursue a new conception of a "favorable business climate." The older notion had stopped with low taxes on corporations and a cold shoulder to unions. Now it was recognized that tomorrow's industries would be R&D- and knowledge-intensive, with global linkages, and thus attracted only to states whose governments were dedicated to strong educational systems, infrastructure, and public services. In this conception, the state would make no effort to arrange a particular industrial portfolio; let that come in over the borders. This was the California model after Governor George Dukmejian replaced Jerry Brown in 1982 and shifted economic development efforts toward aggressive overseas marketing of California's climate, both business and seasonal.

Those who like the term *Industrial Strategy* would like this model—"targeting the process," with government making no judgments on what product, technology, or locales would flourish. Still, targeting sectors kept creeping in. States in the forefront of the new movement invariably heard from advisory commissions in the recommendation, for example, that they improve educational systems. What could be more sector-neutral? The education most esteemed was not in art or history but in math, science, and technology, and although it was occasionally claimed that higher technologies were evenhanded in their benefits, as adept at reviving older industries as at spawning new ones, the new strategies targeted despite themselves. The California Commission on Industrial Innovation (appointed in late 1981 by Governor Jerry Brown) urged that Pacific Rim state to aim its support at "the cutting edge industries, from semi-conductors to telecommunications to biotechnology." Twenty-nine of the commission's 50 policy suggestions targeted educational programs toward just such industries, which were being anointed as winners. That was one choice; the other choice was the quiet one: to say nothing about autos, steel, waste disposal, and other untargeted sectors.[63]

There were more assertive conceptions of the state role than California's. One regional agency, the Southern Growth Policies Board, was for "hands-on policies" to replace the older "hands-off-business" credo, for a partnership between enterprise and government in which government would share, even often take the lead, in making production process and product decisions, in financial risk-taking, in searching out new markets close by or abroad.[64] Though not turning their backs on the hunt for other states' industrial assets, state governments were reported to be developing, in an uneven pattern across the 50 states, the habit of relying upon their own expertise and a new level of consultation with the private sector. While at least one development agency in every state continued a major effort to lure outside enterprise, there were now collateral efforts to stimulate indigenous enterprise. States were beginning to look inward, working with local resources that the market had somehow failed to shape into productive and commercial reality. "The buffalo hunt [for industries from other states] is a dying breed," a North Carolina development expert exaggerated the new trend. "Those states that are going to be successful are those that will grow their own buffalo." [65]

Many states targeted what they took to be promising sectors, identifying "certain industries likely both to provide high economic development benefits and to flourish in that particular state's environment." [66] Wisconsin at one point declared that it would give special attention to food processing, papermaking, and printing; Nevada chose high-tech firms in communications, financial, and insurance services; Michigan, automobiles and their suppliers, the manufacture of fiberglass motor homes. The underlying assumption in such targeting of sectors was the existence of a capital, labor, or information gap hampering the success of the riskier ventures, especially in states not well served by national venture capital markets, strong universities, or export traditions. The venture capital gap was thought especially important, and by 1985 18 states, Connecticut and Massachusetts in the forefront, had created a range of lending instruments, from state-owned venture capital corporations making equity investments to product development corporations.

States also expanded their general support for R&D—"research is the oil and gas of our future" said a Texas governor, marking the shift in thinking—with 33 states reporting some form of high-technology support.[67] Research grants to universities or tax credits to private research firms were widespread, but states also established incubator facilities (75 in operation by 1984) to nurture research firms or small manufacturing companies. Research-oriented industrial parks near Stanford University and in North Carolina's piedmont were the pattern for 150 others around the country. Assuming that the capitalist spirit was, as Alexander Hamilton had said long ago, "wayward and timid," state development officials and politicians nudged local manufacturers toward more aggressive export efforts by opening trade offices abroad, distributing analyses of foreign markets, and financing export programs. All governors and many mayors became familiar with international air routes and the hotels and business leadership of Tokyo, Paris, Mexico City.[68]

Programs springing up within 50 jurisdictions fell into no simple pattern, but there seemed two principal models—California and Michigan. In California, SED policy aimed to communicate to capitalists within or outside state borders that the Golden State was congenial to enterprise, offering a well-managed set of public services, chief among them educating the citizenry for a high-technology future. High-tech buffaloes were obviously especially welcome, but the state government had no process or institutions for shaping the size or behavior of the herd; Tennessee and other states followed this more passive of the new activist SED strategies.

Another general direction was taken in many states in the older manufacturing heartland, where New Deal liberalism had been strong but was evolving in different and uncertain directions. A visitor to Michigan in 1986 remarked the changes in government-business relationships there since the early 1970s. Formerly there had been "a smug arrogance" in the automobile industry, little serious research and scant contact with the universities, except to hire their graduates. As for the government, its "principal actions were to pile taxes and regulations on the industry." None of that could be found in the mid-1980s. The visitor in 1986 noted that the state government spent millions for engineering facilities at the flagship university campus at Ann Arbor, and financed the start-up of robotics and machine vision companies. The state's top universities, unlike the past, "interact . . with companies large and small."[69]

Other states in the industrial heartland, such as Pennsylvania and New York, pursued versions of this strategy; but the public would soon know most about one of them, the Massachusetts of Michael Dukakis, two-term governor and the Democrats' 1988 presidential nominee. Connecticut may have moved first (in 1972) to establish a state-size version of the RFC, but in Massachusetts the entrepreneurial state had its most vigorous early expression. Massachusetts finally galvanized itself into action because of the prolonged postwar erosion of its textile, apparel, and leather industries.

In their haste skipping the vital first step of a "strategic audit" of their state's economy—a step that Michigan, for example, had taken with great thoroughness—Massachusetts' policy reformers and business activists churned out program and institutional innovations aimed at what was thought to be the chief problem, venture finance, and building on assumed strengths—an educated labor force and the Boston-based university research talents. The assumptions were dubious, for the state had unusually aggressive private financial markets, and its public education systems and job-training programs were weak links; but basic assumptions take on importance only in the long term, while energy and program ingenuity were at once visibly impressive.[70]

Governor Dukakis, along with thousands of Bay State policy and business activists, poured enormous time and energy into such new institutions as the Office of State Planning, which in 1976 produced the first vision of the commonwealth's new SED policy; the Wednesday Morning Breakfast Group; the Massachusetts Task Force on Capital Formation; the Massachusetts Technology Development Corporation; the Massachusetts Industrial Finance Agency; the Community Development Finance Corporation; the Massachusetts High Technology Council; the Governor's Commission on the Future of Mature Industries; Centers of Excellence; and, largest idea of all but not enacted, MassBank (the Massachusetts Development Bank).

This incomplete list of institutions created to deal with economic development reflected Massachusetts' efforts to build along the lines of the second Industrial Policy model, one that grounds its operations in a more thickly organized two-way communication between government and private sector in which public policymakers no longer intend to be either antagonistic or gratefully reactive. "The trend," wrote the authors of the *Directory of Incentives for Business Investment and Development,* "is increasing selectivity, targeting, self-awareness, and . . . the premeditated nature of state programs."[71] Paralleling these policy measures was an economic resurgence that caught national attention. Governor Dukakis, who had been the second governor to lead in the new directions but the most vigorous, claimed that his policies had caused the improvement. His version of what government could do, in partnership with business, to turn economic slump into revival was at the core of his 1988 presidential candidacy and campaign. These positive interpretations of Bay State economic history would change with stunning rapidity after 1989, when Massachusetts entered an economic slump and Dukakis presided over a budgetary

debacle. This reversal suggests that judgments on the states' new development strategies should not be made so quickly.

### Assessment of the 50 Substitutes for National IP

Governor Bruce Babbitt was not confessing a peculiar Arizona deviation
but defining a general trend when he said that the recommendations of
development commissions in 27 states in each case "amount to a state
industrial policy." "While the national debate rages on whether we ought
to have an industrial policy," reported a leading student of current developments in state politics, "there isn't a state that doesn't have one, or isn't
putting one together."[72] Here and there, as in Michigan, boldness about
experimentation was matched by caution about labels. A reporter in the
Michigan state capital wrote: "What is developing here is a kind of industrial policy, although Michigan government and business officials shun
use of that term."[73] Two Urban Institute researchers spoke with more
candor and thus more insight: "State and local economic development
programs are an implicit industry policy," not just for these jurisidctions
but for the nation as a whole.[74]

Was it good public policy, this revealed Industrial Policy invented piecemeal by the states? Governors always claimed overall success, and their
opponents claimed otherwise. If anything is clear it is that the verdict on
the new entrepreneurial states should not come from the fickle sentiments of voters. Some governors associated with aggressive SED policy of
the new sort were rewarded at the polls, but Jerry Brown in California
derived little advantage from his innovative efforts in this area, and
Michael Dukakis was both reelected and defeated by the voters. "It is very
difficult to translate economic development programs into political capital," a student of 50 states' experience could conclude in 1989.[75]

As to the economic results, these will be slow in coming and difficult to
assess. At the outset, contemporary media carried mixed evidence. In
North Carolina, for example, the state-funded Microelectrics Center,
humming along on $82 million of taxpayers' funds with another $17 million from industry, was criticized by nearby university researchers as cap-
tive to industry perspectives, and thus as falling short of its full innovative
potential.[76] In Tennessee, a winning bid for General Motors' "Saturn"
plant promised 6,000 "new" jobs and a $200 million annual payroll at
Spring Hill in central Tennessee. The project soured around the edges by
mid-decade, however, as GM delayed full investment in view of the com-

pany's economic difficulties, and Spring Hill residents became increasingly indignant at a host of environmental, transportation, and housing problems they had not been told to expect from this boon arranged by their government in Nashville.[77]

Like the governors' claims, these scattered reports were anecdotal evidence of policy results. An OTA study found these experiments "too recent and too varied to evaluate systematically" and viewed the few evaluations sponsored by state governments as "inconclusive and contradictory." Studying only state programs to advance "high technology" capacities and industries, the agency found that 85 percent of the 153 state programs established in 1979–1982 had not been evaluated at all by the governments paying for them.[78] Governor Babbitt of Arizona, an enthusiastic booster of the new direction in SED policy, admitted in 1984 that "it is still too early to evaluate" it all, and conceded that somebody, somewhere, ought to ask if the 50 states were engaged in much duplicative spending. Only in the case of educational reforms did he predict net gains everywhere.[79]

Of course, the problem was not simply that it was early, the programs new and spread over nearly all the states. It was also difficult to evaluate state policies long in existence, since the states had always lagged far behind the federal government in program evaluation, and private-sector policy analysts much preferred to study and write about national policy. The nation's economists, too, overwhelmingly preferred national and international economies for study, and macroeconomic to microeconomic issues. Even when analysts begin to address the problem of evaluation, "data are hard to come by . . . Evaluative techniques are inadequate . . . A major task of description, evaluation, and theory building lies ahead."[80]

Yet even in the infancy of the evaluation effort, certain findings began to look quite durable. The Massachusetts experience drew considerable attention since the state's governor for eight years of a decade of economic renaissance had been Michael Dukakis. He had claimed, in the long campaign from Democratic primaries to his November 1988 defeat, that "his" policies accounted for "the Massachusetts miracle." His political opponents asserted that his economic policies were of no help or were actually harmful. Policy analysts soon offered a sounder view. The economic revival on which Dukakis' presidential hopes rode was regional, though uneven (western Massachusetts had not fully shared in it), and a major factor in rapid growth rates had been the inflow, from Reagan's Pentagon, of twice the national average per capita defense spending. The state government's new SED policies "may have helped at the margin to sustain the state's revival once it began," two analysts concluded.[81] It is possible that the content of policy may be less important than the "tone" of the policy process—the extolling of entrepreneurship, efficiency, and creativity; the communication of confidence in a positive future.[82] This is a policy component just as is money or other subsidies, but it is the most difficult to measure.

Early evaluations of SED policy thus conveyed a mildly positive assessment with multiple caveats and qualifications. State governmental efforts to stimulate development within their borders, shifting industrial structure in advantageous ways in the process, were no magic bullet. Many factors must combine felicitously. SED policies could at best have made a small positive contribution, stretched over much time, and not even that contribution was assured if large international economic forces were adverse. Some states employed the new approaches to development and continued to experience general economic difficulties—Texas, the timber economies in Washington and Oregon, West Virginia. Using government to steer economies toward different and better configurations was slow work, the outcomes always uncertain. Sensing the shaky foundations of the achievement of a decade of change, in which state economic policy had been broken free of exclusive reliance upon smokestack chasing and given a more positive conception and imaginative set of tools, the Southern Growth Policies Board called in 1986 for "patient money and the public's willingness to accept long-term strategies."[83] The board had in mind a public educated to the need to accept a certain rate of failures, the mistakes weeded out by careful program analysis. Industrial policymaking was no easier at the grass roots than in Washington. It was merely possible to call it by its name.

## A Century after Bryce: Still Unconscious Philosophers

The curious separation between belief and practice and between national and local politics that Lord Bryce had described in *The American Commonwealth* was perhaps the only feature of American life unchanged a century later. The states were still the homes of unconscious philosophers, building a new political economy without theory, to all appearances oblivious to the gales of free-market ideology. At the very same time in Washington free marketeers were routing the idea that Industrial Policy ought to be recognized and organized. The "layer cake" image of American intergovernmental relations had never seemed so apt as in the new economic policy. In the 50 state capitals (or the vast majority of them) American pragmatists blended activist government with the private sector in an effort to accelerate as well as guide economic change.

There is little study of the actual policy debates preceding the new initiatives of the entrepreneurial state, but the observations of two scholars in 1978 seem to have held true through the 1980s. "No aspect of economic policy has been more poorly argued or documented" than incentives to business, said Bennett Harrison and Sandra Kanter after finding in state hearings and reports "virtually no articulated criticism accessible to politicians."[84] An activist scholar, a University of Wisconsin professor, also testified: "I sat on the Wisconsin economic development commission for a year, listening to them plan for the future. Not once did I hear any reference to economic theory. Certainly no one objected that government couldn't or shouldn't be trying to pick winners or guide the economy. They weren't guided by any theory. They just asked, 'What's happening over in Illinois, or in Michigan? What's working?'"[85]

Contrast this with what happened when, in the 1980s, Americans who lived in states where industrial policies were optimistically piled upon one another elected some of their neighbors to Congress. Upon arrival many of these people were transformed into doctrinal and vigilant opponents of the idea that governments could or should do what was being done so enthusiastically back home in Sacramento, Harrisburg, or Raleigh. Indeed, people who lived in Virginia and Maryland but worked in the District of Columbia lived in one world by day and the other by night. In the states where they slept and spent weekends, government was "aggressive and interventionist, in direct contradiction to what is happening in national politics." Merely by commuting to their daily work stations, these Americans moved to a very different place, where "the rhetoric of the free market, voluntarism, privatization, and deregulation reign."[86]

Bryce did not profess to understand this curious separation between one America and another, between belief and practice, or why it appeared to be fixed by the boundaries set by federalism rather than by class, religion, or education. One hundred years later we have the same puzzlement.

## The States' Accomplice: Reagan's Washington

This account suggests two horizontal layers of de facto Industrial Policy cake, state-local and federal, in the metaphor of that leading student of the evolution of American federalism, Morton Grodzins. The traditional image of American federalism assumed that the state and local governmental terrain had sharply differentiated functions and no sustained interchanges with the national state in Washington. This was not true even in the nineteenth century, Grodzins pointed out, and the evolution of intergovernmental relations in the twentieth century required the substitution of a marble cake analogy. Distinct zones of activity never existed. In the modern era the blending of responsibilities and functions is far advanced in virtually all areas—even in nineteenth-century strongholds of local governmental authority, education, highways, and police.

Also in economic development policy. The federal authorities not only have their own industrial policies but also encourage and partially pay for those at work in the 50 states. In 1983 state and local governments spent $8.6 billion in federal money on economic development programs per se. Another $12.8 billion was spent on infrastructure, much of it directly tied to industrial targeting. Another $4 billion (a tax expenditure) was directed to targeted industries by way of the IDB subsidy, a source of funding that had escalated sharply over the past two decades (from $5.7 billion in 1975, to $14.2 billion by 1980, to $22.8 billion by 1983). Beyond these expenditures, the Small Business Administration held annual conferences with state officials on how to aid small firms, the Department of Commerce and Eximbank helped states with export promotion activities, and much state-directed R&D spending involved federal money. The state part of the revealed IP was heavily financed from Ronald Reagan's Treasury Department and genially promoted throughout the executive branch.[87]

For opponents of targeting and all the rest of the Industrial Policy aspiration, the discovery of federal complicity in so many state ventures at arranging the industrial landscape and portfolio was a call for reform. Even if one had no settled opinion on Industrial Policy, there were reasons for concern at the revelation that officials in Washington were lavishly contributing to a host of economic development subsidies that were distributed by local officials constrained by no national goals or accountability. IDBs, the most expensive bill that the states annually sent to Washington, were a universally condemned method of financing intergovernmental programs. When the Congressional Budget Office had, at the request of Congress, taken the first close look at this device, it found that the drain on the federal treasury had increased fivefold since 1975, financing, among other things, McDonald's hamburger and K-Mart chains, a topless bar, golf courses, and a "dirty book store" in Philadelphia.[88] The agency suggested that the federal government exert more control over the states' targeting, specifying in the law certain business sectors to be assisted, limiting issuance of IDBs, or eliminating them completely. It worried that such subsidies, especially export promotion, might violate international trade rules and invite foreign complaints. Congress, in 1982 and 1984, chose to make minor restrictions. Washington was a partner to state industrial policies, but had no goals, and looked the other way.[89]

## The Debate's Winner: America's Two-in-One Revealed IP

After the political defeat of the IP idea in 1984, two separately layered systems of Industrial Policy remained in place. Their main outlines and tendencies were visible to any interested party. The federal Industrial Policy of the 1980s was illegitimate but influential, slipping toward even greater Pentagon and protectionist influence. The state-sponsored component of the revealed IP was smaller in total impact but was growing, had no useful critics and little analysis. The two layers shared the economic development function. Fifty governors, state councils, and legislative committees attempted to manage the scattered pieces in their layer of the revealed Industrial Policy of America. No one managed the top layer at all. As Lord Bryce had learned, this was the American way. The product: unconscious Industrial Policy.

# CHAPTER 10

# Doing without Industrial Policy

The Administration will not engage in industrial policy, period.

Michael J. Boskin, Chairman,
Council of Economic Advisers (1989)

The tide will turn on industrial policy.

Laura D'Andrea Tyson,
Harvard University (1990)

The issue will never die.

Fred Branfman, Director,
Rebuild America (1990)

The policy decision of mid-1984, confirmed by the November election, was to refrain from passing a law or otherwise "establishing" an Industrial Policy for the United States. This was not a decision not to "have" an IP. It was a decision not to recognize or manage the one in place. Choosing not to have anything to do with an official IP left the nation with its unofficial one.

There was a tendency to see this episode in the way that Americans perceived all contests. A winner of the debate had been declared, and the contest was over. In a summary article in the influential *Journal of Economic Literature* in early 1986, R. D. Norton wrote that "the Reagan revolution sealed the issue, ruling out a U.S. industrial policy for years to come."[1]

Two errors ride that statement. Sealed the issue? Norton must have meant, sealed the *term*. The term *Industrial Policy*, which had never fully satisfied even its popularizers, was rarely heard as Norton surveyed the scene in 1986. In that sense only, the debate was over. Lester Thurow published *The Zero-Sum Solution* late in 1985 and confined "the case for

Industrial Polices" to one chapter, where he offered suggestions for the design of institutions to produce a national "vision" through tripartite consultation, subsidize civilian industrial R&D, conduct public development banking, and manage industrial triage. Yet most of the book was devoted to analysis of the global economy, American saving habits, the values animating the work force and managerial elites.[2] In a 1987 book Robert Reich framed the solutions to the nation's economic problems in terms of cultural values, and the term *industrial policy* appeared only on one page.[3] Apparently, the leading advocates of what a journalist in 1986 recalled as "the leaden Washington phrase 'industrial policy'" had concluded that the term had collected intractable liabilities.[4] Reich thought that Industrial Policy, unfortunately, "had become almost synonymous with saving our declining industries," and Thurow concluded that it "had got too tied up with a federal development bank."[5] Terminology had been a lightning rod for ideology and blocked further progress. For Thurow, "if the words 'a competitiveness policy' are less controversial, let's all agree to use them from now on out."[6]

Not even its friends would call its name, and Industrial Policy slipped away—as terminology. The Democratic party appointed a policy commission in the aftermath of the humbling defeats of November 1984, and its 1986 report did not use the term, or anything resembling it. The document found that "strong, independent families are the centerpiece of Democratic domestic policy." Economic development was said to be mainly a state and local concern.[7]

Yet the underlying economic realities of expanding global competition and industrial transformation remained, as globalization of economic life continued to agitate the issues of sectoral decline and national industrial portfolio, pushing them back onto the public agenda from which they had been removed in the latter half of 1984.

### The American Economy after the
### Death of Industrial Policy

The most intensely scrutinized economy in the world continued to draw diverse and contradictory appraisals. "Informed opinion, the best opinion," wrote Berkeley's Stephen Cohen and John Zysman in 1987, "is utterly confused . . . There are interpretations to satisfy just about every opinion, every interest, and every mood."[8] The *New Republic* inaugurated a feature, "Notebook," built around the media's confused reading of American trends, pairing headlines that were flatly contradictory, such as:

"Inflation Fears Easing" (*San Francisco Chronicle,* page 1)
"Inflation Pressures Build" (same paper, page 4)[9]

The administration's official view of economic trends remained as it had been since the resumption of growth in early 1983, that a robust and self-correcting American capitalist system was handling all challenges. The "Great American Job Machine," Reagan officials' favorite term for the economy, continued to expand from 1985 through the end of the Reagan term, adding in the president's words "nearly 19 million jobs" since the trough of 1982.[10] By the end of 1988, the U.S. economy reached its 73rd month of consecutive expansion, exceeded only by the Vietnam War–driven 106-month growth of the 1960s.

This had been accomplished with negligible inflation. If employment in manufacturing edged slightly downward across the 1980s, this was, in the view of Reagan's Council of Economic Advisers, merely a sign of a natural and beneficial shift toward services, reminiscent of the happy evolution of American agriculture.[11] Some industries, or firms within troubled industries, were displaying remarkable vigor. Ford Motor Company and Harley-Davidson had made good use of temporary import quotas to improve product lines and sales; minimills in steel doubled their capacity from 1975 to 1985 and were said to hold the key to the future for a steel industry; news of high-technology industrial expansion came from Massachusetts and other parts of the Northeast, and a Honda-owned and -managed auto plant in Marysville, Ohio, announced in the spring of 1987 that it would soon export American-made cars to Japan.[12]

This was the cheerful view from the administration, and some of the fragments of evidence that were offered to confirm it. That perspective was shared in parts of the business and academic worlds, and was apparently persuasive to the millions of investors who pushed stock price averages through the Dow Jones 1,000 index in late 1984 and through 1,800 in the spring of 1986, to 2,700 by October 1987.

The crash came at the end of October, erasing $500 billion or 24 percent of the value of stocks, lending credence to those who had for some time been taking a pessimistic view of economic trends. Prosperity had quite evidently been borrowed, and the ledgers showed two fast-rising deficits. Driving the demand-side recovery of 1983–1988 had required unprecedented levels of federal borrowing, while the American consumer had enjoyed a period unique in the national experience, essentially an agreement by Japanese and other exporters to accept indefinitely a 3:2 ratio between what they shipped to the United States and what they would take as goods in return.

When merchandise trade deficits first appeared in 1972, they were small and were easily paid for by earnings from years of overseas investment, so that the balance on current account was positive. By the early 1980s, however, the gap and the volumes involved quietly and relentlessly transformed the nation's accounts. The first half of the 1980s established a pattern of export stagnation at just above $200 billion, while imports surpassed $300 billion, an arresting ratio matching $3 of consumption to every $2 of production. American imports in 1985 amounted to 35 percent of all the manufactured goods consumed at home, and the nation amassed a merchandise trade deficit of $148.5 billion. The figure in 1986 reached $170 billion, and the tiny high-tech surplus of 1985, $3.6 billion, became a $2.2 billion deficit in 1986, with imports exceeding exports in professional and scientific instruments, communications equipment, and electrical components.[13] Former Federal Reserve chairman Arthur Burns termed these developments "awesomely different from anything experienced in the past"; that is, history offered no sure guide to what lay ahead.[14]

Correction of such imbalance must eventually come through the mechanisms of currency adjustment. No nation consuming $3 worth of imported things while exporting only $2 worth would forever be subsidized by the international community. More U.S. currency would flow abroad than would be returned by American export or other earnings, financial markets would take note, the dollar would cheapen against other currencies and reduce Americans' ability to buy imports. Eventually the dollar would not buy so many Hondas or Taiwanese shoes; Iowa corn and Detroit-built cars would not fetch so many yen or marks. Imports would drop as U.S. dollars had less purchasing power, and exports would expand, though bringing lower prices. Such international trade adjustments would have ended the Import 3–Export 2 binge, leaving a lowered American standard of living. It would then be evident, as it had not been during the happy 3-for-2 days, that the American economy had weakened relative to others.

This was the expected process, but events did not follow textbook forecasts. For reasons peculiar to the international economic environment of the 1980s, foreigners did not weaken U.S. currency by moving promptly from dollars to other assets at the first appearance of substantial trade imbalances. Instead, overseas investors, finding America the most stable and accessible of capitalist societies, continued to bolster the dollar with purchases of dollar-denominated things—the huge quantities of federal paper being issued to cover the budget shortfalls; American real estate, companies, securities. The dollar thus remained strong against the currencies of other trading partners longer than economic theory predicted, extending far into the 1980s the period in which imports could become entrenched within the U.S. economy. The dollar reached a peak in early 1985 (fetching 262 yen and 10.5 francs) and began a steady decline to a temporary plateau in mid-1988 (bringing 128 yen and 5.7 francs). By the end of Reagan's second term the dollar had lost one-third of its pre-1985 value on international currency markets.[15]

The trade gap responded to these exchange rate realignments more slowly and sluggishly than predicted. The merchandise trade deficit for 1986 was a towering $152.6 billion, increasing in 1987 to $153 billion. Only in 1988 did a rise in exports begin to reduce such deficits, in the teeth of continuing high imports and the first negative balance on services and interest payments in 30 years of record keeping. The trade deficit for 1988, though finally lower than the year before, was a formidable $137 billion.[16]

Thus the inevitable rebalancing of U.S. trade accounts was postponed until the 1990s, and an artificial prosperity was extended. This postponement of corrections would eventually have costs that could be broadly anticipated. Sustaining an expansion with large federal deficits had not only piled up a debt of unprecedented size, but for the first time in the twentieth century moved much of it offshore. Our formerly internal mortgage had been quickly internationalized. By the spring of 1985, borrowing had been so massive and prolonged that the leading nation of the free world had transformed itself from the globe's largest creditor to the largest debtor, erasing in 5 years a 70-year accumulation of overseas assets. Most economic writers in Reagan's last year in office estimated that the U.S. debt to foreigners reached $420 billion at the beginning of 1987; it reached $664 billion at the end of 1989. Close to $60 billion a year went abroad just as interest payments.[17]

Where was the American economy going? It was "growing," the Reagan administration would point out each year after 1982, going "up," at least in size, and had been doing so for more months in a row than was the historic norm. But it was no longer getting richer (per capita), and it might indeed be getting poorer. New York banker Peter G. Peterson, a Republican and former secretary of commerce, gathered the bad news in a trenchant article in the October 1987 *Atlantic Monthly*, an essay half-seriously said to have precipitated the stock market collapse later that month.[18]

Peterson and others made much of the dramatic shift to world debtor status as a result of budgetary and trade deficits, but they were alarmed by trends more fundamental than the trade imbalance, which some economist can always predict will correct itself in time, or the external debt, which any economic historian can confirm was far higher in the late nineteenth century as America vaulted to world leadership.[19] Overall productivity growth rates, which had surged ahead in manufacturing, especially when the 1983 recovery began, had stagnated by 1985–1986. Nonfarm business productivity increased by only 0.7 percent in 1986; manufacturing productivity fell that year from an encouraging 4.3 percent to 2 percent by 1989, the second consecutive year in which the U.S. trailed all the 11 other industrialized countries. Overall multifactor productivity growth in 1987 was only 0.9 percent, almost the lowest growth rate of all industrial nations. Two Brookings authors looking at national productivity performance in 1973–1986 saw a "startling . . . collapse . . . a crisis." [20] Savings rates had followed a similar pattern in the 1980s, rising somewhat in 1983–1984 when Reagan said they should, but falling in 1985 to the lowest rate in 35 years and slipping further (to a mere 3.9 percent of disposable income) in 1986.[21]

As the Reagan era neared an end, only the president's own economists still saw no real problems in basic trends. In most assessments, the economic prospects were troubled, and many spoke of debts to be paid: "A short-term decline in the standard of living of the American people is inevitable," wrote James Fallows, "since the nation had chosen subsidized consumption now, in return for a lower standard of living in the future.[22] An MIT group studied the economy from a "bottom-up" angle of vision, examining the nation's production system with special attention to eight basic industries, and found "that American industry indeed shows worrisome signs of weakness" and that "relative to other nations and relative to its own history, America does indeed have a serious productivity problem." [23] The announcement and description of relative and possibly absolute decline boosted sober, to some even gloomy books by Paul Kennedy, David Calleo, Walter Russell Mead, and Benjamin Friedman to broad attention and readership.[24]

## Along with Macro-Trend Worries, Structural Worries

The path from mounting trade deficits to huge federal deficits and low national savings rates was direct and short, and the designated culprits obviously guilty. But structural developments kept the strings of the IP debate vibrating as the Reagan era moved toward its close. Among the winning notions in the 1984 contest of ideas had been the conviction that the structure of the economy took care of itself. "The progression of an economy such as America's from agriculture to manufacturing to services is a natural change," announced Reagan's 1985 *Economic Report*. Or, in the New York Stock Exchange's view, "a strong manufacturing sector is not a requisite for a prosperous economy."[25] Or recall Herbert Stein's happy acceptance of a trading relationship with Japan in which "Dallas" tapes were exchanged for Japanese cars and computers. Occasionally it had been said that a handful of "national security" sectors required custodial treatment. Orthodox thought had finessed that issue during the 1980–1984 debate. Outside these rare national security industries, if there were any, markets were always arranging tomorrow's best industrial structure.

It fell to a Japanese industrialist, Akio Morita, head of Sony Corporation, to provide a rallying concept for those alarmed about the U.S. economy's structural transformation. American industry was becoming the home of "the hollow corporation," Morita observed, and *Business Week* made his descriptive phrase a headline issue in March 1986.[26] That spring *Business Week* editors were, if anything, more worried than they had been six years earlier, when their special issue on Industrial Policy may be said to have begun the debate. They reported Morita's view, and their own dark suspicion, that although American manufacturing seemed to be holding its own if one looked at its percentage of GNP, such figures concealed a fundamental weakening. Final sales and earnings recorded by American multinational corporations, often in joint ventures with Japanese firms, sustained an optimistic outlook and bolstered stock market confidence. Behind these figures, however, was a geographic rearrangement of the production process which seemed to bode ill for the future. Product initiation remained—for the time being—in the United States; increasingly, sales and service took place again within American borders. As Robert Reich put it, "We take charge of the two ends of the production process . . . the Japanese concentrate on the complex manufacturing process in between."[27] The center of gravity of manufacturing prowess was shifting offshore, even though American-based firms were recording the final sale of the product. *Business Week*, Reich, and a growing collection of others saw the nation shipping overseas not only a portion of our manufacturing process but something more important—engineering, design, and production skills with their linkages to upstream product ideas and downstream marketing.[28]

A detailed exploration of the composition of national economic portfolio came with Stephen Cohen and John Zysman's *Manufacturing Matters* (1987), a vigorous attack upon Daniel Bell's vision of a postindustrial services economy replacing the grimy industrial system. To the Berkeley authors, conventional economics had forgotten what developmental economics had always known, that economies are nets of linkages of skills and functions. Because U.S. agriculture had not shifted offshore, but had mechanized and remained a major sector, service jobs remained in its web of linkages to strengthen the economy. Employment in pizza parlors was "loosely" tied to agriculture and would probably survive if all farming moved to Mexico, but the agricultural chemical industry was "tightly" linked, requiring proximity to the production in the fields. By Cohen and Zysman's estimates, American manufacturing was tightly linked to 40-60 million service jobs—not just joined in the sense that manufacturing wages allowed the purchase of hamburgers and dental care, but directly linked to goods production, usually upstream from that process. Allow the industrial base to slip offshore, and many of these high-paying service jobs would eventually if not immediately drain out of the American economy.

In this analysis, the emerging services-based economy, with here and there a few profitable "hollow" (manufacturing done overseas) manufacturing corporations, would not bring rising living standards. Instead, it "may be a way of spreading around economic stagnation, as we take in each other's linen for wash."[29] Manufacturing matters, industrial structure matters, and trends moving through both were increasingly serious. "American manufacturing has never been in more trouble than it is now," was the first sentence of an Office of Technology Assessment study published in 1990, and the arrival in 1986 of the first trade deficit in high-technology products, reflecting weakening performance from electronic equipment from semiconductors through computers and automatic data processing equipment, indicated that competitive pressures were being felt across the range of industries from old to new.[30]

Did the emerging consensus on industrial trends and their serious implications revive Industrial Policy? The aversion to the term persisted through the second half of the decade, and the broadening awareness of the deep social roots of lagging economic performance meant that the "what is to be done" section at the end of virtually all books and reports urged action in quadrants 1 and 2, in social values and science, technology and management, with the usual scolding of the government for its fiscal irresponsibility in quadrant 3 (see Figure 1). An MIT study of eight industries urged remedies for six flaws, ranging from "short time horizons" to "neglect of human resources," and only last came "government and industry at cross-purposes."[31] Whatever that implied, public policy could not be indifferent to economic storm signals, and a strong case had been made that this meant it could not be indifferent to economic structure. Such arguments in the second half of the decade sustained a rationale for some sort of policy realignment. David Halberstam, writing of the global and especially the Japanese-American economic conflict from the perspective of the automobile industry, found "in America . . . in 1985 . . . the unsettling sense that a crisis existed and had not been faced."[32]

### Replacing IP: Can Trade Policy Substitute?

With such troubled economic weather, the concerns that had come together under the IP rubric sought another channel. It had often been predicted that if IP were not established as a potentially positive channel of remedial action during eras of rapid industrial change, political pressures would flow toward protectionism. And so they did, in Reagan's second term.

A renewed importance for trade policy had not seemed likely at the end of 1984, for the Trade and Tariff Act passed late in the year had, in the words of I. M. Destler, "cleared the decks of major trade issues requiring statutory attention."[33] But foreign trade continued to require political attention, given the behavior of imports and exports. When the trade deficit of 1984 was calculated at $123 billion, nearly a third of it recorded with Japan, Congress returned in a protectionist, retaliatory mood. Democrats in the House pushed several legislative ideas, including conventional import curbs for specific industries such as textiles or shoes, but also a requirement that the executive branch more frequently make access to U.S. markets conditional upon trade partners' actual record of U.S. imports, a clear challenge to the principles underlying the General Agreement on Tariffs and Trade (GATT). For most of 1985 the Reagan administration seemed passive or unconcerned. The president let months slip by before appointing a special trade representative to replace William Brock, and he clearly valued the strategic alliance with Japan and his "Ron-Yasu" relationship with Prime Minister Yasuhiro Nakasone far more than any opening of the Japanese market. Absent gestures from the administration to ease the pressures, Congress surprised itself by passing a protectionist bill in the fall with special help for textiles, shoes, and copper.

Finally aware that it was losing control of the trade issue, the administration sent Treasury Secretary James Baker III to New York in September to make the now historic announcement that five major industrial nations jointly called for a weaker dollar, and took an increasingly tougher stance vis-à-vis imports in general and Japan in particular. The era of relatively free trade since World War II had never seemed in such jeopardy as in the mid-1980s, with world trade stagnating, overcapacity plaguing most industries, and fierce domestic political pressures massing behind restriction.[34]

This mounting preoccupation with trade politics should have called attention to the lost advantages of the Industrial Policy framework. As a channel for policy deliberation on the array of matters affecting national economic competitiveness, trade policy seemed a dead end. Of the entire arsenal of policy tools available to deal with industrial change, it left out too much—fiscal policy, monetary policy, regulation, R&D policy, education, labor force retraining, and antitrust. It seemed entirely negative, with no connection to positive steps toward economic development.

Yet it seemed the only channel available through the rest of the Reagan term. Congress had dropped Industrial Policy, and Competitiveness had no focus. So industrial rescuers would work with trade policy, and attempt to shape it to serve broader purposes than mere protection.

No responsible public figure advocated or defended protection. The conventional wisdom, deeply entrenched, held that the potential of trade policy was virtually always negative, essentially synonymous with "protectionism." It was a policy that blocked desired imports, a political mistake that must simply be patiently contained while trade forces, which were invariably beneficial, found ways around barriers.

Many in Congress, and some publicists, had for some time been denying that the aggressive restrictionism they advocated was in fact the discredited, simple protectionism of Smoot-Hawley days. Retaliation against imports could and should be undertaken as market-opening tools, used

in tit-for-tat bargaining to lead toward lower trade barriers on all sides—
especially in Japan. Equally, the export-promotion side of trade policy
was said to offer an avenue for a variety of export subsidies to the fast-
developing sunrise industries of the future. Such arguments were in the
mid-1980s gaining some support in the academic community, where
trade was a specialty and the conventional wisdom was increasingly
suspect.

In conventional Ricardian trade theory, comparative advantage derives
from factor endowments; it is not and cannot be created by governments.
Thus state subsidies to exporting industries are not a threat to other nations' industries or well-being. They are simply a stupid mistake, a subsidy to receiving consumers. Nobel Prize–winning economist Milton
Friedman illustrated this belief in a remark he made on his television program on the principles of capitalism. If a country wished to subsidize its
products and offer them in the United States, Friedman thought, we
should buy as many of these artifically cheap items as possible and enjoy
the subsidy. Some of our domestic industries might shrink under the pressure of cheaper items from abroad, but the benefit to consumers was what
counted. The composition of national industry was not a policy concern,
but a matter best left to markets. If the foreigners woke up and ceased
their subsidies, domestic industries would revive again.[35]

During the IP discussion this orthodoxy received major challenge.
Robert Reich, Lester Thurow, and other writers had argued that "dynamic comparative advantage" might be created for certain knowledge-
intensive industries or firms by governments. The state could push
selected sunrise industries rapidly down the learning curve behind early
barriers to competition, reaping dynamic economies of scale and building
an unsurmountable technological lead. A subsidized Japanese export, entering U.S. markets, might be one of Milton Friedman's gifts, or, if the
sponsoring government were astute, it might also be a Trojan horse, entering on a strategic mission.[36]

The foundations of this view were historical, grounded chiefly in the
experience of the Japanese and the "Asian Tigers" Hong Kong, Taiwan,
Singapore, and South Korea. During the four-year IP debate it had lacked
an acceptable theoretical foundation, and most economic and trade professionals saw it as dangerous heresy. All this changed very rapidly in the
second half of the decade, as "new wave" or "strategic trade theory"
gained adherents and depth, convincing even some former doubters that

there was theoretical grounding for experimentation, with certain export-oriented industrial policies at certain times offering a net positive contribution to national (though perhaps not net international) welfare.[37]

Even those who concluded that "strategic trade theory" opened a window of opportunity for governmental activism in quadrant 4 (see Figure 1) were also quick to point out its limits. The information requirements for successful state intervention were high; retaliation might soon erase national welfare gains; the threat of global protectionism made this a risky business. And there were other difficulties. The trade policy machinery was inherently reactive. The Harley-Davidson motorcycle company came to governmental attention not because it was being watched as a vital industry but because it complained of imports and demanded relief. The company's subsequent revival, after protection came in 1983, was a source of some Reaganite pride, although the administration had not initiated action. No one had identified making motorcycles as a strategic industry.

Despite these handicaps, trade policy was all the Democrats had as a vehicle for intellectual and political assault upon the administration in Reagan's second term. Thus the 99th (1985–86) and 100th (1987–88) Congresses compiled a record containing much trade policymaking, which some called protectionism and others defended as "aggressively market-opening." Stripped to the essentials, a trade policy reform bill was incubated in 1986, worked its way to passage in both houses by the spring of 1988, and was vetoed by Reagan in May. Adjustments were made, and the 1,100-page Omnibus Trade and Competitiveness Act of 1988 was signed by Reagan in August.

We are not interested in all the details of this 1,100-page goliath, but in looking inside the Trojan horse of trade policy reform to see if Industrial Policy rode within. And so it did, in several forms. Early in 1985 Congressman John LaFalce and other House Democrats attached a Council on Industrial Competitiveness to ongoing trade legislation—this time leaving out the Bank. Even this was denounced in a Mobil Oil ad as a "backdoor to the discredited belief that government should plan the economy," and the House leadership lost interest. Senator Jeff Bingaman (Dem., N.M.) chaired a Senate Democratic working group and put forward a proposal for a Competitiveness Policy Council which received sufficient business support to slip into the trade bill of 1988 and avoid a Reagan vote. The Council embodied the Forum concept, was an independent body composed of 12 members heavily weighted to the private sector (9), and charged with identifying sectoral problems, developing and recommending corrective strategies—when necessary by convening sectoral subcouncils—and preparing an annual report.[38] Part of the IP architecture was suddenly in place.

Indeed, the 1988 trade law, with its 30 new federal offices or panels and its 100 new reports to Congress and public, actually bristled with pieces of industrial policy (a plant-closing prenotification law passed separately, Reagan declining to veto). Commentators on this denouement of a long second-term battle over trade policy thought they were observing merely a confused and confusing narrow escape from protectionism. They failed to see how much industrial policy had just been planted across the federal landscape. The new trade policy regime had been thrown together by many parenting policy entrepreneurs, was designed without thought of a coordinating center, and would require years for assessment. Yet 1988 had been a big year for industrial policies as they rode the back of trade policies, though not a good year for IP as a dream of coordination.

### Organizing around "Competitiveness"

Trade policy, moving into the vacuum left by the 1984 disappearance of the concept of Industrial Policy, could not entirely fill it. Democrats, and those Republicans convinced that Reaganomics was inadequate, continued the search for an alternative framework for national economic policy. Apart from their political defects, trade and industrial policies were limited to quadrant 4. The concept of Competitiveness offered hope of a larger framework for discussion in Reagan's second term—a vehicle for the sense of economic urgency widely felt in business and political circles, for a crusade to produce public- and private-sector reforms amounting to a strategic response to the new competition, but without the discomforts of targeting.

Reagan's second term coincided with an enlightening exploration of this possibility. As before, the lead was taken by Democrats. Whatever Competitiveness meant in policy terms, it was, to House Speaker Jim Wright, "the dominant economic issue of the remaining years of the twentieth century."[39] The Democratic Leadership Council, centrists in search of their own program, met in December 1986 and reported the development of "a competitiveness index" that conveyed bad news about the American economy in world trade. Before the end of the year a bipartisan 170-member Congressional Caucus on Competitiveness had been formed, and a month later Ronald Reagan appeared to be responding. The president, in the words of one journalist, made "the consensus on competitiveness . . . complete" when his January 1987 State of the Union address embraced the issue and the White House cobbled together a 1,600-page "Competitiveness Bill" conveying familiar ideas about pro-tecting intellectual property, more R&D spending, and other such unof-fending staples.[40]

By this time the president was not trusted to follow up seriously on much of anything, and he did not appear to sense that most of America's business leadership, high-tech as well as smokestack, was now deeply alarmed by underlying trends and looking to Washington for leadership. Reagan had ignored the Young Commission report, and for months Young remained loyally patient in his offices at Hewlett-Packard. A year and four months after the commission had placed its worrisome findings on the president's desk, 30 Democratic and Republican senators impa-tiently introduced a joint resolution to force the administration to report within 60 days on its (non)response to a commission it had appointed. By the autumn of 1986, Young had tired of waiting and formed the Council on Competitiveness of prominent business, labor, and academic leaders, rented an office on Pennsylvania Avenue just two blocks from the White House, and began to issue reports repeating earlier warnings about Amer-ica's declining world economic position. The *Washington Post* reported an evolving coalition on Competitiveness, with members ranging from the American Business Conference (whose 100 members were high-growth corporations not expected to be alarmed about the economic future), four congressional caucuses, the National Academy of Engineering, the Democratic Center for National Policy, and the National Association of Manufacturers.[41]

The competitiveness rubric appeared for a time to have absorbed and transcended IP, offering an idea broad—or diffuse—enough to suit both Reagan and Lane Kirkland. Reporters at the outset had difficulty finding critics of the new concept, whatever it meant. ("The thing has become a hype without much substance," was Kevin Phillips' observation.)[42] The working definition of Competitiveness became that of the Young Com-mission: "The degree to which a nation, under free and fair market condi-tions, produces goods and services that meet the test of international markets while simultaneously maintaining and expanding the real in-comes of its citizens."[43]

That sounded like a goal, but what was the strategy to reach it? Here the advocates of Competitiveness, at least as represented by John Young's Council on Competitiveness, attempted to transcend the earlier debate. The remedies for an eroding industrial position were not to be sought in quadrant 4, through activist intervention in sectors. Instead, the desired public policy reforms seemed to lie in quadrant 3, in economywide measures, and there was much exhortation about awakening and revival directed toward corporation executives, unionists, and educators in quadrants 1 and 2.

Framing the issues in this way gave the talk about Competitiveness a timely emphasis upon quadrant 3's fiscal follies, which were widely denounced through the mid- and later 1980s as budgetary deficits mounted. This was a congenial theme in virtually all quarters, as were the exhortations to develop public and private policies encouraging more saving, larger investments in education, infrastructure, and R&D, and the like.

Where did this leave Industrial Policy? Outwardly, it had been finessed, left behind. Competitiveness spokesmen carried forward IP's stress upon the continuing erosion of industrial strength and the inadequacy of the reforms of the early Reagan years, but their policy critique focused primarily on defects in fiscal policy, education, and the levels and focus of R&D effort. These broad themes gained the Competitiveness idea many mild endorsements, and virtually no enemies. It was a collection of responsible-sounding ideas about macroeconomic policies and what corporation heads should do to prepare the nation's current and rising work force to compete. Ignoring IP, Competitiveness simply left the de facto IP intact down in quadrant 4, in its far-flung grapple with sectoral development.

This decision to handle the sectoral policy issue by ignoring it carried opportunity costs which were little discussed. If there was much misdirection of effort, with both tactical and strategic errors, in America's vast and scattered industrial policies (whose high-technology components had drifted under the wing of the Defense Department), then the decision to continue to manage them prevented the pursuit of some desirable objectives. To some, the benefits potentially available from confronting the de facto IP derived from strategic coordination; to others, from the pruning of inefficiencies and the release of market forces. Both were difficult to pursue with the problem in the closet.

The Competitiveness framework of the latter half of the 1980s, seeing more problems than opportunities in the sectoral interventions of governments, made Industrial Policy the uninvited fourth member of the U.S.

team, as the Competitiveness strategy fielded players in only three quadrants. Japan, Korea, West Germany, and the other major trading economies fielded full teams.

## The Persistence of Sectoral Interventions, 1985–1988

Industrial policies ignored, however, were not banished, and sectoral policy concerns and decisions kept breaking through. In 1985, the Democrats attempted to sustain their sponsorship, as we have seen. Each time the House of Representatives formulated or passed a trade bill, the Democrats attached a rider establishing an institutional beachhead for overall management of sectoral interventions—usually a permanent "Industrial Competitiveness Council" or "Council on Industrial Competitiveness," with a suggestion for the creation of sectoral subcouncils. They did not, however, attach a Bank. Congressman LaFalce voiced in 1986 the lessons learned in 1984: "A bank would not fly, will not fly and that . . . was the excess baggage" from RFC history which he and his colleagues would not carry forward next time.[44]

But Democrats could only propose, and were actually losing the initiative on a topic they had chiefly invented. The Reagan administration, led not by the White House but by other parts of the executive branch, was moving inexorably toward the enlargement of existing interventions and the establishment of new ones. Officials in the Commerce Department had been pressing for more sectoral activism as early as 1982. More aggressive was the Pentagon, which had grown increasingly concerned with the technological health of certain of its client industries and the specter of dependence upon Asian electronics suppliers. The Department of Defense in the second Reagan term increasingly displayed a "national industrial portfolio" outlook similar to that practiced in Japan and advocated by people the administration thought of as enemies.

The forcing events were crises in two formerly vigorous American industries with national security linkages—machine tools and semiconductors. The American machine tool industry—deploying the machines that make the machines that make screws, bolts, and rings, as well as the presses, drills, casters, and robots—was unquestionably the best in the world in the 1960s. It was not a large industry, smaller than paint and dyes or barber's equipment, but its prima facie link to national security had brought it to the government's attention early in the Cold War. Thus there was a long-standing industrial policy for this sector—chiefly decades of procurement which shaped the industry's product, supplemented by the Air Force's Management Technology program, supplemented by export controls to prevent the Soviets from acquiring valuable tools and technology. These policy instruments aimed at the same thing: military—not commercial—supremacy. There was of course a machine tool industrial policy in Japan, with civilian, commercial ends. It was designed to propel the Japanese industry to overtake and surpass the U.S. industry.

This goal, as measured by world sales, was apparently accomplished in 1986, when Japanese imports rose in the United States to 40 percent of market share. A leading American conglomerate owning Burgmaster and other machine tool makers, Houdaille Industries, filed a trade complaint in 1982 before the U.S. International Trade Commission (USITC). Its brief, a 720-page document based upon months of skillful research in Japan by Houdaille's lawyers, was hailed as the best description of how Japanese industrial policy works for a targeted sector. Priced initially at $1,250 and a hot seller in Washington when the Office of the U.S. Trade Representative published it at $15, the Houdaille petition charged Japan (essentially, MITI) with having fostered a powerful cartel of machine tool makers, using tax advantages, loans, R&D assistance, and the nation's formidable trade barriers to penetrate world and American markets at the direct expense of Houdaille's firms. Houdaille demanded import relief under a radical proposition that Japan's industrial policies for machine tools constituted a violation of trade law. The issue worked its way upward through the trade policy machinery to the cabinet, which divided. The decision was then passed to President Reagan, who decided the matter after hearing the appeal of "his friend," Prime Minister Nakasone. Houdaille's petition was rejected, the slump in machine tools continued, and in 1986 Houdaille began to divest itself of its machine tools group, shutting down Burgmaster and auctioning off its equipment. It was the end of the 42-year career of one of American manufacturing's crown jewels.

Houdaille's machine tool components had been dismembered, it claimed, because the Japanese had both an effective industrial policy for these "mother machines" and a powerful Washington lobbying arm, while the Reagan administration contributed its mix of passivity, ideological objections to trade activism, and fear of offending the Japanese. In Reagan's second term, however, the Pentagon became increasingly concerned at the national security implications of a shrinking U.S. machine tool industry, and in 1986 the president reversed himself and forced the Japanese to limit their machine tool exports, while the Defense Department committed $15 million to a new consortium of U.S. machine tool companies which by 1988 had produced something hitherto found only abroad, a national center for manufacturing process R&D National Center for Manufacturing Sciences funded both by the Defense Department and a coalition of U.S. firms.[45]

It might have come too late, even if the effort turned out to be well designed. As Reagan left office, the Japanese assault upon (mostly) the lower end and the German push from the high end of the machine tool market pressed hard upon the market share of American firms, leading an MIT task force to conclude in 1988 that "the American machine-tool industry is dissolving."[46]

Too late or not, this was industrial policy out in the open, invented within the executive branch. As for Houdaille, it was in trouble not only because of Japanese manufacturing skills and industrial policy, but also because a leveraged buyout in 1979 had loaded the company up with debt, and because Houdaille had mismanaged Burgmaster after acquiring it in 1965. In the view of Max Holland, historian of Burgmaster's rise and fall, it was the American industrial policy that hurt more than the Japanese: "The Pentagon functioned as a perverse and much more powerful MITI, through its procurement policies," which "lured the industry into two-tiered R&D," producing custom machines for the Pentagon instead of concentrating all attention on standardized, economical, numerically controlled machines for commercial sale. An amalgam of Pentagon procurement and tax laws encouraging leveraged buyouts, "Current U.S. industrial policy is a debacle."[47]

### Semiconductors: A Loser-Fixing
### Industrial Policy for the 1980s

The American semiconductor chip industry, producing "the rice of the electronic age and the crude oil of the twenty-first century," had as late as 1975 what looked like an insurmountable lead in silicon chip design and production.[48] U.S. firms held a 60 percent market share and dominated every production category. But the Japanese had targeted the industry, and by 1986 they claimed 90 percent of the world market share for the most familiar type of chip, the static and dynamic random access memory (RAM); and for chips of all types the U.S. world share had dropped to

43 percent, behind Japan's 46 percent.[49] By 1987 the top three semiconductor producers in the world were Japanese. Well before this, victory was sensed in Tokyo and, uncharacteristically, announced. Seventeen Japanese firms "declared victory" in an ad placed in *Scientific American* in October 1981.[50]

Certainly they overwhelmingly dominated RAM chip making, and by the second half of the decade only IBM and AT&T still made such chips (for their own use) inside the United States. American chip buyers thus relied entirely on Japanese RAMs, which were both cheaper and more reliable than those made at home. American semiconductor firms still led in microprocessors and some logic devices including linear circuits, and in the more specialized EPROM (electrical, programmable read-only memory) chips. But the Japanese aimed at supremacy in these products too, intending not only to become the low-cost producer of all RAM chips but also to dominate upstream in the production of machines that made the chips and the materials going into them.[51]

By 1985 the U.S. semiconductor industry was losing $2 billion a year and beginning a layoff of some 25,000 employees, and an industry built by cowboy entrepreneurs without significant government assistance asked for government help—from the trade machinery of the USITC and the Department of Commerce, where import relief and access to Japanese markets might possibly be won. Congressional pressures forced the president to announce the formation of a cabinet-level "strike force" on Japanese semiconductor imports, but the administration found itself deeply divided. All industries are of equal value, said the government's economists, and if this one is failing it must be a managerial failure. Japanese industrial policy may target Nippon's semiconductor industry for assistance, but this should be seen as a subsidy to American consumers of cheap chips. The State Department's view was, Don't offend the Japanese with objections to their odd economic behavior, for they are important allies. The National Security Council worried that vigorous trade complaints or retaliation, which the semiconductor producers (but not consumers) in the United States were demanding, might make the Japanese withdraw support for SDI. And to Commerce Secretary Baldrige's recommendation that the president enforce the law against Japanese dumping, someone from the State Department said: "If we do this, are we moving toward an industrial policy?"[52]

Indeed they were, and did. The president did not want to offend his friend Nakasone, but in a March 1986 finding the USITC confirmed massive dumping of chips. A trade accord with Tokyo was negotiated, aiming to end Japanese dumping (which they had not conceded); but the controls were leaky, and the Japanese market for U.S. chips was not opening. The beleaguered industry was no Houdaille, ready to quit the field. It aggressively knocked upon the right governmental doors when the White House proved unresponsive. Meetings of semiconductor industry and Department of Commerce officials in 1986 began to incubate the idea of a multifirm research consortium, and from the Pentagon the Defense Science Board Task Force reported in early 1987 that the U.S. semiconductor industry was slipping away, with major national security implications. Already, 21 critical military systems were built around chips made only in Japan, a nation ahead of the United States in 25 key semiconductor technologies and evenly matched in 8 more. Defense contractors making sophisticated military hardware would soon depend entirely upon Asians for supplies of those tiny, vital electronic brains imprinted upon silicon wafers.[53]

"National security" was criterion enough on which to pick this former winner as target for an aggressive industrial policy, to prevent it from becoming a loser. In March 1987 the president announced unprecedented sanctions in the form of tariffs as high as 300 percent upon a range of Japanese imports, and although these were soon eased, the administration was ready to move beyond protectionism. Another task force was convened to study the semiconductor industry, and by the end of the year Congress had approved $100 million to fund a new entity to match Japan, Inc., to be called Sematech, based in Austin, Texas. This industry-sponsored, government-sanctioned and -subsidized organization with a $250 million annual budget would pool manufacturing knowledge and conduct joint R&D efforts. American semiconductor industrial policy had taken on a new heft and prominence, despite doubts that neither government nor industry quite knew what it should be doing.

For one thing, the problem involved several industries linked together, with the Japanese beginning to excel in all of them at once. The threat to American-based chip producers came to official notice first, but upstream were companies that supplied the chip-making firms with sophisticated equipment and silicon materials, and these too were losing ground to Japanese competitors. The policy assignment led toward the nurturing of several related industries, and it was not clear that temporary import quotas and a research consortium would be sufficient. The industry, cultural heartland of the entrepreneurial mentality, was being moved by events toward cooperation. A National Advisory Committee on the Semi-conductor Industry, mandated in the 1988 Trade Act, in 1990 urged a major effort to rebuild the nation's consumer electronics industry, with a government bank for "patient capital," and new tax and trade laws to nurse back to life an industry that had substantially moved offshore. Welcome to industrial policy.[54]

## Against Our Principles, Deeper into Sectoral Targeting

The Reagan administration's machine tool and semiconductor industrial policy activism was spasmodic, but one was surprised to see the bear ride the bike at all, even if badly. The administration continued to resist the rising clamor from high-technology businesses urging some sort of major plan centered on the Competitiveness issue. Michael Porter, of the Harvard Business School and member of the Young Commission and Council on Competitiveness, complained in *Fortune* magazine that "the administration . . . seems to believe that the mere acknowledgment of a problem is the first step to greater governmental intervention in the economy."[55] Since it did not recognize any problem within American manufacturing that dollar depreciation would not solve, the administration confined its occasionally expressed concerns about industrial competitiveness to isolated actions. The cherished tax reform plans of 1985–1986 were conceived in such disregard of their effects upon manufacturing as to produce what journalists called "a cry of rage . . . from parts of the nation's industrial midsection," confirming the absence of any forceful industrial viewpoint in the inner circles of policymaking.[56]

Yet on other issues at other times, the impulse to pick sectoral winners proved irresistible. The president, doubtless advised to show some signs of responsiveness to what a former science adviser called "the 'C' word that we'll be hearing so much of during the next twelve months—'competitiveness,'" took a sudden enthusiasm for "superconductivity" research. In 1987 Reagan announced an 11-point plan to speed up American commercialization of what an excited scientific community hoped to be breakthroughs in the discovery of materials conducting electricity with no resistance. He took three cabinet secretaries to Kitty Hawk, North Carolina, to announce the formation of a new Council on Superconductivity and of $150 million in new R&D money to be disbursed (predictably) by the Department of Defense, along with new research centers, patent revisions, and the like.[57]

This was all the White House could or would produce—industrial politics in spasms, not continuous policy leadership. Both the Department of Commerce and the Pentagon moved into this vacuum, the former moving as early as 1986 to identify new technologies with special promise for commercial application by the year 2000. Commerce, lacking a mandate to take or even suggest winner-picking actions, limited itself instead to listing ten barriers to commercialization which somebody should attack. It had been Commerce Department talks with industrial leaders that led to the Sematech initiative, but the department lacked the funds to launch the government's side of the partnership. This opening was exploited by the Pentagon's small and respected R&D funding agency, Defense Advanced Research Projects Agency, which was not in the Pentagon building itself but two subway stops away. By the close of the Reagan presidency, DARPA had moved, partially by choice and in part "propelled" by congressional frustration with administration inactivity, "into the role of venture capitalist for America's high-technology industries," visibly enough that the agency emerged from 25 years of relative obscurity and was sometimes termed "America's Answer to Japan's MITI."[58] DARPA was taking the lead not only in the Sematech consortium but also in efforts to spur American progress in high-definition television, superconductors, and other advanced electronic technologies. The agency's activism reflected a growing concern at higher levels in the Pentagon and encouraged from Capitol Hill, that in its procurement and R&D activities the Defense Department had for so long neglected the "defense-industrial base" that national security considerations forced reorientation of DOD attention toward the health of the civilian industrial sector. In July 1988, DOD issued a study recommending the creation of new institutions to meet the problem, including a "production base advocate" in the Pentagon, a Defense Manufacturing Board, and a new data base on industrial developments.[59]

Yet Pentagon-led Industrial Policy seemed to many a problem dressed up as a solution. A leading student of those patterns, former deputy assistant secretary of defense Jacques Gansler, noted that firms producing for the Defense Department would find that DOD's entrenched habit of "maximizing performance regardless of cost" was "a philosophical virus that could infect the commercial side of the business." Could the Pentagon transform itself into an agency "to help the private sector compete in the highly competitive global market"? Gansler thought no informed person believed this feasible, but the Pentagon was "the most politically acceptable and available organization to do it." "The Defense Department is not where it should be," thought the president of the National Academy of Engineering.[60]

Many believed that the Department of Commerce ought to do that job, or a "civilian DARPA," an idea put in legislative form by Senator John Glenn (Dem., Ohio) in 1989. Meanwhile DARPA found that its newly assumed role as planner for at least the high-technology side of U.S. industry exposed it to closer congressional scrutiny and impatience. Senator Bingaman, convinced that DARPA was not funding enough of the emerging technologies spoken of in congressional hearings, demanded that DOD list its top technological priorities and assess the promise of U.S. industry in their development. In the Pentagon, an aggressive new undersecretary (formerly with General Motors) mobilized efforts to develop a system for monitoring the performance of 215 individual industries, pressed for a shift in procurement to favor commercially available components and for ways to support any major industry threatened by foreign competition. Winner-picking, loser-fixing, welcome to Industrial Policy.[61]

Thus an administration convinced that both theory and history proved that governments couldn't pick winners was, in its second term, driven even deeper into quadrant 4 activism by mounting evidence that the Japanese were successfully steering not by Western economic theory but by a history lesson to the effect that governments sometimes can. There was a marked preference under Reagan for national security rationales and high-technology ventures, but as 1988 came to a close the government had moved deeply into the largest losing-industry bailout in history, as it looked at what it thought were price tages of $50–100 billion attached to the rescue of the nation's savings and loan industry.

Still the administration, speaking in its last months mostly through presidential nominee (and Reagan's successor) George Bush, insisted that the Industrial Policy proposals coming forward again from the Democratic nominee and proud sponsor of "the Massachusetts miracle," Michael Dukakis, were unthinkable innovations that should again be defeated at the polls. Dukakis did indeed advocate what *Newsweek* magazine, two weeks before the election, summarized as "a form of quasi-planning that Democrats called 'industrial policy' before they got scared of the phrase"; but his advisers downplayed the issue. Industrial policies were the answer to 40 percent of the nation's economic problems, estimated Dukakis's adviser Robert Reich, macropolicies the other 60 percent.[62] "George Bush does not have an industrial policy," asserted a Bush aide, but in 1988 the media knew better: "Bush has proposed at least seven of them" in the form of tax breaks, *Newsweek* observed.[63]

So the fig leaf had fallen away as Ronald Reagan ended his term of office, leaving more industrial policies in place than Carter had discovered when he reviewed these creatures in the summer of 1980. The Bush presidency stretched the story into the 1990s, in ways both familiar and novel. As before, relentless economic competition, especially from Japan, activated a coalition of business leaders, congressional Democrats, and activists in Bush's own Defense and Commerce Departments. Industrial policy proposals sprouted like kudzu, and, as before, a Republican presidency staffed by free-market ideologues in high places continued to denounce this Industrial Policy idea that had been killed in 1984.

The principal difference noticeable to anyone who had followed this issue through the decade was the preoccupation with high technology and the part of the economy likely to be transformed and expanded, or literally created, by it. It was only a year after the first high-technology trade deficit in 1986 that Sematech had been formed with federal encouragement and a $100 million annual contribution. By the time George Bush replaced Reagan, the shaky prospects of the U.S. semiconductor industry led to a larger idea—a government-industry partnership to revive the entire American consumer electronics industry, semiconductors easily riding forward in the wake. Called by one journalist "the commercial equivalent of the Manhattan Project," the proposal targeted high-definition television (HDTV) as the Japanese had already done, on the assumption that this was one of those rare leading-edge technologies with the capacity to open vast new markets and transform existing ones.[64] But since it was also one in which uncertainty, high risk, and large capital requirements would cause private industry to underinvest, governments could shorten development times.

To speak of the consumer electronics industry was to invoke a recent past that appeared to convey a strong message. As the MIT industrial study put it, "the history of consumer electronics is a history of successive retreat by American firms," which abandoned the manufacture of radios to the Japanese in the early 1970s, then VCRs, calculators, video games, telephones, virtually all television production, until by the end of the 1980s only 5 percent of the industry resided with the United States.[65]

Now, a new set of technologies made possible HDTV, digital imaging that not only produced far sharper imagery but also, some predicted, would allow TVs to become computers, and vice versa. The Commerce

Department predicted in 1989 that a $140 billion market would open up over 20 years; electronics industry spokesmen predicted three times that; and some foresaw that the technology would affect not only reception but also transmission, storage, processing, and replay of images and data—a staggering market opening. HDTV could be seen as a great opportunity, but given the history of the past two decades in electronics a disturbing pattern seemed evident. Faltering U.S. efforts to understand and apply HDTV technology looked like the last defeat in the great 30-year electronics war conducted between Japan with its national strategy and an America officially (but not unofficially) without one. Trade journals and the general media expressed dismay at the possibility that the struggle over this technology had opened the final round of the Japanese invasion and capture of the entire U.S. electronics industry.[66] Semiconductors would go, with the machines that made them, then computers, telecommunications, artifical intelligence. The Department of Defense, reporting annually on critical technologies, as required by Congress, in 1990 found Japan on a par or significantly ahead in 8 of the 20 top technologies (the Soviets ahead only in one).[67]

Such prospects spurred the demand that government and industry fashion a response. In the spring of 1989 a major group of electronic firms asked for larger DARPA grants for HDTV research (agency funding was already at $10 million a year) and a $1 billion loan guarantee. DARPA had long been active in financing R&D projects with no obvious or direct military significance, especially under Director Craig Fields, and the Pentagon's Defense Science Board, worried about the "defense industrial base," in late 1988 called for an Industrial Policy Committee—no euphemism for them—reflecting the military's "new found interests in the economy," which were "of truly staggering scope," in one journalist's assessment. "National security sells. Industrial Policy doesn't," a Pentagon official observed.[68]

DARPA's Fields and Commerce Secretary Robert Mosbacher were especially outspoken advocates of "a cohesive and comprehensive industrial policy," with HDTV a high priority, in the early days of the Bush administration. But their campaign drew the attention of Richard Darman, head of the Office of Budget and Management; Michael J. Boskin, chairman of the Council of Economic Advisers; and especially John Sununu, White House chief of staff. Mosbacher was called to the White House for a rebuke. "We told him it is not our policy to talk up a single slice of industry," Sununu told the press; "rather than identify preferred slices of the system, we ought to make changes that help the whole system be responsive." In private, they told Mosbacher that he was sounding like Michael Dukakis.[69] White House forces wanted HDTV and X-ray lithography projects at DARPA cut, and cast doubts on Sematech. In George Bush's America, we do not do Industrial Policy. Fields was forced out of his job in early 1990.

"We need a national religious conversion," Fields wrote in a letter not intended for the disclosure that came in the *New York Times* in the early fall of 1989, but "anyone who proposes any ideas for solving the competitiveness problem can be silenced by accusing him of supporting 'industrial policy.'"[70]

HDTV would continue to evolve, without a concerted or energetic federal push. But of course the government still influenced the outcome in important ways, primarily through the anticipated 1991 decision of the Federal Communications Commission as to production and broadcast standards. The administration continued to attempt to draw a clear line where none could be drawn, between the area where it would be active and the area where it would never, never go. It would target "generic" technologies at the "pre-competitive" stage, when no particular industries benefited from R&D and other supports; and when "national security" seemed involved—a wandering border. These distinctions were useful principles, but they left a blurred zone of practice. In fact up to its waist in industrial policies, the administration fitfully denounced them, a sure sign that it would have difficulty with those under its care.[71] Congressional forces pushed for more spending on what sounded to them like "critical technologies" whether they affected an existing particular industry or not, sought to get a clearer science and technology policy out of the Office of Science and Technology Policy, and increased DARPA's budget.[72]

Policy remained "in irons," the sailors' term for a boat hanging indecisively between tacks. Robert Kuttner would observe that the IP debate had come "far more complex, interesting, and consequential than the industrial-policy arguments of a decade ago."[73] This positive assessment must have rested not only upon the high-technology focus ("serious debate . . . about the future of America's technological jewels") but also upon the degree to which the right questions were being asked. Legitimate and tough questions were raised as to whether HDTV was a lead technology spawning many industries, and, if so, how federal intervention could improve market outcomes, in this and in the larger panorama of science and technology policy.[74] Was DARPA the right command unit for a strategic response in high technology? In an informed and penetrating analysis of the prospects in 1990 for American manufacturing ("American manufacturing has never been in more trouble than it is now, and the government is dozing at the switch"), OTA offered a concise history of sectoral targeting. The purpose of the examples provided was not to prove that government could or could not benefit from experience ("The argument cannot and could not be resolved by counting up successes and failures"), but to show on the basis of that experience "how to design institutions that are open to counsel from and collaboration with industry and other interests, but avoid becoming their captives." *Making Things Better* marshaled the insights of experience to offer suggestions for the design of a civilian DARPA, urging modest expectations and long time horizons.[75]

Thus the 1980s ended with more of the right questions being asked than a decade earlier, along with more thoughtful answers. Former doubters of governmental intervention were beginning to swing around to a more pragmatic, activist policy stance, whatever their differences on how and where to act.[76]

Still, this more interesting and complex debate did not seem to have been more consequential, for the government remained divided and the electronics industry uncertain (also divided). The president appointed Vice-President Dan Quayle to head a cabinet-level Council on Competitiveness that had a murky mandate and no staff, and Bush otherwise took no position. In the meantime his closest aides responded to issues in the old ideological categories, misreading or denying the American experience with economic policy affecting sectors, right up to the time of their own tenure. A government that was and always had been involved in microeconomic policy could not make its engagement strategic, because it denied the fact and legitimacy of its influence upon industrial structure. It steadfastly insisted there was an area called "the free market," where resources were always correctly allocated, and which time and change did not corrupt. Mosbacher himself, back on the White House team, was to say: "If the private sector doesn't want to pursue this [HDTV] without massive infusions from government, there is nothing we can do." The "private" sector! In their minds a pristine conception, a place immaculately conceived, its time horizons, structure, work-force skills and exposure to foreign competition untainted by public policy. One must simply have faith in it. Said Sununu: "There are enough examples of companies that are making it to confirm the fact that the fundamental system is sound."[77]

A foremost student of the electronics industry found a way to say that he could not believe his ears: "It's impossible to have this discussion any-where in Europe," Berkeley's Michael Borrus observed. "They just shake their heads incredulously and ask, What on earth can the U.S. govern-ment be debating?"[78] Parts of the government and surrounding policy community were debating what had changed over time and what should be done about it, but presidential advisers were still dug in at their Magi-not line, debating ideals, ideology. This turned the issue into one pecu-liarly American, as perceived by one journalist in 1989: "Is it possible to develop an industrial policy without calling it that?"[79]

## Looking Back

To come out at this place a decade after Jimmy Carter first faced the sec-toral issue was not what anyone had wanted. We have traced a protracted public policy blunder of a special kind. This was not a straightforward case of the selection of the "wrong" policy, in that either the ends or the means (or both) were subsequently found to be flawed. Rather, what had persisted across a decade of economic deterioration was a sustained and profound misconception of the nature of the policy choice itself. The op-tions were not as seen, either to vote sectoral policies in or out, up or down. Framing the issue in that way had been self-defeating. Industrial policies were not the swine flu vaccination program, or national Policy toward the arts. Some policy areas in the modern United States may con-ceivably be "terminated." But eliminating all policies affecting industrial sectors? Except to an iron-willed libertarian, this would be inconceiv-able. Like economic or foreign policies, all governments have industrial policies.

This accepted, there remained many choices, but they were confined to one range: how may this thing we have discovered—uncoordinated in-dustrial policies that add up to an inferior Industrial Policy—be managed toward improvement?

The choice was not framed in this way by the policy system, and mis-definition of the issue was followed by policy ineptitude, a familiar se-quence. Thus four years of discussion focused upon IP, and another four, devoted mainly to the effort to make "competitiveness" serve the evident need for substantial economic policy redirection, had produced in 1984 and confirmed from 1985 to 1988 a stubbornly incompetent decision not to have what we had despite ourselves. The revealed IP survived, secure in its camouflaging dispersal. It bore the telltale marks of design by a committee of senile Washington lobbyists, advised by Asian exporters, if one looked closely at its elements and effects. These were not easily assessed, scattered as they were. Also deployed was a congeries of state and local industrial policies aspiring to shape industrial structure.

Taken together, this revealed IP was not what anyone on any side of the issue had wanted. That it was there at all represented defeat for one school. That it fell so far short of strategic purpose or positive effect handed defeat to everyone else and the public at large. Amid worldwide industrial transformation the United States was "without a standing government capacity to understand competitive dynamics and to intervene judiciously," in the succinct summary of Laura Tyson and John Zysman, with the result that "policy will remain hastily formulated in response to political pressures of the moment, without an understanding of the market issues at hand." [80]

Doubtless there had been some social learning along the way, but the tangible result of it all was a 1984 decision to deny reality and leave policy in disarray. Industrial Policy had been rebuffed; Industrial Policy bestrode the economy, effectively concealed, scattered, untransparent, unacknowledged, unmanaged.

Everyone had lost the Industrial Policy debate.


### Understanding Policy Failure: A Case Study

How to explain this policy outcome? A good place to begin is with U.S. public policy history, which discloses many precedents for this decision to disavow, ignore, and nonmanage important cross-agency policy areas. Similar decisions had been reached after lengthy debate over urban development (result: no National Urban Policy), national growth (no National Growth or Population Policy), energy (no National Energy Policy). Many interests were best served by this choice of scatteration and avoidance, which is a major reason the system so often chooses it. But the configuration of forces at work is not always the same.

In the case of Industrial Policy, a president of the United States was opposed to every form the idea took, out of ideological convictions widely shared and at the peak of their influence. As the IP idea gained momentum, Ronald Reagan, in his first and most puissant phase, headed an administration animated by remarkable ideological agreement. Also, skepticism about this protean new idea was broadly based, ranging out to business and the Academy, to well-known Democratic economists at the

Brookings Institution. The Democratic presidential nominee and the House Democratic leadership, initially receptive or enthusiastic, either rejected the Industrial Policy idea by the spring of 1984, or shunned it because so many other people seem to be doing so.

With hindsight, it might be said that proponents did not appreciate how inaccessible this IP concept was to casual and even some serious listeners. This complex, many-versioned idea with its awkward, conversation-chilling name was difficult to shape to the needs of electoral politics, where, unfortunately, its friends first wished to use it. When simplified, and attributed magical powers, IP raised suspicion among intelligent and cautious people. If described in its complexities, possible variations, and inherent limitations, it was politically enfeebled and soon glazing to the layperson's eyes. Correctly understood, Industrial Policy was no magic bullet and produced its results slowly. It could carry only part of the burden of economic policy influence; even Robert Reich would suggest only 40 percent.

Yet IP, even if exerting up to 40 percent of the government's economic influencing, was a boldly interventionist 40 percent, expressing a degree of economic nationalism not associated with the 60 percent of measures that were macroeconomic. Thus it aroused novel hopes and fears at the same time. The idea of realigning the policies in quadrant 4 for a greater degree of government-business cooperation and a more strategic cast implied a move toward a large change in political economy. Such innovations, in the American setting, tend not to come without crisis. But no crisis came, or none was broadly perceived, in the Reagan years. If American industry was weakening and the overall economy with it, it was dying by a thousand cuts, in Lester Thurow's metaphor, in critical condition without a crisis.

These obstacles in the path of the IP idea still seem an insufficient explanation for what happened—or did not happen. The economy shook off the deep recession of 1981–82, the auto industry became profitable again, and the steel industry stabilized as a viable cripple behind import restrictions and "voluntary" foreign restraint. Even in the election year, however, distress lingered in communities dependent upon plants making farm machinery, steel, machine tools; agriculture reported high bankruptcy rates; even the Silicon Valley's computer chip industry reported red ink and declining sales. There was bad news enough to nourish the search for non-Reaganite general strategies for what must be done, and the swelling IP debate was the result. It remains to be explained why this new idea, on which so much attention had been lavished, fell out of discussion as quickly as it did.

For the Industrial Policy concept in one form or another was convincing, or at least appealing, to many people. Journalists and other pundits thought it exactly suited to the Democrats' needs in the 1980s. In one version or another, it was embraced by heads of corporations and unions, academics, by one count 17 separate study commissions, and for a time, ardently, by Walter Mondale and most of the other Democratic presidential hopefuls.

On the way to the election, however, the Industrial Policy idea in all of its forms passed through a forum of intense public debate. Under intellectual attack, its support eroded among Democrats, who presumably sensed enthusiasm waning also among the public at large, as the Rhode Island vote could be interpreted. The concept of IP, in 1980 fresh and promising, had by 1984 come to be broadly seen as somehow implausible or dubious. By mid-1984 business-oriented task forces and publicists were converging on the hope of an industrial strategy to apply to all sectors. Yet, recognizing the persistence of sectoral policies and that some sectors were more important than others, 17 groups had urged the creation of a mechanism for systematic analysis of industrial policies and issues. The policy machinery at the outer edges was moving toward a rational choice, to take the process steps required to understand the substantive alternatives.

By then it was campaign season, and there was no political opening. Decision would not follow from or be based on the emerging centrist agreement among involved elites from capital, labor, politics, and the Academy. "The government," the ultimate policy deciders, did not respond to the first-stage consensus that had materialized; it did nothing.

### History: Policy Arbiter with a Bias

The facts of the IP debate do not fully explain why this new idea collapsed so quickly. History holds the missing key to these nondecisions.

In the most obvious sense, Americans' traditional suspicion of the state has throughout the history of the republic worked against the evolution toward more social management, a more planned polity. Industrial Policy was a form of planning, and the ancient antiplanning heritage was especially robust in the 1980s.

History leaned against the IP wind in other ways. The years from the end of World War II to 1980 provided a long experience of unchallenged industrial preeminence, and the nation was profoundly unready for sustained difficulties generated by overseas industrial competitors. Nearly half a century had entrenched the habit of orienting public policy toward the population seen as consumers rather than producers. All the new economic policy framework ideas—IP, Industrial Strategy, and Competitiveness—asked for radical change in that habit, and none made much headway in the first half of the 1980s.

Also a handicap, to Industrial Policy especially, was the inherited American view of "government . . . as a referee and not a player, coach, or manager."[81]

These legacies of the American past shaped this policy debate, as all others. History exerted its influence here as the past itself: a stream of national values and behavior still containing much hostility to planning, assumptions of national invincibility, and policy preoccupation with consumer demand and jobs rather than the engines of development on the supply side. Their influence was evident to contemporaries, especially to frustrated industrial planners who felt their constraints.

Yet the debate also exposed the influence of history in a form not acknowledged and rarely recognized even by students of the policy process—another and little-studied form of past-power, the past as source of half-baked "lessons" with which to pummel an ill-prepared opponent and befuddle an ignorant public. And this form of history's engagement was not a neutral player as the status quo was assaulted by reformers.

## History Teachings in the IP Debate

Throughout this episode the many lessons of the past were used like stepping-stones through the cataracts of debate about industrial decline and remedial policy. The primary usage was a resort to simplistic analogy, some event from American or overseas history said to "prove" that Industrial Policy would or would not work. In this mode, history was marshaled for battle, its troops of analogies reinforcing the soldiers of ideology. Sharply pointed history lessons were launched from all sides and, based on identical events, were used to defend antithetical propositions.

The most successful wielder of history in this dispute was the ideology of Government Can't. It was composed of several connected convictions: that IP meant bigger government, especially more attempts at picking winners and salvaging losers; that government doesn't work, especially in guiding economic development; that markets do this work efficiently; and that if we defeat the IP idea (and the Democrats, which is virtually the same thing), IP and industrial policies will not happen. Then the economy will return to Number Oneness.

Such views could have been stated simply as truths derived from economic principles, unvarying in all times and places. Indeed, this was done, but neoclassical economic ideology is arid stuff. Even its adherents understand by now that in American public life most people simply do not believe or understand the true principles underlying the capitalist system.

To the rescue, an indispensable ally—history analogies, lending a hand with potent, compact lessons. The past as it turns out, is a compliant ally, and willingly allows itself to teach or be said to teach the same truths as our economic and political faiths. But it has the authority of real life, of the experiences of our forebears. Many arguers in the IP debate called upon history in this way, and on all sides—from adoption to rejection—of the issue.

The weight of the past eventually was to press more heavily on the scales of discouragement and rejection than on those of encouragement and experimentation. History lessons smothered IP in its maximalist versions, but also in the minimalist forms, even as a mechanism for Industrial Policy analysis.

Does history indeed teach those lessons, and does it teach in these ways?

# PART III

# The Past Speaking to the Future

# CHAPTER 11

# Using and Misusing History

Who controls the past controls the future: who controls the
present controls the past.

George Orwell, *1984*

One would expect people to remember the past and imagine
the future. But in fact, when discoursing or writing about history, they imagine it in terms of their own experience, and
when trying to gauge the future they cite supposed analogies
from the past; 'til, by a double process of repetition, they
imagine the past and remember the future.

Sir Lewis Namier, *Conflicts*

In the end, the question on which Industrial Policy pivoted was whether
the industrial structure of particular places (nations, regions within nations) should be determined by the existing, market-government mix of
forces or, given the results being produced, by a more explicit, purposeful
one. The decision to drift with the status quo may not, in the perspective
of time, rank as high as other policy fumblings of the 1980s—the costly
confusions carried into Central America, the Star Wars delusion, the irresponsible resort to foreign-financed deficits to postpone hard budgetary
choices. But an opportunity to begin sustained scrutiny of what we were
doing beneath the hypocritical denials was rebuffed, during a debate
flawed by myths, amnesia, ignorance, and, above all, simplistic brandish-
ing of historical analogies. The result was a policy impasse satisfactory to
no one. It was a story of postponement that allowed protectionism to
flourish and industrial decay to find many new niches. Explaining this
postponement leads us to the role of history lessons.

## The Dangers of Analogizing

We begin life learning that history teaches by analogy. When we encounter something similar to remembered experience, we form a picture of

what should come next. Experience, however, also makes us aware that reasoning by simple analogy—expecting past outcomes to predict future ones—is tricky business. When Heraclitus observed that we can never step twice into the same river, he simply took note that nothing is ever the same as it was. Rivers change, as does the self who crosses them. Mark Twain provided yet another lesson: "We should be careful to get out of an experience only the wisdom that is in it—and stop there, lest we be like the cat that sits down on a hot stove lid. She will never sit down on a hot stove lid again—and that is well, but also she will never sit down on a cold one."[1] The cat misused the comparative method, of which the historical analogy is one form; it analogized. The cat used one experience to predict all future ones.

The value of an analogy depends crucially upon our understanding of its limits, and our vocabulary betrays a widespread confusion. To say "History proves . . ." rather than "History suggests . . ." is to make a fraudulent claim. "No amount of analogy can prove anything in history," commented British historian G. R. Elton.[2] Similar conditions are followed by similar outcomes only when the entire web of causation is immune to any change—or when some changes exactly offset others. Since change is pervasive, relentless, and rarely exactly offsetting, analogies between past and future events are inherently risky as predictors.

It seems odd that we are not more suspicious of analogies, since we employ them lavishly in the effort to manipulate the thoughts and actions of others. At the extreme, Aristotle considered that history was not a valid form of reasoning and regarded it as fit only for the arts of deliberate persuasion.[3] A deft and plausible analogy to some past event had the value of instantly legitimating one's own position and piling a burden of proof upon the opponent. Similarly, Richard Neustadt has said that people employ analogies only to persuade others or for personal comfort; they use analogies as "battering rams or Linus' blankets."[4] Either way, repeated often enough, they become myths.

## The New History of History's Misuses

Neustadt's and Aristotle's disdain notwithstanding, the persistence of analogies in the arsenal of rhetoric offers impressive evidence that minds are moved, or thought to be moved, by historical analogy. In public policymaking, as we have already seen, they surface in predecision rhetoric (in which the uncommitted are manipulated), as well as during and after the decision, as justification. Arthur Schlesinger, Jr., has commented that the question whether historical references are "the source of policies, or . . . the source of arguments designed to vindicate policies adopted for antecedent reasons" is "in the abstract, insoluble."[5] To discover whether ideas about what history teaches function as legitimaters to persuade, or as foundations of decision, we must look to particular cases.

Fortunately, there is a growing body of research on the question. In 1972, in his pioneering *Lessons of the Past,* Harvard historian Ernest R. May analyzed the misuses of history in presidential decision making from the 1930s to the Vietnam intervention, where he found a long series of foreign policy miscalculations rooted in faulty analogies.[6] May penetrated beyond the official rationales found in state papers, where references to history might be dismissed as mere rhetoric, with no connection to the structure of thought of those in power. He assessed also the internal and informal evidence, where there was far less necessity for dissimulation. Here, unmistakably, history lessons shaped decisions. Later, they appeared again as rationales, for public consumption. Either way, history became a steady source of mistaken policy. In 1986 May and Neustadt, in *Thinking in Time,* greatly expanded the analysis and surveyed more than 30 other cases.[7] A handful were examples of astute learning from the past, as in Franklin D. Roosevelt's handling of the politics of Social Security. Most, however, involved mistakes with varying degrees of costliness.

Occasionally a leader was led into error by knowing little history and making little pretense of thinking historically. Jimmy Carter's administration, for example, commenced work with the mistaken assumption that his "First Hundred Days" would, like Roosevelt's in the spring of 1933, afford an opportunity for quick passage of a large reform program. The administration's secret formulation of an energy plan demonstrated a simpler kind of blunder: ignorance of relevant history. Any knowledge at all of the history of relations between the federal government and the fossil fuels industries would have reminded energy planners that extensive consultative mechanisms linked government and petroleum industry executives through half a century of federal regulation and subsidy. Of all U.S. industries, petroleum and coal mining, and the congressional committees that guarded policy in the energy area, were the least likely to respond to administrative fiat. Carter broke with that heritage tradition of consultation without even knowing it, let alone estimating the costs.[8]

In the majority of cases, however, faulty analogy was the root of error. There was Harry Truman's misjudgment that in Korea he faced a situation similar to Hitler's challenge, which the Allies mishandled at Munich; Lyndon B. Johnson's unsuccessful struggle to escape entanglement in a Vietnam conflict that to him, his advisers, and the public looked very much like the China whose "loss" had hurt the Democrats so badly in 1949; Gerald R. Ford's mistake in the swine flu inoculation program as he took advice from a medical bureaucracy whose most influential memory (unknown to Ford) was the great (and "preventable") influenza epidemic of 1918.

The May and Neustadt books are mainstays in the growing number of studies on the influence of historical assumptions in American policy-making—notably in the areas of constitutional law, social welfare, and immigration policy.[9]

More important perhaps than any books in alerting the public to the mischievous powers of history lessons has been the presidential performance of Ronald Reagan. He was the master of using simple history lessons in political rhetoric, especially in attaching the blame for every social ailment from recession to welfare fraud to any liberal Democrat of whatever age and background. Of course, any politician's rhetoric bristles with references to the glories of the past, back to which he can lead us, and to the recent disasters brought upon us by his opponent's policies. But it was soon obvious to even casual observers that Reagan used history not merely to persuade but also to reach decisions. He appeared to decide most questions by reference to simple analogies to a few deep-seated and unexamined memories or near-memories. Often these had to do with national events, but more typically they derived from his own personal past.

We will better understand Reagan's mentality when time opens the archives and permits more studied appraisals, but his early biographers have made a beginning. Central American policy appears to have been at the center of the president's attention, and he was guided there by applied history of his own fashioning. "In an administration where analogy too often substitutes for thought," wrote Reagan biographer Lou Cannon in the spring of 1985, the Nicaraguan rebel forces labeled "contras" were, in the president's mind as well as in his rhetoric, "likened to the Founding Fathers, the Hungarian Freedom Fighters, and the French Resistance." This was because Reagan "is a romantic who looks at the ill-trained and not necessarily democratic contra forces and sees the Continental armies at Valley Forge."[10] Reagan's mind, in former budget director David Stockman's observation, did not take its direction from a plan or blueprint, but from certain interpretations of his own experience, which found sufficient substantiation if "validated by an anecdote from his personal history."[11]

Those who would understand how the White House remained fixated upon the battle to overturn an isolated Marxist regime in a small, poor country while our own economy slid deeper into a chasm of debt and industrial weakness will need an ear for the pivotal analogies that aligned the Reagan mentality. In a 1986 speech on the counterrevolutionary "contras" upon whom the administration lavished such ill-advised and occasionally illegal succor, Reagan specified the sort of history he steered by. His own presidency should be seen as a campaign in an old struggle that began with the Truman Doctrine, whereby a president acted "just in time to save that country from the closing grip of a Communist tyranny." John F. Kennedy was told by Clare Booth Luce, Reagan recalled, that the only question to be asked of his presidency was whether he "stopped the Communists" or not.[12] Luce, no historian, had, in Reagan's view, asked the only historical question that mattered, and it was one Reagan wished to answer in the affirmative in Nicaragua. As Kant observed in his *Critique of Pure Reason*, "All error has its origin in resemblance."

### "The Terrible Burden of the Past"

Given the misuses made of history in policy formulation, one wonders if reflection upon the past helps human decision making, particularly in times of rapid change. The historian Herbert Butterfield, in pondering the animosities sweeping through Ireland and their nurturance by historical memory, remarked: "One must wonder sometimes whether it would not have been better if men could have . . . thrown off the terrible burden of the past, so that they could face the future without encumbrances."[13] Nearer to our own time and troubles, the Pulitzer Prize–winning historian David Donald observed that because "the age of abundance has ended" for America, the habits ingrained in us by our history make "the 'lessons' taught by the American past . . . today not merely irrelevant but dangerous."[14]

Donald's skepticism is well founded. The more we learn about the use of history lessons in policymaking, the less we are inclined to welcome their influence. The generals of policy continue to fight the last war, plunging into misjudgment by failing to understand what historian C. Vann Woodward calls "the built-in obsolescence of the lessons taught by historians."[15] Some errors induced in significant degree by misapplied history are minor and forgettable. Others are life-threatening, to individuals, groups, nations.

Americans have special reason to believe that knowing and pondering the past can inform and steady human judgment about what to do tomorrow. The men at Philadelphia in 1789 had studied what James Madison called "the fugitive and turbulent existence of . . . ancient republics," making good use of their classical educations and drawing upon the Library Company of Philadelphia's 5,000-volume collection, approximately one-third of it classified under "Memory" (history, geography). What they learned from historical studies, by their own account, helped to produce that summer of remarkable policymaking.[16]

However central to the American experience, this apparent link between historical study and sound policymaking is only one swallow, not a summer. Have humans made port more often than run upon shoals, with history as a pilot? We can say little with confidence about the balance sheet, for study of the matter has not been rigorous. Errors minor and disastrous are undeniable in the record, with various kinds of historical misuse—analogizing, mindless extrapolation of past trends, reliance upon dangerous myths, neglect of useful lessons—deeply embedded in the cumulating stratum of human decisions.

Learning from the past is difficult enough in stable times, but our own era compounds the hazards by changing the situational elements so rapidly and relentlessly. "As soon as you learn the lessons," said a political campaign consultant whose specialty is the volatile electoral behavior of Americans in the 1980s, "you lose—because the lessons always change." One of his colleagues added: "We always fight the last war. There's always an effort to apply those lessons to the next time. And the next time is not going to be like the last time."[17]

## Disciplining Analogies

Can this skepticism of analogies be carried too far? Not long ago, hearing my exposition on the dangers of analogies, the redoubtable Nelson Polsby thundered: "No land wars in Asia! Don't invade Russia in the wintertime!"

The point was well made. We direct our lives by reference to experience, by past lessons learned and stored as unexamined maxims, and we could not function otherwise. Most of these lessons, most of the time, are durably reliable. Mark Twain also reminded us that while history does not repeat itself, it sometimes rhymes. Analogies may and often do carry something useful, almost a promise, of a pattern bound to repeat.

Nevertheless, comparison of the remembered with the prospective remains important and indispensable. The future is always uncertain, and as we ponder it, like cases will and should attract us, for they have certain uses. On trivial matters not much involving the quirky human race, analogizing saves mental energy, to be expended more profitably elsewhere. The sun rises every morning, and it confirms expectations. It rises because of causal forces at work, and a time will come when those forces will change. Then, after much faithful service, the analogy will finally mislead. Few presumed past lessons, in addition, apply so reliably to the problems ahead as the rising of the sun. Analogies must be used, but prevented from becoming analogizing. How, then, do we domesticate historical comparison without analogizing into eventual error?

Ernest May and Richard Neustadt offer one simple method for disciplining analogies into aids to rational choice rather than rhetorical legitimaters of delusion. When an analogy surfaces in decision making, they suggest a parallel listing of *Ls* and *Ds*, the "Likes and Differences" between the past episode to be harvested of lessons and the future to be shaped.[18] Almost at once this interrogation undermines false analogies. Occasions initially thought to be comparable tend to bend apart, become significantly different, and at once questions frame themselves. An analogy between past and present circumstances is thus transformed from an answer machine to a question generator, inviting an analysis that reveals, not formulas for what "will work," but indications of just what is at work. We should make analogies toil for a while before acting upon any knowledge gleaned from them; be prepared for no answers at all out of certain pasts; and always expect that the history lessons large enough to stay in the net must be held as tentative and conditional goods.

### Using the Past: The R&D Record

Analogizing was the major misuse of history in the argument over industrial decline and policy response. But here and there were found more encouraging and instructive efforts to see ahead by examining analogous experience.

When the IP debate heated up, for example, the advocates of a different governmental role were much interested in enlarging and redirecting the federal R&D effort. They made frequent reference to the use of the R&D tool by Japan's Ministry of Industry and Trade as MITI piled up an enviable postwar record of winner-sponsoring. U.S. history also yielded evidence of winner-picking through federal funding of R&D in American agriculture and in support for the aerospace and computer industries. Thus IP proponents offered history lessons to embolden the developmental state. Opponents, however, called attention to the lavish waste of resources upon the French Concorde or the synfuels program, past failures that predicted a similar future.

The level of argument had stabilized at counteranalogizing. Was better history, or better application, available? In this case, it was. The exemplary historical analysis of Yale economist Richard Nelson and associates was published in the chronological middle of the first IP debate, in 1982–83.

In 1979 Nelson had been a consultant in the Carter administration's review of industrial innovation and national policy. He was struck by the "inadequate recognition that the United States has had a long history of policies aimed at stimulating innovation." Given the "progressive inconclusiveness" of recent economic theory about "the appropriate role for government" in this area, it was time to "recount some of that history and attempt to draw lessons." Seven major U.S. industries were selected for comparative study by experts who knew each industry well. Nelson drew together the "lessons from American history" in a book published in 1982 and a *Science* article (written with Richard Langlois) in 1983, comparing the U.S. experience with that of four other industrial nations.[19]

Technological innovation, so far as it is understood ("Innovation remains a rather mysterious process," wrote one student of the matter in 1978), has many identified sources.[20] These go beyond R&D efforts to include a competitive industrial structure, labor-management relations fostering creativity, and social protection of the property rights of innovators. Investment in research and development to achieve new products or production processes is, however, assigned a central if unpredictable role in innovation. Nelson concentrated on the half of all American R&D that was either conducted or paid for by the government. Here, in the richly complex record, he found examples of policy success—the U.S. semiconductor and computer industries, for example, which were "enormously helped in their early days by . . . the Department of Defense" both as a source of R&D funding and as a reliable early buyer of products.[21]

These two successful examples of sectoral targeting through R&D support fit within one of three public-sector R&D models favorably associated in the past with innovation made to run ahead of what the civilian market was producing. When the government is the user-demander, as with semiconductors, computer technology, aircraft, or Tennessee Valley

Authority high dams and generators, and its own expertise is high, government spending for in-house or contractual R&D produces effective technological innovation, and there are commercial spillovers. The success rate seemed also reasonably high in a second kind of arrangement, in which the government sponsored "generic" and nonproprietary R&D of the sort that was one or two steps away from commercialization, a space where private businesses were hesitant. A third approach was occasionally successful, a clientele-oriented—or -dominated—program of applied research such as that conducted in the agricultural sector by the vast decentralized system in place since the late nineteenth century.

Because no model always "worked," Nelson went on to mine other outcomes from history, carrying different lessons. Innovation often refused to occur when governmental spending attempted to call it forth. There was abundant historical evidence that technological innovation is erratic, cannot be reliably planned, may spurt ahead when not nurtured by governments, or may lag even though the state fertilizes innovation with funds.

The historical record also yielded up evidence that was, "for a change, unequivocal," in Nelson's words, evidence that led to a "uniquely negative" verdict on the effort of governments to engage in "picking winners" for the next round of commercial (as distinct from military) success.[22] Federal agencies without sufficient technical expertise, isolated from either the scientific community or the needs of users or both, have compiled a record heavy with frustration. The landmarks include the Supersonic Transport, the Synfuels Corporation, the housing designs promoted by the Department of Housing and Urban Development in Operation Breakthrough, and the gas-cooled nuclear reactors to which the British government was so loyal.

Emerging from a subsequent survey of experience with government-sponsored R&D programs, Nelson offered no simple generalizations. Every outcome, whether technological innovation was spurred or proved refractory, was found to be attached to the special circumstances of the industry, the technological problem, the approach chosen. In Nelson's view, history taught the state, among other things but in front of the rest, a certain humility. Innovation is irregular, a black box filled with surprises. Experience argues for hedged commitments, constant reappraisal, maintenance of options, pluralism of advice and decision makers. "It is very hard to tease out from the historical record clear-cut lessons that are applicable to future policy decisions," he confessed, though "some judgments may be offered" which political leaders eager for bold formulas would probably find "insipid."[23]

The nuanced history lesson sifted out by Nelson, probably due to be seen more as irritating than as insipid, might be summarized as, "Err on the side of caution" when committing the state to funding R&D for purposes of spurring economic development. He had shown a distinct lack of interest in pursuing one aspect of the issue, the clear evidence especially from the Japanese experience that governments can learn how to improve performance in their technology-nurturing role. If such institutional learning took place, it in itself would alter the mix of factors in the future. In Nelson's view, the U.S. executive branch "at the present time" lacked the civil service talent or the heritage of political resistance to private-sector manipulation that would encourage public managers to a more active role in economic development. He offered no suggestions for moving beyond those limitations, some of which are plainly those of time and place and not inherent in the nature of democratic regimes. Nelson implied that the histories he analyzed would constrain all future R&D policy; yet his own work, if read by the right people, might help to alter state capacity, and thus release the future to improve away from the past.[24]

### Chrysler as History Lesson

No case of industrial policymaking was more difficult for either proponents or opponents of IP to use as ammunition than that episode so recent as to preclude its proper assessment, the Chrysler Corporation bailout. In the spirited conversations of the 1980s on the proper role of government, the surest way to make even the most ideologically committed arguer uncomfortable was to raise the Chrysler case. What did it mean? It was difficult to find anyone who thought that governments should go around routinely offering federal money to protect auto company executives and their shareholders from managerial mistakes, or from being on the wrong side of market trends. By a narrow margin and after lively argument, government decided that the failing Chrysler Corporation was a special case. A company teetering on the edge of bankruptcy in 1979 was aided by the state. That company broke even in 1982, and in 1984 sold 2 million vehicles and recorded a $2.4 billion profit, paying back the government-guaranteed loans seven years ahead of schedule, in the process contributing a folk hero to the ranks of America's captains of industry.[25]

Opponents of the IP idea did not like the Chrysler episode in principle. But they were reluctant to cite the bailout as a "history proves," especially in 1983–84. There was too much evidence that, this time, government policy had "worked." Yet IP advocates were equally uneasy, hesitant to cite Chrysler as a model for the restructuring interventions they thought the state should engineer on a continuing basis. Interpretation of the episode was uncertain and slow to form. Then in 1985, declaring that the bailout was an occasion "rich enough to offer evidence, if harvested selectively, to support almost any conclusion that ideology dictates," and that "an unexamined success is a perilous precedent," Robert Reich and John Donahue produced the first substantial historical appraisal in *New Deals: The Chrysler Revival and the American System.*[26]

When a team of federal policymakers next contemplates the impending failure of a large American corporation, a collapse the government is implored to prevent, what "lessons" may they find in *New Deals?* Some readers, knowing a coauthor of the book to be perhaps the most prolific of the advocates of Industrial Policy, might have expected to find history manipulated into a marching order for federal intervention. If so, they were mistaken. We may turn to the book for useful history.

Did the bailout "work"? After narrating the history, which is in itself a good yarn charged with high stakes and strong personalities, the historians supply no simple answer. In a final chapter, "Beyond Chrysler," they offered a set of insights of uncertain applicability. The auto firm survived, prospered, added 83,900 American jobs to the economy in 1985 after the entire 1979 payroll of 121,800 had been said by some to be in jeopardy. Uncertainties cloud this employment balance sheet, for a bankruptcy workout would have spared some unknown portion of Chrysler's production facilities still in operation, even if under other ownership. The public made some profit on the deal, as things turned out, and stood in no financial risk. It was said that the government made the ordeal of negotiating the aid and reporting to the Loan Board so painful that the rescue set no attractive precedent to other firms.

Did these favorable outcomes "prove" that the government was indeed learning to monitor and bargain with troubled firms and communities for the restructuring that the marketplace sometimes could not produce? Was Chrysler an available analogy to encourage other such ad hoc rescues, or even institutionalization of the process?

This first book-length case history would not offer that as a lesson. There was too much on the other side of the ledger. The company's strong performance owed much to falling interest rates in the early 1980s and to the Reagan administration's negotiation of the "voluntary" auto export limits with Japan. The principal beneficiaries had been stockholders, management, and senior labor. The costs of Chrysler's shrinkage had fallen upon one-third of the company's workers and the communities in which they lived. "Key participants in the bailout," Reich and Donahue learned in interviews, people who should have been proud of the result and eager for its repetition, "contend that while the rescue worked this time it offers no model for other cases."[27]

Demonstrating a rare sensitivity to institutional change, which interested them more than whether economic principles had been violated, the Chrysler bailout historians asked what lessons had probably been absorbed by major actors in the American economy who were participants in or observers of this last major bailout of the 1970s. Their guesses about this were based upon scanty evidence, but they established important lines of inquiry. Bankers may have learned from the episode to turn to federal (or, in the case of the rescue of International Harvester, to state and local) government more readily as bankruptcy workouts proceeded. Labor may have briefly accepted the necessity to think more in terms of shared risks and rewards, moving a bit toward profit-sharing and board representation and away from wage demands. Federal officials who took part in the intricate negotiations may have learned that bailouts should always be conditional upon concessions by all parties, which the civil service in Treasury, Commerce, and parts of the White House were rapidly learning how to broker.

By first asking what the Chrysler bailout taught those who passed through it, Reich and Donahue were pursuing the "Likes and Differences" test. They understood that major events, especially those tinged with trauma, enter the stream of time and change the future as long as the memory of them remains alive. Different parties to the transaction remembered it differently, but on the whole the episode appears to have entered the memory of the government, company executives, suppliers, bankers, and the retained workers as a positive experience, a success. The historians arrived at another view, a mixed judgment in which the benefits of an averted major bankruptcy were offset by substantial costs and risks. One-third of the Chrysler work force was eventually discharged, and uncounted others were not hired in enterprises squeezed out of access to capital as $1.2 billion was channeled to Chrysler.

So what did history teach? If a major company again teetered on the edge of bankruptcy, policymakers after 1985 could turn to a written history of the Chrysler rescue of 1979–1983. In that story, Reich and Donahue conceded, could be found a somewhat encouraging record of how to bail out a large manufacturing corporation. The story invited emulation in at least one fundamental sense. The Carter government's tough insistence upon concessions from all parties contrasted favorably with earlier bailouts such as the Lockheed case, as well as with the Reagan administration's free gift to Chrysler (and all U.S. auto companies) of quotas on Japanese imports.

The history of Chrysler aid did not, however, tell policymakers whether to go down that road again if a major company called for help: "The Chrysler episode offers worthy lessons on how to preserve companies . . . but it is less illuminating about why—or when—we should want to." Reich and Donahue found the precedent disturbing at points, especially in the spectacle of Paul Volcker and G. William Miller bullying banks and unions to consent to economic decisions that the chairman of the Federal Reserve Board and the secretary of the Treasury were not appointed to make. Bailouts conducted by negotiation among federal officials, corporation executives, lawyers, investment and commercial bankers also leave parts of the labor force and the communities in which they reside as the unconsulted parties bearing the larger costs. Could we not, they asked, "invent other means" by which government may ease industrial adjustment, so that the risks and costs are more equitably shared? [28]

These bailout and R&D histories had yielded insights into the dynamics at work but no formulas, guiding questions but no eternal rules. These questions would be more valuable to future deciders than any summary report claiming that the government's intervention "worked" or "didn't work." Both studies had the distinguishing feature of any historical policy analysis that aspires to illuminate the future without descending to the seductions of analogizing—the appetite for specific details of each story as it moved through evolving time and shifting context.

### Useful Historians

Nelson, Reich, and Donahue, policy analysts trained in economics and law, ably reconstructed some recent policy experience for its implication for the future. These studies were unusually useful for any interested policymaker, as they were consciously shaped by an applied purpose. Near them on the shelves of the Library of Congress and other repositories of scholarship were many case histories of governmental efforts at spurring economic development in the United States. Consider only a selective sample of those policy histories published during the 1980–1985 cycle of the IP debate.

David A. Hounshell's *From the American System to Mass Production* showed that the federal armories of the early nineteenth century were the sites of much of the young republic's most influential technological innovations in manufacturing.[29] The government was quite evidently pushing economic development ahead. Innovations from the armories were disseminated through the clock, woodworking, and other early industries, extending down the decades even to farm machinery and autos, until by the end of the nineteenth century "the American System of manufacturing," as it came to be called in Europe, was ready for its run to world preeminence. But Hounshell did not urge this experience of successful industrial policy as proof that more federal armories could continue to be founts of innovation. The device had been right for its time, yet the federal government was not again able to invent a hothouse for technological innovation in the nineteenth century, despite several tries.

What of federal agricultural policy, so frequently cited as a sustained and unambiguous success? Had it been so, and what were its applications? Some IP debaters had found in the history of agricultural policy a confirmation that government could nudge troubled, "loser" industries toward world domination along the rails of R&D spending, special credit institutions, and a range of other tools. Did the agricultural historians agree? A leading scholar, Gilbert Fite, published two histories during the IP debate.[30] He depicted federal policy mostly in a beneficial role, germinating in the land-grant colleges and dispersing through the Agricultural Extension Service many of the technological and other innovations that brought such stupendous agricultural productivity in the 1980s. But this achievement was clouded by costs. Fite reported on some of them— chiefly, the painful dislodgment of millions of people from livelihoods and preferred rural habitats, with virtually no governmental buffering or transitional assistance. Another historian publishing in 1984, Pete Daniels, was even more critical of the result of the agricultural transformation engineered by national policy. The government had helped to hasten the decimation of a valuable rural culture and encouraged "larger farms, mammoth implements, killer chemicals . . . debt and bankruptcy."[31]

In agriculture, then, Washington had helped to fashion a winning industry. But the experience hardly qualified as a model for the future. Historians had amply documented the human suffering of the mass of displaced rural laborers and their dependents who attracted remedial governmental attention only fleetingly in the 1930s. Historians noticed, and environmentalists emphasized, the vulnerability of the resultant system. American agriculture in the 1980s was a sector unsustainable in anything like its current soil-eroding, petroleum-dependent, pesticide- and herbicide-addicted, monoculturally deployed forms. Policy success was entwined with policy failures.

A team of scholars at Georgetown University combined several histories in *Under Pressure: U.S. Industry and the Challenges of Structural Adjustment* (1985). In an effort to learn whether federal policies impeded or facilitated structural adjustments within industries, they studied hand tools, industrial fasteners, forgings, petrochemicals, pharmaceuticals, general aviation, and furniture. Here were seven industries, seven different policy engagements, more than seven different learnings. Scrutinized in this way, policy was graded as a mixture of "downside and upside." The government had been of much assistance (mainly through R&D) to pharmaceuticals, and the analyst of that record urged even greater support for this "basic industry." That same government had unresponsively stood aside as the Japanese took strategic aim at the industrial fastener (nuts/bolts/screws) industry in 1964 and by the early 1980s had cut its world market share in half and destroyed 7,000 jobs. This sectoral passivity in Washington was bad industrial policy, at least to the industrial fastener spokesmen who wanted more helpful involvement by the national government. The Georgetown scholars found few general lessons to be derived from this mixed set of outcomes. An import-invaded sector should be given a policy package including subsidies only where "the U.S. has a clear comparative advantage in the world market," if this can be known. Retraining the displaced labor force should receive higher priority than it did in the past.[32]

The energy sector was of surpassing importance, and two excellent histories of federal energy policy were published in the 1980s. John Clark looked at fossil fuel policies from 1900 to 1946, found their origins in energy company requests for help, and characterized the government's performance as inconsistent, uninformed by any concept of the public interest, essentially purposeless.[33] His history strongly implied that the government's weak representation of the national interest was at the root of energy policy inadequacies. Richard Vietor's history ran from 1945 to the 1980s, concluding that "the government's domestic policies for fossil fuels

generally failed" to achieve either their stated goals or any other unintended or correlative goals that appear desirable in retrospect.[34] Industrial policy in the energy industries over time reduced efficiency, brought
minimal gains in equity, failed even to stabilize the sector, and flunked
the test of promoting national security as well.

This sounded like a history lesson "against" industrial policy in any
energy sector. Not so. Vietor assumed that the energy industries and the
government would remain enmeshed, and that policy would be more
successful if both sides better understood the legitimacy of the other's role
and the limitations under which both operated. Markets are powerful,
and market-conforming methods of intervention need more emphasis in
policy formulation, since the government was going to intervene in any
event. For its part, the private sector in times of scarcity, when profits are
high, tends to forget that market failures are pervasive, because energy
corporations neglect the importance of public goods such as equity, security, or planning for the longer term. Vietor found in this history no magic
bullet for improved policymaking but expressed some hopes for more intelligent use of the sectoral advisory councils for the continuous exchange
of information and views.

Do such histories instruct the policymakers that targeting sectors
"works"? The answer seems to be that it works sometimes, in some respects, by some measures, and does "not work" at other times, in other
respects, by other measures. Industries and situations differ, and the general lessons available are few, though valuable: that an intricate meshing
of private and public has long been the reality, so that governmental sectoral policies weave their way through the daily life of production and
trade and have for decades; that such policies are rarely imposed on business but are typically cast and defined through collaboration between
capital and government, amounting to a considerable corporatist tradition
obscured by occasional spasms of conflict; that market forces, when their
power is underestimated (as it usually is), tend to flow around policy barriers and defeat policy ends. A critical variable in the success of economic
development policies is the government's administrative capacity, meaning not just an experienced and skilled civil service but also the ability to
sustain the policy effort despite changes of government.[35]

These are indispensable insights, even though they amount to an am-
ber light before the policy vehicle, rather than the simple red or green preferred by deciders in a hurry. Policy case histories, especially when
constructed over time rather than sliced horizontally out of it, deserve a

larger role in American policymaking. Had they been studied, the IP debate would have been transformed in two important respects: no one could have pretended that the United States was now choosing whether to have sectoral policies, and no one could have flatly asserted that history proves that they work, or don't work. These cul-de-sacs sealed off, greater progress might have been possible.

### Calling upon Historians

Policy case histories do not apply themselves to the future, but require interpretation. If the lay decider is busy, and a slow reader, and books are equivocal and numerous, why not call in the experts who wrote them?

In the autumn of 1983 the Business Roundtable established a task force to study and deflate this new IP idea and took the unusual step of hiring the historian William Becker, of George Washington University, to write a paper on the light shed by history. His monograph supplied the Roundtable task force with the most sophisticated and extensive analysis of the Reconstruction Finance Corporation, National Recovery Administration, and the record of tripartite industrial councils yet supplied to the Industrial Policy community. Becker would not vote "against" IP on the basis of his review; he confined himself to observing that the RFC and NRA histories, especially, were "not particularly encouraging." The task force used stronger language; reinterpreting the scholar's interpretation: "The historical experience with the allocation of capital from above . . . does not engender any optimism that the LaFalce and AFL-CIO bank proposals will be any more successful."[36]

Bringing a historian into the discussion of contemporary issues led to the idea of inviting more than one. At an advanced point in the IP debate, it finally occurred to someone that Industrial Policy was an aspect of political economy, which had a history and also historians. At an American Enterprise Institute (AEI) conference on Industrial Policy in Washington in early November 1984, two leading historians of U.S. economic policymaking in the twentieth century—Thomas McCraw of Harvard and Ellis Hawley of the University of Iowa—spoke about history's lessons, and a third—James T. Patterson of Brown—offered commentary.

Afterward I heard a cluster of staffers from Capitol Hill pronounce this first panel round of the conference a "draw." This expressed political Washington's sense at the time that the only real issue was whether to be "for" or "against" IP, and that neither side could derive any advantage from what the history experts had just said. For my part, I thought it no draw. My score was: history—99; analogizing—0.

McCraw, an expert on economic regulation, must have pleased one part of his audience and made another uneasy when he pointed out that the term *Industrial Policy* was at least a century old, and the topic itself—how national governments can advance economic progress—as old as European mercantilism. He noted that the American nation may have been born in rebellion against mercantilism but promptly began to practice state-promoted economic development itself. Until the late nineteenth century this was an uncoordinated system, with most of the action at the state level, but McCraw credited these efforts, taken as a whole, with accelerating economic development. The overall economic effect of one major policy tool over the entire national experience, the protective tariff, remains a puzzle after more than a century of study. In McCraw's view, however, the "internal improvements," or infrastructure spending urged so prominently by Alexander Hamilton and Henry Clay and funded more aggressively by the states than by the puny federal government, had helped the home market expansion that nurtured American industrialization. McCraw also concluded that antitrust activities, commencing with passage of the Sherman Act in 1890, had produced, in the prime years of industrialization (1890–1920), "a therapeutic effect, an ironic and mostly unintended promotion of efficiency." This efficiency was achieved by driving firms in certain industries toward rationalization and vertical integration rather than to the legally exposed "loose horizontal combinations" that had seemed satisfactory before antitrust laws. In these same years, he thought, federal support for agriculture accelerated beneficial change in that sector. McCraw concluded: "What were the lessons . . . ? Here the historian must become wary. Like most of my professional colleagues, I am reluctant to draw broad, present-day implications from the past. The only true lesson of history, someone once said, is that there are none. I do not believe it can be shown from historical evidence that tariffs, internal improvements, or antitrust laws are always either effective or ineffective in promoting economic growth. The result always depends upon the context."[37]

This stance should not have surprised readers of McCraw's *Prophets of Regulation,* where he had written: "All overarching theories and heroic generalizations about 'Regulation' (with a capital R) run an extremely high risk of being in error . . . Even though much of regulatory history is tinged with apparent failure, regulation cannot properly be said either to have 'failed' or 'succeeded' in an overall historical sense. Instead, individual regulatory experiences and episodes must be judged against a standard true to the particular historical moment."[38] Nor can we say, McCraw thought, that the courts had "failed." Historical reality was not captured in such generalizations. They might serve politics, but they would mislead policy. "Industrial policies" of the tariff/antitrust/internal improvements variety had sometimes been a stimulus to general economic advance, though chasteningly often in ways that had not been foreseen or intended. But even this was no unvarying lesson for tomorrow; "there are none."[39]

Ellis Hawley, author of a brilliant series of studies of the political economy in the interwar years, understood Industrial Policy to mean more than merely the sum of the government's sectoral interventions, but "a national policy aimed at developing or retrenching selected industries," with a "planning and coordinating mechanism" doing the targeting. Given this definition, and Hawley's assignment to look to the twentieth-century experience, he found that the United States in the interwar years "was not as innocent of industrial policy as is commonly assumed."[40]

For there had developed in the 1920s, nurtured by the experience of wartime mobilization, a vision held by a group of "master architects" who aimed at a new form of capitalism, a new political-economic system. The lead was taken by Herbert Hoover, both as secretary of commerce (1920–1928) and as president (1928–1932), joined by top civil servants in the Forest Service, Bureau of Mines, Geological Survey, and the Agriculture Department. These government officials developed close ties to counterparts in professional and philanthropic bodies in private life. Theirs was a vision of a capitalism rationalized and pressed more rapidly toward economic efficiency by a loose form of planning, its public policy tools a mixture of macroeconomics (improved economic statistics, countercyclical public works spending) complemented by vigorous efforts to remedy selected sectoral problems. This system turned on no planning document or agency, but rather upon, in Hawley's words, "moral leadership . . . selective technical assistance, and networks for mobilizing . . . private power." It was "something approaching what we now call industrial policy," but not "a full-fledged industrial policy apparatus" such as could be found in Japan and France after World War II.[41] But this Hoover-inspired complex resembled MITI, Hawley thought, at least in its commingling of private and public sectors, its committee and conference systems working at the task of consensus building, its corporatist tendency to establish centers of power apart from legislatures or parties.

Through this system, mechanisms for sectoral intervention were created in the 1920s for several "problem industries"—lumber, housing, oil and coal, railroad and shipping, agriculture—and among what would be called sunrise sectors such as aviation, radio, motion pictures. Did these interventions work? Hawley was willing to state that "probably they can . . . be credited with some contribution to better economic performance." But there were clear failures in coal and agriculture in the 1920s and "a tendency" for such interventions to slip from the developmental function toward protectionism.[42]

This new system did not entrench itself or become permanent. A two-term presidency for Hoover would have provided a major testing time for such sectoral interventions with their supply-side focus. Instead, the experiment was swamped by the Great Depression, for which the new system was ill matched. It yielded to a regime more willing to enlarge state power in all directions. The New Deal would expand industry-specific programs and laws, becoming even more deeply involved in the regulation and promotion of the oil, coal, shipping, transportation, and agricultural sectors. For two years under the NRA an attempt was made to manipulate wages, prices, and other elements of more than 500 industries. This was a bath of industrial policies, each administered by some interpenetration of private and public officials in corporatist mechanisms. Was this also, at last, IP, arriving in the 1930s?

Hawley would not call it that, for the pressures for intervention created a fragmented pattern, policies without central Policy. Roosevelt, who yearned to bring strategic direction to governmental activities in all fields, could not impose a planning pattern on the New Deal's sectoral involvements any more than he could for public works, land use, or other dimensions of the government's vast activities. Although the two-year experience of the NRA might be called America's first IP, Hawley correctly described it as a disjointed apparatus neither aimed at nor capable of selecting industries for boosting or retrenchment. Roosevelt's efforts to create planning mechanisms were resisted, stretched out, eventually defeated and terminated.

Hawley's survey of those 20 interwar years found "examples of microeconomic intervention that offer some encouragement for those who insist that such institutions can be effective in the American context." On the other hand, the antimanagerial, antiplanning strain in American culture remained always durable and vigorous. Absent a national crisis, industrial policy–like initiatives "have been difficult to institutionalize and legitimize." Devising and implementing Industrial Policy in the United

States "promises to be anything but an easy task," the historian noted. "One informed by such experience would seem obliged to argue . . . [for] a thorough exploration of options more compatible with the persisting antimanagerial components of America's polity and political culture."[43]

The past, they held, offered both encouragement and discouragement for both the sectoral policy activists and those who were sure that governments could not do useful work at that level. Historians had not gone so far as to say that the weight of evidence from experience rested equally on the side of the negative and the encouraging. They offered no final tally on past policies, and in any event they explicitly warned that history could not foretell the future.

Some in the Washington audience were heard to judge the experts' advice as irritatingly equivocal. Perhaps the indeterminacy of the panel of historians that November morning owed to the complexity of the issue at hand—Industrial Policy, a conceptual tropical rain forest. Perhaps the wrong historians had been invited. Or, perhaps, all historians were hopeless as advisers on the problems of today and tomorrow?

To assume so is the dominant tradition. The federal government has a long record of relying upon expert advice. Natural scientists came first, to map and survey the West and to develop new agricultural techniques; the social sciences came later, anthropologists working on Indian affairs, psychologists advising the armed services on testing or the Central Intelligence Agency on counterinsurgency, economists claiming their very own Council of Economic Advisers in 1947 and after. But historians? They have played a very minor, and intermittent, role on the edges of the policy process. Governments have called upon historians for their expertise at earlier times. President Woodrow Wilson commissioned "The Inquiry" as he prepared for the Versailles Treaty talks of 1919, and this body of scholars included historians. The "Violence Commission" headed by Milton Eisenhower arranged for a volume of historical essays as it probed the causes of the presidential assassinations and generalized violence of the late 1960s. Congress paid for a study of the history of presidential "misconduct" when pondering the Watergate scandals. John Kennedy brought a historian (Arthur M. Schlesinger, Jr.) into the White House, as did Lyndon Johnson (Eric Goldman), though in both cases they assigned the scholars to work mostly on nonhistorical duties. Ronald Reagan invited a historian (Edmund Morris) to follow him about and write a presidential biography from the inside.

These examples call attention to a sort of tradition of historians engaged with national policy. Until recently it was an intermittent tradition that probably made most historians uneasy. As the 1980s arrived, the name "public historian" had been devised to designate a growing body of trained historians working in nonacademic settings—for corporations, governments, or for general hire. Most public historians worked in archives or historic preservation, or prepared institutional biographies, but a policy role was evolving. The historians long employed by the Department of Agriculture to answer questions from the public and minor officials found themselves assessing past policies as a part of the larger decision stream. The Army, Navy, and Air Force always utilized historians to prepare studies of battle groups or bases. In the mid-1980s, however, the director of the Air Force Historical Office reported that his office was receiving more questions from and engagement with top Air Force strategists who were becoming aware of the importance of institutional memory. In the Central Intelligence Agency and the Defense Department, in the Department of Energy, the Army Corps of Engineers, and elsewhere across the federal bureaucracy, historians were engaged in work that touched the policy process. The U.S. Army gathered historians at, among other places, Fort Leavenworth, Kansas, to research battlefield lessons to guide officer training at the Center for Army Lessons Learned. Courts were increasingly hiring historians to testify as expert witnesses on everything from water law to Indian claims to whether Sears, Roebuck and Company was guilty of discriminating against women in its pay and promotion practices.[44]

A few historians and their allies have begun to press for larger policy roles. The planner Peter Hall has argued that historians should be centrally involved in the strategic planning function, for their training prepared them superbly to draft the scenarios with which planners could frame the future.[45]

Going further, historian Robert Kelley of the University of California, Santa Barbara, founder of the first graduate program to train public historians, aspired to something more permanent, wide-ranging, and close to the presidency. At his urging, a joint letter from 21 distinguished American historians went to President-elect Jimmy Carter on November 3, 1976, stating: "It is time, we believe, for the national government to begin thinking historically about the problems it must solve." This was to some extent already being done, but through "hasty and shallow . . . use," with bad analogies and inaccurately stated precedents leading to "poorly-considered policies." Professional historians were ready, as the economists had been when called upon to staff the Council of Economic

Advisers in 1946, to improve governmental use of history. One model might be a Panel of Historical Consultants to "conduct studies for you, or reach out to the profession to have them conducted . . . The historical method is now ready to be put to use as an aid to decision-making." The letter to Carter left to the future the precise delineation of functions that a council or panel might perform—preparing background papers upon request, suggesting experts to be tapped for these or other purposes, writing an annual report, writing strategic planning scenarios.[46]

### Doubts about "Court" Historians

Informally, some historians were skeptical about the idea, and happy that Jimmy Carter did not even answer the "Kelley letter." Historians should not work for government, in this view—at least, not in connection with decision making, even if some archival or case-history writing services were permissible. A Council of Historians would only embarrass the profession, either through occasional blunders or through repeated servility. This had been the result, certainly in recent years, of a Council of Economic Advisers, whose inability to foretell the future was annually evident.

And, as with the economists in Ronald Reagan's CEA especially, historians would be tempted to become, and some would become, propagandists for the regime. They would write favorable case studies of their paymasters' favorite programs; upon demand, they might even analogize, offer their professional authority that some piece of history indeed "proves." This suspicion finds some support in history, as one discovers upon reading the monographs by George Blakey (1970) and Carol Gruber (1975) on the National Board for Historical Service during World War I, which too often lent historians' expertise to the uses of governmental propaganda.[47]

Along with the anticipated compromises of professional integrity, historians aspiring to future-shaping policy roles could also expect to expose themselves to occasional ridicule. Other academic experts, serving as legislative consultants or court witnesses, have provided a spectacle of self-contradiction and absurd statements that average people know to be nonsense. This has been especially embarrassing, professionally, to psychologists and psychiatrists, whose clinical judgments are charged with being no better than those of laypeople, while both are consistently outperformed by simple actuarial calculations.[48]

To historians of this mind, it was a bit of good luck that the profession has not been invited into such activity and is not institutionalized in an office down the hall from the president, where it might be routinely consulted and certainly would be implicated in and obliged to defend decision making on public policy. Policy is, after all, an effort to peer into and manipulate the future. Some historians aggressively assert the profession's incompetence in looking forward. More, I suspect, believe that the past confers some useful wisdom to those who must make policy decisions, but would have to admit that historians have not readied themselves for policy service to the modern state, as have the "policy sciences" such as economics, political science, psychology, sociology. Historians are thinly deployed along the line of modern policy experience, and usually do not link their findings with contemporary policy concerns. Since they often shun a theoretical framework, either on principle or by habit, they tend to pile their narrative case histories atop one another without responding to the questions either of the theoretical or applied policy research community. "Their work runs along innumerable separate paths which rarely connect," two historians of social policy have recently observed.[49] These limitations are compounded when it is realized that the discipline of history in America has (probably) never been in a period of such internal confusion as the 1970s and 1980s. Historians in recent years have been increasingly divided internally as to subject matter and methodology, have lost their working consensus upon the elements of a common national story. Epistemological confusion was deepened as the deconstructionist critique raised questions whether historical accounts could possibly bear any relationship to reality.[50]

Perhaps Jimmy Carter knew that many historians were opposed to a policy role, that historian Bruce Stave spoke for his colleagues when he wrote: "Our responsibility is not to policymakers, but to laity, public, not to confirm but to be critical of the policymakers and of their political scientists."[51] The president did not answer Kelley's invitation. Governments and historians remain uneasy partners. Some policymaking bodies, finding a historian in their midst, are simply baffled. Historian John Demos, appointed to the Carnegie Council on Children, found that no one, including himself, knew what to do with his expertise, which "seemed inherently less practical, more diffuse, and more esoteric than the others" and "to lead nowhere in particular." Indeed, they hardly seemed to need him, as the other council members usually opened a new line of discussion with their own "historical preface" which invariably served to legitimize some policy option about to be endorsed.[52]

Some policymakers are more actively hostile to historians than this. "Historians are dangerous, and capable of turning everything topsy-turvy. They have to be watched," said Nikita Khrushchev in 1956.[53] "When I have a problem, I want it addressed," was one executive's terse summary of why that type of academic should not be invited to assist in corporate policymaking: "Historians bleed too much."[54] This must refer to the academicians' alleged inability to move quickly to decision without lengthy pondering of every relevant fact, combined with the assumption that all historian-experts are academicians, which is no longer true. The depth of politicians' skepticism about the usefulness of historians was revealed when Congressman Claude Pepper in 1982 urged the House to establish the office of House Historian. A long dispute ensued, and many objections piled up—not all of them budgetary. One member confessed that he could not tell from the debate "whether we are talking about hiring a historian or a PR man or a psychiatrist." "All we are asking is one historian," Pepper protested. The vote was 230 to 97 against.[55]

## History, with or without Historians, in Policymaking

Despite reservations on both sides, the collaboration is expanding. Both the formal, institutionalized policy engagement of historians and their role as critics of policy substance and policy logic are on the increase. Historians have many useful roles as a consequence—archival management, preparation of institutional histories and custody of institutional memory, scenario building with planners, interrogation of visible and invisible analogies.

Yet wherever historical expertise is located in and around the policy process, the lay deciders will be the end-users of historical insight and will not be especially deferential to this new set of experts. When the subject is atomic physics, or the molecular biology at the foundation of genetic engineering, inexpert politicians rarely attempt to construct independent view of the science itself. Yet when the lessons of the recent and remembered past arrive in the stream of deciding—which is every time, and from front to end of it—policymakers show no reluctance to practice history interpretation without a license or much thought of the need for expert assistance. However significant the advisory role that might ever be accorded historical expertise, the lay policymaker will operate from Everyman's confidence in herself as historical interpreter. Given this reality, the first line of improvement, and the last, lies in lay education.

Sound education in the liberal arts has long been advised as a way of deepening "the historical perspective" of all citizens, especially those making policy decisions. Going one step closer to the realm of policy decision, in some of the graduate schools of public policy and schools of business, most notably at Harvard and the University of North Carolina at Chapel Hill, the policy uses of history are directly addressed in the curricula, engaging that still-neglected question: How is the lay decider to apply—and, avoid misapplying—history, to his or her choices? [56]

How, indeed, could the misapplication of history have been avoided in the matter of what was once called Industrial Policy? And if policymakers will have other chances, how to apply the lessons of experience?

CHAPTER 12

# Improving on the 1980s

The Democratic State has yet to be equipped for carrying
those enormous burdens of administration which the needs of
this industrial age are so fast accumulating.

Woodrow Wilson,
"Science of Administration"

Inept and failing national policy sometimes seemed the defining theme of
the 1980s. It took the form of postponement of what was plainly required
and not technically formidable (reining in budgetary imbalance, bringing
illegal immigration under control), willful neglect of what was known to
be just over the horizon (energy shortages, global warming, doubling of
world population), and outright error (Central American policy, savings
and loan regulation). Industrial policymaking was another such area of
inferior performance, though overshadowed by macroeconomic policy
ineptitude. National policy in both cases drifted, in the midst of a global
economic transformation. The hive of industrial policies in quadrant 4,
along with the macroeconomic policies in quadrant 3 (see Figure 1),
remained beyond the reach of increasingly numerous and frustrated reformers. The shift to the congenially nonpartisan terminology of competitiveness did not produce a sense of direction to economic policy during
Reagan's second term, and the drift continued under his successor. The
economic erosion went on, the eventual price of correction piling higher.

The search for better results in this and other important policy logjams
preoccupies many minds. Improvement will come, analysts tell us, after
changes in electoral processes, or in quality of leadership, or in the Constitution itself, or in societal values, or other variables much argued about.
It is the special focus of this book to direct attention toward a neglected
zone of trouble, and hence of potential improvement: our way of using
history. The failings and increasingly erratic quality of the American policy and political systems have many sources, but a major and little-
appreciated source of mistakes is too much of one way of using history,
and too little of other, less familiar ways.

### Less of One Kind of History, More of Another

Imagine an Industrial Policy debate in a policy community wiser in the hazards, and benefits, of history-using.

It is 1979–80 again. *Business Week* or an enthusiastic investment banker from New York spurs a discussion by declaring that the federal government should orchestrate a regeneration of older industries and the spawning of tomorrow's champions, thus restoring unchallenged American number-oneness through Industrial Policy. Both American and Japanese histories, it is asserted, "prove" this goal to be within reach.

The claims of these early advocates of a new idea are met with universal skepticism. It is not that the policy community knows the cited history lessons to be false—stories of gloriously successful RFCs, agricultural nurturings, computer industries coaxed into life in the United States, and, in Japan, MITI miracles end to end. The policy community does not know much U.S. history, and virtually nothing of Japan, past or present. The skeptical reception has a sturdier basis. Just as everyone knows by now that the world is not flat, every participant in American policymaking, from the electorate inward through the rings of policy analysts to congresspersons, knows that history does not "prove" anything about the future. Any legislator who can recite the Pledge of Allegiance is equally ready on the floor of Congress with rules for history-using: "As a noted historian has said, no amount of analogy can prove anything about the future," or, "At times like these we must remember the words of a great historian, when he said: 'Lessons of the past! An unfortunate phrase which so clutters the field and misleads that the idea that history either "teaches" or "portends" deserves instant death.'"[1] We may be congresspersons or staff, one heard them say, but we are not dummies, to be swayed by theories that the past predicts the future. For even if the past is as you say, hot stove lids may have cooled.

Yet the new idea, the discovery of the existence of industrial policies and the notion that they are of unsuspected potential importance, deserves a better introduction. For the concept fills a need, providing a necessary terminology for discussing something visible in Japan and Europe but hidden and denied in the United States. The concept has work to do, but it must come forward more responsibly. Given the widespread skepticism about future-predicting based upon historical analogies, those who wish to make claims for or against the new idea must cast their arguments, especially the history-based arguments, in a more discriminating way. Proponents of IP quickly recognize this, and one hears a different message: "On balance, and more often than not, the government's resort to industrial policies in the past has spurred economic development ahead of market outcomes, or around them. The implication of this is that these experiences, while they do not predict their repetition, do invite confidence in similar policy initiatives today, a time when we badly need a strategic approach to industrial structure."

Here is a proposition that deserves examination. So is the counterclaim which is immediately heard, that the historical pattern on balance is not as has been asserted, but displays mostly disappointing results. The nature and implications of sectoral policy experience are at issue—what that history is, whether it contains guidance for this different world today and tomorrow.

In these terms the IP concept goes forward into a broadening discussion. Do sector-specific policies have a long history in the United States, and have they mostly "worked" or "not worked"? More important to decision makers, what does this evidence suggest about our options today?

The policy community is not defenseless before rival and contradictory historical claims from journalists, bankers, and other glib analogizers. Historians are at once called upon, since laypeople are soon over their heads in these references to distant events. Historians are no longer foreign to policymaking and thus unready to bring their expertise to bear. U.S. history, they find and communicate, contains hundreds upon hundreds of industrial policies with a wide variety of outcomes, intended and unintended.

Intervening in sectoral development turns out to have been an ancient habit for American governments, federal and state. If the question is whether they "worked" or "did not work," research already done on them allows us to say that the answer is mixed—if by "work" one means achieving congressional ends. There are some interesting patterns in both successful and disappointing outcomes, and therefore something to be learned there for those not seeking formulas. In any event, now that industrial policies are out of the closet it does not take a historian to find them still swarming about even in the Washington of Ronald Reagan and especially in the states, and they seem likely to continue with us for a long time.

Now what path to take? A fragmented entity has been identified in the United States, and official versions of it are visible abroad. Many of our economic ills are laid to the interaction of these, some foreigners having learned to do well what we deny doing at all. Should something new be done with our sectoral interventions, something strategic instead of the piecemeal tinkering of the past? What are the likely gains, risks, the most promising procedures?

Cautiously seeking common ground, 17 citizens' task forces propose "process reforms" to institutionalize the analysis of this elusive new animal, to provide a vantage point from which to gain oversight. Since there is no consensus on what the nation's Industrial Policy ought to do, we should be able to agree that the de facto IP is in fact doing something, daily, *faute de mieux,* and ought to be brought under scrutiny and control. The status quo is unacceptable, both to those who would scale these creatures back and/or change them, and to those who would enlarge and/or change the role of sectoral intervention. Both lack the means. No one is in charge, and the official policy is denial, so that there can be no effective scaling back, or enlarging, or redirecting. Without process reforms, the government's sectoral policies are in hiding. They are collected in one place only at the level of the corporation, which encounters governmental policy as focused upon itself, where the product or service is created and sold. But in Washington sectoral policies are streams of law and administrative rule-making cutting across departments and agencies, never focused, thus eluding overall analysis and management. A new management regime is the first step toward whatever strategy one favors with regard to sectoral targeting. The scalers-back would gain the institutional means to grasp and shrink this dispersed de facto IP when their moment of authority arrives, or the activists gain the means to expand it, given their turn. Either way, there is a need to see the quarry out in the open.

*What* process reforms? Here at last we begin that long-delayed and necessary American debate over Industrial Policy—not whether but how to manage this scattered activity. Proposals are heard for the analytical capability to assess industrial sectors. The Department of Commerce has a base that might be expanded; CEA might take on such an assignment, or a new cabinet department, a "blue-eyed MITI." The president also needs policy coordination, some form of Council, built around sectors rather than around trade, or science and technology, or the defense-industrial base. Congress, lacking a composite view of industrial sectors, needs an appropriate committee structure. Those who cherish transparency for any number of good reasons want a reporting cycle, from executive branch units to Congress and public.

Beyond analysis and coordination of these long-standing and uncoordinated activities, some propose tripartite institutions for the exchange of information between private and public sectors, versions of Iacocca's "little old Forum" where visions of the industrial future might take form. Since certain sunrise technologies and their resultant industries are now understood to be so important to national security that DARPA nurtures them with no clear mandate, a "civilian DARPA" is proposed. The absence of an effective mechanism to analyze foreign investment for potential harm to the U.S. industrial portfolio finds critics with institutional suggestions. Since the diffusion of technological innovation is acknowledged as an American weakness, an "industrial extension service" commends itself.

All such institutional innovations remain within the boundaries of minimalist IP—emphasizing analysis, some taking the next step to coordination, but advisory rather than operating responsibilities for Council and Forum and modest, exploratory aspirations. The central purpose is a "strategic audit" of economic conditions and America's industrial portfolio, such as was the foundation for decision making in states like Pennsylvania which pioneered in the entrepreneurial role. No one anywhere near the center of discussion is greatly enthusiastic about an RFC-type Bank as credit window and restructuring clinic for declining industries, or operating authority for the Forum.[2]

We have reached this point in policy understanding in five pages, while the U.S. policy system has flailed about in sterile disputes through at least three presidential terms. One difference was that no promises of president-electing, nation-saving miracles came attached to the IP idea. This was because, in our scenario, the policy community understood that such was not the historical record and, further, was not ready to believe that it would have proved anything about tomorrow even if the past held unambiguous successes. And there were no counterarguments in the form of false claims of national virginity with regard to industrial policies, since they were quickly found to be historically absurd. None of this rhetoric could survive in our imagined history-savvy political culture. This scenario was different from the story recounted in the first ten chapters here, because there was less of one kind of history, more of another.

To continue the scenario: the call for reforms to find out what our IP is and does is not accompanied by predictions of instant salvation (or damnation). Democrats see no political capital in the notion of setting up the capability for the analysis of something so complex as our national collection of sectoral policies. They accept the dictum of a foremost student of recent state-level industrial policymaking that "it is very difficult to translate economic development programs into political capital."[3] The IP idea plays no part in the presidential politics of 1983–84.

If Ronald Reagan notices these modest proposals to establish some sort of White House presidential assistant or Office of Industrial Policy Analysis with an annual report, he is told by his staff that he objects on the ground that sin in Washington should be denounced, not studied, even if after denunciation it continues to thrive within his own administration. He agrees, especially if IP analysis comes attached to some new and visible structure like a civilian DARPA doing what the military DARPA has busily been doing under Reagan's nose. In such a case, some time must pass, since, in Lester Thurow's words: "No industrial policy mechanism can work without the active support and cooperation of the President of the United States. If he is opposed or indifferent, the idea is not viable in our political structure."[4] In time the Great Ideologist passes from the scene, and some pragmatic successor quietly accepts or even endorses the idea of managing industrial policies. Most of the public pays little attention.

U.S. Industrial Policy is unchanged, in all but one aspect. Neither enlarged nor curbed, it simply has become official and institutionalized (some R&D decisions may have been shifted away from the Defense Department). As with monetary policy after the reforms of 1913 establishing the Federal Reserve System, as with environmental policy in 1969–70, when the Democrats enacted NEPA and Richard Nixon set up the Environmental Protection Agency and began a series of annual reports, Industrial Policy would be something both parties acknowledged. Institutional learning would run in a deeper, clearer channel. Scalers-back and invigorators of industrial policies would now have a framework for discussion and corrective action.

This is an improvement on what the 1980s gave us, a more advanced starting point for the 1990s. Dullards may always manage to turn improved machinery to inferior ends, and produce worse rather than better sectoral interventions. Bad industrial policies may lie ahead; certainly some poor ones lie astern. But flawed policies would now be more exposed to a larger group of interests, and responsibility for them located in a chain of command leading to the president. Sectoral interventions would become increasingly transparent, a gain for honesty and self-knowledge. Above all, the competitiveness imperative would not find quadrant 4 such uncharted and forbidden terrain.

### Industrial Policy out of Hiding—What Road Ahead?

Within the Minimalist framework the important questions can now be addressed. Instead of lingering on the question "Should we have an Industrial Policy?" there is a focus on its proper goals, how to achieve them and not go in wrong directions. Shaping the inevitable sectoral policies of the future will always be an assignment conducted amid conflicts of interest and ideology, as well as international pressures. But in this proposed rearrangement of the way in which history engages policy there will be less of one kind of history and more of another, meaning less support for ideology and more concrete and learning-oriented investigations of economic policy experience. Policy case studies are valued for the comparative questions they stimulate, for the retrieval of institutional and program memories, for reminders of the importance of concrete, ever-changing local detail.

Clearly, this scenario involves a larger role for historical expertise and little or none for analogizing for political ends. Yet the role of midwife of history's gifts can and should not be entrusted only to the experts. There is much to be taken from history that needs no such mediation.

Can we look ahead by looking back? Alice's Queen sensed as much when claiming that "it's a poor sort of memory that only works backwards." We will never be able to predict the future precisely, but there are ways of thinking about the past which promise to improve our average. When we have given up the habit of ransacking history for formulas or models, we are ready for more limited predictive benefits. These reside in the processes of thought by which the past is reconstructed and made intelligible, and are available as aids to laypeople without the mediation of experts. They are essentially the arts of positioning in time and contemporary context. In recognizing this, laypeople may appropriate from historians something more useful than their endless stories.[5]

### Positioning America in Time and Context

How do we read our place in political-economic time, and translate that positioning into insight applied to Industrial Policy decisions?

The 1980s have been a school in the globalization of economics, and in a harder subect, its implications. The mysterious chemistry of economic development has been catalyzed far outside the regions bordering the

North Atlantic. So gradually as to escape the American public's notice until the 1980s, the global stock of productive industrial-capitalist trading societies has been vastly enlarged. The world has come inside the American gates, our market for goods and even for services merging with the world market for the first time in history. "For the first time in history"— another way of saying, something for which people are ill-prepared by experience.

Now that Americans must compete across the range of industries and technologies, it is painfully evident that our recent history might be said to have unprepared us to compete with the best of our competitors, developmental states leading nations of greater social solidarity and discipline. American economic leaders cannot remember when they were not dedicated to immediate consumer gratification and short-term financial rather than institutional measures of corporate and industrial achievement. Political leaders have for half a century lacked any sense of national purpose beyond an anti-Soviet obsession with expensive imperial-military obligations attached.

In this new internationalized economy, the United States can no longer trust to luck, destiny, or inherited priorities. It must relearn how to orient its policy to national economic development in the broadest sense. Where, now, are the crucial levers on the wealth-making machinery?

The debate over Industrial Policy, as continued under the rubric of competitiveness, performed a vital service, though not with great efficiency. It located the crucial levers as the values, assumptions, and behavior at work in all the quadrants—in the private sector's social and corporate realms (quadrants 1 and 2), in the public sector's macroeconomic policies (quadrant 3), and in sectoral policies (quadrant 4).

All quadrants are not necessarily equal. Nations appear to prosper mostly because of endowments in quadrants 1 and 2, where economic performance is shaped by cultural values and private-sector institutions. Kazushi Ohkawa and Henry Rosovsky have called this "social capability," a complex endowment of cultural qualities, human institutions, and relationships whose origins and nurture they admit to be "a puzzle."[6] More than a century earlier, John Stuart Mill had identified "the moral attitudes" of the people as the heart of economic success.[7] Thrift, frugality, and honesty were the factors underlined by Nathan Rosenberg and L. E. Birdzell, Jr., in their timely 1985 study, *How the West Grew Rich*.[8] Economic and cultural historians disagree about the weight and rank order of factors, but they are in broad agreement that the foundations of strong economic performance rest in culture, that amalgam of values, institutions, and habits. The observation so often made in the 1980s, that the Japanese regard the corporation as a living institution and the Americans regard it as a fungible asset denominated in today's currency, underlined one important social trait related to national success which had little to do with and would not be easily corrected by public policy.

While all this is true, something else is also true. The sources of economic progress are multiple and, whatever may have been true before the modern era, are now government matters. The IP debate took place during a time, ironically, when errors in fiscal and regulatory (mainly S&L and banking) policy demonstrated that quadrants 3 and 4 are of large importance too. Quadrant 3 is the domain of economywide policies affecting human, physical, and liquid capital, and the legal framework imposed upon market forces. Quadrant 4 policies work through smaller, sector-specific levers and deliver results on a more extended calendar, for better or worse—which are the only two choices.

The stakes for America's future in quadrant 4 were much clearer by the end of the 1980s than at the beginning, one decided benefit of the IP debate. The nation's industrial portfolio, especially what Michael Porter has called the favorable "clustering" of advancing industries so important to comparative international strength, was being continuously decided by the interplay of markets with policies made in the United States (in Washington, and in most state capitals) and abroad.[9] Opinion was decidedly shifting as the 1990s began; former skeptics were beginning to acknowledge that, as the Japanese and others deployed their industrial policies and we deployed ours, the United States was clearly losing not only the older industries but also its edge in high technology.[10] Not only had the merchandise trade deficit surged from $26 billion in 1980 to $108 billion by 1989, totaling $863.7 across the Reagan decade, but a surplus in high-technology goods steadily shrank until the account dipped into deficit by 1986 and hovered in that zone thereafter. By the end of the 1980s only one U.S. company produced color television sets, most of them assembled in Mexico; no videocassette recorders were made in the United States, no facsimile machines, or compact disc players; a huge battle raged over semiconductors and computers.[11]

The connection between eroding strength in leading-edge industries and a declining future standard of living for Americans was evident, but it was turned into tomorrow's problem by the discovery of debt's potential as an aid to procrastination. On its borrowing and import binge in the 1980s the U.S. economy had evaded the rules, postponing the consequences. But borrowing $10 billion a month to finance imports and budget deficits was unsustainable in the long term, especially since the 1980s were the Indian summer of the oil crisis and would certainly give way to higher energy bills ahead. Our external debt, $2 trillion in 1990, was easily the largest in the world, having grown recently at an annual rate of $100–150 billion. Apart from the questions about foreign direct investment and "Who owns America?" or reductions in future living standards implied in rising levels of debt service, both slowly felt pains, there was the "hard landing" scenario. A sudden flight of foreign capital might lead to drastic dollar devaluation and inflation, followed by recession and shrinkage of the world's largest economy, a surge of global protectionism, Third World debt default, and worldwide economic catastrophe.

A happier alternative was sketched in 1988 by C. Fred Bergsten and his colleagues at the Institute for International Economics. A swing of up to $200 billion in the U.S. trade balance must occur, to stabilize or reduce the cumulating foreign-held U.S. debt, the trigger of the hard landing scenario. The means to this end was a combination of U.S. fiscal responsibility with an export drive necessarily targeted at and consciously absorbed mostly by the rich countries who should be consuming more—Japan, West Germany, and the newly industrialized Asian countries. Export gains must come mainly by expansion of the 80 percent of merchandise trade which is manufactured goods; service-sector export surpluses are small and not quickly or easily raised.[12]

To steer this course, macroeconomic corrections to shrink the internal and external deficit were an urgent priority. But if we must export more and import less, arranging this vast adjustment required not only higher private and public savings at home, but also negotiating such shifts with trading partners who—along with some domestic interests—have strong short-term interests in the status quo. U.S. trade policy must become more aggressive and strategically sophisticated, a risky new path to the traditional U.S. goal of an expanding rather than a protection- and depression-shrunk volume of world trade. As always, when trade politics assumes more visibility and importance, it pulls industrial policies and eventually the overall management of quadrant 4 out of the shadows.

## The New Trade Politics:
## At Our Initiative, Reforming Your Structure

When Congress and import-besieged elements of the business and labor communities secured passage of the trade law of 1988, the executive branch was reluctantly driven toward the concept of "managed trade," with actual export-import results rising in importance against the goal of maintaining the fragile negotiating process on which the postwar expansion of trade had rested. The "Super 301" clause forced U.S. trade officials to designate those countries with unfair trade barriers, and required retaliation if negotiations failed to bring a remedy. Brazil and India were designated, along with, inevitably, the nation that in 1989 accounted for approximately half of America's trade deficit—Japan. Alarmed at the prospect of futile negotiations with the Japanese, followed by mandatory enforcement of quotas and tariffs, clumsy tools that enriched foreign manufacturers and harmed American importers, someone in the Treasury Department revived "an old Japanese idea" for broad talks on the "structural impediments" impeding trade. The Structural Impediments Initiative (SII) brought U.S. and Japanese trade officials together early in the summer of 1989 and closed a year later. These remarkable talks appear to signal a new era.[13]

Before this, U.S. trade negotiation was a combination of a guiding strategy—the ritualistic endorsement of freer trade along with adherence to and broadening of GATT rules—and a contradictory tactic—frequent resort to bilateral sector arrangements (textiles, steel, autos) in which even the great American free trader entered into deals involving quotas and other limits on competition. Yet all our talk and all the negotiated truces did not stem the steady rise of the trade deficit, and those who in the early 1980s blamed the exchange rates confronted the fact that the dollar fell 30 percent after its high in 1985 and ended the decade at postwar lows against the yen and mark. Yet the trade deficit remained over $100 billion annually. Currency realignment did not do what it was supposed to do, and dogged insistence on enforcing and expanding GATT rules seemed to promise results only in the long run in which we are all dead.

Patience wore thin, the intellectual underpinnings of faith in the old theories eroded, and time brought the 1988 trade law, more resolute language from U.S. trade officials, and SII—the appearance, at least, of a new

U.S. strategy. Still present was the commitment to freer trade achieved through stricter enforcement of GATT rules, even broadening them to cover agriculture, financial services, intellectual property, and government procurement. These were tied up in the Uruguay round of trade talks, which might bring such laudable goals many steps closer, or throw the participating nations back into a confusion of bilateral and regional negotiations whose result no one could foresee. But newly present in the form of the SII talks were not only hard words about retaliation if Japanese markets did not accept more American-made space satellites, supercomputers, and lumber, but also a determination to pry into and expose all the dirty secrets of Japan's industrial policies. So far as can be told from press accounts, U.S. negotiators complained of laws allowing collusion among Japanese corporations in setting prices and allocating sales, and regulations protecting small-store owners from retail chains. They found themselves insisting that the Tokyo government stimulate consumer buying power, even stipulating increased spending on housing and public works. This intrusion into Japan's internal affairs was, not surprisingly, matched by Japanese criticism of ours. Their language was not published, but Japanese negotiators apparently criticized U.S. saving rates, budgetary deficits, and poorly trained and motivated workers. It seems that Japanese pressure was a large factor in forcing President Bush to reverse himself and agree to higher taxes in June 1990.[14]

Trade negotiations are transformed when conducted in this way. Once there were international issues and domestic ones; now they merge as "intermestic." Trade conflicts become tutors and critics about internal arrangements, about effective and ineffective, "fair" and "unfair" policies in quadrants 3 and 4, from fiscal to monetary to land use to antitrust to education. The SII talks, so far as can be discerned, did not place on the table the entire range of industrial policies with which we should now be familiar—R&D, taxes, loan-guarantee subsidies to particular industries, procurement. But it is difficult to see how the logic of the SII negotiations can continue to spare them. Aside from complaints about lazy workers, such talks amount to governments agreeing: we attack your quadrant 3 and 4 activities, and then you can attack ours.

If there is to be more of this in the future, the absence in the United States of Industrial Policy—managing strategies and institutions will become even more indefensible. Bilateral, regional, or GATT-level talks about "structural impediments" will always find the United States handicapped and governmental capacities asymmetrical. President Bush and

Prime Minister Toshiki Kaifu, drawn into trade talks on this rare occasion, could speak for their country's fiscal and (in Bush's case, without full authority) monetary policies. And when quadrant 4 matters come up, MITI can speak for Japanese sectoral strategies. But U.S. trade negotiators cannot confidently speak for their country's sectoral policies or objectives, not only because we officially have none but also because trade officials' authority does not include much that the Japanese (and others) will in time complain about—including R&D spending, cartels, procurements, and more. Such negotiations expose the president's lack of quadrant 4 management institutions.

Further, they beg for international rules for the harmonization of all internal policies affecting trade, rules now lacking in GATT. We have already begun discriminating between industrial policies that are acceptable and those that are not, and we cannot go very far in this direction without a sure and continuous understanding of our own sectoral interventions, which we will be obliged to defend.

A recent Twentieth Century Fund report, *The Free Trade Debate*, found the new rules unformulated but the basic principles reasonably clear. Industrial policies, we have learned, can be either zero-sum or positive-sum. Protection is the former, labor force adjustment measures are the latter, and government-spurred innovation is a gray area. When does government R&D support for exporting industries that in time threaten to destroy "basic" or "strategic" industries overseas become a reverse sort of structural impediment? What is zero-sum to one may be positive-sum to another, since the rules are not clear. In any event, it should be clear on all sides that what your trade partners should not be doing, now that we are all poking around looking for structural impediments, is devising zero-sum industrial policies down in quadrant 4.

The prospect of foreign heads of state helping to force American presidents to raise taxes when informed opinion in the U.S. had been unable to produce this much-needed result is a surprising and, one may hope, serendipitous new element in national policymaking. It has its parallel in quadrant 4. There, the menace was not presidents (and others) with no spine for fiscal responsibility, but the specter of industrial policies that were uniformly, wrongheadedly, protectionist. As economist Gary Hufbauer recently wrote, a commitment to letting the free market decide important sectoral matters, such as in what region or even in what country things will be produced, may be called the "White Knight" of the story. Governmental interference to accelerate or deflect market forces in selected sectors is "the Prince of Darkness," for these are actions "very likely to be captured by producer groups." Despite the clarity of these ancient principles, by which IP was always condemned, Hufbauer reveals how far orthodox thinking has shifted. For he conceded that the Prince was with us despite all, and, apparently remembering that economists have always acknowledged that when the ideal was unattainable the mind should turn to the second best, suggested that there might be two models of sectoral intervention. The "history of the Multifiber Agreement stands as its own warning against comparable arrangements in other sectors," he wrote of one of the Dark Princes. But recent efforts by the government to play a lead role in semiconductor industry development through Sematech, while too young to go to the jury, might represent a new, successful, not even dark model.[15]

Might the Japanese and others now be coming to the rescue, as structural impediment–type trade talks are repeated? For the weight of such talks should necessarily come down on the side of positive-sum industrial policies, preferring the adaptive and tolerating most of the innovative varieties. American industrial policymakers might gain some right-thinking allies abroad, tipping the balance from third to second best, and a not-so-Dark Prince of structural strategy.

## Assessing the Possible

Whatever party is in power with whatever agenda, our industrial policies will be under increasing pressure to become either a helpful part of a strategy that shrinks our trade deficit, or the other option, a protectionist and thus trade- and prosperity-constricting policy influence.

In view of the high stakes, some may ask, why such modest designs? If "thinking historically" suggests the institutionalization of Industrial Policy, why not large hopes for immediate, election-winning "industrial revitalization" through state-spurred development? Why not also crank up the Bank, to consolidate and give strategic thrust to the many federal and state credit programs already inhabiting the landscape of American capitalism?

A justification for choice of the minimalist position could be constructed on the grounds of political realism; Reagan's vice-president is still in the White House. But if some political transformation brought to office an energetic Roosevelt or Kennedy type with a taste for bold departures, he or she should ask: Where are we in time—economic, but also and most important for policy, governmental time?

Claims like "the government can" or its analytic equivalent, "the government can't," are hopelessly static. Governments, like other things human, move through time and do not remain the same, any more than the societies over which they preside. There is political development just as there is economic development—also political undevelopment, unraveling, declining competence. It is centrally important, in contemplating some new governmental assignment, to estimate the state's capacities for the task.

Consider two levels of American government and their oddly divergent development. The governments of the 50 states were widely credited with having made rapid strides from a general incompetence at midcentury toward modernization and efficacy, with the most rapid progress occurring in the 1960s and 1970s. It was then, not at the beginning of this curve of improvement, that states took on new responsibilities in economic development and sectoral promotion. One may hope that the industrial policy activism of the states in the 1980s may have been matched by the requisite capacity.

The opposite trend, however, is evident at the national level. The Washington government through those same decades has drifted more deeply into what political scientist James MacGregor Burns long ago called a "deadlock" in which decisive and sustained governmental interventions to shape society were increasingly unlikely.

The sources of a generalized governmental debility were a complex matter and one much discussed, with the best summary that of political scientist James Sundquist:

> For the last decade or two, the political scene has changed profoundly, and the changes all militate against governmental effectiveness. Four of the trends, all interrelated, affect the government's ability to formulate policy: the disintegration of political parties, the popularization of presidential nominations, the rejection by Congress of presidential leadership, and fragmentation of authority in Congress that prevents its development as an alternative source of policy integration and leadership. A fifth trend is the gradual deterioration of administrative capability.[16]

Even some enthusiasts of IP acknowledged the evident erosion of the abilities of the government upon which they were pressing this new task. Ira Magaziner and Robert Reich wrote in an early book advocating IP:

> The difficulties that stand in the way . . . should not be underestimated. Unlike Japan and many West European countries, the United States

lacks the tradition of an expert and independent civil service that could provide the business community and the general public with a high level of advice to achieve the sort of consensus upon which industrial policy must rest . . . consensus forming institutions in United States society have deteriorated over the last two decades. Political parties, civic organizations, religious organizations, charities, and other broad groups have been replaced in recent years by special interest organizations . . . coalitions are fleeting, attention spans are short . . . There is so much "noise" in the system . . . In short, the U.S. is not a nation of planners.[17]

These discouraging thoughts did not, in the end, discourage Magaziner and Reich. Yet even as the debate over IP advanced, the federal government's competence underwent further broad erosion. True, there was under Reagan the appearance of a remarkable purposiveness, at least in the executive branch. But the purposiveness was aimed at program-dismantling and agenda-emptying rather than at the far more difficult task of altering the surrounding society. Below the level of political appointees, the standing civil service outside the Pentagon experienced demoralizing budget and salary cuts and a steady message from the White House that most of the government was not a national asset.

A foremost student of the executive branch, Hugh Heclo, assessed the government's particular capacity for industrial policymaking during the Reagan administration, describing the lack of a core of senior civil servants with sectoral expertise and a sense of legitimate mission as a "hollow center." Microeconomic expertise had always been thin in Washington, and it was Heclo's impression that this deficiency was becoming worse through the 1980s. Many units that would have to be involved in industrial policymaking, such as the Department of Justice, had essentially none of the required economic expertise and no interest in acquiring it. Very few international trade professionals at the federal level understood the labor adjustment side of the problem. And those few civil servants who might have wished to develop the required expertise would find their task more difficult as the Reagan administration made major cuts in the operations of the Bureau of Labor Statistics, blocked BLS studies of industrial closing, and made repeated and somewhat successful efforts to reduce the gathering and distribution of economic statistics across the nondefense agencies of government.[18]

Heclo did not address the apparent enhancement of sectoral expertise in the Office of the U.S. Trade Representative (and, to a lesser degree, the International Trade Commission and the trade apparatus within Commerce) under Reagan (and Carter), where other observers found an improving grasp of industrial details and especially of Japanese industrial structure. But even in these corners of the Reagan executive branch, where technical expertise was found to improve, there prevailed the deferential governmental style that was peculiarly American (some would say, Anglo-Saxon), what two scholars of U.S. trade policies called a "basically reactive mode."[19] The trade professionals in USTR were more numerous and better informed in 1990 than in 1978 or 1968, but they resembled their predecessors in their uncertainty whether they should go beyond administering the byzantine provisions of the trade laws to, like MITI, actually decide what the strategic goals of trade policy ought to be, sector by sector and overall.

This added up to governmental machinery that, to Heclo in 1984, was slipping toward even greater incapacity for coordinating the complexities of sectoral policies. In 1986 Heclo told a reporter that Reagan "has restored the presidency as an institution after a run of basically three failed presidents," but with the important qualification that it was much easier to make the presidency appear vigorous and effective when the assignment did not include solving problems or managing the government but merely the task of exuding optimism while crippling entire agencies and programs. Reagan's achievement, then, was measured entirely in personal rather than institutional terms and precariously survived despite what Heclo bluntly called "unparalleled economic mismanagement."[20]

Shortly after this interview came the Reagan government's embarrassing disarray at the Reyjkavik summit; then the "Irangate" episode, which forced top officials, including Vice-President Bush, to declare that they had not known what was going on, and into 1988 a cascade of defense procurement scandals and weapons system cost-overruns bringing a widening recognition that the administration was incompetent even on the national security side. The CIA had clearly been out of control through most of the Reagan presidency; the president went through five national security advisers in five years, only the last (Frank Carlucci, 1987–1988) being a professional; and the secretary of state had been screened from clandestine public and private foreign policymaking.

These mileposts of incompetence in the military and national security functions were especially evident in the second term of an administration whose first four years had been made uncomfortable by news reports of bumbling at the top of and demoralization down through the Environmental Protection Agency, the Internal Revenue Service in 1985 losing thousands of taxpayers' returns and forced by budget cuts to shrink their enforcement effort, the Immigration and Naturalization Service swamped at the border where it admitted that it could detain only one in three or four illegal entrants, the usually reliable bureaucracy in the Department of Agriculture producing during Reagan's tenure two new farm program revisions that raised federal costs sixfold and failed in every major objective, the Council of Economic Advisers limping for months with only one member while the president was known to be pondering its termination. Heclo's listing of the weakening powers of the American state in the 1980s had been impressive, but incomplete and understated. Ronald Reagan, in fact, had presided over a progressive deterioration of the capacity of the state in virtually all areas of the executive branch, including even his beloved defense. The United States was moving in the stream of time, but not in a direction encouraging to the Industrial Policy ambitions swirling in the political air.

These trends toward a weakening spring of government would not be dramatically reversed by a mere presidential election in 1988 or 1992, especially one confirming a little-changed Republican party in office. A seasoned veteran of presidential struggles to improve the competence of U.S. government, Stuart Eizenstat, reminded Democrats that the Reagan changes would have considerable durability. The Californian had brought a cadre of free-market ideologues with him to Washington, and they would remain entrenched in all but the topmost levels of the federal bureaucracy, and in the surrounding policy mills, whoever was elected president in 1988. They were people with a long-term commitment that included hostility to industrial policymaking, and "any administration in the future—Democratic or Republican—will have to face a bureaucracy considerably shifted to the right, and very consciously so." It would take more than one election, Eizenstat foresaw, and more than a few years of dedicated sifting and replacing in the civil service to soften this ideological deposit within and around the Permanent Government.[21]

Equally sobering findings could be reported of Congress, which proved incapable of making the modest financial adjustments necessary to reinforce the foundations of the Social Security system, so that a national commission had to be called in for the task. The same solution was used for study of the basing mode of the MX missile, and was attempted also in order to extricate Congress from a painful and confused Central American policy dilemma, though without success. The congressional budgetary process was so infirm that in not one single year following the 1974 Budget Act was Congress able to pass all 13 appropriation bills. For fiscal 1987 it was forced to operate the entire government on continuing resolutions, while leaving a 1986 deficit of $180 billion. Three times in the 1980s a budget deadlock forced the government to shut down all but emergency services. *Time* magazine felt obliged to use its cover in late 1989 to ask, "Is Government Dead?"[22]

### "Using the Time"

Such trends strengthen the skepticism about Washington's ability suddenly to match the strategic genius of Tokyo. Stubborn facts attested to critical governmental incapacities. But what else was true? Toward the end of the Reagan era the climate of opinion seemed subtly to be changing, as if a weather front had passed through. This was, at least, the judgment of the Democratic party's presidential aspirants and of both parties' ultimate nominees, all of whom sensed public uneasiness with governmental disorder and placed considerable stress through 1987–88 upon promises to restore "competence."

The strength of this wind beginning to gust toward restoration of the national government's policy capacities will be known when historians write histories improving upon our guesses. Heclo himself did not believe that the sobering deterioration of governmental capacity must or would be irreversible. "What is is not necessarily what can be," he had written at the end of his review of governmental trends. He sensed that the historical wind might be veering around to gather behind rather than beat against the ideal of competent and activist government. As early as mid-decade there seemed to emerge among serious students of the Industrial Policy question "a recognition of the need for improving such capacities" that afforded "the common ground" on which to make some intellectual and eventually institutional progress.[23]

"You must use the time," William Diebold, Jr., had written, early in the IP discussion. He referred to the necessity that any reprieves from marketplace pressures that might be granted to national industries by government should be temporary, the time bought by policy intervention to be used for economic change. But the time should be used for political change as well; as Robert Solow saw it, study of relatively successful IP abroad indicated that "evolved organizations appear as the critical social resource."[24] The flow of time had for a decade or two been toward a deterioration of state capacity. Did the trend persist, or might it be turned another way, and used for the restoration and construction of at least some elements of governmental capability?

Here, again, Heclo suggested positive directions. The IP debate had been marred by incessant pontification about what history "proved" about the inability of U.S. national (curiously, not state and local) governments to make rational allocative decisions. We should instead, Heclo urged, "regard the capacities of government as a variable rather than as an absolute constant," regard the abundant historical episodes of policy error as counseling "prudence, not resignation," and take such steps as were both politically and "socially administrable" within the existing limitations. Those limitations themselves might be pushed outward.[25]

What were the particular capacities called for by industrial policymaking? In his view, the assignment of strategic direction of the national industrial portfolio required that the state be more purposive, knowing what it wants rather than invariably deferring to private-sector demands. It must have a "self-monitoring" capability, so that the directing center of government knows what the parts are doing, and can coordinate actions. It must have a great deal of practical knowledge of sectors, and develop "bargaining acumen," for it will be constantly calculating and allocating quids pro quo. And since Industrial Policy might be called "tough love for the economic system," there must be a systematic way for government to conduct the bargaining that must lead to those necessary concessions and adjustments that no party to the discussion would have accepted in the traditional political corridors. This implies "procedural predictability" to build trust and memory, "encouraging people to aggregate rather than merely to mobilize their interests."[26]

Heclo had some suggestions about how to move in these directions. First, undersell what might be accomplished, even in the best of circumstances, through microeconomic interventions. Probably we should not use emotion-raising words like *Industrial Policy* at all, but some "sleep-inducing" terminology such as "the management of microeconomic programs."[27] Heclo clearly preferred not to use IP again as a weapon in presidential politics. This mistake had made a lightning rod of an important policy area especially vulnerable to disruption by sharp swings in party support such as have periodically unsettled British micropolicy.

Two immediate steps he thought useful. At present, the government too frequently did not have the ability to judge the case made by claimants for sectoral assistance. Remembering that industrial policies are "not something that gets made" but "a process that gets learned," Heclo urged the creation of an analytic unit in the executive branch, and a quiet invigoration of the existing network of sectoral forums.[28] He also urged reform of the top levels of the federal civil service. This idea, born 100 years earlier, was stirring in Washington even as he wrote.[29]

I have devoted some attention to Heclo's spartanly minimalist version of an Industrial Policy not to endorse its substance but to commend the mode of reasoning which led toward it. His small beachhead for learning how to conduct the strategic industrial interventions we are now performing willy-nilly was based on a meticulous and also time-aware assessment of the state's capacities. Sensitive to time, Heclo rejected a static conception of governmental competence in favor of a learning-curve conception in which limits bequeathed by the past to the present should be regarded as something to be both respected and transcended.

More of the right kind of history use.

## Positioning the American State

Is concluding that it is time to create mechanisms (not including a Bank) to manage sectoral interventions that are now adrift and denied "nothing to get excited about," in Charles Schultze's words?

In a sense, such steps should be reassuringly familiar. The idea of moving industrial policymaking somewhat more out of congressional hands and into more technocratic and quasi-independent institutions is akin to the evolution of the tariff and of the issues of money and credit. A central and reliably exciting issue to the larger American public through the nineteenth century, the tariff from 1911 to 1934 was moved substantially out of the public mind and at another remove from congressional scrutiny. The same process of detachment took place for monetary policy beginning in 1913, with the establishment of a quasi-autonomous Federal Reserve System. Since Congress makes industrial policies now, scattering their administration across the executive branch agencies, creating a management system within the executive branch in many respects would represent a similar policy evolution. Is that exciting? If it helps to improve economic performance, promoting adjustment and innovation more often than erecting walls against change, if it leads to "tough love for the industrial system," which in our dynamic times much needs it, then this should be modestly exciting to citizens who are aware of it.

Probably this is not what Schultze had in mind. Is Industrial Policy, even in a restricted version, something more than just another shift of power over a highly technical policy area out of congressional hands and into some quasi-autonomous body or bodies floating in or near the executive branch? Is there afoot a shift in political economy, from the American "weak state" model toward "strong state" Planning—a prospect exciting to all the combatants in the debate, if in different ways?

Peter Eisinger, astute observer of the flourishing state-level experiments with "strategic economic development," found in them "a clear departure" from the weak-state model, "the seeds of a genuine transformation of the American political economy." [30]

Looking ahead on such matters is uncommonly hard. Many have seen Planning coming to the U.S. on many occasions, myself among them. All were wrong in at least their timing, though one recalls that Robert Maynard Hutchins answered a question about his error in predicting a third, nuclear war by citing the historian who turned aside a question about the French Revolution with the remark "It's too early to tell." [31] Certainly the sustained efforts of a powerful, popular president, Franklin D. Roosevelt, could not graft Planning upon the U.S. system, for when the dust of the New Deal settled a "Broker State" political economy had emerged, in journalist John Chamberlain's phrase. [32] In that system, still within the weak state model by comparison with European systems, the government did not look ahead, aiming at coherent strategic objectives. Instead, the Broker State orchestrated the conflict of organized interest groups. Washington was not the site of a government with its own purposes, but of a sort of modified marketplace, a "parallelogram of pressures" or place of political exchange where groups within the economy and society brought their special problems and bargained for state-conferred benefits. The economy aimed itself; the government's role was to ensure that it did not slow down, too much, for too long. The style of policymaking was incremental and piecemeal, the government's time horizon close in, timed to the electoral cycle. It displayed a weak sense of an overriding public interest and a deferential reliance upon the electorate's, and in particular large corporations', private agenda. It was a reactive system, flexible and responsive to its admirers, aimless and without vision to its detractors. Those who predicted that it would be replaced by Planning, as FDR had urgently wished and several of his successors in various degrees hoped for, always underestimated the momentum of our antistatist past and the power of our private agendas. The Broker State was alive and well in Washington toward the end of Reagan's presidency, by the testimony of former businessman and Reagan trade negotiator Clyde Prestowitz: "There is no government in Washington. It is just a bunch of interests." [33]

Such a statement would come as no surprise to anyone acquainted with the scholarship on the history of the American state in the industrial era. Washington, like London, has been the home of the weak-state model, as Tokyo and Paris are leading examples of capitals of strong states that have survived over a century of turbulent change. The social sources of the American preference for our own version of a weak state are formidable indeed, and their persistence should have calmed the fears of those who announced that Congressman John LaFalce and Walter Mondale were within one election of planting an Industrial Policy–led strong state upon American soil. But if reflection upon our nation's antistatist traditions also suggests continuing high levels of incompetence and the impossibility of governmental autonomy from corporations or whatever interest is thought to wield irresistible political power in the United States, consult the history again. Our weak-state historical record is filled with strong-state moments, is a past stirring with other possibilities.[34]

Remembering this should sharpen our eye for recent trends that might affect state capacity. In Hugh Heclo's list of the four capacities of government most especially called for by the industrial policymaking assignment, "purposiveness" came first. There can be no significant shift in U.S. political economy without more of it; and, as the Cold War fades, leaving U.S. national government without the only overriding purpose of the postwar era, a substitute has emerged in the form of foreigners, coming to the U.S. gates with their consumer-enriching industry and potentially skill-eroding wares. When the business cycle turns down and the borrowing party is over, a stronger sense of governmental and social purpose will surely coalesce around some form of the competitiveness theme. Many voices have all but asked for an enabling economic crisis.

The Industrial Policy debate produced talk of another necessary ingredient of a more purposive state in matters of economics, a "new consensus" on a revised public philosophy to replace that working set of priorities and convictions hammered together during the New Deal and World War II and by the 1980s in disarray. In the early 1980s, when Reagan seemed poised to overturn all the barriers to business enterprise that had been erected since the 1930s, the call for consensus most often sounded as a call to unionists and environmentalists to lay down their arms, for the state to retreat from the expensive and misguided luxuries of welfarism and to get on with being "a service sector for firms," as one writer had described the state in Japan.[35]

Consensus approached in this way produced only discord. Labor, communities, environmentalists would not consent, and formulated different industrial policies, protective of their interests. Business and civic cultures, in Robert Reich's term, seemed during the IP debate as starkly opposed as ever. Even the "business community" was not, it turned out, consensual. Older industries had a different idea of policy consensus from entrepreneurs in the Silicon Valley. How to make Industrial Policy out of such divisions?

But a close reading of the discussion reveals the gradual emergence and broadening, as the 1980s advanced, of at least an elite agreement that the contest with foreigners required some adjustment of historic positions. Much of the shifting of position came, it seems, as the left-of-center constituencies moved rightward. Democrats, especially younger ones from the South and West, liberal academics, some unionists, and others were clearly moving upon supply-side ground, which was a fundamental if quiet reorientation. Instead of always talking about jobs, which was another way of saying that workers' income was what mattered, they now agreed that the prior goal must be successful products—that is, sales and profits, to which jobs come attached. And the market was conceded to be a force to be respected, not only for its sheer power but because it transmitted signals that marked the main paths of efficiency. The new mood among liberals and workers suggested the acceptance of market-driven industrial changes—so long as labor was not expected to bear the entire brunt of the effort to compete with the Brazilians and Koreans, so long as community disruption was decently and resourcefully resisted, so long as international competition did not become a quest for which society would accept the most noxious environmental pollution, and so long as management acknowledged the efficiency gains to be had from enlarged labor-force participation and a flatter pyramid of material rewards.

If in fact it proves to be deep and enduring, this was a notable shift in social priorities on the American center-left. As for the business community, diverse as it was, there seemed to be a compensatory shift away from the demands for an absolute end of the burdens of environmental regulation and of taxation which had been heard at the beginning of the Reagan era. Those eight years nurtured a certain business realism about how much of the old order could be dismantled. Business taxes were indeed drastically lowered and unions further weakened, but environmental regulation had to be conceded an even larger place and turned over to professionals. A plant closing prenotification law was accepted by Reagan and most of the business community in the struggle around the 1988 trade bill, and one heard less about the inability of corporations to compete with Taiwanese firms allowed to pollute and to fire workers summarily. No interested party, in the end, was expected to win, or be asked to capitulate, across its entire agenda, though most of the readjustment of expectations came from liberals and labor. One could see the common ground more clearly as terminology changed. The IP idea as formulated and heard in the 1980s set people to imagining grounds of conflict, but the competitiveness idea acted as the ark that all creatures could board, two by two.

Does this degree of ideological convergence amount to an opening for policy change which was obscured by the temporary ability of a few people in the Reagan and Bush administrations to keep their fingers in the dike? Hugh Heclo, speaking as one of those who saw a small such opening, and knowing that the rallying concept of competitiveness did not eliminate sectoral policies but would necessarily have to include them, advised a disguise of soporific nomenclature and the assignment of industrial policies to a technocratic elite—nothing to get overly excited about. We could make progress on the IP question only if we depoliticized it and took the few bipartisan steps toward management on which reasonable people had already quietly agreed. This was surely astute advice, given the political climate in which Heclo assessed what was possible; but was the decision on Industrial Policy inherently a system-changing decision of large dimensions and thus inevitably ideological and available as a pivotal issue in presidential election seasons?

As we know from the debate, IP was in fact a magnet for larger ambitions than Heclo's hopes for unheralded bureaucratic beachheads. Some continued to see IP in this way even after Mondale's political judgment that it should not ride in the front of the parade. "We could try to sneak it in, pretending that nothing is being changed," thought Harvard's George Lodge, but that would create "a legitimacy gap" in which "changes will be made, but clumsily, in haste, desperation, and confusion." "The fact is that the new planning role of the state is virtually upon us," he wrote in another place,̇ "but its ideological underpinnings are still missing." In an analysis of nine countries Lodge and Ezra Vogel found that nations possessing a strong "communitarian" ideology were also the strongest trade competitors, while the U.S. and Great Britain lagged behind, encumbered by their individualistic pasts.[36]

The economic policy debates of the 1980s carried many such appeals for arousing rather than sleep-inducing language, either because an exciting big idea was needed for electing a Democratic president, or because (this was Lodge's view, and Reich's, for example) it was believed that IP without an accompanying broad shift in national priorities and habits would be both ineffective and too easily captured by defensive interests. One could also hear in the vicinity of the IP idea the sounds of a high-voltage if poorly focused current of nationalism. These impulses toward raising the stakes around the Industrial Policy concept sounded like the maximalist ambitions of an earlier time, and were unfortunate for the reception of what sounded like a partisan proposal but was actually a bipartisan discovery requiring a management decision. Organizing our industrial policies will be one step toward a newly strategic role for American government, but both distant and recent experience suggest that this aspect of the issue should not be exaggerated. Calls for firmer "ideological underpinnings" have a dated sound, as if it were still early 1983; plainly, what Lodge meant was more attuned to the evolving moment (1990), an appeal for stronger intellectual underpinnings and efforts at public education on the broader, four-quadrant competitiveness agenda.

Larger ambitions will inevitably attach themselves to the competitiveness theme, augmented by a rising tide of nationalism. Industrial Policy is but a part, with its own important, limited potential, suited at this place in time for the minimalist approach. There remain after more than a decade of discussion many knotty questions tending to confirm Heclo's sense that a period of learning and nonpartisan legitimating, on a small beachhead out of the spotlights, was in order.

Who, to take the largest of them, is to be the senior partner, corporations or the state? This was an especially difficult question in a world in which American corporations produce goods in Taiwan, Japanese firms build cars in Tennessee and California, and the largest corporations of all have no real national home or identification: "I was asked the other day about U.S. competitiveness, and I replied that I don't think about it at all," said a company president. "We at NCR [National Cash Register] think of ourselves as a globally competitive company that happens to be headquartered in the United States." In Robert Reich's words, "the struggle over trade is entering a new phase in which nations and corporations may be on different sides."[37] Governments ought to have a different agenda from corporations, an overriding one, and possess a healthy autonomy from the pressures of any interest group. Governments and citizens should remember the important partial truth in Alexander Hamilton's comment that capital is wayward and timid. The reality is that increasingly in the United States they do not. The conviction that governments have a different agenda, which only sometimes coincides with that of "American" firms, is virtually exhausted in the one of the two political parties that has sometimes put this belief forward in modern times. In the United States, corporation executives typically do not see it this way, and even governmental officials often do not. There is still work ahead to clarify "Who is Us?" (Robert Reich's phrase). Are our government's chief clients in sectoral interventions and economic development generally to be only "American" firms no matter where they locate production facilities? Or, since corporations must operate in an increasingly borderless economy while borders and what is within them remain of special importance to the nation state, should government's clients be seen primarily as entities more geographically and emotionally tied to American workers, producing communities, posterity? With such questions inadequately discussed even after a decade of debate, minimalist beginnings need not be unchallenging or wasted time.[38]

## History—Hindering the New?

This brief reconnaissance of our place in economic and political time suggests the timeliness of an explicit but minimalist Industrial Policy as a part of a competitiveness framework for U.S. economic policy generally. A reading of time and context is made to speak here for policy innovation, but of a cautious and limited sort, policy decisions to be steered more firmly by designated technocratic elites among whom business agendas may be expected to exercise a large influence. Some would call this a conservative reformist counsel, in both senses of that term. Modest changes are judged to be desirable, but even those thought possible might well be described as steps to the right, social change confined within older patterns. Those versions of IP not seen as positioned for launching are schemes for grand economic renewal through full-throttle Bank, Council, and Forum, whether led by the Rohatyns and Iacoccas or formed on the left around worker control of the workplace as well as the boardroom. Things to get excited about.

Is history always so numbing of large departures? When we find history in policymaking, shall we say of it the reverse of what Macauley once said of the American Constitution, that it is all anchor and no sail?

This is a question stitched throughout the entire fabric of human thought, and the answers we give to it tell more about our mood as we answer it than about the problem itself, which re-ensnares every generation. Many thinkers have concluded that history, meant as part of the human experience that we remember, is on balance and inherently the enemy of human daring and innovation. We may see this in classic form in Friedrich Nietzsche's 1874 essay, "On the Uses and Disadvantages of History for Life." Writing in a Germany just moving from fragmentation toward some larger unity and world role, and ardent to spark enthusiasm for moving ahead, Nietzsche wrote that "when the historical sense reigns without restraint, and all its consequences are realized, it uproots the future because it destroys illusions" with its stories of man's limits and mistakes. History "undervalues that which is becoming" and "hinders any firm resolve to attempt something new." He said this as and because European historical thought looked back to the splendor of the classical world, and thus conveyed to the nineteenth-century European mind "this paralyzing belief that humanity is already declining." [39]

The extraordinarily wide-minded economist Albert O. Hirschman has extended one of these themes, pointing out that groups and nations could not launch and carry to completion any large enterprise without what he calls "the hiding hand" that conceals from them how costly and painful the effort will be.[40] Knowing history's details would pull away the hiding hand and wring the daring out of peoples. The policy analyst Henry J. Aaron gave the complaint a new and poignant formulation, arguing in *Politics and the Professors* (1978) that social science research expressed in policy case histories is inherently a conservative force. Aaron was especially interested in the historical record of the War on Poverty, which at the time of his writing had produced a decade of studies conveying the message that the effort was a failure from the start. Such histories reinforced the coming conservative counterrevolution and its passivity with regard to the persistence of poverty. Their bias came because policy history researchers, in Aaron's view, build their careers upon the retrospective exposure of disappointing gaps between intentions and results. Policy history analysts reported on failed projects with a special relish because of professional incentives, thus helping promote an unjustified but deep skepticism about public policy itself. "The process by which [policy history] research and experimentation is created," wrote Aaron, "corrodes the kind of simple faiths on which political movements are built." A student of corporate decision making agreed. Whether embodied in research studies or in remembered experience, "the bias of history is to pessimism," wrote Professor Dick Levin of policymaking (in this case, long-range planning) in American business.[41]

These complaints express one view of the influence that knowledge of the past is said to exert upon policy. There are other ways to see the matter. Nietzsche himself saw another possibility. "We must know the right time to forget as well as the right time to remember . . . to see when it is necessary to feel historically and when unhistorically," for "we do need history for life and action," the past serving as an indispensable source of myths to nerve humanity to great deeds.[42] According to Henry Kissinger, onetime historian, his perception of the sudden possibility of a great diplomatic breakthrough in U.S.-Chinese relations in the early 1970s was based in his sense of the historical evolution of great power politics. And Franklin D. Roosevelt, architect of the New Deal era of energy and innovation, was guided through the crisis of the Great Depression by a conception of American history as an inevitable progression from the frontier individualism of the nineteenth century to a more collectivist social order capable of enforcing the husbandry of the nation's soil and forestry resources.[43]

Thinking historically about the Industrial Policy idea in the 1990s means, along with the pondering of policy histories that will not repeat, along with a relish for distinguishing detail and a suspicion of abstract theory, that we position the elements of the issue in time and context. The sense of historical positioning that commends a minimalist beginning also brings into view contextual linkages that might, in the end, excite even senior Brookings fellows.

## Economic Development and Widening Engagements

The four lines that give us the quadrants allow us to see sectoral policy's home down in quadrant 4, but they mislead by suggesting boundaries. If the planning or, as Americans prefer, strategic instinct is introduced there, will it stay modestly and unexcitingly confined there, doing the hard, slow, mostly un-newsworthy work of imagining and pursuing an ever-better industrial portfolio? Then why did Peter Eisinger conclude that state economic development policy (SED) contained the seed of a new political economy? He was not alone in seeing that economic development as an imperative has an integrative potential at least matching that of the last major goal of U.S. public officials, staying ahead of the Soviet Union. Two students of New York State argue that the new SED policy there, by contrast with the older budget policy, becomes "the vital center to which all other policy areas—budget, energy, infrastructure, environment, regulation, education and crime—had to be related."[44]

The suggestion possesses an inner logic. David Osborne, after his survey of recent state development efforts, anticipated that technological innovation "will inevitably create problems in other areas," such as job displacement, so that development policy "should ideally be complemented by a 'social adjustment' strategy to help people and communities adjust."[45] We have bits of such a "social adjustment" strategy now in a halfhearted commitment to worker retraining and in plant closing pre-notification, but larger connections might be made. "Our nation is at risk," began the April 1983 report of the National Commission on Excellence in Education: "Our once unchallenged preeminence in commerce, industry, science, and technological innovation is being overtaken by competitors throughout the world."[46] The nation's educators saw the linkage between their classrooms and any serious campaign for competitive industries. Economic power should not be seen only as a collection of corporations whose books show profits, but more broadly as based in a work force whose educational resources, cultural values, and habits of shop-floor participation make it highly innovative and attuned to the new technologies and the market they make possible. If there are 60 million functional illiterates in the United States, if our engineering schools must look abroad for more than half the students they will graduate, and if the high school dropout rate for Hispanic students is four times higher than the national average, these and other local issues or nonissues are in practice connected to any competitiveness campaign.

Linkages will be discovered in other directions. The environmentalist community chided the Industrial Policy debaters for economic planning devoid of the ecological dimensions of Americans' well-being.[47] Even as economic policy discussion reached a concurrence that a rising standard of living in the United States required a constant national upgrading of the skills of the work force, immigration policy lost control of the borders and doubled the annual population growth by admissions of chiefly low-skilled, non-English-speaking, and poorly educated migrants from the Third and Fourth Worlds. As Congress moved toward modest revision of legal immigration policy in 1989–90 it began to dawn on some of the more alert participants that a commitment to economic competitiveness was a poor fit with an immigration selection system based almost entirely on family reunification and refugee admissions, leaving only 6 percent of available visas to those selected according to labor market concerns.[48] Social policy, in all directions, was pulled toward absorption into economic development policy. If a short, minimalist step toward Industrial Policy establishes a position from which these larger connections are seen, in time this newly invigorated and focused industrial viewpoint may not be easily confined to quadrant 4. The planning regime established for industrial structure, and any created for competitiveness in general, will have some tendency to be ambitious for wider authority. Our history suggests that if this occurs it will, at some point, be something to get excited about.

### Past as Prologue: The Final Excitement of Industrial Policy

As the United States and Britain conferred in 1945 over postwar reconstruction, they agreed that expanded world trade was a central objective and fashioned a set of new institutions that proved to be aids to those ends—principally a new international monetary regime designed at Bretton Woods, and the General Agreement on Tariffs and Trade. These are familiar because still in one way or another on the scene, but a piece of that postwar design fell out of history. The International Trade Organization (ITO), sponsored by the United States and a prominent part of the Havana Charter signed by many nations in the spring of 1948, was called by President Truman in 1949 "an integral part of the larger program" and "an essential forward step." The ITO was to be the organized expression of the freer trade commitment, the secretariat without which GATT was only a series of episodic meetings at which trade officials would wrangle. The ITO was to gather information on trading nations' domestic economies, exposing the existence of cartels and other governmental policies that impeded trade expansion directly or indirectly. Its charter did not contain the term, but the ITO was plainly meant to be an instrumentality capable of analyzing industrial policies internationally so that when it came time for GATT-level bargaining there would be more on the table than the traditional tariffs and quotas and a more comprehensive approach to trade issues.[49]

There was resistance to the ITO idea in the United States, where isolationists in the Republican party expressed fear that it might become a "super-state." After the Republican victories in the congressional elections of 1950, obscured by MacArthur's retreat from the Yalu River in Korea, the U.S. government announced that it would not resubmit the ITO treaty to the Senate.

The process of industrial policymaking may yet work its way forward to that past idea, which will be a novelty only to those who have forgotten that history. A handful of IP commentators saw and said, as the debate went on, that the reality of worldwide industrial policies required an international forum in which these often-protectionist activities could be made transparent and influenced toward developmental rather than defensive forms—harmonization, it is frequently called. Presumably, though no one seems to have a clear idea of just how this would work, the GATT talks would be supplemented by a framework for pressuring all nations' industrial policies in the direction of the innovation-spurring or the adaptive type, designed to ease nations out of sectors in which comparative advantage has been lost or to agree to shrink worldwide capacity. Plainly preservationist policies would stand condemned, and judgments would have to be rendered on those subsidized export industries whose purpose was "predatory" rather than innovation-spurring. A uniform method of calculating the extent of subsidies has been suggested, as well as publicity about the negative impacts now hidden.[50] At the least there would be sustained international pressure to exert some discipline upon this tool of national policy which is so readily tilted from constructive purposes to the uses of trade warring.

Here we know we are thinking with some aid from history, for notice the ironies. Industrial Policy was resisted as a familiar augmentation of state power, but economist Charles Kindleberger has astutely argued that an international forum as sketched here, coming into being only after the United States set aside its hypocrisy and established a minimalist beginning, would represent at once an evolution toward more government internationally while permitting selective movement toward less government nationally. In that regime, many industrial policies would come under international pressure for elimination. The irony is viewed from another angle by another perceptive observer, Raymond Vernon, who pointed out that to equip ourselves to negotiate more-open markets, the United States might face the ironic necessity "first of all to equip the U.S. government with more powers for the control or promotion of foreign trade than it now possesses." The only pathway to fewer, more defensible industrial policies may turn out to be a stronger, more purposive and strategic state, itself an ironic route to a stronger international legal regime as trading neomercantilist states discover that in certain respects (in Vernon's words again) "nations are no longer very manageable as economic units."[51]

But then the eternal truth about history that so many seek is not that the past repeats itself, predicts, or "proves," but that it will surprise. This may translate to some as the ultimate caution, but it carries also an emboldening possibility, that doors may not remain always closed. This paradox, stated long ago, carries a hint of encouragement for those hoping that the way ahead is not known by those who claim certainty and who envision only small changes:

> And the end that men looked for cometh not
> And a path is there where no man thought
> So hath it fallen here.[52]

# Notes

# Index

# Notes

## Introduction

1. "Yes, We're Down," *Business Week*, December 17, 1990, p. 62; Paul Krugman, *The Age of Diminishing Expectations: U.S. Economic Policy in the 1990s* (Cambridge, Mass.: Massachusetts Institute of Technology Press, 1990).
2. Quoted in T. M. Knox, *Hegel's Philosophy of Right* (Oxford: Clarendon Press, 1942), p. 13.
3. Nelson Polsby and Geoffrey Smith, *British Government and Its Discontents* (New York: Basic Books, 1981), 171.

## 1. The New Economic Order

1. Henry Luce, Editorial, *Life*, February 17, 1941, p. 41.
2. *Economic Report of the President: 1964* (Washington, D.C.: Government Printing Office, 1965), p. 1.
3. U.S. Bureau of the Census, *Statistical Abstract of the United States: 1985* (Washington, D.C.: Government Printing Office, 1986), pp. 427–463.
4. Frank A. Weil, "The Best Defense Is a Good Economy," *Washington Post*, May 25, 1980, p. D1.
5. This discussion draws especially from Robert O. Keohane, *After Hegemony: Cooperation and Discord in the World Political Economy* (Princeton: Princeton University Press, 1984); and I. M. Destler, *American Trade Politics: System under Stress* (New York and Washington, D.C.: Twentieth Century Fund and Institute for International Economics, 1986), esp. chaps. 1 and 2.
6. This account draws especially upon Irving B. Kravis et al., eds., *World Production and Income: International Comparisons of Real Gross Product* (Baltimore: Johns Hopkins University Press, 1982); World Bank Staff, *World Bank Report, 1984* (New York: Oxford University Press, 1984); U.S. Bureau of the Census, *Statistical Abstract: 1985;* and President's Commission on Industrial Competitiveness (PCIC), *Global Competition: The New Reality,* 2 vols. (Washington, D.C.: Government Printing Office, 1985).
7. See the annual *Economic Report of the President* for the years 1977–1983 (Washington, D.C.: Government Printing Office); U.S. Department of Commerce, *International Economic Indicators* (Washington, D.C.: Government Printing Office, 1983);

PCIC, *Global Competition*; U.S. Department of Commerce, International Trade Administration, *U.S. Competitiveness in the International Economy* (Washington, D.C.: Government Printing Office, 1981); U.S. Bureau of the Census, *Statistical Abstract: 1985;* Bruce R. Scott and George C. Lodge, eds., *U.S. Competitiveness in the World Economy* (Cambridge, Mass.: Harvard Business School Press, 1985).

8. Quoted in Clyde Prestowitz, Jr., *Trading Places: How We Allowed Japan to Take the Lead* (New York: Basic Books, 1988), p. 39. Prestowitz was a U.S. trade negotiator during the early 1980s.

9. See William H. Branson, "Industrial Policy and U.S. International Trade," in *Toward a New U.S. Industrial Policy?* ed. M. L. Wachter and S. M. Wachter (Philadelphia: University of Pennsylvania Press, 1983). This discussion also draws upon the annual *Economic Report of the President,* especially for the years 1977–1983; PCIC, *Global Competition;* Scott and Lodge, *U.S. Competitiveness;* Business Week Team, *The Reindustrialization of America* (New York: McGraw-Hill, 1982); Ira Magaziner and Robert Reich, *Minding America's Business* (New York: Vintage, 1982); Paul R. Lawrence and Davis Dyer, *Renewing American Industry* (New York: Free Press, 1982); and U.S. Bureau of the Census, *Statistical Abstract of the United States: 1989* (Washington, D.C.: Government Printing Office, 1989).

10. Kissinger quoted in David Rockefeller, "America's Future: A Question of Strength and Will," *Atlantic Community Quarterly* 17 (Spring 1979), 14.

11. See especially Robert B. Reich, "Industrial Evolution," *Democracy* 3 (Summer 1983), 10–20; Scott and Lodge, *U.S. Competitiveness;* and Destler, *American Trade Politics.*

12. Destler, *American Trade Politics,* p. 76. See also Paul R. Krugman, ed., *Strategic Trade Policy and the New International Economics* (Cambridge, Mass.: MIT Press, 1986), table 9.1, pp. 212–213.

13. Joseph Schumpeter, *Capitalism, Socialism, and Democracy* (New York: Harper Brothers, 1942), p. 169.

14. See Raymond Vernon, "International Investment and International Trade in the Product Cycle," *Quarterly Journal of Economics* 80 (May 1966), 190–207.

15. See Daniel Bell, *The Coming of Post-Industrial Society* (New York: Basic Books, 1973).

16. For the comparative estimates of per capita income, see Organization for Economic Cooperation and Development (OECD), *National Accounts: Main Aggregates,* vol. I (Brussels, 1984), p. 86; also Destler, *American Trade Politics,* pp. 159–160.

17. Parsons quoted in Daniel P. Moynihan, interview, *American Heritage,* October–November 1986, p. 36.

18. Lester C. Thurow, "The Productivity Problem," *Technology Review* 83 (November–December 1980), 41.

19. For comparative productivity rates, see *Economic Report of the President: 1980* (Washington, D.C.: Government Printing Office, 1981); National Council on Employment Policy, *Labor Force and Productivity Measurements: Danger Ahead* (Washington, D.C.: Government Printing Office, 1982); Howard Leichter, "National Productivity: A Comparative Perspective," in *Productivity and Public Policy,* ed. Marc Holzer and Stuart S. Nagel (Washington, D.C.: Sage, 1984); Martin Neil Baily, "Capital, Innovation, and U.S. Productivity Growth" (Paper presented in

Paris, March 5, 1984). For a "moderately comforting assessment of U.S. productivity rates" which is in fact not very comforting, see William J. Baumol, "Is There a U.S. Productivity Crisis?" *Science,* February 3, 1989, pp. 611–615.

20. Baily, "Capital, Innovation, and Productivity Growth," pp. 2–3.

21. See especially Lester C. Thurow, *The Zero-Sum Society: Distribution and the Possibilities for Economic Change* (New York: Basic Books, 1980).

22. See especially Edward F. Denison, *Accounting for Slower Economic Growth: The U.S. in the 1970s* (Washington, D.C.: Brookings Institution, 1979); idem, "Explanations of Declining Productivity Growth," *Survey of Current Business* 59 (1979), 1–24; John W. Kendrick, "Productivity Trends in the U.S.," in *Lagging Productivity Growth: Causes and Remedies,* ed. Shlomo Maital and Noah M. Meltz (Cambridge, Mass.: Ballinger, 1980); Thurow, "The Productivity Problem," pp. 41–51; U.S. Department of Labor, Bureau of Labor Statistics, *Handbook of Labor Statistics* for 1980–1984 (Washington, D.C.: Government Printing Office, 1980–1984) and *Monthly Labor Review* for 1980–1988; John W. Kendrick and E. S. Grossman, *Productivity in the U.S.: Trends and Cycles* (Baltimore: Johns Hopkins University Press, 1980); Victor Perlo, "The False Claim of Declining Productivity and Its Political Uses," *Science and Society* 46 (1982), 284–327; Kathleen Newland, "Productivity: The New Economic Context," in *Worldwatch Paper 49* (Washington, D.C.: Worldwatch Institute, 1982); Martin Neil Baily, "The Productivity Growth Slowdown by Industry," *Brookings Papers on Economic Activity* 2 (1982), 423–454; Virgil H. Ketterling, "Economic Performance of U.S. Industries, 1973–1981," in U.S. Department of Commerce, Bureau of Industrial Economics, *U.S. Industrial Outlook* (Washington, D.C.: Government Printing Office, 1983); Arnold Packer and Arthur F. Neef, "The International Context," in U.S. Department of Labor, Bureau of Labor Statistics, *A Bureau of Labor Statistics Reader on Productivity* (Washington, D.C.: Government Printing Office, 1983); William J. Baumol, "On Productivity Growth in the Long Run," *Atlantic Economic Journal,* September 12, 1984, pp. 10–25; Michael R. Darby, "The U.S. Productivity Slowdown: A Case of Statistical Myopia," *American Economic Review* 74 (1984), 301–322; and William J. Baumol and Kenneth McLennan, eds. *Productivity Growth and U.S. Competitiveness* (New York: Oxford University Press, 1985).

23. Edward F. Denison, "The Puzzling Setback to Productivity Growth," *Challenge,* November–December 1980, p. 3.

24. Thurow, *The Zero-Sum Society,* pp. 40, 51.

25. I capitalize *Planning* to distinguish it from city planning, corporate planning, and other systematic but limited efforts to arrange a different future.

26. Herbert Stein, *Presidential Economics* (New York: Simon and Schuster, 1984), p. 318.

27. For the Planning movement of these years, see Otis L. Graham, Jr., *Toward a Planned Society: From Roosevelt to Nixon* (New York: Oxford University Press, 1976); Herbert Stein, "Economic Planning and the Improvement of Economic Policy," in *The Politics of Planning,* ed. Bruce Briggs (San Francisco: Institute for Contemporary Studies, 1976); and David E. Wilson, *The National Planning Idea in U.S. Public Policy: Five Alternative Approaches* (Boulder: Westview Press, 1982).

28. Charles L. Brown quoted in *Washington Post,* September 12, 1982, p. H1.

29. On national growth and urban policies of the 1970s, see Graham, *Toward a Planned Society;* idem, "America's Size and Shape: Federal Growth Policy from Humphrey to Reagan" (Paper presented at the Woodrow Wilson Center for Scholars, June 12, 1983); Advisory Committee on National Growth Policy Processes, *Forging America's Future* (Washington, D.C.: Government Printing Office, 1976); Anthony Downs, "Urban Policy," in *Setting National Priorities: The 1979 Budget,* ed. Joseph Pechman (Washington, D.C.: Brookings Institution, 1978); Royce Hanson, *The Evolution of National Urban Policy, 1970–1980: Lessons from the Past* (Washington, D.C.: National Academy Press, 1982).

30. William Diebold believes that Taussig was the first to use the term. Wrote Taussig: "Hence President McKinley, in calling the extra session of 1897, asked Congress to deal solely with the import duties and the revenue. The two questions of industrial policy and of legislation for revenue ought, indeed, to be considered separately"; Frank W. Taussig, *The Tariff History of the United States,* 7th ed. (New York: G. P. Putnam's Sons, 1923), p. 325. Diebold thinks these words actually were written in 1898; he has found the term in a memo from Taussig to Woodrow Wilson toward the end of World War I; Diebold, *Industrial Policy as an International Issue* (New York: McGraw-Hill, 1980), p. 200. In James M. Swank's *The Industrial Policies of Great Britain and the United States* (Philadelphia: J. B. Lippincott, 1976), the term appears merely as a synonym for tariff policy, which seems also to have been Taussig's usage.

   According to Chalmers Johnson, "The contemporary idea of Industrial Policy is of Japanese origin (although the Japanese claim to have gotten it long ago from the Americans . . .)"; see Johnson, ed., "Introduction," in *The Industrial Policy Debate* (San Francisco: Institute for Contemporary Studies, 1984), pp. 5–6; and Hiroya Ueno, "Industrial Policy: Its Role and Limits," *Journal of Japanese Trade and Industry,* July–August 1983, pp. 34–37. The term occurs in the minutes of a Twentieth Century Fund conference held late in 1931, at which economists were urged to "grapple with specific suggestions of national or industrial policy"; Meredith Givens and Evans Clark to James Harvey Rogers, December 4, 1931, Rogers manuscripts, Yale University Library. The banker Eugene Staley wrote in 1944: "The most feasible and also the most constructive alternative to restrictive intervention by the State is not non-intervention (laissez-faire) but intervention of a more constructive kind—namely, a positive programme of industrial adaptation"; *World Economic Development* (Montreal: International Labour Office, 1944), p. 177.

31. The U.S. Bureau of the Census' *Standard Industrial Classification Manual: 1987* (Washington, D.C.: Government Printing Office, 1988) requires 704 pages to list all industrial sectors, and 194 pages for manufacturing ("establishments engaged in mechanical or chemical transformation of materials or substances into new products") (p. 67). On services, see James B. Quinn, "The Impact of Technology in the Service Sector," in *Technology and Global Industry,* ed. B. R. Guile and Harvey Brooks (Washington, D.C.: National Academy Press, 1987); and D. I. Riddle and Kristopher J. Brown, "From Complacency to Strategy: Retaining World Class Competitiveness in Services," in *Global Competitiveness,* ed. Martin K. Starr (New York: W. W. Norton, 1988).

32. Declaration by Robert Schuman, French minister for foreign affairs, Paris, May 9, 1951, in Dean Acheson, *Present at the Creation: My Years in the State Department* (New York: W. W. Norton, 1969), p. 383. For an early and intelligent discussion, see Lawrence G. Franko, "Industrial Policies in Western Europe: Solution or Problem?" *World Economy,* January 1979, pp. 31–50.

33. For the history of developmental economics, see Albert O. Hirschman, "Rise and Decline of Developmental Economics," in *Essays in Trespassing: Economics to Politics and Beyond* (Cambridge, Mass.: Harvard University Press, 1981); Paul W. Streeten, "Development Ideas in Historical Perspective," in *Toward a New Strategy for Development,* Rothko Chapel Colloquium (New York: Pergamon, 1979); and Gerald M. Meier and Dudley Seers, eds., *Pioneers in Development* (New York: Oxford University Press, 1984).

34. John Maynard Keynes, *The General Theory of Employment, Interest, and Money* (New York: Harcourt, Brace, 1936), p. 379.

35. William Diebold, Jr., *The United States and the Industrial World: American Foreign Economic Policy in the 1970s* (New York: Praeger, 1972), p. 452.

36. The Advisory Committee on National Growth Policy Processes, *Forging America's Future,* stated that "the executive office needs a new sectoral economic staff . . . to follow and analyze key sectors of the private economy" (p. 36).

37. William G. Watson, *A Primer on the Economics of Industrial Policy* (Ottawa: Ontario Economic Council, 1983), p. 69.

38. Ibid., p. 70.

39. Mancur Olson, "Supply Side Economics, Industrial Policy, and Rational Ignorance," in Claude Barfield and William A. Schambra, eds., *The Politics of Industrial Policy* (Washington, D.C.: American Enterprise Institute, 1986), pp. 265–266.

40. Wildavsky, ibid., p. 266.

## 2. Emergence of the Industrial Policy Idea

1. Arthur M. Schlesinger, Jr., *Robert Kennedy and His Times* (Boston: Houghton Mifflin, 1978), p. 226.

2. On the troubles of the steel industry in the postwar era, see Robert W. Crandall, *The U.S. Steel Industry in Recurrent Crisis: Policy Options in a Competitive World* (Washington, D.C.: Brookings Institution, 1981); Michael Borrus, "The Politics of Competitive Erosion in the Steel Industry," in *American Industry in International Competition,* ed. John Zysman and Laura Tyson (Ithaca: Cornell University Press, 1983); Zoltan J. Acs, *The Changing Structure of the U.S. Economy: Lessons from the Steel Industry* (New York: Praeger, 1984); Paul A. Tiffany, "The Roots of Decline: Business-Government Relations in the American Steel Industry, 1945–1960," *Journal of Economic History* 44 (1984), 407–419; Donald F. Barnett and Robert W. Crandall, *Up from the Ashes: The Rise of the Steel Minimill in the United States* (Washington, D.C.: Brookings Institution, 1986); John P. Hoerr, *And the Wolf Finally Came: The Decline of the American Steel Industry* (Pittsburgh: University of Pittsburgh Press, 1988); Mark Reutter, "The Rise and Decline of Big Steel," *Wilson Quarterly* 12 (1988), 46085; and Thomas R. Howell et al., *Steel and the State* (Boulder: Westview, 1988).

3. On the Carter administration and the Solomon Plan for steel, see U.S. Federal Trade Commission, *The United States Steel Industry and Its International Rivals* (Washington, D.C., 1977), chap. 2, p. 5; Anthony M. Solomon, *Report to the President: A Comprehensive Program for the Steel Industry* (Washington, D.C.: Government Printing Office, 1977); F. Gerard Adams and Lawrence R. Klein, eds., *Industrial Policies for Growth and Competitiveness* (Lexington, Mass.: Lexington Books, 1983); Jeffrey A. Hart, "An Industrial Policy for the U.S." (Paper presented at the annual meeting of the American Association for the Advancement of Science, 1982); William T. Hogan, *World Steel in the 1980s: A Case of Survival* (Lexington, Mass.: Lexington Books, 1983); Borrus, "The Politics of Competitive Erosion."

4. William J. Diebold, *Industrial Policy as an International Issue* (New York: McGraw-Hill, 1980), p. 116.

5. Gail Schwartz and Pat Choate, *Being Number One: Rebuilding the U.S. Economy* (Lexington, Mass.: Lexington Books, 1980): pp. 95–97.

6. *Economic Report of the President, 1986* (Washington, D.C.: Government Printing Office, 1986), pp. 114–115.

7. Donald F. Barnett and Louis Schorsch, *Steel: Upheaval in a Basic Industry* (Cambridge, Mass.: Ballinger, 1983), chap. 9: see also Crandall, *The U.S. Steel Industry in Recurrent Crisis;* and Hoerr, *And the Wolf Finally Came.*

8. Jimmy Carter, *Keeping Faith: The Memoirs of a President* (New York: Bantam Books, 1982).

9. See "Report of the Study Group on Presidential Transition: Special Annex: The 1976 Transition" (Institute of Politics, John F. Kennedy School of Government, Harvard University, October 1980).

10. For a succinct history of trade policy, see I. M. Destler, *American Trade Politics: System under Stress* (New York and Washington, D.C.: Twentieth Century Fund and Institute for International Economics, 1986).

11. Ibid., p. 11.

12. U.S. Senate, Committee on Finance, *Trade Agreements Act of 1979*, 96th Cong., 1st sess. (Washington, D.C.: Government Printing Office, 1979), pp. 268–269.

13. Congressional Quarterly, *President Carter: 1979* (Washington, D.C., 1980), p. 59A.

14. U.S. Bureau of the Census, *Historical Statistics of the United States: Colonial Times to 1957* (Washington, D.C.: Government Printing Office, 1960), p. 542.

15. U.S. International Trade Commission, *Twenty-fifth Annual Report of the President of the United States on the Trade Agreements Program, 1980–1981* (Washington, D.C.: Government Printing Office, 1982), pp. 20–25.

16. On trade patterns and issues under Carter, see Robert B. Reich, "Industries in Distress," *New Republic,* May 9, 1981; idem, "Industrial Evolution," *Democracy* 3 (Summer 1983), 10–20; U.S. Department of Commerce, *International Economic Indicators and Highlights of U.S. Export and Import Trade* (Washington, D.C.: Government Printing Office, 1983); and Judith Goldstein, "The Politics of Trade: Institutions of Protection," *American Political Science Review* 80 (1986), 169–181.

17. "The New Export Policy Works Like the Old—Badly," *Business Week,* July 21, 1980, pp. 88–91.

18. On Carter's urban and national growth policies, see Otis L. Graham, Jr., "Amer-

ica's Size and Shape: Federal Growth Policy from Humphrey to Reagan" (Paper presented at the Woodrow Wilson Center for Scholars, June 21, 1983); and Michael E. Bell and Paul S. Lande, eds., *Regional Dimensions of Industrial Policy* (Lexington, Mass.: Lexington Books, 1982).

19. See Robert B. Reich and John Donahue, "Lessons from the Chrysler Bailout," *California Management Review* 27 (Summer 1985), 157–183.
20. Iacocca quoted ibid., pp. 120–121.
21. O'Neill quoted in U.S. Congress, *Congressional Record,* October 16, 1979, p. H12222.
22. "Chrysler Wins $3.5 Billion U.S. 'Bailout,'" *Congressional Quarterly,* February 1980, pp. 53–55.
23. On Carter's supply-side efforts, see *Public Papers of the Presidents: Jimmy Carter, 1979* (Washington, D.C.: Government Printing Office, 1980); President's Commission on Industrial Competitiveness, *Global Competition: The New Reality,* 2 vols. (Washington, D.C.: Government Printing Office, 1985); Wendy Schact, *Industrial Innovation and High Technology Development* (Washington, D.C.: Government Printing Office, 1981); Claude E. Barfield, *Science Policy from Ford to Reagan* (Washington, D.C.: American Enterprise Institute, 1982).
24. "Innovation and American Industry: What Went Wrong?" *Center Magazine* 12 (November–December 1979), 7–40.
25. Gilpin quoted in Walter Goldstein, ed., *Planning, Politics, and the Public Interest* (New York: Columbia University Press, 1978), p. 140.
26. George McAlmon, "American Manufacturers Are Losing World Markets," *Center Magazine* 12 (November–December 1979), 9.
27. Jordan Baruch, memo, June 14, 1979, Domestic Policy Staff Papers, box 186, Jimmy Carter Library, Atlanta (hereafter cited as DPS Papers). Carter's proposals on industrial innovation came in a speech of October 31, 1979.
28. Goldschmidt to Miller, July 14, 1980, "DOT File," George Eads Papers (Eads's possession; hereafter cited as Eads Papers).
29. Orin Kramer to Stuart Eizenstat, July 7, 1980, Eads Papers; Kramer to Eizenstat, n.d., DPS Papers, box 268.
30. Jaskinowski, speech to a Madrid symposium, May 9, 1980, DPS Papers, box 37.
31. Arnold Packer to George Eads and Jerry Jasinowski, February 21, 1980, Eads Papers.
32. Frank Press to Jimmy Carter, August 20, 1980, DPS file, box 192, Carter Papers. Jasinowski was also speaking publicly for "a more positive kind of industrial policy, one I would describe as a policy of supporting the winners, the growth sectors of our economy"; and "the business community must form a core of industrial policy advocates"; Jasinowski, "A New Industrial Strategy," speech to the Semiconductor Association, 27 Sept. 1979, DPS Papers, box 29.
33. Robert Hamrin, summary of a Los Angeles meeting on Industrial Strategy, June 18, 1980, President's Committee for an Agenda for the Eighties, DPS Papers, box 4.
34. Peter J. Solomon, memo to Deputies, July 21, 1980, Eads Papers.
35. Anonymous memo from CEA staff, July 15, 1980, Eads Papers.
36. Paul Krugman, "Foreign Experience with Industrial Policy: A Critical Review," draft, July 5, 1980, Eads Papers.

37. In 1974 Eads had been named executive director of a commission that liberal planners in Congress had pushed upon Richard Nixon in the hope that the unanticipated oil crisis might create a climate in which a national Planning institution might be established to improve foresight. Nixon stacked the National Commission on Supplies and Shortages with "conservatives," who still believed that "free markets" could handle all decisions about the national future. The only support for Planning came from the report of a unit attached to the commission by Senator Hubert Humphrey. *Forging America's Future* (Washington, D.C.: Government Printing Office, 1976), the report of the awkwardly titled Advisory Committee on National Growth Policy Processes, offered a cogent argument for and design of an indicative Planning system. It included one of the earliest suggestions that the CEA develop sectoral expertise and monitoring. Thus George Eads's education in sectoral and regional policy issues—where he was remembered as "a conservative"—was extensive. This account of the work of the EPG and the Deputies Group draws upon the author's interview with George Eads, July 25, 1985, College Park, Maryland.

38. George Eads and Jerry Jasinowski, memo for EPG principals on "Industrial Policy," June 12, 1980, Eads Papers.

39. The quotations in the next five paragraphs are from ibid.

40. Adam Clymer, "Carter's Vision of America: The President Talks about His Goals for a Second Term," *New York Times Magazine*, July 21, 1980, p. 14. See also Edward Cowan, "Auto Aid Study and 'Industrial Policy,'" *New York Times*, May 20, 1980, pp. D1, D5; and U.S. Department of Labor, Office of Foreign Economic Research, *Report of the President on U.S. Competitiveness* (Washington, D.C.: Government Printing Office, 1980).

41. Eads and Jasinowski, memo for EPG principals.

42. Amitai Etzioni, "The Father of Reindustrialization Speaks," *Christian Science Monitor*, October 17, 1980, p. 23.

43. Stuart Eizenstat to Jimmy Carter, n.d., DPS Papers, box 192, Carter Library.

44. Amitai Etzioni, "Reindustrialization: View from the Source," *New York Times*, June 29, 1980, p. F16. See also idem, "Rebuilding Our Economic Foundations," *Business Week*, August 25, 1980, p. 16; idem, "Reindustrialization of America," *Science*, August 22, 1980, p. 863; idem, "Riding a Whirlwind," *Society*, March–April 1982, pp. 29–35.

45. "Kennedy Plan Aims to Revive Economy," *New York Times*, May 21, 1980, p. 26.

46. Edward Cowan, "Carter Economic Renewal Plan," *New York Times*, August 22, 1980, p. B4. "We have got to go beyond reindustrialization," Carter's press secretary, Jody Powell, told reporters; quoted in "Carter's Plan for United States Industry," *Time*, September 1, 1980, p. 40.

47. See *Weekly Compilation of Presidential Documents, Administration of Jimmy Carter: 1980* (August 28, 1980) (Washington, D.C.: Government Printing Office, 1981), pp. 1585–91; Congressional Quarterly, *President Carter: 1979*, p. 15; Dale Tate, "Carter Economic Plan: A Timely Melange," *Congressional Quarterly Weekly Reports*, August 30, 1980, pp. 2563–65; Rochelle Stanfield, "Don't Call It Economic Stimulus, Call It Economic Renewal," *National Journal*, September 5, 1980,

pp. 1468–72; "Fact Sheet: Economic Program for the Eighties," Office of the White House Press Secretary, August 28, 1980, Carter Papers.

48. See U.S. House of Representatives, Committee on the Budget, *President's Economic Revitalization Program,* 96th Cong., 2d sess. (Washington, D.C.: Government Printing Office, 1980); and Clyde Farnsworth, "Reviving Industry: The Search for a Policy," *New York Times,* August 18–22, 1980.
49. "A Leaf out of Europe's Industrial Book," *The Economist,* August 9, 1980, p. 21.
50. *Weekly Compilation of Presidential Documents: 1980,* pp. 1585–87.

### 3. Ousted from Washington

1. John Pinder, ed., *National Industrial Strategies and the World Economy* (London: Allenheld, Osmun, 1982), p. 178.
2. Frank A. Weil, "The U.S. Needs an Industrial Policy," *Fortune,* March 1980, pp. 149–150; "The Reindustrialization of America," *Business Week,* June 30, 1980, pp. 56–138.
3. "Reindustrialization of America," pp. 56, 9, 55, 88.
4. Ibid., p. 88. See also Editors of Business Week, *The Reindustrialization of America* (New York, 1982).
5. Edwin J. Bowers, "Can All Sides Agree on an Industrial Policy?" *Iron Age,* July 1980, pp. 27–29.
6. Robert Levy, "Business Views 'Reindustrialization,'" *Dun's Review,* October 1980, pp. 90–92.
7. Clyde Farnsworth, "Reviving Industry: The Search for a Policy," *New York Times,* August 18, 1980, p. D8.
8. U.S. House of Representatives, Committee on Banking, Finance and Urban Affairs, Subcommittee on the City, *Urban Revitalization Policy,* 96th Cong., 2d sess. (Washington, D.C.: Government Printing Office, 1980), pp. 6–7, 65–66. See also Pat Choate and Gail Schwartz, *Being Number One* (Lexington, Mass.: Lexington Books, 1980), pp. 1, 2, 98.
9. Philip Caldwell, "The U.S. Must Strengthen Its Competitiveness," *Harvard Business Review,* January–February 1981, p. 76.
10. Gresser quoted in U.S. House of Representatives, Committee on Ways and Means, Subcommittee on Trade, *High Technology and Japanese Industrial Policy: A Strategy for U.S. Policymakers,* 96th Cong., 2d sess. (Washington, D.C.: Government Printing Office, 1980), p. 28.
11. "Reindustrialization of America," p. 55.
12. And would include Ezra F. Vogel, *Japan As Number One: Lessons for America* (Cambridge, Mass.: Harvard University Press, 1979); Nabutaka Ike, *Japan: The New Superstate* (Chicago: W. H. Freeman, 1974); Herman Kahn and Herbert Passin, *Japanese Challenge: The Success and Failures of Economic Success* (New York: T. Y. Crowell, 1979); and Frank Gibney, *Fragile Superpower* (New York: W. W. Norton, 1979).
13. Neal Peirce and Carol Steinbach, "Reindustrialization—A Foreign Word to Hard-Pressed American Workers," *National Journal,* October 10, 1980, p. 1784.

14. Farnsworth, "Reviving Industry," p. D1.
15. Charls Walker to author, March 4, 1984.
16. Peter Behr, "Senate Demands Congress Produce an Industrial Policy," *Washington Post*, August 9, 1980, pp. F7–8.
17. "Text of Democratic Party Platform," *Congressional Quarterly Weekly Reports*, August 16, 1980, pp. 2390–91.
18. President's Commission for a National Agenda for the Eighties, *A National Agenda for the Eighties* (Washington, D.C.: Government Printing Office, 1981), pp. 22, 35, and esp. chap. 3.
19. *Economic Report of the President: 1981* (Washington, D.C.: Government Printing Office, 1981), pp. 127–130.
20. Ibid., pp. 130, 127, 129.
21. Jimmy Carter, *Keeping Faith: Memoirs of a President* (New York: Bantam, 1982).
22. Walt W. Rostow, *Getting from Here to There* (New York: McGraw-Hill, 1978), pp. 186–187.
23. "Felix Rohatyn," *Current Biography*, May 1978, pp. 349–352; see also Ralph Nader and William Taylor, *The Big Boys: Power and Position in American Business* (New York: Pantheon, 1986).
24. Felix G. Rohatyn, "Public-Private Partnerships to Stave off Disaster," *Harvard Business Review*, November–December 1979, pp. 6–10.
25. Felix Rohatyn, "The State of the Nation's Industry—All Talk and No Action," *Washington Post*, July 20, 1980, p. D1.
26. Felix Rohatyn, "Reconstructing America," *New York Review of Books*, March 5, 1981, pp. 18–19; idem, "The Coming Emergency and What Can Be Done about It," ibid., December 4, 1980, pp. 20–25.
27. Rohatyn, "The Coming Emergency," 24, 20.
28. "Interview with Lester C. Thurow," *U.S. News and World Report*, September 22, 1980, pp. 61–62.
29. Sidney Lens, "Deindustrialization: Panacea or Threat?" *The Progressive*, November 1980, pp. 44, 46.
30. William Wolman, "The Left-Wing Perimeter of Reindustrialization," *Business Week*, November 17, 1980, p. 12.
31. Ronald Muller, *Revitalizing America: Politics for Prosperity* (New York: Simon and Schuster, 1980), pp. 242, 277.
32. Gar Alperovitz and Jeff Faux, "Who Is to Take Which Bitter Pill?" *New York Times*, August 4, 1980, p. D1.
33. Joseph E. Coberly, Jr., "With the Government for a Partner, Who Needs Enemies?" *Dun's Review*, September 1980, p. 109.
34. Proxmire quoted in *What's Next?* November 1980, p. 2.
35. James Fallows, "American Industry: What Ails It, How to Save It," *Atlantic Monthly*, September 1980, pp. 45–47.
36. William J. Diebold, *Industrial Policy as an International Issue* (New York: McGraw-Hill, 1980), pp. ix, 20.
37. OECD, *The Aims and Instruments of Industrial Policy: A Comparative Study* (Brussels, 1975), pp. 18–19.

38. Diebold, *Industrial Policy as International Issue,* pp. 23, 114, 207, 259–261. See also John Pinder, Takashi Hosomi, and William Diebold, *Industrial Policy and the International Economy* (New York: Trilateral Commission, 1979).
39. Jerry J. Jasinowski, "Impressions from the Industrial Policy Debate," in U.S. Department of Commerce, *1981 U.S. Industrial Outlook* (Washington, D.C.: Government Printing Office, 1981), p. xv.
40. William Diebold to author, March 26, 1985.

## 4. Pundits at Floodtide

1. *Encyclopedia Britannica Book of the Year: 1981* (Chicago: Encyclopedia Britannica, 1982), pp. 312–326.
2. U.S. Bureau of the Census, *Statistical Abstract of the United States: 1984* (Washington, D.C.: Government Printing Office, 1984), pp. 442, 445–450; *Economic Report of the President: 1983* (Washington, D.C.: Government Printing Office, 1983), pp. 17–29; ibid. (Washington, D.C.: Government Printing Office, 1983), pp. 131–138.
3. *Economic Report of the President: 1982,* pp. 192–196; U.S. Bureau of the Census, *Statistical Abstract: 1984,* pp. 445–450; *Britannica Book of the Year: 1981,* pp. 314–318.
4. *Economic Report of the President: 1983,* p. 124.
5. Ibid., pp. 3–10, 124–33; U.S. Bureau of the Census, *Statistical Abstract of the United States: 1985* (Washington, D.C.: Government Printing Office, 1984), pp. 106–107, 800–803; ibid., *1988* (Washington, D.C.: Government Printing Office, 1986), pp. 381–383; *Encyclopedia Britannica Book of the Year: 1982* (Chicago: Encyclopedia Britannica, 1983), pp. 313–315; Charles F. Stone and Isabel V. Sawhill, *Economic Policy in the Reagan Years* (Washington, D.C.: Urban Institute, 1984), pp. 1–25.
6. *New York Times,* January 6, 1982, sec. 12, p. 32. A. F. Ehrbar, "Grasping the New Unemployment," *Fortune,* May 16, 1983, pp. 107–112. See also William Serrin, "Collapse of Our Industrial Heartland," *New York Times Magazine,* June 6, 1982, pp. 42–43.
7. Max L. Carey, "Occupational Employment Growth through 1990," *Monthly Labor Review,* August 1981, pp. 48–49; see also U.S. Department of Labor, Bureau of Labor Statistics, *Occupational Outlook Handbook, 1982–83* (Washington, D.C.: Government Printing Office, 1982), pp. 13–19.
8. Review of Ira Magaziner and Robert Reich, *Minding America's Business* (New York: Vintage, 1982), in *Foreign Affairs,* Summer 1982, p. 1190.
9. Thomas J. Peters and Robert H. Waterman, Jr., *In Search of Excellence: Lessons from America's Best-Run Companies* (New York: Harper & Row, 1982).
10. See especially Robert H. Hayes and William J. Abernathy, "Managing Our Way to Economic Decline," *Harvard Business Review,* July–August 1980, pp. 67–77; David Vogel, "America's Management Crisis," *New Republic,* February 7, 1981; James O'Toole, *Making America Work: Productivity and Responsibility* (New York: Continuum, 1981); William J. Abernathy, Kim Clark, and Alan Kantrow, eds., *Industrial Renaissance: Producing a Competitive Future for America* (New York: Basic

Books, 1983); and Paul R. Lawrence and Davis Dyer, *Renewing American Industry* (New York: Free Press, 1983).

11. Magaziner and Reich, *Minding America's Business,* pp. 90–106, 330.

12. R. D. Norton, "Industrial Policy and American Renewal," *Journal of Economic Literature* 24 (1986), 4.

13. Magaziner and Reich, *Minding America's Business,* p. 370.

14. Ibid., p. 378.

15. Lester C. Thurow, "How to Rescue a Drowning Economy," *New York Review of Books,* April 1, 1982, p. 3.

16. Robert B. Reich, *The Next American Frontier* (New York: Times Books, 1983).

17. This is the same idea explored in Arthur Okun's influential book, *Equality and Efficiency: The Big Tradeoff* (Washington, D.C.: Brookings Institution, 1975). Though it is unclear how much debt he owed to recent writing in American history, Reich's theme of a "civic culture" struggling for dominance against a "business culture" resembles a controversy among historians over a "classical republicanism" suspicious of commercial values, and always in conflict with a "Lockean" or individualist-commercial ethos. The seminal book in the new appreciation of the influence of classic republicanism is J. G. A. Pocock, *The Machiavellian Moment: Florentine Political Thought and the Atlantic Republic Tradition* (Princeton: Princeton University Press, 1975); see also Lance Banning, *The Jeffersonian Persuasion* (Ithaca: Cornell University Press, 1978); and the work of Dorothy Ross, James Henretta, and Garry Wills, reviewed in Isaac Kramnick, "Republican Revisionism Revisited," *American Historical Review* 87 (1982), 629–664. For critics, see Joyce Appleby, *Capitalism and a New Social Order: The Republican Vision of the 1790s* (New York: New York University Press, 1984); and John P. Diggins, *The Lost Soul of American Politics: Virtue, Self-Interest, and the Foundations of Liberalism* (New York: Basic Books, 1984).

18. Robert B. Reich, "The Next American Frontier," *Atlantic Monthly,* April 1983, p. 102; idem, *Next American Frontier,* p. 13.

19. Reich, *Next American Frontier,* p. 119.

20. For brief popular introductions to institutionalist economics see Robert Kuttner, "The Poverty of Economics," *Atlantic Monthly,* February 1985, pp. 74–84; and Martin Bronfenbrenner, "Early American Leaders—Institutional and Critical Traditions," *American Economic Review* 75 (1985), 13–27.

21. Reich, *Next American Frontier,* pp. 139, 133, 140.

22. Ibid., p. 170.

23. Ibid., pp. 206–207.

24. Ibid., p. 134. "Since the late 1960s America's economy has been slowly unraveling" (p. 3), "the social fabric is slowly unraveling" (p. 280), he wrote in *Next American Frontier.* Earlier, "There is increasing danger that the American economy may unravel"; "Industries in Distress," *New Republic,* May 9, 1981, p. 19. See also Reich, "Industrial Evolution," *Democracy* 3 (Summer 1983), 20. Goethe quoted in Will Durant, *The Story of Philosophy* (Boston: Little, Brown, 1953), p. 300.

25. Reich, "The Next American Frontier," p. 102.

26. Ibid., p. 103.

27. Reich, *Next American Frontier,* pp. 135, 227.

28. Ibid., pp. 239–245, 276. For a fuller exposition of his ideas on the design of IP, see Robert B. Reich, "Making Industrial Policy," *Foreign Affairs,* Spring 1982, pp. 852–881; and idem, "Industrial Policy: Ten Concrete, Practical Steps to Building a Dynamic Economy," *New Republic,* March 31, 1982, pp. 28–31.

29. Reich, *Next American Frontier,* pp. 246–249, 266.

30. Ibid., pp. 280, 275.

31. Randall Rothenberg, "Mr. Industrial Policy: The Democrats' Latest Answer to Reaganomics Is the Brainchild of a Diminutive Harvard Professor Named Robert Reich," *Esquire,* May 1983, pp. 95–97.

32. Robert B. Reich, "The Liberal Promise of Prosperity," *New Republic,* February 21, 1981, pp. 21, 23.

33. Robert A. Solo, "Melman and Reich on Industrial Policy," *Economic Development and Cultural Change* 34 (January 1986), 383. It was said that Reich had borrowed without credits from Charles F. Sabel, *Work and Politics: The Division of Labor in Industry* (Cambridge, Mass.: Harvard University Press, 1982), a book conceived a short distance from Reich's office. Sabel had written that "Fordism" had met its successor in the more flexible high-technology cottage industries flourishing in Italy along the Adriatic coast. See Sharon Churcher, "How New Is Reich's Frontier?" *New York,* June 13, 1983, p. 13; and Robert J. Samuelson, "The Policy Peddlers," *Harper's,* June 1983, pp. 60–65. Randall Rothenberg reported complaints that "the details are hazy . . . recommendations lack rigor"; "Mr. Industrial Policy," p. 233.

34. Barry Bluestone and Bennett Harrison, *The Deindustrialization of America: Plant Closings, Community Abandonment, and the Dismantling of Basic Industry* (New York: Basic Books, 1982), pp. 3, 5–6.

35. Ibid., pp. 32–35; see also Congressional Budget Office, *Dislocated Workers: Issues and Federal Options* (Washington, D.C.: Government Printing Office, 1982).

36. Bluestone and Harrison, *Deindustrialization,* pp. 27, 193–194.

37. Ibid., pp. 195, 213, 243–244. See also Bennett Harrison, "The International Movement for Prenotification of Plant Closures," *Industrial Relations* 23 (1984), 387–409; Richard B. McKenzie, *Restrictions on Business Mobility* (Washington, D.C.: American Enterprise Institute, 1979); and idem, *Fugitive Industry: The Economics and Politics of Deindustrialization* (Cambridge, Mass.: Ballinger, 1984).

38. For the critical reception of *The Deindustrialization of America,* see Robert Z. Lawrence, "Is Trade Deindustrializating America? A Medium-Term Perspective," *Brookings Papers on Economic Activity* 1 (1983), 129–161; idem, "The Myth of U.S. Deindustrialization," *Challenge,* November–December 1983, pp. 12–21; idem, "Sectoral Shifts and the Size of the Middle Class," *Brookings Review* 3 (1984), 3–11; for rebuttal see Barry Bluestone, "Is Deindustrialization a Myth?" *Annals of the American Academy of Political and Social Science,* September 1984, pp. 39–51; idem, "Is Deindustrialization a Myth?" in *Deindustrialization,* ed. Gene F. Summers (Washington, D.C.: American Academy of Political and Social Science, 1984). For the view that Bluestone and Harrison were not radical enough, see Richard Peet, "The Deindustrialization of America," *Antipode,* 1982, pp. 47–53.

39. Samuel Bowles, David M. Gordon, and Thomas E. Weisskopf, *Beyond the Waste*

*Land: A Democratic Alternative to Economic Decline* (Garden City, N.Y.: Anchor, 1983). This was a book about economic decline, productivity, and even—briefly—re-industrialization, corporatism, and "the Japanese 'miracle.'" It did not, however, use the term *industrial policy,* and gave almost no coverage of sector development or policies. It was one of those interesting books on the economic trends of the contemporary world which fall at the edge of, and complement, the literature of IP as I have tried to circumscribe it.

40. Michael Kinsley, "The Double Felix," *New Republic,* March 25, 1984, p. 29.

## 5. Industrial Visions and History Lessons

1. Center for National Policy, *Restoring American Competitiveness: Proposals for an Industrial Policy* (Washington, D.C., 1984), pp. 8, 9, 10. The director of the study was Professor Lewis B. Kaden of Columbia University Law School.

    The Board would have three functions. The first would be "to evaluate and advise the President and Congress on key sectors of the economy that deserve special consideration, based on the nation's interest in growth, employment and competitiveness." Second, "In . . . limited cases, the Board could participate and assist in the preparation, through negotiation among all affected interests, of a package of mutually reinforcing actions designed to improve the long-term competitiveness of that industry . . . [to] include both public and private actions, and to recommend governmental actions, not to direct them." Finally, "The Board's only direct authority would be as the policymaking body for certain federal industrial credit assistant programs . . . under the aegis of a new Industrial Finance Administration." The board, composed of twelve to fifteen members from government, business, and labor, would be situated in the Executive Office of the President (pp. 13–14.)

2. The IFA "would operate under the jurisdiction of the IDB. It would be empowered to extend loans, guarantees, and other forms of assistance to companies, industries, and, perhaps in some cases, to state or local government agencies, but only as part of a development strategy adopted by the Board." IFA assistance "would in all cases be limited to no more than 50 percent of necessary funds . . . a crucial negotiating chip in obtaining participation by private lenders." In designing the IFA, the group studied "the successful record of the World Bank and the Federal National Mortgage Association" (ibid., pp. 14–15). See also Peter Kilborn, "Plan to Revive Industrial Vigor Urged in Study," *New York Times,* January 1, 1984, pp. 1, 28.

3. Lester C. Thurow, *The Case for Industrial Policies* (Washington, D.C.: Center for National Policy, 1984), p. 5.

4. Lester Thurow, "Down with the Dollar," *Newsweek,* August 8, 1983, p. 66; idem, *Case for Industrial Policies,* pp. 7, 13.

5. Thurow, *Case for Industrial Policies,* pp. 3, 4–5.

6. Ibid., pp. 8–9. See also Thurow, "Farms: A Policy Success," *Newsweek,* May 16, 1983, p. 78.

7. U.S. House of Representatives, Committee on Banking, Finance and Urban Affairs, Subcommittee on Economic Stabilization, *Industrial Policy,* 98th Cong., 1st sess., 5 vols. (Washington, D.C.: Government Printing Office, 1983), I, 110.

8. Elisha P. Douglass, *The Coming Age of American Business: Three Centuries of Enterprise, 1600–1900* (Chapel Hill: University of North Carolina Press, 1971), pp. 224–239.

9. In addition to Douglass, see Carter Goodrich, *Government Promotion of American Canals and Railroads, 1800–1890* (New York: Columbia University Press, 1960); and Ronald Shaw, *Erie Water West: A History of the Erie Canal, 1792–1854* (Lexington: University of Kentucky Press, 1966).

10. Richard Bolling and John Bowles, *America's Competitive Edge: How to Get Our Country Moving Again* (New York: McGraw-Hill, 1982), esp. pp. 1–44. For a more critical and current view see William U. Chandler, *The Myth of TVA* (Cambridge, Mass.: Ballinger, 1984); and Erwin R. Hargrove and Paul K. Conkin, eds., *TVA: Fifty Years of Grass-Roots Bureaucracy* (Urbana: University of Illinois Press, 1983).

11. William Diebold, Jr., "Past and Future Industrial Policies in the U.S.," in *National Industrial Strategies and the World Economy*, ed. John Pinder (London: Allenheld, Osmun, 1982), p. 182.

12. I have adapted to my own uses similar four-quadrant schematics found in William Abernathy, Kim Clark, and Alan Kantrow, eds., *Industrial Renaissance: Producing a Competitive Future for America* (New York: Basic Books, 1983), p. 4, and Robert H. Hayes and Steven C. Wheelwright, *Restoring Our Competitive Edge: Competing through Manufacturing* (New York: John Wiley & Sons, 1984), pp. 392–393.

13. Bush quoted in "Beating the System," *New Republic*, November 5, 1990, p. 8.

14. Thurow, *Case for Industrial Policies*, pp. 17, 6.

15. Center for National Policy, *Restoring American Competitiveness*, p. 9.

16. Thurow quoted in House Subcommittee for Economic Stabilization, *Industrial Policy*, I, 169. See also Lester C. Thurow, "Losing the Economic Race," *New York Review of Books*, September 27, 1984, pp. 28–31; idem, "The Case for Industrial Policy," *Newsweek*, January 9, 1984, p. 79.

17. Fred P. Graham, conversation with author, June 24, 1983.

18. Parker quoted in Gavin Wright, *Old South, New South: Revolutions in the Southern Economy since the Civil War* (Stanford: Stanford University Press, 1986), p. 4. Parker's objection to such a perspective was that it mistakenly equated nations with economies.

19. Ezra F. Vogel, *Japan as Number One: Lessons for America* (Cambridge, Mass.: Harvard University Press, 1979).

20. Barry Bluestone and Bennett Harrison, *The Deindustrialization of America: Plant Closings, Community Abandonment, and the Dismantling of Basic Industry* (New York: Basic Books, 1982), p. 5.

21. David McKay and Wyn Grant, "Industrial Policies in OECD Countries: An Overview," *Journal of Public Policy* 3 (Feburary 1983), 3. The components of that index were real rate of GDP growth, offset by unemployment and inflation rates. Other measures are easily imaginable, over other periods, and in some of them the U.S. economy appears to have been reasonably strong. If one contrasts the gross domestic product (GDP) growth rates of the twenty-four nations of the OECD, one finds the U.S. economy growing at a slightly slower-than-average rate (less than 5 percent) in 1961–1973 but at the average rate (2.5 percent) in 1974–1980; OECD, *National Accounts, 1951–1980* (Paris, 1982).

22. Robert Kuttner, "The Declining Middle," *Atlantic Monthly*, July 1983, pp. 60–72. See also Lucy S. Gordon, *Are Middle Level Jobs Disappearing?* (Washington, D.C.:

AFL-CIO, 1983); Emma Rothschild, "Reagan and the Real America," *New York Review of Books,* February 5, 1981, pp. 11–18; Eileen L. Collins and Lucretia D. Tanner, eds., *American Jobs and the Changing Industrial Base* (Cambridge, Mass.: Ballinger, 1984); and Robert Z. Lawrence, "Sectoral Shifts and the Size of the Middle Class," *Brookings Review* 3 (1984), 3–11.

23. F. Markley Roberts, "A Labor Perspective on Technological Change," in Collins and Tanner, *American Jobs,* p. 195.

24. Laura Tyson and John Zysman, eds., *American Industry in International Competition: Government Politics, and Corporate Strategies* (Ithaca: Cornell University Press, 1983), pp. 8–9.

25. Stuart E. Eizenstat, "Designing a Workable and Effective Industrial Policy," typescript of address at Charleston, W.Va., November 3, 1983, p. 5 (author's possession).

26. Labor-Industry Coalition for International Trade, *International Trade, Industrial Policies, and the Future of American Industry* (Washington, D.C., 1983).

27. John Pinder, Takashi Hosomi, and William Diebold, *Industrial Policy and the International Economy* (New York: New York University Press, 1979). The authors of this study preferred the term *structural policies* despite their title, but the latter term did not take hold.

28. For assessments of foreign Industrial Policies in print from 1970 to 1980, see OECD, *Industrial Policies of Fourteen Member Countries* (Paris, 1971); OECD, *The Aims and Instruments of Industrial Policy: A Comparative Study* (Paris, 1975); OECD, *Selected Industrial Policy Instruments: Objectives and Scope* (Paris, 1978); European Economic Community, *Industrial Policy in the Community* (Brussels, 1970); Lawrence G. Franko, *European Industrial Policy: Past, Present, and Future* (Paris: OECD, 1980); and Steven J. Warnecke and Ezra N. Suleiman, eds., *Industrial Policies in Western Europe* (New York: Praeger, 1975).

29. Sheila K. Johnson, *American Attitudes toward Japan, 1941–1975* (Washington, D.C.: American Enterprise Institute, 1975), pp. 95, 107.

30. Dulles quoted in U.S. Department of State, *Foreign Relations, 1952–54,* vol. XIV (Washington, D.C.: Government Printing Office, 1985), pp. 1724–25. For a recent account of racial stereotypes on both sides of the Pacific, see John Dower, *War without Mercy: Race and Power in the Pacific War* (New York: Pantheon, 1986).

31. Thomas K. McCraw, ed., *America versus Japan* (Cambridge, Mass.: Harvard Business School Press, 1986), pp. 1–33.

32. Louis Kraar, "How the Japanese Mount That Export Blitz," *Fortune,* September 19, 1970, p. 129.

33. See, for example, William G. Ouichi, *Theory Z: How American Business Can Meet the Japanese Challenge* (Reading, Mass.: Addison-Wesley, 1981); and Richard Tanner Pascale and Anthony G. Athos, *The Art of Japanese Management: Applications for American Executives* (New York: Warner Books, 1982).

34. Vogel, *Japan as Number One,* pp. 161, 59.

35. Koji Taira, "Industrial Policy and Employment in Japan," *Current History,* November 1983, p. 364. See also Christopher Madison, "Industrial Policy, Japanese Style," *National Journal,* February 26, 1983.

36. Chalmers A. Johnson, *MITI and the Japanese Miracle: The Growth of Industrial Policy, 1925–1975* (Stanford: Stanford University Press, 1982).

37. Chalmers A. Johnson, "The Policy Dilemmas of America's Response to the Challenge of Japan," Occasional Paper 14 (Woodrow Wilson International Center for Scholars, East Asia Program, January 1983), p. 3.

38. Royal Commission on Depression of Trade and Industry, *Final Report,* 3 vols. (London, 1886). See Michael Davenport, "Industrial Policy in the United Kingdom," in *Industrial Policies for Growth and Competitiveness,* ed. F. Gerard Adams and Lawrence R. Klein (Lexington, Mass.: Lexington Books, 1983).

39. Sidney Pollard, *The Wasting of the British Economy* (New York: St. Martin's Press, 1982), p. 2. See also Pollard, *Britain's Prime and Britain's Decline: The British Economy 1870–1914* (New York: Routledge, Chapman and Hall, 1989).

40. Stephen Blank and Paul Sacks, "If at First You Don't Succeed, Don't Try Again: Industrial Policy in Britain," in *Industrial Vitalization: Toward a National Industrial Policy,* ed. Margaret E. Dewar (New York: Pergamon, 1982), p. 210. See also Richard E. Caves and Lawrence B. Krause, eds., *Britain's Economic Performance* (Washington, D.C.: Brookings Institution, 1980); and Aaron L. Friedberg, *The Weary Titan: Britain and the Experience of Relative Decline 1895–1905* (Princeton: Princeton University Press, 1988).

41. Franko, *European Industrial Policy,* p. 34. See also Brian Hindley, *State Investment Companies in Western Europe: Picking Winners or Backing Losers?* (New York: St. Martin's Press for the Trade Policy Research Center, 1983).

42. Arthur Knight, "Industrial Policy," in *Changing Perceptions of Economic Policy,* ed. Frances Cairncross (London: Methuen, 1981), p. 136.

43. Abernathy, Clark, and Kantrow, *Industrial Renaissance,* pp. 9–10.

44. Henry Rosovsky, "Introduction," in Bolling and Bowles, *America's Competitive Edge,* pp. xii–xiii.

45. Pollard, *Wasting of the British Economy,* pp. 185, 188–89, 191.

46. Blank and Sacks, "If at First," p. 236.

47. Davenport, "Industrial Policy in United Kingdom," p. 331.

48. Geoffrey Smith and Nelson W. Polsby, *British Government and Its Discontents* (New York: Basic Books, 1981), p. 174.

    Even in England in the 1980s, some businessmen, writers, and staunch civil servants in economics ministries urged yet another try to get industrial policies right. William Gwyn contrasted these "Pragmatists," who thought that changes in public policy could yet be devised which might correct the slide, with the "Jeremiahs," who saw fundamental social flaws that were beyond the reach of policy. See William Gwyn, "Jeremiahs and Pragmatists," in *Britain: Progress and Decline,* ed. William Gwyn and Richard Rose (New Orleans: Tulane University Press, 1980); and Jack Hayward and Michael Watson, eds., *Planning, Politics, and Public Policy: The British, French, and Italian Experiences* (London: Cambridge University Press, 1975).

## 6. Alternative Designs

1. *Modernizers* and *Preservationists* are the terms used by R. D. Norton, "Industrial Policy and American Renewal," *Journal of Economic Literature,* March 1986, p. 4.

2. "Interview, William Diebold, Jr.: Industrial Policy as an International Issue," *Challenge*, January–February 1981, p. 31; John Pinder, Takashi Hosomi, and William Diebold, *Industrial Policy and the International Economy* (New York: New York University Press, 1979), p. 326.

3. Robert Solow, "Wheeling and Dealing for the Common Good," *New York Times Book Review*, February 5, 1984, p. 11.

4. Randall Rothenberg, *The Neo-Liberals* (New York: Simon and Schuster, 1984), p. 233. See also Robert B. Reich and John D. Donahue, *New Deals: The Chrysler Revival and the American System* (New York: Times Books, 1985).

5. "We need the RFC both for the short-run and long-run problems," Etzioni told a House subcommittee in 1983; U.S. House of Representatives, Committee on Banking, Finance and Urban Affairs, Subcommittee on General Oversight and Renegotiation, *Establishment of a National Development Bank and Related Matters*, 98th Cong., 1st sess. (Washington, D.C.: Government Printing Office, 1983), p. 134.

6. "Interview: Adlai E. Stevenson: Reindustrialization," *Challenge*, January–February 1981, pp. 40–44.

7. Felix Rohatyn, "Reconstructing America," *New York Review of Books*, March 5, 1981, pp. 16, 18.

8. Ibid., p. 18; Lester C. Thurow, "How to Rescue a Drowning Economy," *New York Review of Books*, April 1, 1982, p. 4.

9. U.S. Congress, Joint Economic Committee, *The 1982 Joint Economic Report*, 97th Cong., 2d sess. (Washington, D.C.: Government Printing Office, 1983), p. 110. See also Richard Corrigan, "Democrats Seek an Industrial Policy in Time for the Next Election Campaign," *National Journal*, June 11, 1983.

10. Solow, "Wheeling and Dealing," p. 11.

11. Pinder, Hosomi, and Diebold, *Industrial Policy and International Economy*, pp. 327–330.

12. *The Need for U.S. Industrial Objectives: A Report of the Industrial Objectives Panel of the Economic Policy Council of UNA-USA* (New York: United Nations Association, 1982), p. 5.

13. "Interview: William Diebold," p. 31.

14. Bruce Scott, in U.S. House of Representatives, Committee on Banking, Finance and Urban Affairs, Subcomittee on Economic Stabilization, *Industrial Policy*, 98th Cong., 1st sess., 5 vols. (Washington, D.C.: Government Printing Office, 1983), I, 429.

15. John Zysman and Stephen S. Cohen, "Double or Nothing: Open Trade and Competitive Industry," *Foreign Affairs*, Summer 1983, p. 1137.

16. Kennedy quoted in U.S. Congress, Joint Economic Committee, *The 1983 Joint Economic Report*, 98th Cong., 1st sess. (Washington, D.C.: Government Printing Office, 1983), pp. 93–94.

17. Frank A. Weil, "Industrial Policy: A Process in Need of a Federal Industrial Coordination Board," *Law and Policy in International Business* 14 (1983), 981. Weil's design for the FICB drew heavily upon what he learned from a review of U.S. and European history since World War II. See also Weil, "Policy for Industry," *New York Times*, March 28, 1982, p. F2.

18. Robert B. Reich, "Making Industrial Policy," *Foreign Affairs,* Spring 1982, pp. 876–877.

19. Center for National Policy, *Restoring American Competitiveness: Proposals for an Industrial Policy* (Washington, D.C., 1984), pp. 7–15.

20. Stephen S. Cohen, "Industrial Policy and East Coast Myopia," *New York Times,* August 28, 1983, p. D69; David Osborne, *State Technology Programs: A Preliminary Analysis of Lessons Learned* (Washington, D.C.: Council of State Policy and Planning Agencies, 1989).

21. Weil, "Policy for Industry."

22. For a useful summary of the institutional innovations proposed from 1981 to 1983 by various private and public study groups, see Business–Higher Education Forum, *America's Competitive Challenge* (Washington, D.C., 1983), apps. A and B.

23. John Latona in U.S. Senate, Committee on Banking, Housing and Urban Affairs, Subcommittees on International Finance and Monetary Policy, *Foreign Industrial Targeting,* 98th Cong., 1st sess. (Washington, D.C.: Government Printing Office, 1983), p. 108.

24. House Subcommittee on Economic Stabilization, *Industrial Policy,* I, 135–156.

25. Stanley Modic, "A U.S. Industrial Policy," *Business Week,* November 14, 1983, p. 7; see also Jerry Jasinowski in *Toward a New U.S. Industrial Policy,* ed. M. L. Wachter and S. M. Wachter (Philadelphia: University of Pennsylvania Press, 1982). An industrial strategy of this sort, policy change without institutional change, was endorsed in 1983 by, among others, chief executives David Mahoney of Norton Simon, Lee Iacocca of Chrysler (who expressed support for an RFC), and Edward Jefferson of Du Pont. See "Talking Up an Industrial Policy," *Newsweek,* April 4, 1983, pp. 66–67.

26. Scott quoted in House Subcommittee on Economic Stabilization, *Industrial Policy,* I, 430–431.

27. Center for National Policy, *Restoring American Competitiveness,* p. 8.

28. Felix Rohatyn, *The Twenty-Year Century* (New York: Random House, 1982), p. 4.

29. LaFalce quoted in House Subcommittee on Economic Stabilization, *Industrial Policy,* I, 499.

30. Cantor quoted in House Subcommittee on General Oversight and Renegotiation, *Establishment of National Development Bank,* p. 220; Roemer quoted ibid., p. 229.

31. Ira Magaziner, interview, *Providence Journal,* December 18, 1983, p. 9.

32. Testimony by Milan Stone on behalf of the AFL-CIO, House Subcommittee on Economic Stabilization, *Industrial Policy,* I, 288–302; United Auto Workers news release, "UAW Calls for Industrial Policy Geared to Full Employment and Balanced Growth," September 28, 1983.

33. Ira Magaziner and Robert Reich, *Minding America's Business* (New York: Vintage, 1982), pp. 377–378.

34. William Diebold, Jr., "Past and Future Industrial Policies in the U.S., in *National Industrial Strategies and the World Economy,* ed. John Pinder (London: Allenheld, Osmun, 1982), p. 182.

35. Scott quoted in House Subcommittee on Economic Stabilization, *Industrial Policy,* I, 422.

36. William K. Krist, "The U.S. Response to Foreign Industrial Policies," *National Journal,* January 22, 1983, p. 201.

37. Bergsten and LaFalce quoted in Subcommittee on Economic Stabilization, *Industrial Policy,* I, 87–93.

38. Scott quoted ibid., p. 430.

39. John Zysman and Laura Tyson, eds., *American Industry in International Competition* (Ithaca: Cornell University Press, 1983), p. 470.

40. *Economic Report of the President: 1982* (Washington, D.C.: Government Printing Office, 1983); U.S. International Trade Commission, *Annual Report of the International Trade Commission* for 1974–1983 (Washington, D.C.: Government Printing Office, 1974–1983).

41. Bureau of the Census, *Statistical Abstract of the United States: 1984* (Washington, D.C.: Government Printing Office, 1983); *Economic Report of the President* for 1981–1983 (Washington, D.C.: Government Printing Office, 1982–1984); John L. Palmer and Isabel V. Sawhill, eds., *The Reagan Experiment* (Washington, D.C.: Urban Institute, 1982); Charles F. Stone and Isabel V. Sawhill, eds., *Economic Policy in the Reagan Years* (Washington, D.C.: Urban Institute, 1984); John W. Kendrick, "Productivity, Costs, and Prices: Outlook for 1983–1984," *AEI Economist,* January 1983; Martin Neil Baily, "Will Productivity Growth Recover? Has It Done So Already?" *American Economic Association Papers and Proceedings* 74 (1984), 234–235.

42. Morton Kondracke, "Liberalism's Brave New World," *Public Opinion,* April/May 1982, pp. 2–5.

43. Rothenberg, *The Neo-Liberals,* p. 221.

44. Wirth quoted in Sidney Blumenthal, "Drafting a Democratic Industrial Plan," *New York Times Magazine,* August 28, 1983, p. 53; LaFalce quoted in Corrigan, "Democrats Seek an Industrial Policy," pp. 1221–22.

45. Gary Hart, *A New Democracy* (New York: William Morrow, 1982), pp. 46–47; quoted in *Raleigh News and Observer,* October 19, 1983, p. 6. Hart, too, uttered the obligatory words: "an industrial strategy is not . . . central economic planning, and it is not Japanese-style 'picking the winners' or 'propping up the losers' . . . we need a new process, initiated by the President, to create long-term agreements by management, labor, financial markets, and government designed to help our major industries become more competitive in the changing international economy"; *A New Democracy,* p. 48.

46. Monroe W. Karmin, "Industrial Policy: What Is It? Do We Need One?" *U.S. News and World Report,* October 3, 1983, p. 45.

47. U.S. Congress, House Democratic Caucus, Committee on Party Effectiveness, *Rebuilding the Road to Opportunity: A Democratic Direction for the 1980s* (Washington, D.C.: Government Printing Office, 1982). See also the subsequent House Democratic Caucus (Gillis W. Long and Robert S. Strauss, cochairmen), *Renewing America's Promise: A Democratic Blueprint for Our Nation's Future* (Washington, D.C.: Government Printing Office, 1984), esp. chaps. 3–6; and Ross K. Baker, "The Bittersweet Courtship of Congressional Democrats and Industrial Policy" (Paper presented to the Midwest Political Science Association, April 11, 1986).

48. U.S. Senate Democratic Caucus Task Force, *Jobs for the Future: A Democratic Agenda*

(Washington, D.C.: Government Printing Office, 1983), pp. 7, 15–16. For a review of five manifestoes from the Democrats, see James K. Galbraith, "Congress and the Industrial Policy Debate," in *Industrial Policy: Business and Politics in the United States and France,* ed. Sharon Zukin (New York: Praeger, 1987).

49. Carolyn Kay Brancato et al., *Industrial Policy in the 98th Congress,* Issue Brief IB83125 (Washington, D.C.: Congressional Research Service, 1985).
50. Heritage Foundation, "Industrial Policy: A Summary of Bills before Congress," *Issue Brief* 96, July 12, 1983.
51. Wirth quoted in Karmin, "Industrial Policy," p. 46; I. M. Destler, *American Trade Politics: System under Stress* (New York and Washington, D.C.: Twentieth Century Fund and Institute for International Economics, 1986), pp. 2–3.
52. The hearing record is found in House Subcommittee on Economic Stabilization, *Industrial Policy.* For analysis of this legislative history, see Stewart Auerbach, "Industrial Policy," *Washington Post,* June 29, 1983, p. F1; Baker, "Bittersweet Courtship"; Blumenthal, "Drafting a Democratic Industrial Plan"; and William Schneider, "Industrial Policy: It All Depends on How It's Sold to the Voters," *National Journal,* September 17, 1983, p. 96.
53. Regan quoted in Kenneth Noble, "Regan Belittles the Idea of U.S. Industrial Policy," *New York Times,* October 15, 1983, p. 46.
54. Hamilton quoted in, for example, F. Gerard Adams and Lawrence R. Klein, eds., *Industrial Policies for Growth and Competitiveness* (Lexington, Mass.: Lexington Books, 1983), p. 91, followed by a lengthy review of "industrial policies" adopted in the long span of U.S. history; see also Chalmers A. Johnson, ed., *The Industrial Policy Debate* (San Francisco: Institute for Contemporary Studies, 1984), p. 17.
55. Kirkland quoted in House Subcommittee on Economic Stabilization, *Industrial Policy,* IV, 83.
56. Rohatyn quoted ibid., p. 169.
57. Gail Schwartz and Pat Choate, *Being Number One: Rebuilding the U.S. Economy* (Lexington, Mass.: Lexington Books, 1980), pp. 109, 111.
58. Lester C. Thurow, *The Case for Industrial Policies* (Washington, D.C.: Center for National Policy, 1984), pp. 8–9.
59. "Revitalization," *Business Week,* pp. 42–43.
60. Julian Gresser, in U.S. House of Representatives, Committee on Ways and Means, Subcommittee on Trade, *High Technology and Japanese Industrial Policy: A Strategy for U.S. Policymakers,* 96th Cong., 2d sess. (Washington, D.C.: Government Printing Office, 1980), pp. 42–43.
61. James Bryce, *The American Commonwealth,* 3d ed. (New York: Macmillan, 1916), p. 593.
62. On the active role of state governments in the economic development of the nation, see Oscar Handlin and Mary Handlin, *Commonwealth: A Study of the Role of Government in the American Economy, Massachusetts, 1774–1861,* rev. ed. (Cambridge, Mass.: Harvard University Press, 1969); Louis Hartz, *Economic Policy and Democratic Thought: Pennsylvania, 1776–1860* (Cambridge, Mass.: Harvard University Press, 1948); James Willard Hurst, *Law and the Conditions of Freedom in the Nineteenth Century United States* (Madison: University of Wisconsin Press, 1956); Robert A. Lively, "The American System: A Review Article," *Business History Re-*

*view,* March 1955, pp. 81–96; E. A. J. Johnson, *The Foundations of American Economic Freedom: Government and Enterprise in the Age of Washington* (Minneapolis: University of Minnesota Press, 1973); Arthur M. Schlesinger, Jr., *The Cycles of American History* (Boston: Houghton Mifflin, 1986); and Harry N. Scheiber, "State Law and 'Industrial Policy' in American Development, 1790–1987," *California Law Review* 75 (January 1987), 415–444.

63. Arthur Conan Doyle, "Silver Blaze," in *The Memoirs of Sherlock Holmes* (New York: Ballantine, 1975), p. 34.

64. Marshall quoted in House Subcommittee on Economic Stabilization, *Industrial Policy,* I, 375–377.

65. David Irons, "Inching toward a National Competitive Strategy," *Harvard Magazine,* November–December 1983, p. 44.

66. LaFalce quoted in House Subcommittee on Economic Stabilization, *Industrial Policy,* V, 244.

67. Krugman quoted in Federal Reserve Board of Kansas City, *Industrial Change and Public Policy* (Kansas City, 1983), p. 123.

68. Ibid., pp. 80, 123–150.

## 7. The Critics

1. Herbert Stein, "Don't Fall for Industrial Policy," *Fortune,* November 14, 1983, p. 78.

2. Donald T. Regan, *Treasury News,* October 14, 1983, pp. 9, 11.

3. Don Lavoie, "Two Varieties of Industrial Policy: A Critique," *Cato Journal,* Fall 1984, p. 458. See also Robert M. Kaus, "Gary Hart's Idea Collection," *New Republic,* March 26, 1983.

4. Bruce Bartlett, "The Best Industrial Policy Is No Industrial Policy," *Competition,* August 1981, p. 12. See also Lavoie, "Two Varieties of Industrial Policy," p. 458.

5. Charles L. Schultze, "Industrial Policy: A Solution in Search of a Problem," *California Management Review* 24 (Summer 1983), 6.

6. *Economic Report of the President: 1984* (Washington, D.C.: Government Printing Office, 1984), pp. 88–94; see esp. chap. 3.

7. New York Stock Exchange (NYSE), *U.S. International Competitiveness: Perception and Reality* (New York, 1984), pp. 32–44, 50, 152; Herbert Stein, "Don't Fall for Industrial Policy," *Fortune,* November 14, 1983, p. 78. That comment took on an ironic edge when the Japanese began buying large pieces of the U.S. movie and TV industries, the first large chunk going to Sony Corp. with its 1989 purchase of Columbia Pictures Entertainment, Inc.

8. NYSE, *U.S. International Competitiveness,* p. 36.

9. Ibid., pp. 42–50.

10. Robert Z. Lawrence, *Can America Compete?* (Washington, D.C.: Brookings Institution, 1984), pp. 5, 22.

11. Ibid., pp. 25, 36; Robert Z. Lawrence, "Before Industrial Policy," *New York Times,* November 30, 1983, p. A31.

12. Lawrence, *Can America Compete?* pp. 80–83, 105.

13. Lawrence, "Before Industrial Policy," p. A31. See also Robert Z. Lawrence, "Is

Trade Deindustrializing America? A Medium-Term Perspective," *Brookings Papers on Economic Activity* 1 (1983), 129–161; idem, "The Myth of U.S. Deindustrialization," *Challenge*, November–December 1983, pp. 12–21.

14. Guarini quoted in U.S. House of Representatives, Committee on Banking, Finance and Urban Affairs, 98th Cong., 1st sess., Subcommittee on Economic Stabilization, *Industrial Policy*, 5 vols. (Washington, D.C.: Government Printing Office, 1983), V, 318–319, 323.

15. Murray Weidenbaum and Michael Athey, "What Is the Rust Belt's Problem?" in *The Industrial Policy Debate*, ed. Chalmers A. Johnson (San Francisco: Institute for Contemporary Studies, 1984), p. 128.

16. Melvyn Krauss, "Europeanizing the U.S. Economy: The Enduring Appeal of the Corporatist State," in Johnson, *Industrial Policy Debate*, pp. 72–73, 75.

17. Miller quoted in House Subcommittee on Economic Stabilization, *Industrial Policy*, V, 498.

18. Lundgren quoted ibid., p. 146.

19. James K. Hickel, "The Chrysler Bail-Out Bust," *Backgrounder* (Heritage Foundation) 276 (July 13, 1983). See also Hickel, "Lemon Aid," *Reason*, March 1983, p. 96.

20. Assistant Treasury Secretary Roger Altman quoted in House Subcommittee on Economic Stabilization, *Industrial Policy*, IV, 278–284.

21. GAO quoted ibid., pp. 314–318.

22. Congressman Wright Patman inserted a lengthy history of the agency in the *Congressional Record*, August 1969, pp. 22052–22124; see also Walter Grinder and Alan Fairgate, "The Reconstruction Finance Corporation Rides Again," *Reason*, July 1975, pp. 23–29; and Randall Rothenberg, "An RFC for Today: A Capital Idea," *Inc.*, January 1983.

23. Felix Rohatyn, "Reconstructing America," *New York Review of Books*, March 5, 1981, p. 18.

24. Jesse Jones and Edward Angley, *Fifty Billion Dollars: My Thirteen Years at the RFC, 1932–1945* (New York: Macmillan, 1951).

25. James S. Olson, *Herbert Hoover and the Reconstruction Finance Corporation, 1931–1933* (Ames: Iowa State University Press, 1977); see also idem, *Saving Capitalism: The Reconstruction Finance Corporation and the New Deal, 1933–1940* (Princeton: Princeton University Press, 1988).

26. Lavoie, "Two Varieties of Industrial Policy," pp. 477–478; Thomas J. DiLorenzo, "The Political Economy of National Industrial Policy," *Cato Journal*, Fall 1984, p. 597.

27. Celesta Gentry, "Federal Credit Programs: An Overview of Current Problems and Their Beginnings in the Reconstruction Finance Corporation" (Typescript, U.S. Treasury Department, July 18, 1980), pp. i, 3–5, in George Eads Papers (Eads' possession).

28. Arthur F. Denzau and Clifford M. Hardin, *A National Development Bank: Ghost of the RFC Past* (St. Louis: Center for the Study of American Business, 1984), pp. 1–2.

29. Roberts quoted in U.S. Congress, Joint Economic Committee, *Industrial Policy, Economic Growth, and the Competitiveness of U.S. Industry: Part I*, 98th Cong., 1st sess. (Washington, D.C.: Government Printing Office, 1983), pp. 92, 24–30.

30. Denzau and Hardin, *A National Development Bank,* p. 1. On the revival of an RFC see also Stein, "Don't Fall for Industrial Policy," p. 78; Roger G. Altman and Jeffrey Garten, "The Fallacy of a Modern-Day RFC," *New York Times,* October 9, 1983, p. 6, 9; and Clark Nardinelli, "The RFC's Murky History," *Backgrounder* 317 (October 13, 1983).

31. Business Roundtable Ad Hoc Task Force, *Analysis of the Issues in the National Industrial Policy Debate: Working Papers* (New York, 1984), pp. 118–122.

32. See Gerald T. White, *Billions for Defense: Government Financing by the Defense Plant Corporation during World War II* (Tuskaloosa: University of Alabama Press, 1980).

33. Robert A. Solo, "The Saga of Synthetic Rubber," *Bulletin of the Atomic Scientists* 36 (April 1980), 35; see also U.S. Senate, Committee on the Judiciary, *Synthetic Rubber; A Case Study in Technological Development under Government Direction,* 85th Cong., 2d sess. (Washington, D.C.: Government Printing Office, 1959), written by Robert A. Solo. For a generally concurring account, see Peter J. T. Morris, *The American Synthetic Rubber Research Program* (Philadelphia: University of Pennsylvania Press, 1989).

34. Olson, *Saving Capitalism,* finds its "accomplishments during the 1930s . . . impressive" (p. 225). There still is no adequate RFC history for the period 1940–1952.

35. Stein, "Don't Fall for Industrial Policy," p. 70.

36. For Muller's design for a Bank, see House Subcommittee on Economic Stabilization, *Industrial Policy,* IV, 38–58.

37. Bethune quoted ibid., p. 307.

38. Koji Taira, "Industrial Policy and Employment in Japan," *Current History* 82 (November 1983), 362.

39. Philip H. Trezise, "Industrial Policy Is Not the Major Reason for Japan's Success," *Brookings Review* 2 (Spring 1983), 13–18.

40. William G. Ouchi, *Theory Z: How American Business Can Meet the Japanese Challenge* (Reading, Mass.: Addison-Wesley, 1981); Richard T. Pascale and Anthony G. Athos, *The Art of Japanese Management: Applications for American Executives* (New York: Warner Books, 1982); Robert H. Hayes and Steven Wheelwright, *Restoring Our Competitive Edge: Competing through Manufacturing* (New York: John Wiley & Sons, 1984).

41. Toshimasa Tsuruta, "The Myth of Japan, Inc.," *Technology Review* 86 (July 1983), 46.

42. Jill Hills, "The Industrial Policy of Japan," *Journal of Public Policy* 3 (1983), 79. See also Kazuo Sato, ed., *Industry and Business in Japan* (White Plains, N.Y.: M. E. Sharpe, 1980).

43. "Industrial Policy, Part I: The Japanese Model," in *Manhattan Report on Economic Policy* (Manhattan Institute for Policy Research) 2 (October 1982), 9; Tsuruta, "The Myth," p. 48.

44. Frank Gibney, *Miracle by Design* (New York: Times Books, 1982), p. 143. See also G. C. Allen, *The Japanese Economy* (New York: St. Martin's Press, 1982).

45. George Gilder, "A Supply-Side Economics of the Left," *Public Interest* 72 (Summer 1983), 38.

46. Robert Ozaki, "How Japanese Industrial Policy Works," in Johnson, *Industrial Policy Debate,* p. 51.

47. "America cannot be MITI-ized, nor should it be," said Amitai Etzioni, "The MITI-ization of America?" *Public Interest* 72 (Summer 1983), 47.
48. Murray Sayle, "Japan Victorious," *New York Review of Books,* March 28, 1985, p. 40.
49. Jared Taylor, *Shadows of the Rising Sun: A Critical View of the "Japanese Miracle"* (New York: Morrow, 1983), pp. 21–22, and see esp. chap. 10. Ironically, this was also the view of officials from a major U.S. industry threatened with extinction by MITI targeting. The 1982 petition of the Houdaille machine tool industries for import relief was accompanied by what trade officials acknowledged to be the most meticulous and detailed reconstruction, in English, of the network of subsidies, protection, and strategic encouragement by which MITI formulated industrial policy. Yet Houdaille vice-president John Latona, after telling a congressional committee that Japanese IP worked brilliantly, insisted that it would not be appropriate here. See House Subcommittee on Economic Stabilization, *Industry Policy,* II, 588–604.
50. Brock quoted in House Subcommittee on Economic Stabilization, *Industrial Policy,* V, 296, 366.
51. Paul Krugman, "Foreign Experience with Industrial Policy: A Critical Review," draft, July 5, 1980, pp. 3, 31, Eads Papers.
52. George C. Eads, "Lessons from the U.S. and Elsewhere," in *Toward a New Industrial Policy*, ed. M. L. Wachter and S. M. Wachter (Philadelphia: University of Pennsylvania Press, 1982), pp. 472–479.
53. Krauss, "Europeanizing the U.S. Economy," pp. 74–88.
54. Robert J. Samuelson, "The Policy Peddlers," *Harper's,* June 1983, p. 62.
55. For other assessments of recent European experience with industrial policies, see Juergen Donges, "Industrial Policies in West Germany's Not-So-Market-Oriented Economy," *World Economy,* September 1980, pp. 69–96; Hobart Rowen, "Overcoming Europessimism," *Washington Post National Weekly,* April 23, 1984, pp. D6–9; and Brian Hindley, *State Investment Companies in Western Europe: Picking Winners or Backing Losers?* (New York: St. Martin's Press, 1983), p. xx.
56. Theodore J. Eismeier, "The Case against Industrial Policy," *Journal of Contemporary Studies* 6 (Spring, 1983), 21–22.
57. Stephen Blank and Paul Sacks, "If at First You Don't Succeed, Don't Try Again: Industrial Policy in Britain," in *Industrial Vitalization: Toward a National Industrial Policy,* ed. Margaret E. Dewar (New York: Pergamon, 1982).
58. Eads, "Lessons from the U.S.," pp. 476, 473.
59. Blank and Sacks, "If at First," pp. 209–214.
60. Royal Commission on Depression of Trade and Industry, *Final Report,* 3 vols. (London, 1886).
61. Quoted in G. R. Searle, *The Quest for National Efficiency: A Study in British Politics and Political Thought, 1889–1914* (Oxford: Blackwell, 1971), p. 1.
62. For the British economy before World War I, see Roderick Floud, "Britain, 1860–1914," in *The Economic History of Britain since 1700,* ed. Floud and Donald N. McCloskey, vol. II (Cambridge: Cambridge University Press, 1981); and Donald N. McCloskey, ed., *Essays on a Mature Economy: Britain after 1840* (Princeton: Princeton University Press, 1971).

63. Richard E. Caves and Lawrence B. Krause, *Britain's Economic Performance* (Washington, D.C.: Brookings Institution, 1980), p. 185.

64. Anthony Sampson, *The Changing Anatomy of Britain* (London: Hodder and Stoughton, 1982), p. 69.

65. Peter Jenkins, "Patient Britain: A Century of the 'English Disease,'" *New Republic,* December 23, 1985, p. 16.

66. Martin J. Wiener, *English Culture and the Decline of the Industrial Spirit, 1850–1980* (Cambridge, Mass.: Harvard University Press, 1981).

67. David S. Landes, *The Unbound Prometheus: Technological Change and Industrial Development in Western Europe from 1700 to the Present* (Cambridge, Mass.: Harvard University Press, 1969), pp. 342–358. See also Carlo Cipolla, *The Economic Decline of Empires* (London: Methuen, 1971); D. H. Aldcroft and H. W. Richardson, *The British Economy, 1870–1939* (London: Macmillan, 1969); Bernard Elbaum and William Lazonick, eds., *The Decline of the British Economy* (Oxford: Clarendon Press, 1986).

68. Geoffrey Smith and Nelson W. Polsby, *British Government and Its Discontents* (New York: Basic Books, 1981), pp. 175–176.

69. Landes, *The Unbound Prometheus,* pp. 357, 554.

70. Bernard Nossiter, *Britain: A Future That Works* (Boston: Houghton Mifflin, 1978). See also the observations of John Kenneth Galbraith in Krishan Kumar, "A Future in the Past?" *New Society* 42 (November 1977), 418–419; and David Rose et al., "Economic Restructuring: The British Experience," *Annals of the American Academy of Political and Social Science,* September 1974.

71. Tom Nairn, "The Politics of the New Venice," *New Society* 42 (November 1977), 352.

72. R. James Ball, "Industrial Policy in the United Kingdom," in Wachter and Wachter, *Toward a New Industrial Policy,* pp. 507–508.

73. Herbert Stein, *Presidential Economics* (New York: Simon and Schuster, 1984), p. 321.

74. Albertine quoted in Joint Economic Committee, *Industrial Policy, Economic Growth, and Competitiveness,* p. 5.

75. Baldrige quoted in U.S. Senate, Committee on Finance, *Promotion of High Growth Industries and U.S. Competitiveness,* 98th Cong., 1st sess. (Washington, D.C.: Government Printing Office, 1983), pp. 16–17.

76. Richard McKenzie, "National Industrial Policy: An Overview of the Debate," *Backgrounder* 275 (July 12, 1983), 23.

77. Gerald R. Jantscher, "Lessons from the Maritime Aid Program," in *Industry Vitalization: Toward a National Industrial Policy,* ed. Margaret Dewar (New York: Pergamon, 1982), pp. 111–117.

78. Paul A. Tiffany, "The Roots of Decline: Business-Government Relations in the American Steel Industry, 1945–1960," *Journal of Economic History* 44 (1984), 407.

79. Richard H. K. Vietor, *Energy Policy in American since 1945: A Study of Business-Government Relations* (Cambridge: Cambridge University Press, 1984), chap. 3; see also Richard R. Nelson, ed., *The Moon and the Ghetto* (New York: W. W. Norton, 1977), p. 120.

80. John L. Campbell, *Collapse of an Industry: Nuclear Power and the Contradictions of United States Policy* (Ithaca: Cornell University Press, 1988).

81. Bernard Bellush, *The Failure of the NRA* (New York: W. W. Norton, 1975). On the NRA, see also Ellis W. Hawley, *The New Deal and the Problem of Monopoly* (Princeton: Princeton University Press, 1966); Hawley, "Industrial Policy in the 1920s and 1930s," in *Politics of Industrial Policy,* ed. Claude E. Barfield and William A. Schambra (Washington, D.C.: American Enterprise Institute, 1986); Robert F. Himmelberg, *Origins of the National Recovery Administration* (New York: Fordham University Press, 1976); and Otis L. Graham, Jr., *Toward a Planned Society: From Roosevelt to Nixon* (New York: Oxford University Press, 1976), chap. 1.

82. Walter C. Sellar and Robert J. Yeatman, *1066 and All That: A Memorable History of England* (New York: E. P. Dutton, 1931), p. vii.

83. Wachter and Wachter, *Toward a New Industrial Policy.* Deep skepticism was expressed only by George Eads, former Carter CEA member, and two top Reagan aides, Murray Weidenbaum and Donald Regan.

84. The Brookings Institution, called "long a bastion for liberal Democrats," was thanked for becoming "a hot-bed of anti-industrial policy work" through the writing of Robert Crandall, Robert Lawrence, Philip Trezise, and Charles Schultze, in Bruce Bartlett, "America's New Ideology: Industrial Policy," *American Journal of Economics and Sociology* 44 (January 1985), 7.

85. Dwight R. Lee, "The Faulty Logic of Industrial Policy," 299 (1984), 1.

86. Jasinowski quoted in U.S. Senate, Committee on Finance Subcommittee on Economic Growth, Unemployment and Revenue Sharing, *Future of U.S. Basic Industries,* 98th Cong., 1st sess. (Washington, D.C.: Government Printing Office, 1983), 185.

87. *Economic Report of the President: 1984* (Washington, D.C.: Government Printing Office, 1984), p. 88.

88. Schultze, "Industrial Policy," p. 12; see also Charles L. Schultze, "Industrial Policy: A Dissent," *Brookings Review,* Fall 1983.

89. Jasinowski, interviewed in Stanley J. Modic, "A U.S. Industrial Policy," *Business Week,* November 14, 1983, p. 42; Schultze quoted in Joint Economic Committee, *Industrial Policy, Economic Growth, and Competitiveness,* pt. 3, pp. 2–40.

90. George C. Eads, "Picking Winners and Killing Dogs," pp. 37–38.

91. Lawrence, *Can America Compete?* p. 117.

92. Ibid., pp. 134, 136.

93. Eads quoted in Joint Economic Committee, *Industrial Policy, Economic Growth, and Competitiveness,* pt. 1, pp. 102–104.

94. Schultze quoted ibid., p. 108.

95. Robert W. Crandall, "Can Industrial Policy Work?" *Washington Post Book World,* May 22, 1983, p. 8.

96. Bruce Bartlett, "The Old Politics of a New Industrial Policy," *Wall Street Journal,* April 19, 1983, p. 34.

## 8. The End of the Beginning

1. *Economic Report of the President: 1984* (Washington, D.C.: Government Printing Office), 1984, pp. 1–5.

2. Leslie Wayne, "U.S. Job Surge Envy of Europeans," *International Herald Tribune,*

June 27, 1984, p. 6. See also U.S. Department of Commerce, International Trade Administration, *U.S. Industrial Outlook: 1985* (Washington, D.C.: Government Printing Office, 1985), pp. 29–33.

3. Iacocca quoted in Peter Behr, "Shift toward Services Continues," *Washington Post,* January 13, 1985, pp. F1, F13.

4. John W. Kendrick, "Productivity and Cost Prospects for 1984–1985," *AEI Economist,* April 1984, pp. 7–9. See also Lawrence Fulco, "Productivity and Costs in 1984," *Monthly Labor Review,* June 1985, pp. 40–45; and *Business Week,* October 22, 1984, p. 31.

5. Peter K. Clark, "Productivity and Profits: Are They Really Improving?" *Brookings Papers on Economic Activity* 1 (1984) 133–163. See also Martin Neil Baily, "Will Productivity Growth Recover? Has It Done So Already?" *American Economic Association Papers and Proceedings* 74 (1984), 234–235.

6. "Imports Are Beginning to Hurt," *Business Week,* October 22, 1984, p. 31.

7. U.S. International Trade Commission, *1984 Annual Report* (Washington, D.C.: Office of Public Affairs, 1984), pp. 1–29; Pietro S. Nivola, "The New Protectionism: U.S. Trade Policy in Historical Perspective," *Political Science Quarterly,* 101 (1986), 578.

8. Carl Sandburg, "Chicago," in *Chicago Poems* (New York: Henry Holt, 1916), p. 3.

9. Joseph Kraft, "New Adventure in the National Saga," *Washington Post,* January 15, 1984, p. 16.

10. U.S. Congress, Joint Economic Committee, *The Industrial Policy Movement in the United States: Is It the Answer?* 98th Cong., 2d sess. (Washington, D.C.: Government Printing Office, 1984), pp. x, 4–5.

11. George Cabot Lodge, *The American Disease* (New York: Alfred A. Knopf, 1984). See also G. C. Lodge and W. C. Crum, "U.S. Competitiveness: The Policy Tangle," *Harvard Business Review,* January–February 1955; and Bruce R. Scott and George C. Lodge, eds., *U.S. Competitiveness in the World Economy* (Cambridge, Mass.: Harvard Business School Press, 1985).

12. "Do We Need an Industrial Policy?" *Harper's,* February 1985, pp. 36–48, report of a conference held at Harvard in late 1984; for reports of other exchanges between the four economists, see "The Deindustrialization of America," *Boston Globe,* October 30, 1984, p. 44; and "The Latest Debate about Deindustrialization," *Business Week,* February 6, 1984, p. 12. See also Barry Bluestone, "Is Deindustrialization a Myth?" *Annals of the American Academy of Political and Social Science,* September 1984, pp. 39–51.

13. Robert Z. Lawrence, *Can America Compete?* (Washington, D.C.: Brookings Institution, 1984), pp. 134–137; Lester Thurow, "Losing the Economic Race," *New York Review of Books,* September 27, 1984, pp. 28–31.

14. Otto Eckstein et al., *The DRI Report on U.S. Manufacturing Industries* (New York: McGraw-Hill, 1984), I, 82–101.

15. White House Conference on Productivity, *Productivity Growth: A Better Life for America* (Washington, D.C.: Government Printing Office, 1985), pp. 20–21, 77–85.

16. Julian Gresser, *Partners in Prosperity: Strategic Industries for the U.S. and Japan* (New York: McGraw-Hill, 1984), pp. xiv–xv. Gresser drew upon the work of perhaps

ten economic historians in formulating his argument, and was especially indebted to David S. Landes, *The Unbound Prometheus: Technological Change and Industrial Development in Western Europe from 1700 to the Present* (Cambridge, Mass.: Harvard University Press, 1969).

17. See Robert E. Driscoll and Jack N. Behrman, eds., *National Industrial Policies* (Cambridge, Mass.: Oelgeschlager, Gunn, and Hain, 1984), for essays on Brazil, Canada, France, Japan, Malaysia, Mexico, the Philippines, the Republic of China, Singapore, South Korea, Sweden, the United Kingdom, West Germany, and the United States.

18. Paul R. Krugman, ed., *Strategic Trade Policy and the New International Economics* (Cambridge, Mass.: MIT Press, 1986), p. 5. See also John M. Culbertson, *International Trade and the Future of the West* (Madison, Wis.: Twenty First Century Press, 1984); and Robert Kuttner, "The Poverty of Economics," *Atlantic Monthly,* February 1985, pp. 74–84.

19. "Japan, Then and Now," *OECD Observer* 127 (March 1984), 3.

20. Stanley J. Modic, "It's Just Wishful Thinking," *Industry Week,* October 17, 1983, p. 7.

21. Chalmers Johnson, ed., *The Industrial Policy Debate* (San Francisco: Institute for Contemporary Studies, 1984), p. 19. For Japan's continuing strength, see Thomas K. McCraw, ed., *America Versus Japan* (Cambridge, Mass.: Harvard Business School Press, 1986).

22. Ibid., p. 4.

23. Stuart E. Eizenstat, "Industrial Policy: Not If, but How?" *Fortune,* January 23, 1984, pp. 183–185.

24. Iacocca quoted in U.S. House of Representatives, Committee on Banking, Finance and Urban Affairs, Subcommittee on Economic Stabilization, *Industrial Competitiveness Act,* 98th Cong., 2d sess. (Washington, D.C.: Government Printing Office, 1984), p. 168; and Lee Iacocca with William Novak, *Iacocca: An Autobiography* (New York: Bantam Books, 1984), pp. 199, 330, 329, 316.

25. Bartlett quoted in Johnson, *Industrial Policy Debate,* p. 7; Richard Newfarmer, "Investment Policy," in U.S. Congress, Joint Economic Committee, *Politicies for Industrial Growth in a Competitive World: A Volume of Essays,* 98th Cong., 2d sess. (Washington, D.C.: Government Printing Office, 1984), pp. 18–19.

26. Iacocca quoted in House Subcommittee on Economic Stabilization, *Industrial Competitiveness Act,* pp. 168, 172.

27. Kevin P. Phillips, *Staying on Top: The Business Case for National Industry Strategy* (New York: Random House, 1984), pp. 17–21, 61–78.

28. Ibid., pp. 14–15, 34–35, 44, 57–58, 112–113, 119, 124, 158; idem, "America Must Look Out for Number One," *Washington Post,* December 16, 1984, pp. F1, F4. If there was a boundary separating strategy from policy, Phillips was willing to cross it later, when public opinion would permit. He speculated that "a second stage" might be reached by 1986–87, when the public might permit a National Steel Authority or an Advanced Technology Corporation (*Staying on Top,* pp. 86–87). Or, Industrial Policy.

29. Assar Lindbeck, "Industrial Policy as an Issue in Economic Development," *World Economy* 4 (December 1981), 402.

30. Targeting the process of innovation through tax incentives and support for R&D was urged by Congressman Ed Zschau (R., Calif.), U.S. House of Representatives, Committee on Banking, Finance and Urban Affairs, Subcommittee on Economic Stabilization, *Industrial Policy,* 98th Cong., 1st sess., 5 vols. (Washington, D.C.: Government Printing Office, 1983), V, 157–176; see also U.S. Congress, Joint Economic Committee, *Industrial Policy Movement in the United States: Is It the Answer?* 98th Cong., 1st sess. (Washington, D.C.: Government Printing Office, 1984), app. I.

31. Alfred D. Chandler, Jr., *Strategy and Structure* (Cambridge, Mass.: Harvard University Press, 1962).

32. House Subcommittee on Economic Stabilization, *Industrial Competitiveness Act.* H.R. 4360 also established a Federal Industrial Mortgage Association to improve the secondary market for mortgages for loans to small companies, where the bill's drafters had discovered what they took to be a flaw in capital markets. The Bank was to be capitalized at $8.5 billion. The package was presented as a complement to macroeconomic policy and as an alternative both to "protectionism" and to the option of passively watching our industries be "picked off one by one."

    H.R. 4360 proposed only two of the three basic IP institutions: the tripartite Forum (called a Council) and the Bank. Congressional Democrats had not provided the White House coordinating mechanism (the Council in my usage) LaFalce was attempting to merge tripartism and presidential coordination in his Council, since 4 of the 16 members would either be cabinet officers or state-local elected officials. This hardly met a president's needs for a coordinating mechanism under his control.

33. LaFalce quoted in Richard Corrigan, "Democrats May Set Trap for Themselves with Industrial Policy Package," *National Journal,* May 26, 1984, p. 1039.

34. Hart quoted in *Raleigh News and Observer,* April 23, 1984, p. 5A; Mondale quoted in Randall Rothenburg, "Mr. Industrial Policy," *Esquire,* May 1983, pp. 95–97; see also "Hart Brands Chrysler Bailout as Policy Failure," *Los Angeles Times,* April 25, 1984, p. 114; I. M. Destler, "Protecting Congress or Protecting Trade?" *Foreign Policy,* Spring 1986, pp. 102–105; and Robert M. Kaus, "Gary Hart's Idea Collection," *New Republic,* March 26, 1984.

35. Ross K. Baker, "The Bittersweet Courtship of Congressional Democrats and Industrial Policy" (Paper presented at Midwest Political Science Association meeting, April 11, 1986), pp. 20, 21. See also Simon Lazarus and Robert E. Litan, "The Democrats' Coming Civil War over Industrial Policy," *Atlantic Monthly,* September 1984, pp. 92–98; and Robert W. Russell, "Congress and the Proposed Industrial Policy Structures," in *The Politics of Industrial Policy,* ed. Claude A. Barfield and William Schambra (Washington, D.C.: American Enterprise Institute, 1986).

36. Iaccoca quoted in House Subcommittee on Economic Stabilization, *Industrial Competitiveness Act,* p. 186.

37. John J. LaFalce, interview with author, April 24, 1986.

38. Baker, "Bittersweet Courtship," p. 29.

39. Mondale issues coordinator William Galston, interview with author, February 23, 1987.

40. Senator Edward Kennedy, "Revitalizing the U.S. Economy: The Role of Industrial Strategy," *Journal of Business Strategy* 5 (Summer 1984), 8.

41. Baker, "Bittersweet Courtship," p. 18.

42. Ibid., p. 38.

43. The Rhode Island "Greenhouse Compact" proposed many things, but the title came from one idea, relatively secondary, to establish four "research greenhouses" to "take technologies which are well advanced in basic research and accelerate the process of commercial development"; Rhode Island Strategic Development Commission, *The Greenhouse Compact: Cultivating Rhode Island's Fourth Economy, Executive Summary,* 2 vols. (Providence, 1983), I, 29.

44. Seven of its detailed proposals would affect the targeting of capital resources; seven would change labor, regulatory law, and tax law; five would increase the level and alter the focus of state R&D efforts; one had to do with retraining; and one established the permanent Strategic Development Commission as the implementing agency. This adds up to 22 rather than the commission's 21 recommendations, since I interpret one recommendation as falling in two areas. This was a formidable reform document, both as to politics and economics.

45. Magaziner quoted in *Providence Journal,* December 18, 1983, 3; Rhode Island Strategic Development Commission, *The Greenhouse Compact,* p. 4.

46. Allan Feldman, "Sunset for Industrial Policy," *Policy Review,* Fall 1984, p. 84.

47. Clarke E. Ryder, interview, *Providence Journal-Bulletin,* June 2, 1984, p. A1.

48. Magaziner quoted in "Rhode Island's Greenhouse Compact: Putting Industrial Policy to a Vote," *New York Times,* June 10, 1984, sec. 3, p. 4. See also Hilary Silver, "Is Industrial Policy Possible in the United States? The Defeat of Rhode Island's Greenhouse Compact," *Politics and Society* 15 (1986), 333–368; Thomas J. Anton and Darrell M. West, *Nothing for Something: Popular Reactions to New Industrial Policy* (Providence: A. Alfred Taubman Center for Public Policy and American Institutions, 1985); Nikhilesh Dholakia and Paul Mangiameli, "An Appraisal of Rhode Island's Strategy for Reindustrialization," *Northeast Journal of Business and Economics* 10 (Spring/Summer 1984), 12–28; George Borts, "The Greenhouse Program," *Northeast Journal of Business and Economics* 10 (Spring/Summer 1984), 29–34.

49. Howard Kurtz, "A 'New Idea' Fizzles on Launch," *Washington Post,* July 15, 1984, p. B5.

50. Ibid.; Feldman, "Sunset for Industrial Policy," p. 84; U.S. Congress, Joint Economic Committee, *The Industrial Policy Movement in the United States: Is It the Answer?* (Washington, D.C.: Government Printing Office, 1984), p. 51.

51. Walter Olson, "Industrial Policy from the Grass Roots," *Wall Street Journal,* June 12, 1984, p. 34; Anton and West, *Nothing for Something,* p. 1.

52. John Walsh, "Skirmish on the Industrial Policy Front," *Science,* June 29, 1984, p. 1410; Ronald Brownstein, "A Big Idea Is Back," *National Journal* September 29, 1984, p. 1829.

53. Robert Kuttner, "Revenge of the Democratic Nerds," *New Republic,* October 22, 1984, p. 17. The literature on the 1984 presidential campaign, a campaign judged by two authors as "mindless" and "devoid of content" (see Jack W. Germond and Jules Witcover, *Wake Us When It's Over: Presidential Politics of 1984* [New York: Mac-

millan, 1985], pp. 539–540), is unmarked by the term *Industrial Policy,* let alone any discussion of it. See Austin Ranney, ed., *The American Elections of 1984* (Durham, N.C.: Duke University Press, 1985); Peter Goldman and Tony Fuller, *The Quest for the Presidency* (New York: Bantam Books, 1985); and William A. Henry, *Visions of America: How We Saw the 1984 Election* (Boston: Atlantic Monthly Press, 1985).

54. Strauss quoted in Stuart Auerbach, "Industrial Policy," *Washington Post,* June 29, 1983, p. F1.
55. William Galston, interview with author, February 23, 1987.
56. John J. LaFalce, interview with author, April 24, 1986.
57. Walter Mondale, interview with author, October 21, 1985.
58. Robert Reich to author, January 24, 1985.
59. Magaziner quoted in Adam Smith, "The Cold Truth about a Hot Idea," *Esquire,* October 1984, p. 83.
60. Paul Craig Roberts, "A Tax Scheme to Deindustrialize America," *Wall Street Journal,* December 6, 1984, p. 32.
61. Joseph A. Pechman, "The Treasury Tax Reform Plan: Pro- or Anti-Growth?" *Brookings Review* 4 (Spring 1985), 30–36.
62. President's Commission on Industrial Competitiveness (PCIC), *Global Competition: The New Reality,* 2 vols. (Washington, D.C.: Government Printing Office, 1985), I, 11, 19; II, 10–19; for media reaction, see Peter Behr and David Vise, "Tax Plan Enrages Manufacturers," *Washington Post,* June 2, 1985, pp. F1, F4.
63. PCIC, *Global Competition,* II, 187; I, 31.
64. Ibid., I, 31, 51–60.
65. Colin Norman, "Commission Proposes Science Department," *Science,* March 1, 1985, p. 1017.
66. PCIC, *Global Competition,* II, 247.

## 9. America's Unconscious Industrial Plan

1. William D. Eberle, Richard N. Gardner, and Ann Crittenden, *The Next Four Years: The U.S. and the World Economy* (Lanham, Md.: University Press of America, 1984), p. 11.
2. U.S. Congress, House of Representatives, *Council on Industrial Competitiveness Act,* H.R. 99-579, 99th Cong., 2d sess. (Washington, D.C.: Government Printing Office, 1986), p. 11.
3. Lee Iacocca with William Novak, *Iacocca: An Autobiography* (New York: Bantam Books, 1984), p. 330.
4. Dr. Sheldon Weinig quoted in U.S. House of Representatives, Committee on Banking, Finance and Urban Affairs, Subcommittee on Economic Stabilization, *Industrial Policy,* 98th Cong., 1st sess., 5 vols. (Washington, D.C.: Government Printing Office, 1983), I, 77. For another summary view of our revealed IP, see Robert B. Reich, *Tales of a New America* (New York: Times Books, 1987), pp. 228–231.
5. Phyllis Levinson et al., *The Federal Entrepreneur: The Nation's Implicit Industries Policy* (Washington, D.C.: Urban Institute, 1982), pp. i, 70, 85.

6. Ibid., pp. 132–139. The aids to industries fell into four categories: aids to increase demand (import restrictions, price supports, procurement, etc.), financial sub-sidies (loans, loan guarantees, tax expenditures, etc.), production subsidies (loans for plant construction and equipment, labor retraining, R&D), subsidies to profits (direct payments to parts of air transport, shipping). One of the Urban Institute report's authors, Marc Bendick, said in congressional testimony that only 44 per-cent of the 329 aids to industry were "explicitly targeted" by industry, but that others were targeted by characteristics that were proxies for industry, which ac-counts for the estimate of 81 percent used elsewhere in the report. See House Sub-committee on Economic Stabilization, *Industrial Policy*, I, 535–537.

   The Congressional Budget Office's study, *Federal Support of U.S. Business* (Wash-ington, D.C.: Government Printing Office, 1984), excluded procurement, R&D, and infrastructure subsidies, and even so found federal aids to business costing in the range of $132 billion in 1984.

7. House Subcommittee on Economic Stabilization, *Industrial Policy*, I, 597; Celestea Gentry, "Federal Credit Programs: An Overview of Current Programs and Their Beginning in the Reconstruction Finance Corporation" (Typescript, U.S. Treasury Department, July 18, 1980), in George Eads Papers (Eads's possession); *Economic Report of the President: 1982* (Washington, D.C.: Government Printing Office, 1982), p. 94.

8. Richard E. Feinberg, *Subsidizing Success: The Export-Import Bank in the U.S. Economy* (New York: Cambridge University Press, 1982), pp. 1, 27–31, 25, 131.

9. Nonna A. Noto, *Industrial Policies Implicit in Federal Business Credit Programs* (Wash-ington, D.C.: Congressional Research Service, 1980), p. 35. See also Herman B. Leonard, *Checks Unbalanced: The Quiet Side of Public Funding* (New York: Basic Books, 1986).

10. U.S. Congress, House of Representatives, Committee on Banking, Finance and Ur-ban Affairs, Subcommittee on Economic Stabilization, *The Corporate Tax Code as Industrial Policy*, 98th Cong., 2d sess. (Washington, D.C.: Government Printing Office, 1984), pp. 23–36.

11. Lester C. Thurow, *The Zero-Sum Solution: Building a World-Class American Economy* (New York: Simon and Schuster, 1985), pp. 224–226.

12. Perry D. Quick, "Businesses: Reagan's Industrial Policy," in *The Reagan Record*, ed. John L. Palmer and Isabel V. Sawhill (Washington, D.C.: Urban Institute Press, 1984), p. 301. See also Charles R. Hulten and J. W. Robertson, "Taxation: Our De Facto Industrial Policy," *Urban Institute Policy and Research Report* 14 (Octo-ber 1984), 1–5.

13. Donald T. Regan, address to the National Press Club, December 3, 1984, in U.S. Department of the Treasury, *Press Release*, vol. 263 (Washington, D.C.: Govern-ment Printing Office, 1984).

14. Young quoted in U.S. Congress, House of Representatives, Committee on Banking, Finance and Urban Affairs, Subcommittee on Economic Stabilization, *Report of the President's Commission on Industrial Competitiveness*, 99th Cong., 1st sess. (Washing-ton, D.C.: Government Printing Office, 1985, p. 21.

15. David B. Yoffie, "Protecting World Markets," in *America versus Japan*, ed. Tho-

mas K. McCraw (Cambridge, Mass.: Harvard University Press, 1986), pp. 51–55; see also I. M. Destler, "Protecting Congress or Protecting Trade?" *Foreign Policy,* Spring 1986, pp. 102–105.

16. *Domestication* is the term of Raymond J. Ahearn and Alfred Reitman, "Trade Policy Making in the Congress," in *Recent Issues and Initiatives in the U.S. Trade Policy,* ed. R. E. Baldwin, NBER Conference Report (Boston: National Bureau of Economic Research, 1984).

17. Baker quoted in Hobart Rowen, "Reagan's Trade Problem," *Washington Post,* October 4, 1987, p. H1.

18. In these terms the administration was losing the argument. Robert Crandall of the Brookings Institution estimated that the VERs on Japanese autos added $2,500 to the price of Japanese cars and $800–1,000 to American vehicles; U.S. Senate, Committee on Employment and Productivity, *Impact of Trade on Employment,* 99th Cong., 1st sess. (Washington, D.C.: Government Printing Office, 1985), pp. 254–255. Gary C. Hufbauer and Howard F. Rosen calculated that textile protection cost American consumers $27 billion in 1985, a purchase of American textile jobs at a cost of $20,000–50,000 per job. Protectionism for all major industries cost over $50 billion, they estimated, saving 100,000 jobs; Hufbauer and Rosen, *Trade Policy for Troubled Industries* (Washington, D.C.: Institute for International Economics, 1986), pp. 18–27. For an estimate of $58.5 billion for the cost of all U.S. trade barriers see M. C. Munger and K. A. Rehbein, "The High Cost of Protectionism," *Europe,* May/June 1984, pp. 10–11.

19. William R. Cline, ed., *Trade Policy in the 1980s* (Washington, D.C.: Institution for International Economics, 1983), pp. 217–218.

20. Alan W. Wolff, "International Competitiveness of American Industry: The Role of U.S. Trade Policy," in *U.S. Competitiveness in the World Economy,* ed. Bruce R. Scott and George C. Lodge (Cambridge, Mass.: Harvard Business School Press, 1985), p. 324.

21. President's Scientific Research Board, *Science and Public Policy,* vol. I: *A Program for the Nation* (Washington, D.C.: Government Printing Office, 1947), pp. 10–121; U.S. Bureau of the Census, *Historical Statistics of the United States: Colonial Times to 1957* (Washington, D.C.: Government Printing Office, 1960), p. 965.

22. B. R. Guile and Harvey Brooks, eds., *Technology and Global Industry* (Washington, D.C.: National Academy Press, 1987), p. 193; Kenneth Flamm, "Technology Policy in International Perspective," in U.S. Congress, Joint Economic Committee, *Policies for Industrial Growth in a Competitive World,* 99th Cong., 2d sess. (Washington, D.C.: Government Printing Office, 1984), pp. 29–39.

23. Steve Coll, *The Deal of the Century: The Breakup of AT&T* (New York: Atheneum, 1986), 369.

24. Charles L. Brown, "The AT&T Experience: Implications for a National Industrial Policy," *Journal of Business Strategy* 5 (Summer 1984), 19. See also Peter Temin and Louis Galambos, *The Fall of the Bell System: A Study in Prices and Politics* (Cambridge: Cambridge University Press, 1987); and Alan Stone, *Wrong Number: The Breakup of AT&T* (New York: Basic Books, 1989).

   For a dispute over whether judges or Justice Department lawyers are the least qualified to make decisions on the effects of antitrust adjudication upon technological innovation, see William F. Baxter, "Anti-Trust Law and Technological Innovation," *Issues in Science and Technology*, Winter 1985, with a rejoinder by Daniel Schwartz and J. M. Cooper; also Alfred D. Chandler, Jr., et al., *National Competition Policy: Historians' Perspectives on Antitrust and Government-Business Relationships in the U.S.* (Washington, D.C.: Federal Trade Commission, 1981). David Dale Martin, "The Role of Antitrust in the Industrial Policies of the United States," in U.S. Congress, Joint Economic Committee, *Policies for Industrial Growth in a Competitive World: A Volume of Essays*, 98th Cong., 2d sess. (Washington, D.C.: Government Printing Office, 1984), reviews antitrust law as industrial policy. For tort law as industrial policy, see Peter W. Huber, "The Bhopalization of U.S. Tort Law," *Issues in Science and Technology*, Fall 1985.

25. William G. Ouchi, "The Microeconomic Policy Dialogue," in President's Commission on Industrial Competitiveness (PCIC), *Global Competition: The New Reality*, 2 vols. (Washington, D.C.: Government Printing Office, 1985), II, app. E, pp. 356–357. *The Encyclopedia of Governmental Advisory Organizations 1986–1987* (Washington, D.C.: Gale, 1988) required 860 pages to list 5,000 of such groups, far more than the PCIC had counted.

26. A summary of "employee protection provisions" in federal law is presented in Secretary of Labor's Task Force on Economic Adjustment and Worker Dislocation (Malcolm R. Lovell, Jr., chairman), *Economic Adjustment and Worker Dislocation in a Competitive Society* (Washington, D.C.: Government Printing Office, 1986); see esp. fig. 2.

27. Malcolm R. Lovell, Jr., "An Antidote for Protectionism," *Brookings Review* 3 (Fall 1984), 23.

28. Steve Charnovitz, "Worker Adjustment: The Missing Ingredient in Trade Policy," *California Management Review* 23 (Winter 1986), 167. For critical assessments and suggestions for reform of trade adjustment assistance, see Hufbauer and Rosen, *Trade Policy for Troubled Industries;* J. David Richardson, "Worker Adjustment to U.S. International Trade," in *Trade Policy in the 1980s*, ed. William R. Cline (Washington, D.C.: Institute of International Economics, 1983).

29. Robert B. Reich, "What Kind of Industrial Policy?" *Journal of Business Strategy* 5 (Summer 1984), 10–17; see also the following works by Reich: "Industrial Evolution," *Democracy* 3 (Summer 1983), 10–20; "Playing Tag with Japan," *New York Review of Books*, June 24, 1985, p. 40; "Why Democracy Makes Economic Sense," *New Republic*, December 19, 1983, pp. 25–32; *The Next American Frontier* (New York: Times Books, 1983); "An Industrial Policy of the Right," *Public Interest* 73 (1983), 3–17; "Beyond Free Trade," *Foreign Affairs*, Spring 1983, pp. 773–804; "The Next American Frontier," *Atlantic Monthly*, April 1983, pp. 97–108; "What Is Industrial Policy?" *Harper's*, April 1985; "Toward a New Public Policy," *Atlantic Monthly*, May 1985.

30. Kenneth Flamm, *Targeting the Computer: Government Support and International Competition* (Washington, D.C.: Brookings Institution, 1987), pp. 9, 18.

31. Ibid., p. 18.

32. *New York Times*, April 30, 1973, pp. 1, 17. On DARPA's activities, see Michael R. Gordon, "Will the Pentagon's Ad Hoc 'Industrial Policy' Ultimately Hamper U.S. Industrial Creativity?" *National Journal*, February 26, 1983; Andrew Pollack,

"America's Answer to Japan's MITI," *New York Times*, March 5, 1989, pp. 1, 8. The best source on postwar science and technology policy as it affects industrial development is Richard R. Nelson, *Government and Technological Progress* (New York: Pergamon, 1982).

33. Flamm, *Targeting the Computer*, pp. 170, 193.

34. PCIC, *Global Competition*, I, 38.

35. Harvey Brooks, "The Strategic Defense Initiative as Science Policy," *International Security* 2 (Fall 1986), 170, 183.

36. Bernard J. O'Keefe, "The SDI and American R&D," *International Security* 2 (Fall 1986), 191–192.

37. Bruce Steinberg, "The Military Boost to Industry," *Fortune*, April 30, 1984, pp. 42–48.

38. Jacques Gansler, "Integrating Civilian and Military Industry," *Issues in Science and Technology*, Fall 1988, p. 69; see also concurring comments on Gansler's essay in *Issues in Science and Technology*, Spring 1989, pp. 18–20.

39. O'Keefe, "SDI and American R&D," pp. 191–192.

40. Melman quoted in Fred Hiatt and Rick Atkinson, "The Hidden Costs of the Defense Buildup," *Washington Post Weekly Edition*, December 1, 1985, p. 10. See also Seymour Melman, *Profits without Production* (New York: Alfred A. Knopf, 1983).

41. Scott quoted in House Subcommittee on Economic Stabilization, *Industrial Policy*, I, 490.

42. Walter A. McDougall, *The Heavens and the Earth: A Political History of the Space Age* (New York: Basic Books, 1985), p. 230.

43. Paul A. Kennedy, "The (Relative) Decline of America," *The Atlantic*, August 1987, p. 33; see also Kennedy, *The Rise and Fall of the Great Powers* (New York: Random House, 1987).

44. Robert B. Reich, "Bread and Circuits," *New Republic*, August 3, 1987, p. 36.

45. Fitzgerald quoted in "America's Weapons-Driven Industrial Policy Weakens National Security," *Plowshare*, Winter 1986, p. 1; Patrick quoted in U.S. Congress, Joint Economic Committee, *Industrial Policy, Economic Growth, and the Competitiveness of U.S. Industry, Part I*, 98th Cong., 1st sess. (Washington, D.C.: Government Printing Office, 1984), pp. 11, 13.

46. Albert Shaw, "The American State and the American Man," *Contemporary Review* 51 (January–June 1987), 710.

47. Ibid., pp. 696, 711.

48. James Bryce, "Laissez Faire," in *The American Commonwealth* (New York: Macmillan, 1916), pp. 273–277. See also William S. Brock, *Investigation and Responsibility: Public Responsibility in the U.S., 1865–1900* (New York: Cambridge University Press, 1984); and Richard Sylla, "The Progressive Era and the Political Economy of Big Government" (Paper presented at a conference on Robert Higg's *Crisis and Leviathan*, Stanford, Calif., October 1986).

49. "States Strive to Lure High Technology Firms," *Raleigh News and Observer*, August 17, 1983, p. 6A.

50. Walter Olson, "Industrial Policy from the Grass Roots," *Wall Street Journal*, June 12, 1984, p. 30.

51. "States Work, Entice Business," *Chapel Hill Newspaper*, March 29, 1987, p. 220.

52. For state-level economic development activities before and after the Civil War, see Harry N. Scheiber, "State Law and 'Industrial Policy' in American Development, 1790–1987," *California Law Review*, January 1987, pp. 415–444. On the interwar origins of state economic development programs and their immediate postwar evolution, see George B. Tindall, *The Emergence of the New South, 1913–1945* (Baton Rouge: Louisiana State University Press, 1967); Albert Lepawsky, *State Planning and Economic Development in the South* (Washington, D.C.: National Planning Association, 1949); and James Cobb, *The Selling of the South* (Knoxville: University of Tennessee Press, 1982).

53. This discussion draws extensively upon Peter K. Eisinger, "High Tech Employment and Economic Development," Report for Wisconsin Strategic Development Commission (Madison, Wis., 1986); Eisinger, *The Rise of the Entrepreneurial State: State and Local Economic Development Policy in the United States* (Madison: University of Wisconsin Press, 1988). See Herbert Jacob and Kenneth Vines, eds., *Politics in the American States* (Boston: Little, Brown, 1965).

54. A critical view of state and local economic development programs is Robert Goodman, *The Last Entrepreneurs: America's Regional War for Jobs and Dollars* (New York: Simon and Schuster, 1979).

55. Thornburgh quoted in Peter K. Eisinger, "The Rise of the Entrepreneurial State in Economic Development" (Discussion paper, A. Alfred Taubman Center, Brown University), p. 1.

56. Eisinger, *Rise of the Entrepreneurial State*, p. 157; U.S. Congress, Joint Committee on Taxation, *Tax Reform Proposals: Tax Treatment of State and Local Government Bonds* (Washington, D.C.: Government Printing Office, 1985). See also Larry C. Ledebur and David W. Rasmussen, "Let's Try a Federalist Industrial Policy," *Challenge*, November–December 1983, pp. 58–60.

57. Eisinger, *Rise of the Entrepreneurial State*, p. 2.

58. National Association of State Development Agencies (NASDA), *User's Guide to State Industrial Incentives* (Washington, D.C.: Urban Institute Press, 1983); NASDA, *Directory of Incentives for Business Investment and Development in the U.S.: A State by State Guide*, 2d ed., rev. (Washington, D.C.: Urban Institute Press, 1986), pp. 1–4; Warren Brown, "Parts Are New Target in Japanese Invasion of U.S. Auto Industry," *Washington Post*, June 23, 1988, p. 2E.

59. See Eisinger, *Rise of the Entrepreneurial State*. See also David Osborne, *Laboratories of Democracy* (Boston: Harvard Business School Press, 1988); and Harvey A. Goldstein, ed., *The State and Local Industrial Policy Question* (Washington, D.C.: American Planning Association Press, 1987).

60. Goodman, *The Last Entrepreneurs*.

61. David Birch, *The Job Generation Process* (Cambridge, Mass.: MIT Program on Neighborhood and Regional Change, 1979); idem, *Job Creation in America: How Our Smallest Companies Put the Most People to Work* (New York: Free Press, 1987). Birch's findings are placed in doubt by Charles Brown, James Hamilton, and James Medoff, *Employers Large and Small* (Cambridge, Mass.: Harvard University Press, 1990). Reviews of academic research on SED policy are found in Bennett Harrison and Sandra Kanter, "The Political Economy of States' Job-Creation," *American Institute of Planners Journal*, October 1978; Roger Schmenner, *Making Business*

*Location Decisions* (Englewood Cliffs, N.J.: Prentice-Hall, 1982); and Michael Kieschnick, "Taxes and Growth: Business Incentives and Economic Development" in *State Taxation Policy*, ed. Michael Barker (Durham, N.C.: Duke University Press, 1983).

62. Governor Bruce Babbitt, "The States and the Reindustrialization of America," *Issues in Science and Technology*, Fall 1984, pp. 85–86; Eisinger, "Rise of the Entrepreneurial State," p. 27.

63. California Commission on Industrial Innovation, *Winning Technologies: A New Industrial Strategy for California and the Nation: Final Report* (Sacramento: Office of the Governor, 1982), pp. 1, 6, 18. For case studies of California and other states, see R. Scott Fosler, ed., *The New Economic Role of American States* (New York: Oxford University Press, 1988); and Osborne, *Laboratories of Democracy.*

64. Southern Growth Policies Board, *Halfway Home and a Long Way to Go*, Report of the 1986 Commission on the Future of the South (Research Triangle Park, N.C., 1986), p. 23. This singular document, felicitously written by University of North Carolina, Chapel Hill, novelist Doris Betts, is a fine example of working with local talent.

65. Kenny Johnson, editorial, *Raleigh News and Observer*, December 10, 1986, p. 18C.

66. Eisinger, "Rise of the Entrepreneurial State," p. 27.

67. Scott Jaschik, "Universities' Hi-Tech Pacts with Industry Are Marred by Politics, Poor Planning, and Hype," *Chronicles of Higher Education*, March 12, 1986, p. 16.

68. This account draws especially on Eisinger, *Rise of the Entrepreneurial State;* Fosler, *New Economic Role;* Osborne, *Laboratories of Democracy;* Rochelle L. Stanfield, "An Industrial Policy for Cities and States," *National Journal*, February 26, 1983; Mel Dubnick, "American States and the Industrial Policy Debate," *Policy Studies Review* 4 (August 1984), 22–27; Peter Bernstein, "States Are Going Down Industrial Policy Lane," *Fortune*, March 5, 1984; Larry C. Ledebur, "The Role of State Economic Development Programs in National Industrial Policy," in *Revitalizing the U.S. Economy*, ed. F. Stevens Redburn, Terry F. Buss, and Larry C. Ledebur (New York: Praeger, 1986); and Ledebur and David Rasmussen, "The Role of State Economic Development Programs in National Industry Policy," *Policy Studies Journal* 13 (June 1985), 4–13.

69. Philip H. Abelson, "Global Manufacturing Competition," *Science*, June 6, 1986, p. 1181; James Barron, "States Back Risky Ventures in Effort to Create New Jobs," *New York Times*, June 23, 1986, pp. 1, 9.

70. Osborne, *Laboratories of Democracy*, chap. 6.

71. NASDA, *Directory of Incentives*, p. 4.

72. Neal Peirce, "Dukakis Leads the Way," *Boston Globe*, September 4, 1983, p. 7.

73. Warren Brown, "Michigan's Battered Economy on the Mend," *Washington Post*, July 29, 1984, p. G1.

74. Ledebur and Rasmussen, "Let's Try a Federalist Industrial Policy," p. 58.

75. Osborne, *Laboratories of Democracy*, p. 78.

76. Monte Basgall, "Microchip Research: Balancing Industry and Education," *Raleigh News and Observer*, April 26, 1987, pp. D1, 5.

77. "The Tennessee Lessons of Saturn," *Forum* 11 (Spring 1987), 6–40.

78. U.S. Office of Technology Assessment, *Technology, Innovation, and Regional Economic Development* (Washington, D.C.: Government Printing Office, 1984).

79. Babbitt, "The States and Reindustrialization," p. 93.

80. Fosler, *New Economic Role*, p. 315.

81. Ronald Ferguson and Helen Ladd, "Massachusetts," in Fosler, *New Economic Role*, pp. 21, 34. For assessments of Massachusetts SED see Scott Jaschik, "States Trying to Assess Economic Program," *Chronicle of Higher Education*, June 3, 1987; Mickey Kaus, "A Hard Look at Dukakis's 'Massachusetts Miracle,'" *Newsweek*, February 22, 1988; Osborne, *Laboratories of Democracy*, chap. 6; and David Lampe, *the Massachusetts Miracle: High Technology and Economic Revitalization* (Cambridge, Mass.: MIT Press, 1988).

82. Eisinger, *New Entrepreneurial State*, pp. 10–15.

83. Southern Growth Policies Board, *Half Way Home*, p. 23.

84. Harrison and Kanter, "Political Economy of States' Job-Creation," p. 424.

85. Peter Eisinger, interview with author, December 18, 1985.

86. Eisinger, *New Entrepreneurial State*, p. 19.

87. Congressional Budget Office, *The Federal Role in State Industrial Development Programs* (Washington, D.C.: Government Printing Office, 1984), pp. xvii, 13–14, 22–27, 35. See also Richard B. McKenzie, "A Threat of Industrial Blackmail," *Backgrounder* 237 (1982).

88. Congressional Budget Office, *Small Issue Industrial Revenue Bonds* (Washington, D.C.: Government Printing Office, 1981).

89. David Rasmussen and Larry Ledebur proposed a "federalist industrial policy" in which the $10 billion spent by Washington in 1981 on IDBs alone would instead become a guaranteed loan program that the states could direct toward locally selected high-risk ventures in new technologies; "The Role of State Economic Development Programs in National Industrial Policy," in Redburn, Buss, and Ledebur, *Revitalizing the U.S. Economy*. For critical reviews of IDB use by local governments, see John M. Kline, *State Government Influence in U.S. International Economic Policy* (Lexington, Mass.: Lexington Books, 1983); and James M. Verdier, "Advising Congressional Decision-Makers," *Journal of Policy Analysis and Management* 3 (Spring 1984).

## 10. Doing without Industrial Policy

1. R. D. Norton, "Industrial Policy and American Renewal," *Journal of Economic Literature* 24 (March 1986), 1.

2. Lester C. Thurow, *The Zero-Sum Solution: Building a World-Class American Economy* (New York: Simon and Schuster, 1985).

3. Robert B. Reich, *Tales of a New America* (New York: Times Books, 1987), p. 231.

4. Noel Epstein, "You Want to Compete with Japan? Ask Ohio," *Washington Post*, June 24, 1986, p. D1–2.

5. Robert B. Reich, "What Is 'Industrial Policy?'" *Harper's*, April 1985, pp. 6, 71; Thurow, *Zero-Sum Solution*, p. 298. "Now that the notion of industrial policy has lost some of its immediate political appeal, we may have an opportunity to learn

something about it," was Reich's sage observation (Reich, "What Is Industrial Policy?," p. 5.)

6. Thurow, *Zero-Sum Solution*, p. 298.
7. Democratic Policy Commission, *New Choices in a Changing America* (Washington, D.C., 1986), p. 1.
8. Stephen Cohen and John Zysman, *Manufacturing Matters: The Myth of the Post-Industrial Economy* (New York: Basic Books, 1987), p. xii.
9. "Notebook," *New Republic,* October 10, 1989, p. 9.
10. *Economic Report of the President: 1989* (Washington, D.C.: Government Printing Office, 1989), p. 7.
11. Ibid., pp. 41–111.
12. *Economic Report of the President: 1988* (Washington, D.C.: Government Printing Office, 1988), p. 20; *Economic Report of the President: 1989,* pp. 1–10; T. J. Lueck, "Signs of Economic Revival Abound in Northeast," *New York Times,* June 23, 1985, pp. 1, 20; "Firing Up the Land of Low-Tech," *Newsweek,* December 9, 1985, p. 55; and James Risen, "Japan Targets—Japan," *Philadelphia Enquirer,* April 4, 1987, pp. 1, 14.
13. U.S. Department of Commerce, International Trade Administration (ITA), *U.S. Trade: Performance in 1985 and Outlook* (Washington, D.C.: Government Printing Office, 1986), pp. xx–25; Council on Competitiveness, *America's Competitive Crisis: Confronting the New Reality* (Washington, D.C.: 1987), pp. v–15.
14. Arthur Burns, "The American Trade Deficit," *Foreign Affairs,* Summer 1984, p. 1068.
15. *Economic Report of the President: 1989,* pp. 118–121.
16. ITA, *United States Foreign Trade Highlights: 1985* (Washington, D.C.: Government Printing Office, 1986); ITA, *U.S. Foreign Trade Highlights: 1988;* U.S. Bureau of the Census, *Statistical Abstract of the United States: 1989* (Washington, D.C.: Government Printing Office, 1990), pp. 788–789; Council of Economic Advisers, *Economic Indicators: February 1990* (Washington, D.C.: Government Printing Office, 1990), p. 35.
17. "U.S. Net Foreign Debt rises to $664 Billion," *Washington Post,* July 3, 1990, p. D1. Useful summaries of economic trends in the second half of the 1980s are Council on Competitiveness, *America's Competitive Crisis,* pp. 1–25, Bruce R. Scott, "U.S. Competitiveness in the World Economy: An Update" (Harvard University Graduate School of Business Administration, February 1987); George L. Perry, "Getting Back on Track: An Economic Observer," *Brookings Review* 5 (Spring 1987).
18. Peter G. Peterson, "The Morning After," *Atlantic Monthly,* October 1987.
19. Yale historian Paul Kennedy's article "The (Relative) Decline of America," *Atlantic Monthly,* August 1987, added historical weight to Peterson's jeremiad. The extent of the pessimism of late 1987 is reflected in the conversion of Tom Peters, coauthor of the best-selling *In Search of Excellence: Lessons from America's Best-Run Companies* (New York: Harper & Row, 1982), to the view that "there are no excellent companies"; see Cindy Skrzycki, "Tom Peters Now Calls U.S. Situation Dire," *Washington Post,* October 18, 1987), pp. H1, H5.
20. Martin Neil Baily and Alok K. Chakrabarti, *Innovation and the Productivity Crisis* (Washington, D.C.: Brookings Institution, 1988), pp. 1–3; *Monthly Labor Review*

109 (December 1986), 57; 110 (December 1987), 65; 111 (December 1988), 85; Council on Competitiveness, *America's Competitive Crisis*, pp. 8, 24; "The Surge in Factory Productivity Looks like History Now," *Business Week*, October 8, 1990, p. 24.

21. Paul R. Krugman and George Hatsopoulos, "The Problem of U.S. Competitiveness in Manufacturing," *New England Economic Review*, January–February 1987, p. 26.

22. James Fallows, "The Three Fiscal Crises," *Harper's*, September 1985, pp. 18–24.

23. Suzanne Berger et al., "Toward a New Industrial America," *Scientific American*, June 1989, pp. 39–40; Michael L. Dertouzos et al., *Made in America: Regaining the Productive Edge* (Cambridge, Mass.: MIT Press, 1989), p. 8.

24. A review of the leading "declinist" books of the late 1980s, works by Paul Kennedy, David P. Calleo, Robert Gilpin, and Walter Russell Mead, is Jeffrey E. Garten, "Is American Decline Inevitable?" *World Policy Journal*, Winter 1987–88, pp. 151–174; Richard Rosecrance, "Must America Decline?" *Wilson Quarterly*, Autumn 1990, reviews both declinists and antideclinists such as Joseph S. Nye and Henry Nau.

25. Quoted in Cohen and Zysman, *Manufacturing Matters*, pp. 5, 265.

26. "The Hollow Corporation," *Business Week*, March 11, 1986, pp. 34–86. Morita's low regard for American industry and society was more candidly expressed in *"No" to Ieru Nippon* (Tokyo: Kobunsha Publishing, 1989), a slim book published in Japan and coauthored with Shinatro Ishihara, a flamboyant right-wing member of the Diet. A photocopied translation, "The Japan That Can Say No," was quickly circulated in the U.S. with no identification of the translators.

27. Robert B. Reich, "Japan Inc., U.S.A.," *New Republic*, November 28, 1984, pp. 20–22.

28. On the "hollowing of the economy," see Susan Lee and Christie Brown, "The Protean Corporation," *Forbes*, August 24, 1987, pp. 76–79. Although *Business Week* was as full of alarm in 1985 as it had been in 1980, it had shifted position to reflect the debate: "The country does not need a comprehensive industrial policy requiring large-scale governmental intervention in the economy," the editors noted in their story on industrial decline. Then what did it need? To "think strategically"; "The Hollow Corporation," pp. 34, 85.

29. Cohen and Zysman, *Manufacturing Matters*, pp. 4, 12–22, 56, 241. For a concurring opinion, see Eastman Kodak's advertisement, "Oxymoron: Post-Industrial, World-Class Economy," *New Republic*, October 17, 1988, p. 7; Dertouzos et al., *Made in America*, chap. 2.

30. U.S. Office of Technology Assessment, *Making Things Better: Competing in Manufacturing* (Washington, D.C.: Government Printing Office, 1990), p. 1; idem, *Paying the Bill: Manufacturing and America's Trade Deficit* (Washington, D.C.: Government Printing Office, 1988), pp. 66–67. Other cogent assessments of the condition and future of American manufacturing were Laura Tyson, "Competitiveness," in *Global Competitiveness*, ed. Martin K. Starr (New York: W. W. Norton, 1988); and David J. Teece, ed., *The Competitive Challenge: Strategies for Industrial Innovation and Renewal* (Cambridge, Mass.: Ballinger, 1987).

31. Dertouzos et al., *Made in America*, p. 44.

32. David Halberstram, *The Reckoning* (New York: Morrow, 1986), p. 725.

33. I. M. Destler, *American Trade Politics: System under Stress* (New York and Washington, D.C.: Twentieth Century Fund and Institute for International Economics, 1986), p. 232.

34. I. M. Destler, "Protecting Congress or Protecting Trade?" *Foreign Policy,* Spring 1986, pp. 102–105. See also William R. Cline, ed., *Trade Policy in the 1980s* (Washington, D.C.: Institute for International Economics, 1983); Robert Z. Lawrence and Robert E. Litan, *Saving Free Trade: A Pragmatic Approach* (Washington, D.C.: Brookings Institution, 1986); C. M. Aho and J. D. Aronson, *Trade Talks: America Better Listen!* (New York: Council on Foreign Relations, 1985); and Raymond J. Waldmann, *Managed Trade: The New Competition between Nations* (Cambridge, Mass.: Ballinger, 1986).

35. Friedman's view, with a rebuttal, is found in Jagdish N. Bhagwati, "Toward a Policy Synthesis: A Panel Discussion," in Cline, *Trade Policy in the 1980s,* p. 731.

36. The question whether imports were gifts or Trojan horses was addressed in Cohen and Zysman, *Manufacturing Matters,* p. 237. On contemporary ferment in trade policy, see Jagdish N. Bhagwati, *Protectionism* (Cambridge: MIT Press, 1988).

37. A valuable review of the literature on strategic trade theory is Jonathan Eaton and Gene Grossman, *Optimal Trade and Industrial Policy under Oligopoly,* Working Paper 1236 (Cambridge, Mass.: National Bureau of Economic Research, 1986). See also James Brander and B. J. Spencer, "Tariff Protection and Imperfect Competition," in *Monopolistic Competition in International Trade,* ed. Henry K. Kierzkowski (New York: Oxford University Press, 1984); Gene M. Grossman and J. David Richardson, *Strategic U.S. Trade Policy* (Cambridge, Mass.: National Bureau of Economic Research, 1985); Paul R. Krugman, ed., *Strategic Trade Policy and the New International Economics* (Cambridge, Mass.: MIT Press, 1987).

38. Public Law 100-418, Competitiveness Policy Council Act, 102 Stat. 1454–62 August 23, 1988; Bruce Stokes, "Debating about a Trade Council," *National Journal,* June 6, 1988, p. 1489; Ken Jarboe to author, June 5, 1989; Mobil Oil, "What's Wrong with H.R. 4800," *Washington Post,* July 27, 1986, p. D3; Congressional Research Service, *Trade,* Issue Brief 87003 (Washington, D.C., 1988).

39. Wright quoted in Auerbach, "Parties Vie to Embrace American Competitiveness," *Washington Post,* December 21, 1986, pp. K1, K4.

40. Mark Potts, "Reagan Bolsters Competitiveness," *Washington Post,* February 1, 1987, p. H5; Democratic Leadership Council, *Winning in the World Economy: The Economic Competition Index* (Washington, D.C., 1986); Democratic Leadership Council, newsletter, December 1986; presidential message to Congress, January 27, 1987, in *Weekly Compilation of Presidential Documents* 23 (February 2, 1987), 51–52; "Competitiveness Bill Goes to Congress," *Science,* February 27, 1987, p. 967.

    The competitiveness crusade, by contrast to IP, seemed to bring out many allies and no enemies. Teachers of Latin devised a news release arguing that "a 'dead' language may help restore the U.S. work force's competitive edge"; Jesse Grumette, "Study of Latin Is Basic to Knowledge," *Chapel Hill Newspaper,* December 27, 1986, p. 30.

41. *Congressional Record,* April 17, 1986, pp. S4428–34; Mark Potts, "Council on Competitiveness Formed," *Washington Post,* December 3, 1986; "John Young's

Mission," *Industry Week,* February 9, 1987; Council on Competitiveness, *America's Competitive Crisis.* Young was tireless in communicating the message his president and the policy community at large had apparently failed to heed. For anxiety in the business community over declining industrial competitiveness and the administration's torpor, see the account of the press conference held in Washington by the CEO of the Eastman Kodak Company, *Washington Post,* April 22, 1988, p. G1.

42. Phillips quoted in Chris Welles, "The 'Competitiveness Craze': A New Name, an Old Idea," *Business Week,* January 19, 1987, p. 31.

43. President's Commission on Industrial Competitiveness, *Global Competition: The New Reality,* 2 vols. (Washington, D.C.: Government Printing Office, 1985), II, 6.

44. LaFalce quoted in U.S. House of Representatives, Committee on Banking, Finance and Urban Affairs, Subcommittee on Economic Stabilization, *Council on Industrial Competitiveness Act,* H.R. 99-579, 99th Cong., 2d sess. (Washington, D.C.: Government Printing Office, 1986), p. 33.

45. Max Holland, *When the Machine Stopped* (Cambridge, Mass.: Harvard Business School Press, 1989), pp. 180–188. See also U.S. Senate, Committee on Banking, Housing and Urban Affairs, Subcommittee on International Finance and Monetary Policy, *Foreign Industrial Targeting,* 98th Cong., 1st sess. (Washington, D.C.: Government Printing Office, 1983). Houdaille vice-president John Latona, after describing Japanese sectoral policy and demanding a similar U.S. government response, still had reservations: "Do we need some kind of super industrial coordinating what-have-you? I am inclined not to think so" (Holland, p. 108). *Economic Report of the President: 1989,* pp. 247–248. See also Michael Borrus, *Competing for Control: America's Stake in Microelectronics* (Cambridge, Mass.: Ballinger, 1988), p. 259.

46. Dertouzos et al., *Made in America,* p. 20; Max Holland, "Don't Blame the Japanese," *Los Angeles Times Magazine,* July 12, 1987, pp. 16–23; Robert Wrubel, "Out of Tolerance," *Financial World,* July 12, 1988, pp. 34–36; Ralph Winter, "Machine Tool Makers Lose Out to Imports," *Financial World,* August 17, 1987, pp. 1, 8.

47. Holland, *When the Machine Stopped,* pp. 269–270, 276.

48. Clyde Prestowitz, *Trading Places: How We Allowed Japan to Take the Lead* (New York: Basic Books, 1988), p. 26; Council on Competitiveness, "New Consortium Promotes U.S. Manufactures," *Challenge,* January 1988, p. 10.

49. Borrus, *Competing for Control,* pp. 3, 15, 173, 16–17.

50. Prestowitz, *Trading Places,* p. 39.

51. For a concise review of semiconductor industry development and national strategies in the 1980s, see Borrus, *Competing for Control.*

52. Prestowitz, *Trading Places,* p. 59; Mark Potts, "U.S. Chip Industry's Gloomy Future," *Washington Post,* May 10, 1987, p. H1.

53. U.S. Department of Defense, Office of the Undersecretary of Defense for Acquisition, Defense Science Board Task Force, *Report on Semiconductor Dependency* (Washington, D.C.: Government Printing Office, 1987); Andrew Pollack, "U.S. Sees Peril in Japan's Dominance in Chips," *New York Times,* January 5, 1987, pp. 1, 22.

54. John Carey, "Washington, Inc.," *Business Week,* special issue, "Innovation in America," 1989. "Interview: Ian Ross," *Challenge,* December 1989, pp. 1, 6;

Donna Walters, "Can U.S. Consumer Electronics Firms Stage a Comeback?" *Los Angeles Times*, October 21, 1990, D1, D10.

55. Michael Porter, "Why U.S. Business Is Falling Behind," *Fortune*, April 28, 1986, p. 256.

56. Peter Behr and David Vise, "Tax Plan Enrages Manufacturers," *Washington Post*, June 2, 1985, pp. F1, F4.

57. Kim McDonald, "At Supercollider 'Pep Rally,'" *Chronicle of Higher Education*, December 16, 1987; David L. Wheeler, "President Reagan Outlines 11-Point Plan for Commercializing Superconductivity," *Chronicle of Higher Education*, August 5, 1987.

58. Andrew Pollack, "America's Answer to Japan's MITI," *New York Times*, March 5, 1989, sec. 3, pp. 1, 8.

59. "Pentagon's Push to Bolster Competitiveness," *Challenges*, September 1988, p. 2; Committee on the Role of the Manufacturing Technology Program in the Defense Industrial Base, Commission on Engineering and Technical Systems, *Manufacturing Technology: Cornerstone of a Renewed Defense Industrial Base* (Washington, D.C.: Office of the Secretary of Defense, 1987); Defense Science Board, *Use of Commercial Components in Military Equipment* (Washington, D.C.: Office of the Secretary of Defense, 1986), p. 780; "Pentagon's Economic Policy Should Expand, Panel Suggests," *Raleigh News and Observer*, October 19, 1988, p. 11A; David Morrison, "Halting the Erosion," *National Journal*, July 30, 1988, pp. 1968–70.

60. Jacques S. Gansler, "Integrating Civilian and Military Industry," *Issues in Science and Technology*, Fall 1988, pp. 71–72; Pollack, "America's Answer to Japan's MITI," pp. 3, 8; Daniel Greenberg, "Casting the Pentagon as Guide for U.S. Industry Begs for Calamity," *Los Angeles Times*, January 10, 1989, p. II-7.

61. Daniel Charles, "Reformers Seek Broader Military Role in Economy," *Science*, August 12, 1988, pp. 779–81; Colin Norman, "DOD Lists Critical Technologies," *Science*, March 24, 1989, p. 1543; Department of Defense, *The Department of Defense Critical Technologies Plan* (Washington, D.C., 1989).

62. "Beyond Sound Bites," *Newsweek*, October 17, 1988, p. 33; Hobart Rowen, "Dukakis' Perspective on Economy Emerging," *Washington Post*, July 21, 1988, p. A23.

63. "Beyond Sound Bites," p. 33; Paul Bluestein, "The Democrats Aren't Using Their Economists' Script," *Washington Post National Weekly Bulletin*, April 25–May 1, 1988, p. 20. Another voice of the Democratic party was the popular and visible Governor Mario Cuomo of New York. His Commission on Trade and Competitiveness, using the term *industrial policy* only once and with ambivalence, affirmed that a Competitiveness strategy must have a sectoral component, that industries are interdependent and national strategy must look to the total portfolio, that trade relief must be contingent upon industry plans for revitalization, and that sectoral task forces must be formed in industries of strategic importance; Cuomo Commission on Trade and Competitiveness, *The Cuomo Commission Report* (New York: Simon and Schuster, 1988), pp. 132, 162–165.

64. "High Tech's United Front," *U.S. News & World Report*, July 10, 1989, p. 45.

65. Dertouzos et al., *Made in America*, pp. 12–14, 217.

66. Mel Levine, "An Alarm Is Ringing, but Few Are Listening," *Los Angeles Times*, July 18, 1990, p. B7.

67. Department of Defense, *Critical Technologies Plan*.

68. Mackubin T. Owens and William J. Long, "Expand the Military Industrial Complex?" *Orbis,* Fall 1989, pp. 554, 558; Department of Defense, Defense Science Board, *Final Report on the Defense Industrial and Technological Base* (Washington, D.C., 1988).

69. Sununu quoted in "Does the U.S. Need a High-Technology Industrial Policy to Battle Japan, Inc.?" *Business Week,* February 5, 1990, p. 55.

70. Fields quoted in Bob David, "High-Definition TV, Once a Capital Idea, Wanes in Washington," *New York Times,* June 6, 1990, pp. 1, 6.

71. Colleen Cordes, "Congress Presses Bush to Provide Strong Support for the Commercial Development of Technologies," *Chronicle of Higher Education,* July 5, 1990, pp. A19–21.

72. David P. Hamilton, "Technology Policy: Congress Takes the Reins," *Science,* November 9, 1990, p. 747.

73. Robert Kuttner, "The Hands-Off Argument Is Crumbling," *Los Angeles Times,* June 24, 1990, p. M7.

74. Peter Passell, "The Uneasy Case for Subsidy of High Technology Efforts," *New York Times,* August 11, 1989, pp. A1, D2; "Does the U.S. Need?" p. 56.

75. Office of Technology Assessment, *Making Things Better,* pp. 1, 3–4; see especially Executive Summary.

76. See, for example, Paul R. Krugman, "Bush's Team Should Study Creation of Super-Firms," *Los Angeles Times,* June 10, 1990, pp. D1, D7.

77. Mosbacher quoted in Colin Norman, "HDTV: The Technology du Jour," *Science,* May 19, 1989, p. 761; Sununu quoted in "Does the U.S. Need?" p. 59. See also Bruce Stokes, "High-Tech Tussle," *National Journal,* June 22, 1990, pp. 1338–42.

78. Borrus quoted in "Does the U.S. Need?" p. 59.

79. David E. Sanger, "The Technology That the U.S. Doesn't Want Japan to Have," *New York Times,* April 2, 1989, p. 3.

80. Laura Tyson and John Zysman, eds., *American Industry in International Competition: Government, Politics, and Corporate Strategies* (Ithaca: Cornell University Press, 1983), p. 23.

81. Scott, "U.S. Competitiveness in the World Economy," p. 3.

### 11. Using and Misusing History

1. Mark Twain, *Following the Equator* (Hartford: American, 1869), p. 79.

2. Robert W. Fogel and G. R. Elton, *Which Road to the Past? Two Views of History* (Cambridge: Cambridge University Press, 1983), p. 96.

3. *Aristotle's Poetics,* trans. S. H. Butcher (New York: Hill and Wang, 1961), p. 68.

4. Richard E. Neustadt, "Uses of History in Public Policy," *Humanities* 2 (October 1981), 1.

5. Arthur M. Schlesinger, Jr., "The Inscrutability of History," *Encounter,* November 1966, p. 10.

6. Ernest R. May, *Lessons of the Past* (Cambridge, Mass.: Harvard University Press, 1972).

7. Richard E. Neustadt and Ernest R. May, *Thinking in Time: The Uses of History for Decisionmakers* (New York: Free Press, 1986).

8. Even a quick reading of Robert Engler, *The Politics of Oil* (Chicago: University of Chicago Press, 1961), would have supplied sufficient historical knowledge to have raised fundamental questions about the Carter energy policy assumptions. See also Stuart E. Eizenstat, "A Historical 'Memory' for Presidents," *New York Times*, January 14, 1987, p. 27.

9. See George E. Mowry, "The Uses of History by Recent Presidents," *Journal of American History* 53 (1966), 5–18. For history lessons in the hands of judges and lawyers, see Charles Fairman's notable denunciation of Supreme Court justices as historical dunces, "Does the Fourteenth Amendment Incorporate the Bill of Rights?" 2 *Stanford Law Review* 5-139 (1949); idem, *History of the Supreme Court of the United States: Reconstruction and Reunion, 1864–88*, vol. VII (New York: Macmillan, 1971); and Charles A. Miller, *The Supreme Court and the Uses of History* (Cambridge, Mass.: Harvard University Press, 1969). The controversy over the Founders' "original intent" is reviewed in Michael Kent Curtis, *No State Shall Abridge: The Fourteenth Amendment and the Bill of Rights* (Durham, N.C.: Duke University Press, 1986); Leonard W. Levy, *Constitutional Opinions: Aspects of the Bill of Rights* (New York: Oxford University Press, 1985); Traciel V. Reid, "A Critique of Interpretivism and Its Claimed Influence upon Judicial Decision Making," *American Politics Quarterly* 16 (1988), 320–356. See also Paul L. Murphy, "Time to Reclaim: The Current Challenge of American Constitutional History," *American Historical Review* 69 (October 1963), 64–79; Alfred Kelly, "Clio and the Court: An Illicit Love Affair," *Supreme Court Review* 69 (1965), 119–158; and Wilcomb E. Washburn, "The Supreme Court's Use and Abuse of History," *OAH Newsletter*, August 1983, pp. 7–9. For uses and misuses of history in social welfare policy, see Donald T. Critchlow and Ellis W. Hawley, eds., *Federal Social Policy: The Historical Dimension* (Philadelphia: Pennsylvania University Press, 1988); Maris Vinovskis, *An "Epidemic" of Adolescent Pregnancy? Some Historical and Policy Considerations* (New York: Oxford University Press, 1985); and John Demos, "History and the Formation of Social Policy toward Children," in *Past, Present, and Personal* (New York: Oxford University Press, 1986); on immigration policy, see Otis L. Graham, Jr., "Uses and Misuses of History in the Debate over Immigration Reform," *Public Historian* 8 (Spring 1986), 41–64; in foreign affairs, see Francis L. Lowenheim, ed., *The Historian and the Diplomat: The Role of History and Historians in American Foreign Policy* (New York: Harper & Row, 1967).

   Taylor Branch, reviewing the government's increasing engagement in a "war on drugs" and noting that policy discussion of the possibility of drug legalization tended to ignore the history of alcohol prohibition in the 1920s, wrote that "on no other subject except race are we so evasive about our past, and none remains so contemporary"; Branch, "Let Koop Do It," *New Republic*, October 24, 1988, p. 22. However, the research on evasiveness about our past, and other misuses of it, is not so advanced as to confirm Branch's nomination of drug policy as number one history-evader.

   Two journals, *Public Historian* (1978–) and *Journal of Policy History* (1988–), frequently explore the policy uses to which history has been and ought to be put.

10. Lou Cannon, "The Cost of Contra Aid May Be Reagan's Credibility," *San Jose Mercury News*, March 31, 1986, p. 7B.

11. David A. Stockman, *The Triumph of Politics: The Inside Story of the Reagan Revolution* (New York: Harper & Row, 1986), p. 9.
12. "Text of Reagan Speech on the Contras," *New York Times*, March 17, 1986, p. 8. See also Nicholas Lemann, "The Unfinished War," *Atlantic Monthly*, December 1988, p. 37; and Bernard Weinraub, "Test of a Presidency: Reagan's Early Encounters with the Left Seem Key to His Drive to Aid the Contras," *New York Times*, March 18, 1986, pp. 1, 4. The thought processes of Reagan remind us that whereas some uses of analogy are rhetorical and deliberate, others are unexamined and internalized. These are differently dangerous.
13. Herbert Butterfield, *History and Human Relations* (New York: Macmillan, 1952), pp. 166–167.
14. David Herbert Donald, "Our Irrelevant History," *New York Times*, September 8, 1977, p. A26. For a tenth-anniversary review of Donald's skeptical essay, see Michael Skube, "History—A Lesson Still Worth Learning?" *Raleigh News and Observer*, September 27, 1987, pp. D1, D5.
15. C. Vann Woodward, *Thinking Back* (Baton Rouge: Louisiana State University Press, 1986), p. 139.
16. Jack P. Greene, *The Intellectual Heritage of the Constitutional Era: The Delegates' Library* (Philadelphia: Library Company of Philadelphia, 1986), is a compelling account of the historical ideas so central to the Founders' political thought. See also Colin B. Goodykoontz, "The Founding Fathers and Clio," *Pacific Historical Review* 23 (1954), 111–123; and Richard M. Gummere, *The American Colonial Mind and the Classical Tradition* (Cambridge, Mass.: Harvard University Press, 1963).
17. Raymond Strother and Charles Mahe quoted in Charles Green, "The Real Lessons from Election 1986," *Honolulu Star Bulletin and Advertiser*, November 9, 1986, p. A21.
18. Neustadt and May, *Thinking in Time*, pp. 89, 235.
19. Richard R. Nelson, ed., *Government and Technological Progress* (New York: Pergamon, 1982), p. vii; Richard Nelson and Richard Langlois, "Industrial Innovation Policy: Lessons from American History," *Science*, February 18, 1983, p. 814.
20. Franklin A. Long, "Technological Innovation for the U.S. Civilian Economy: The Role of Government," in *Planning, Politics, and the Public Interest*, ed. Walter Goldstein (New York: Columbia University Press, 1978), p. 114.
21. Nelson and Langlois, "Industrial Innovation Policy," p. 817.
22. Ibid., p. 818.
23. Nelson, *Government and Technological Progress*, pp. 454–455.
24. Richard Nelson, *High-Technology Policies: A Five-Nation Comparison* (Washington, D.C.: American Enterprise Institute, 1984), pp. 81, 86–87.
25. Hobart Rowen, "Chrysler's Bailout No Model for an Industrial Policy," *Washington Post*, April 29, 1984, pp. F1, 6; Peter Behr, "When the Taxpayers Saved Lee Iacocca's Bacon, What Did They Get out of It?" *Washington Post*, May 13, 1984, pp. C1–2.
26. Robert B. Reich and John Donahue, *New Deals: The Chrysler Revival and the American System* (New York: Times Books, 1985), pp. 4, 9.
27. Ibid., p. 270.
28. Ibid., pp. 294, 297.

29. David A. Hounshell, *From the American System to Mass Production: 1800–1932* (Baltimore: Johns Hopkins University Press, 1984).

30. Gilbert Fite, *American Farmers: The New Minority* (Bloomington: Indiana University Press, 1981) and *Cotton Fields No More: Southern Agriculture, 1865–1980* (Lexington: University Press of Kentucky, 1984).

31. Pete Daniel, *Breaking the Land* (Urbana: University of Illinois Press, 1985), p. 69. For a vigorous indictment of U.S. agricultural policy, see Jim Hightower, *Hard Tomatoes, Hard Times* (Washington, D.C.: Agribusiness Accountability Project, 1972); and Wendell Berry, *The Unsettling of American Agriculture* (San Francisco: Sierra Club, 1978). Don Hadwiger has pointed out that there have been four reasonably distinct policy regimes in agriculture from the 1860s to the 1980s. This finding makes generalizations suspect. See Don F. Hadwiger, *The Politics of Agricultural Research* (Lincoln: University of Nebraska Press, 1982).

32. Catherine Stirling and John N. Yochelson, eds., *Under Pressure: U.S. Industry and the Challenges of Structural Adjustment* (Boulder, Colo.: Westview Press, 1985), pp. 7, 28.

33. John G. Clark, *Energy and the Federal Government: Fossil Fuel Policies, 1900–1946* (Urbana: University of Illinois Press, 1986), esp. chap. 15 and pp. 384–385.

34. Vietor, *Energy Policy since 1945*, p. 345; and see esp. chap. 14.

35. Other valuable recent case studies with policy implications include Gary C. Hufbauer and Howard F. Rosen, *Trade Policy for Troubled Industries* (Washington, D.C.: Institute for International Economics, 1986), who analyze 31 case studies of special protection; and Gerald R. Jantscher, "Lessons from the Maritime Aid Program," in *Urbanization, Responses, and Policies,* ed. David Dewar (Cape Town: Urban Problems Research Unit, 1982). For the interpenetration of public and private realms, see Louis Galambos and Joseph Pratt, *The Rise of the Corporate Commonwealth* (New York: Basic Books, 1970); and Ellis W. Hawley, "The Discovery and Study of a 'Corporate Liberalism,'" *Business Week Review* 52 (Autumn 1978), 309–320.

36. The Business Roundtable Ad Hoc Task Force, *Analysis of the Issues in the National Industrial Policy Debate: Working Papers* (New York, 1984), pp. 125, 21.

37. Thomas K. McCraw, "Mercantilism and the Market: Antecedents of American Industrial Policy," in *The Politics of Industrial Policy,* ed. Claude E. Barfield and William A. Schambra (Washington, D.C.: American Enterprise Institute, 1986), p. 55.

38. Thomas K. McCraw, *Prophets of Regulation* (Cambridge, Mass.: Harvard University Press, 1984), pp. 301, 308.

39. McCraw, "Mercantilism and the Market," p. 55.

40. Ellis W. Hawley, "'Industrial Policy' in the 1920s and 1930s," in Barfield and Schambra, *Politics of Industrial Policy,* p. 64. See also Alfred D. Chandler, Jr., et al., *National Competition Policy: Historians' Perspectives on Antitrust and Government Business Relationships in the U.S.* (Washington, D.C.: Federal Trade Commission, 1981). In addition to historians of modern political economy, economic historians of larger periods and contexts would have been useful mentors. The debate would have been greatly improved if there had been wide familiarity with the work of

Gibbon and Toynbee, Kondratief and Braudel, as well as contemporaries such as Carlo Cipolla, Charles Kindleberger, David Landes, Angus Maddison, Mancur Olson, Nathan Rosenberg, and Paul Birdzell.

41. Hawley, "'Industrial Policy,'" pp. 66–67.

42. Ibid., pp. 71, 73.

43. Ibid., pp. 79–81.

44. Public history is served by a national association, the National Council for Public History, and a journal, *Public Historian.* On the scope and history of public history, see Robert Kelley, "Public History: Its Origins, Nature, and Prospects," *Public Historian,* Fall 1978, 16–28; Barbara Howe and Emory Kemp, eds., *Public History: An Introduction* (Malabar, Fla.: Krieger, 1986).

45. Peter Hall, *Great Planning Disasters* (Cambridge, Mass.: Harvard University Press, 1977), pp. 69–79.

46. Twenty-one historians to President-elect Jimmy Carter, November 3, 1976, copy in author's possession. Stuart Eizenstat, Carter's domestic policy adviser, does not recall having seen the historians' letter, but has decided on his own that some of the Carter administration's mistakes could have been avoided if there had been "a Secretariat" of "non-political careerists in the White House to consider historical precedents" and to remedy the "blind spot in memory" which is uniquely serious around the presidential office; Eizenstat, "A Historical 'Memory' for Presidents," *New York Times,* January 14, 1987, p. A27.

    For an earlier proposal based on a more traditional model than Kelley's, in which a central Historical Office would coordinate and promote written history, see Louis Morton, "Historians and the Federal Government: A Proposal for a Government-wide Historical Office," *Prologue,* Spring 1971, pp. 3–11. The classic denunciation of "official" or "court" history is B. H. Liddell Hart, "Response and Judgment in Historical Writing," *Military Affairs* 23 (Spring 1959).

47. See George T. Blakey, *Historians on the Homefront: American Propagandists for the Great War* (Lexington: University Press of Kentucky, 1970); Carol S. Gruber, *Mars and Minerva: World War I and the Uses of the Higher Learning in America* (Baton Rouge: Louisiana State University Press, 1973).

48. See David Faust and Jay Ziskin, "The Expert Witness in Psychiatry and Psychology," *Science,* July 1, 1988, pp. 1–5, a devastating review of research on clinical judgment by psychiatrists.

49. Critchlow and Hawley, *Federal Social Policy,* p. 10.

50. For a review of the troubled condition of contemporary historiography, see Bernard Bailyn, "The Challenge of Modern Historiography," *American Historical Review,* 1982; Thomas Bender, "Wholes and Parts: The Need for Synthesis in American History," *Journal of American History* 73 (June 1986), 120–136; and the entire issue of *American Historical Review,* June 1989.

51. Bruce M. Stave, ed., *Modern Industrial Cities* (New York: Sage, 1984), p. 14.

52. Demos, "History and Social Policy," pp. 202, 208–209.

53. Khrushchev quoted in Marc Ferro, *The Use and Abuse of History, or How the Past Is Taught* (London: Routledge and Kegan Paul, 1981), p. 114.

54. David J. Rothman and Stanton Wheeler, eds., *Social History and Social Policy* (New

York: Academic Press, 1981), p. 5. Other heads of state, at other times, have expressed the opposite sentiment, as when President Lyndon Johnson responded to Bill Moyers' question:

> *Moyers:* "If you could talk to anybody, just sit there with your shoes off and talk, who would you like to talk to?"
>
> *LBJ:* "I'd like to talk to Toynbee."
>
> *Moyers:* "Why?"
>
> *LBJ:* "He could help me understand what I'm up against in Vietnam. It's that God Damn slate that you find when you walk into this office. You know, it wasn't written by Kennedy, and it wasn't written by Eisenhower, it was written by history. And I just don't understand it."

Richard L. Schott, interview with Bill Moyers, June 20, 1978, pp. 39–40, Lyndon Baines Johnson Library, Austin, Texas.

55. *Congressional Record,* December 17, 1982, pp. H10183-89. The U.S. Senate established a Senate Historical office in 1985.

56. See Otis L. Graham, Jr., "The Uses and Misuses of History: Roles in Policy Making," *Public Historian* 5 (1983), 5–19.

## 12. Improving on the 1980s

1. Geoffrey Elton, in Robert W. Fogel and G. R. Elton, *Which Road to the Past? Two Views of History* (New Haven: Yale University Press, 1984), p. 96; François Bedarida, "The Modern Historian's Dilemma," *Economic History Review* 40 (1987), 342–343.

2. Among the voluminous suggestions for the configuration of the Council, Forum, and Bank functions, see Stuart E. Eizenstat, "Designing a Workable and Effective Industrial Policy" (typescript of address at Charleston, W.Va., November 3, 1983; author's possession), for placement of the "coordinating unit" in the Domestic Policy Staff; Kenneth Flamm, *Targeting the Computer: Government Support and International Competition* (Washington, D.C.: Brookings Institution, 1987) for a "civilian DARPA," an idea endorsed in legislation by Senator John Glenn (D., Ohio) along with a transformation of the Department of Commerce into the Department of Industry and Technology. Fred C. Bergsten, *America in the World Economy: A Strategy for the 1990s* (Washington, D.C.: Institute for International Economics, 1989), reminded that the Council on Competitiveness, enacted in the Omnibus Trade Act of 1988, might serve the needed functions if it were ever established. A different approach came from the American Academy of Arts and Sciences, which organized an interdisciplinary research project to discover "the best administrative, structural and operational procedures" of "an agency needed to fund . . . selected high leverage areas of civilian technology and engineering research and development" by studying selected "technologies with long-term payoffs"; Leo L. Beranek et al., "Civilian Technology Department," *Science,* May 25, 1990, pp. 941–942. An argument for continuing to rely upon DARPA may be found in Jacques Gansler, "Integrating Civilian and Military Industry," *Issues in Science and Technology,* Fall 1988, pp. 66–78.

3. David E. Osborne, *Laboratories of Democracy* (Boston: Harvard Business School Press, 1988), p. 79.

4. Lester C. Thurow, *The Case for Industrial Policies* (Washington, D.C.: Center for National Policy, 1984), p. 21.

5. For elaboration on time and context in policymaking, see Otis L. Graham, Jr., "The Uses and Misuses of History," and Richard E. Neustadt and Ernest R. May, *Thinking in Time: The Uses of History for Decisionmakers* (New York: Free Press, 1986).

6. Kazushi Ohkawa and Henry Rosovsky, *Japanese Economic Growth: Trend Acceleration in the 20th Century* (Stanford: Stanford University Press, 1973), esp. chap. 9.

7. John Stuart Mill, *Essays on Some Unsettled Questions of Political Economy* (1848; reprint, London: London School of Economics, 1948).

8. Nathan Rosenberg and L. E. Birdzell, Jr., *How the West Grew Rich: The Economic Transformation of the Industrial World* (New York: Basic Books, 1985).

9. Michael E. Porter, *The Competitive Advantage of Nations* (New York: Free Press, 1990).

10. On Porter's "industrial clusters" as historically and potentially established through the help of carefully targeted industrial policies, see Paul R. Krugman, "Bush's Team Should Study Creation of Super-Firms," *Los Angeles Times,* October 6, 1990, pp. D1, D7.

11. U.S. Office of Technology Assessment, *Paying the Bill: Manufacturing and America's Trade Deficit* (Washington, D.C.: Government Printing Office, 1988), pp. 1–5.

12. The discussion here owes much to Bergsten, *America in the World Economy,* esp. pp. 12–13. In this book, eight chapters on macroeconomic corrections surround one on the required microeconomic measures, which include invigorated programs in worker adjustment and a Council on Competitiveness "to develop projections for the future of key American industries and to assess the impact on them of the policies of foreign governments. These analyses would provide baselines against which to judge industry requests for import relief or other government assistance" (p. 12). Industrial Policy occupies one-ninth of the book. See also C. Michael Aho and Marc Levinson, *After Reagan: Confronting the Changed World Economy* (New York: Council on Foreign Relations, 1988); and Alan W. Wolff, "International Competitiveness of American Industry," in *U.S. Competitiveness in the World Economy,* ed. Bruce Scott and George C. Lodge (Cambridge, Mass.: Harvard Business School Press, 1988).

13. Bruce Stokes, "Talking with Tokyo Worthwhile?" *National Journal,* June 3, 1989, p. 1367; Elizabeth Weir, "U.S. Plies Uncharted Waters in Effort to Open Markets," *Congressional Quarterly Weekly Report,* May 20, 1989, pp. 1170–74.

14. Ronald Elving, "Japan Pledges to Lift Barriers: Congress Will Wait and See," *Congressional Quarterly Weekly Report,* April 7, 1990, p. 1054.

15. Twentieth Century Fund Task Force on the Future of American Trade Policy, *The Free Trade Debate* (New York: Priority Press, 1990); see especially the "background paper" by Gary C. Hufbauer, chap. 4, "Sector Arrangements: Prince of Darkness." For a dark view of recent semiconductor industrial policy, see Robert Z. Lawrence and Charles L. Schultze, eds., *An American Trade Strategy: Options for the 1990s* (Washington, D.C.: Brookings Institution, 1990), pp. 29–33.

16. James L. Sundquist quoted in Donald L. Robinson, ed., *Reforming American Gov-*

*ernment: Papers of the Committee on the Constitutional System* (Boulder: Westview Press, 1985), p. 87. See also Sundquist, *Constitutional Reform and Effective Government* (Washington, D.C.: Brookings Institution, 1986), for the argument that the absence of strong political parties is the core source of governmental debility in the United States. For discussion see Mark P. Petracca et al., "Proposal for Constitutional Reform: An Evaluation of the Committee on the Constitutional System," *Presidential Studies Quarterly* 20 (Summer 1990).

For steps toward a theory of government failure to match the sophistication reached by the theory of market failures, see Charles Wolf, Jr., *"Non-market Failure" Revisited: The Anatomy and Physiology of Government Deficiencies* (Santa Monica, Calif.: Rand Corporation, 1981); and Wolf, *Markets or Governments: Choosing between Imperfect Alternatives* (Cambridge, Mass.: MIT Press, 1988).

17. Ira Magaziner and Robert B. Reich, *Minding America's Business* (New York: Vintage, 1982), pp. 377–378.

18. Hugh Heclo, "Industrial Policy and the Executive Capacities of Government," in *The Politics of Industrial Policy,* ed. Claude E. Barfield and William A. Schambra (Washington, D.C.: American Enterprise Institute, 1986), pp. 303–310. See also Harry Bernstein, "Bureau of Labor Statistics Facing More Cuts," *Los Angeles Times,* August 28, 1985, sec. IV, p. 1.

19. The U.S. International Trade Administration turned out annual "competitive assessments" of sectors such as roller bearings, commuter aircraft, and certain vegetables grown in the Great Lake states, and the USITC did reviews and forecasts for 350 industries; these reports appeared more frequently during the 1980s. For the persistence of confusion among trade professionals as to what they should be trying to achieve, see William H. Branson and Alvin K. Klevorick, "Strategic Behavior and Trade Policy," in *Strategic Trade Policy and the New International Economics,* ed. Paul R. Krugman (Cambridge, Mass.: MIT Press, 1986).

20. Hugh Heclo quoted in Bernard Weinraub, "The Reagan Legacy," *New York Times Magazine,* June 22, 1986, p. 16; Heclo, "Industrial Policy and Executive Capacities," p. 293.

21. Eizenstat quoted in Weinraub, "Reagan Legacy," p. 14. "Permanent Government" is a term used by Arthur Schlesinger, Jr.

22. *Time,* October 23, 1989. See also Thomas E. Mann, "Breaking the Political Impasse," in *Setting National Priorities: Policy for the Nineties,* ed. Henry J. Aaron (Washington, D.C.: Brookings Institution, 1990).

23. Heclo, "Industrial Policy and Executive Capacities," p. 293.

24. Robert A. Solow, "Lessons from Elsewhere," in *American Economic Policy: Problems and Prospects,* ed. Gar Alperovitz and Roger Skurski (South Bend, Ind.: Notre Dame University Press, 1984), p. 52.

25. Heclo, "Industrial Policy and Executive Capacities," pp. 301–303. Martha Derthick, after reviewing administrative breakdowns in the Social Security Administration, the Internal Revenue Service, and the Immigration and Naturalization Service, recommended that Congress not legislate without administrative capacity or "state of the agency reports"; Derthick, *Agency under Stress: The Social Security Administration in American Government* (Washington, D.C.: Brookings Institution, 1990).

26. Heclo, "Industrial Policy and Executive Capabilities," p. 202.

27. Ibid., p. 311.

28. Ibid. Heclo recognized the need for "forums in which key public and private makers of public policy can explore joint concerns" but was wary of the "grand coalition" or national Forum approach, since the United States "has a sorry record in the area of national forum building." This was a history lesson, but Heclo in this case gave no supporting evidence. For a positive view of governmental capacities, see Steven Kelman, *Making Public Policy: A Hopeful View of American Government* (New York: Basic Books, 1987).

29. See Hugh Heclo, *A Government of Strangers: Executive Politics in Washington* (Cambridge, Mass.: Harvard University Press, 1977). Every presidential election in the United States sweeps out of positions in the executive agencies some 4,000 political appointees, effectively a turnover of a tenth of the supergrade-level members of the executive population. A consequence is institutional disruption, discontinuity, and a heavy injection of the partisan agenda of the president or, more typically, of some economic interest group being paid off for electoral support. To that degree the American state is rendered the more transient, amateurish, and short-memoried. In Great Britain, by contrast, a prime minister makes perhaps 75 political appointments, a French president no more than 150. Don A. Cothran finds the American state disrupted by the appointment of 99 percent more political appointees than in other nations; Cothran, "Japanese Bureaucrats and Policy Implementation," *Policy Studies,* Fall 1987, pp. 439–458.

30. Peter K. Eisinger, *The Rise of the Entrepreneurial State: State and Local Economic Development Policy in the United States* (Madison: University of Wisconsin Press, 1988), pp. 8, 342.

31. Harry S. Ashmore, *Unseasonable Truths: The Life of Robert Maynard Hutchins* (Boston: Little, Brown, 1989), p. 541.

32. John Chamberlain, *The American Stakes* (New York: Carrick and Evans, 1941). On the planning aspirations of the New Deal, see Otis L. Graham, Jr., "Franklin D. Roosevelt and the Intended New Deal," in *Essays in Honor of James Macgregor Burns,* ed. M. R. Beschloss and Thomas E. Cronin (Englewood Cliffs, N.J.: Prentice-Hall, 1989).

33. Clyde Prestowitz, Jr., *Trading Places: How We Allowed Japan to Take the Lead* (New York: Basic Books, 1988), p. 268. On the Planning idea in modern America, see Otis L. Graham, Jr., *Toward a Planned Society: From Roosevelt to Nixon* (New York: Oxford University Press, 1976).

34. For comprehensive review of historical scholarship on modern states, see Peter B. Evans, Dietrich Rueschemeyer, and Theda Skocpol, eds., *Bringing the State Back In* (Cambridge: Cambridge University Press, 1985). For the American state and the conditions and extent of its autonomy, see G. John Ikenberry, David A. Lake, and Michael Mastanduno, eds., *The State and American Foreign Economic Policy* (Ithaca, N.Y.: Cornell University Press, 1988).

35. Assar Lindbeck, "Industrial Policy as an Issue in the Economic Environment," *World Economy* 4 (December 1981), 402.

36. George C. Lodge, *Perestroika for America: Restructuring Business-Government Relations for World Competitiveness* (Cambridge, Mass.: Harvard Business School Press,

1990), p. 210; idem, *The New America Ideology* (New York: Alfred A. Knopf, 1984), p. 288; idem, "It's Time for an American Perestroika," *Atlantic Monthly*, April 1990, pp. 35–36; George C. Lodge and Ezra F. Vogel, eds., *Ideology and National Competitiveness: An Analysis of Nine Countries* (Cambridge, Mass.: Harvard Business School Press, 1987).

37. Louis Uchitelle, "U.S. Manufacturing Flows Abroad," *New York Times*, March 26, 1989, pp. 1, 23. Robert B. Reich, "Rough Trade," *New Republic*, October 31, 1988, p. 38.

38. Robert B. Reich, "Who Is Us?" *Harvard Business Review*, January–February 1990, pp. 53–64; idem, *Tales of a New America* (New York: Basic Books, 1987), chap. 6; idem, "An Outward-Looking Economic Nationalism," *American Prospect* 1 (Spring 1990), 104–113; and Kenichi Ohmae, *Beyond National Borders: Reflections on Japan and the World* (Chicago: Irwin, 1987). See also the exchange between Reich and Laura D. Ryson, "They Are Not Us," *American Prospect* 1 (Winter 1991), 37–53. As this book went to press, Robert Reich had followed the logic of his disillusionment with American firms to a radical reconception of Industrial Policy. See Robert B. Reich, *The Work of Nations: Preparing Ourselves for 21st Century Capitalism* (New York: Alfred A. Knopf, 1991), a sure sign that the IP debate in the 1990s will not lack for intellectual vigor or surprise.

39. Friedrich Nietzsche, "On the Uses and Disadvantages of History for Life," in *Untimely Meditations* (New York: Macmillan, 1983), pp. 95, 75, 101, 116.

40. Albert O. Hirschman, *Exit, Voice, and Loyalty: Response to Decline in Firms, Organizations, and States* (Cambridge, Mass.: Harvard University Press, 1970), p. 96.

41. Henry J. Aaron, *Politics and the Professors: The Great Society in Perspective* (Washington, D.C.: Brookings Institution, 1978), p. 159. Dick Levin, *The Executive's Illustrated Primer of Long-Range Planning* (Englewood Cliffs, N.J.: Prentice-Hall, 1981), p. 6. For a similar view of history, see Robert S. Lynd, *Knowledge for What? The Place of Social Science in American Culture* (Princeton: Princeton University Press, 1939).

42. Nietzsche, "On the Uses of History," p. 169.

43. Henry Kissinger, *White House Years* (Boston: Little, Brown, 1979), pp. 54–65, 685–686. Graham, "Roosevelt and the Intended New Deal."

44. Morton Schoolman and Alvin Magid, eds., *Reindustrialization New York State: Strategies, Implications, Challenges* (New York: State University of New York Press, 1986), pp. 14–15.

45. David Osborne, *State Technology Programs: A Preliminary Analysis of Lessons Learned* (Washington, D.C.: Council of State Policy and Planning Agencies, 1989), p. 7.

46. National Commission on Excellence in Education (David P. Gardner, chairman), *A Nation at Risk: The Imperative for Educational Reform* (Washington, D.C.: Government Printing Office, 1983), p. 1.

47. Seven major environmental groups joined to contribute to the IP debate in Project on Industrial Policy and the Environment (Robert D. Hamrin, coordinator), *America's Economic Future: Environmentalists Broaden the Industrial Policy Debate* (Washington, D.C.: National Resources Defense Council, 1984). See also Robert G. Healy, *America's Industrial Future: An Environmental Perspective* (Washington, D.C.: Conservation Foundation, 1982). Ecologists had at least some influence. George

Lodge spoke of the necessity to "sustain the food chain" of customers, manufacturers, and suppliers; *Perestroika*, p. 68.

48. See George J. Borjas, *Friends or Strangers: The Impact of Immigrants on the U.S. Economy* (New York: Basic Books, 1990).

49. Truman quoted in William Diebold, Jr., *The End of the ITO*, Essays in International Finance, no. 16 (Princeton: Princeton University Press, 1952), pp. 2, 29; the basic book remains Clair Wilcox, *A Charter for World Trade* (New York: Macmillan, 1949).

50. Aho and Levinson, *After Reagan*, pp. 107, 122.

51. Raymond Vernon, *Exploring the Global Economy* (Lanham, Md.: University Press of America, 1985), pp. 23, 25.

52. Euripides, *Medea*, in *Fifteen Greek Plays*, ed. Gilbert Murray (New York: Oxford University Press, 1943), p. 494.

# Index

Donahue, John, 253, 254, 255
Donald, David, 247
Dukakis, Michael, 199, 200, 201, 202, 229
Dulles, John Foster, 85

Eads, George, 40–41, 135–136, 137, 145, 146–147
Economic change, 14–16, 19, 66–67, 119, 140, 196, 209; effects of, 107, 151; resistance to, 139
Economic development, 140, 208, 275–276. *See also* State economic development (SED) policies
Economic Development Administration (EDA), 142
Economic goals, 188, 294; U.S., 7, 36, 64, 113, 178, 292; long-term, 36, 61, 203, 286, 296; short-term, 61, 66, 103, 276, 278; Japanese, 85–86
Economic growth, 16, 81, 92; U.S., 7–8, 10, 72, 89, 108, 116, 121, 209, 211–212; Japanese, 9, 85, 123, 155–156. *See also* Job creation
Economic performance, 83, 276, 277; proposals for improving, 41–42, 61–62, 146, 147, 153, 215; Western European, 93, 136; criteria for, 98; U.S., 167, 229
Economic policies, 3, 8, 9–10, 204, 219, 235, 238, 293; under Carter, 27, 32, 156, 182, 185, 245; under Reagan, 58, 104–105, 165, 168, 220, 269; under Bush, 280–281. *See also* Macroeconomic policies; Microeconomic policies; State economic development (SED) policies
Economic Policy Group (EPG), 38–39, 40, 42
*Economic Report of the President*, 27; (1964), 7; (1980), 51–52; (1981), 59; (1984), 120, 149; (1985), 213
Economic Revitalization Board, 44
Economic stagnation, 13, 18, 210, 212, 214, 216
*Economist*, 44
Education, 89, 139, 267–268, 298; criticism of, 66–67, 92, 221. *See also* Retraining of labor
Education policy, 197, 199, 200, 202
Efficiency, economic, 68, 69, 139, 221, 258, 260, 261, 292; as goal, 64, 98, 134, 178
Eisenhower, Dwight D., 63, 188

Eisinger, Peter, 290, 297
Eizenstat, Stuart, 286; and sectoral policies, 34, 42–43, 156; and IP, 75, 76, 84
Elections: (1980), 43, 50–51, 274; (1984), 112, 148, 159, 160–161, 164–167, 207; (1988), 286, 287
Electronics industry, 222, 277; U.S., 81, 176, 177, 183–184, 186, 236, 250; Japanese, 87; French, 135; government intervention in, 177, 183, 224–227, 228, 230–234. *See also* Semiconductor industry
Elton, G. R., 244
Employment, 16, 60, 214; in manufactures, 13, 73, 120, 122, 149–150, 152, 209. *See also* Job creation; Unemployment
Employment policy, 20, 98, 162, 178
Energy, 8, 17, 19, 27
Energy industries, 196; U.S., 44, 129, 176, 245
Energy policy, 143, 257–258
Entrepreneurial state, 36, 194–201, 273
Environmental policy, 194, 274, 285, 292, 298
EPG. *See* Economic Policy Group
Equity, 68, 69, 70, 71, 72–73, 258
Erie Canal, 78–79, 114
Etzioni, Amitai, 42, 43, 96
Europe. *See* Western Europe
European Economic Community, 30
European Management Forum, 156
Executive branch (Japan), 86, 87
Executive branch (U.S.), 57, 99, 284, 285–286, 288; and trade policy, 30–31, 215; and economic development, 175, 205, 252, 272; and sectoral policies, 222, 251, 289. *See also* Civil service (U.S.); *specific departments, e.g.*, U.S. Department of Commerce
Export-Import Bank, 127, 176, 205
Extractive industries, 21

*Failure of NRA, The* (Bellush), 143
Fallows, James, 212
Faux, Jeff, 56
Federal Communications Commission, 232
*Federal Entrepreneur, The* (Urban Institute), 174
Federalism, 203, 205
Feldman, Allan, 162, 164